All Over

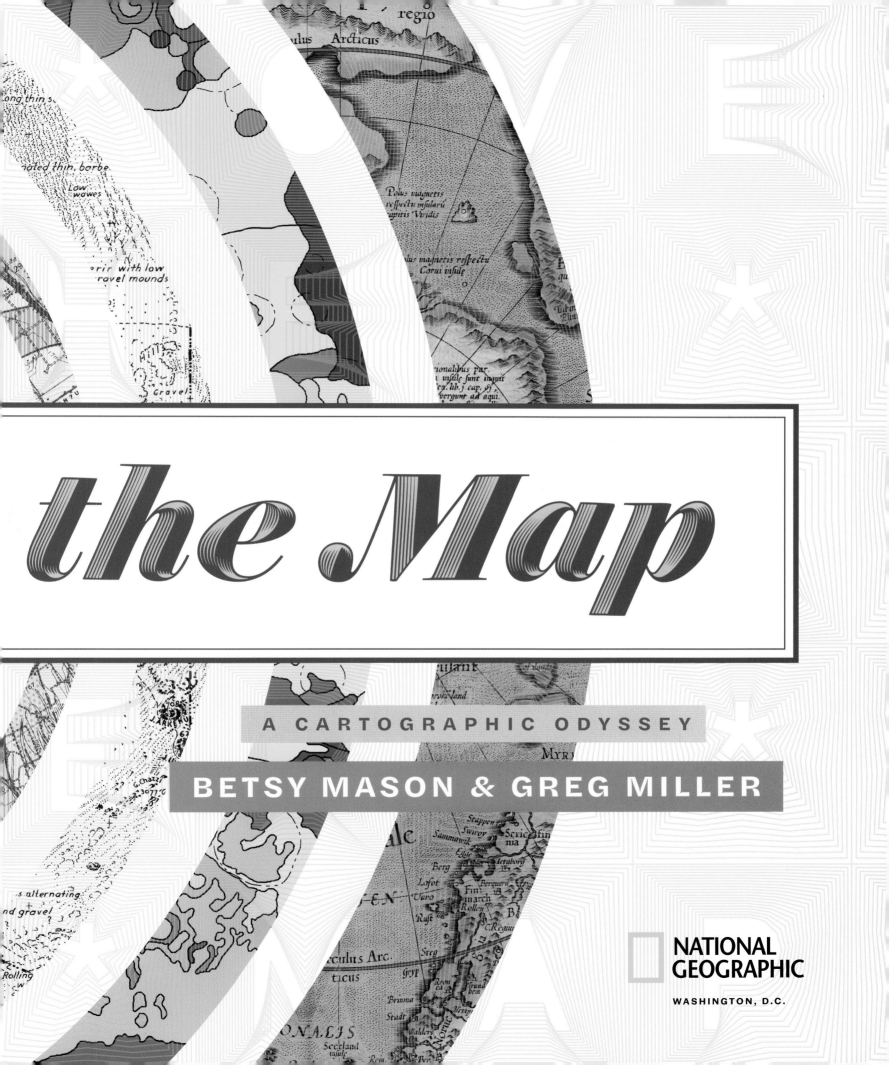

the Map

A CARTOGRAPHIC ODYSSEY

BETSY MASON & GREG MILLER

NATIONAL GEOGRAPHIC

WASHINGTON, D.C.

CONTENTS

ONE DOT PER PERSON
*(2013, Weldon Cooper Center for Public Service,
Rector and Visitors of the University of Virginia)*

Dustin Cable, a former demographic researcher at the University of
Virginia, used 308 million color-coded dots to represent the race
of every person in the United States counted by the 2010 Census.
The detail here shows the segregation of white (blue), black (green),
Asian (red), and Hispanic (orange) neighborhoods in Chicago.

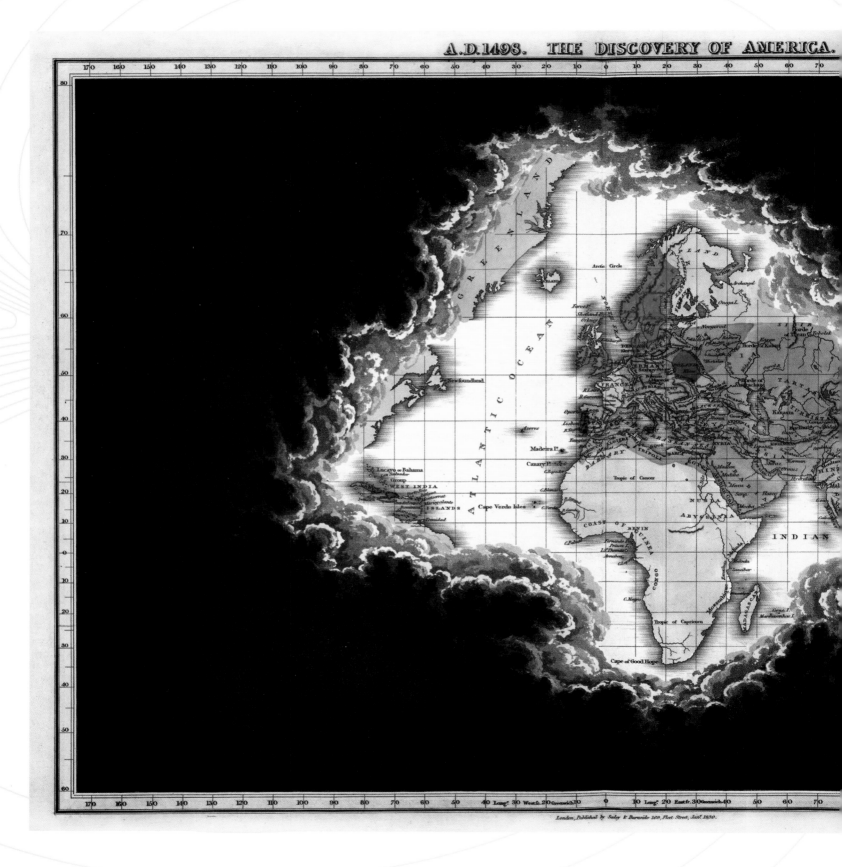

London, Published by Sidey & Burnside 169, Fleet Street, Jan.ʳ 1830.

Introduction

Our brains are built for maps. We humans are visual creatures—we need to picture something to really understand it. For centuries, people have been creating maps for just that purpose, to put down on paper (or parchment, or pixels) a world they're just on the verge of comprehending, or to tell a story that would be hard to tell any other way. Maps are one of the best tools ever invented for illustrating and exchanging ideas.

That's why maps can be so captivating. The best ones catch your eye because there's something intriguing or appealing about how they look and draw you in with the promise of something more: a revelation about the world, a vision of another time or a far-off place, or an interesting story. In this book we've tried, above all else, to highlight maps with good stories behind them.

KNOWLEDGE PARTS THE CLOUDS
(1830, David Rumsey Map Collection, David Rumsey Map Center, Stanford Libraries)

The clouds of ignorance recede as geographical knowledge increases with time in Edward Quin's historical atlas, which uses a series of maps to show which parts of the world were known at different points in history. This map accompanies a chapter detailing important historical events between 1294 and 1498.

One of the most amazing things maps can do is transport you to a different time or place. It's fascinating to see a familiar city as it once was, or as it might have been. Or to see something completely foreign, like a road traveled by shogun and samurai in 17th-century Japan or the underground passages of an early 18th-century Hungarian silver mine where men wielded pickaxes by lamplight.

Maps always reveal something about the biases and ambitions of their makers. To look at a map is to view the world through someone else's eyes—to see the coastline of South America as pirates saw it in the 1600s, or to see American cities as the Soviet military mapped them, in exquisite detail, during the Cold War.

Maps have always been instruments of discovery, revealing something about the world that wasn't readily apparent. Geologists mapping San Francisco after the 1906 earthquake made discoveries that changed their science forever. Other maps included here illustrate fascinating dead ends in the human quest for knowledge, like the idea that the visible lines on the surface of Mars were canals constructed by Martians or that foul-smelling air was the cause of cholera.

Maps can also be a springboard for the imagination and a way to create fantasy worlds or explore places that don't (yet) exist. In doing so they give shape to our greatest hopes and worst fears. Examples in this book include a forward-thinking London stenographer's early 20th-century plans for utopian communities that combined the best of urban and rural living and a 15th-century physician's vision of how the Apocalypse would unfold.

The human impulse to explore, discover, and create works of beauty runs deep through the history of cartography. Several stories in this book show the great measures mapmakers have taken to document the physical landscape and the inventive techniques they've developed to make it come alive.

This map book is different from others you might have on your shelf. We are not experts in cartography or its history; we're journalists with a lifelong love of maps who were eager to learn more. We've spent the past five years following our curiosity; visiting map collections; combing through archives; and interviewing dozens of scholars, curators, collectors, and cartographers who were kind enough to share their time and expertise.

Along the way, we've uncovered intriguing historical maps nobody has bothered to write about before, dug up new stories about iconic maps, and discovered amazing cartographic works in progress. We've shared some of these stories on our blog for National Geographic, All Over the Map, but the vast majority are making their debut here.

Some of these maps come from museums, prestigious universities, and famous collections. But we've gone out of our way to also include maps from less vaunted sources. They've been buried in obscure government reports, long-forgotten scientific papers, private collections, and dusty corners of libraries. Some are products of popular culture, such as one from the blockbuster television series *Game of Thrones*. Others are part of everyday life—the kind you might expect to find in the seat-back pocket of an airplane or that you would tuck into your pocket before hitting the ski slopes.

We've defined what constitutes a map broadly, and a few entries in this book push the boundaries. You'll find beautiful anatomical drawings mapping connections in the brain, for example, as well as a detailed schematic diagram of the Death Star, the infamous superweapon from the *Star Wars* movies.

The chapters ahead are loosely organized by theme, but this book is by no means a systematic overview of the world of maps. We have instead tried to capture the diversity of cartography, from its rich history to its thriving present, from the practical to the fanciful. This is a book written *by* map lovers *for* map lovers (including those who don't yet know they are). It's a lavishly illustrated book of true short stories that happen to be about amazing maps and their makers. We hope you enjoy it.

THE HEIGHT OF CARTOGRAPHY
(1988, National Geographic)

The artistry of the hand-drawn relief on this map of Mount Everest, published as a supplement to the November 1988 issue of *National Geographic,* has yet to be rivaled. The mapping project was led by the renowned explorer and cartographer Bradford Washburn (who also made the Grand Canyon map on page 119), and the relief was done by the Swiss Federal Office of Topography.

WATER

WARS

Charting Rivers and Seas

Throughout human history, waterways have been a source of opportunity and wonder. They beckon with the promise of fortunes that lie beyond the horizon or up the river (tempered, perhaps, by the fear of what might lurk beneath the surface). They've also inspired some of the most intriguing and evocative maps.

Maritime cartography reached a pinnacle in the Netherlands in the 17th century. A thriving and brutally competitive map trade had developed in Amsterdam as mapmakers supplied navigational charts and maps to mariners seeking to capitalize on the booming spice trade (see page 32). In that era of colonial land grabs and ever expanding trade routes, such maps were highly sought after. Halfway around the world, English pirates were raiding Spanish galleons off the Pacific coast of the Americas as much for their maps as for their gold (see page 18).

With time, maritime maps became increasingly scientific, but that didn't diminish their beauty. In 1807 the U.S. Congress authorized the new nation's first coastal survey, jump-starting an arduous, decades-long effort that resulted in beautiful and meticulously accurate maps of American coastlines and harbors (see page 42). Rivers, too, became objects of study. Geologist Harold Fisk's multicolor maps of the ever changing course of the Mississippi are some of the most captivating maps you'll ever see (see page 14).

The maps in this chapter have many stories to tell, but they all reflect the prominent place of waterways in our history and imagination. ➤➤

MARINER'S MIRROR
(1584, Barry Lawrence Ruderman Map Collection, David Rumsey Map Center, Stanford Libraries)

The 16th-century *Spiegel der Zeevaerdt (Mariner's Mirror)* was the first printed atlas of nautical charts and sailing instructions. It was created by a Dutch sea captain and cartographer named Lucas Janszoon Waghenaer (this type of book became known in English as a "waggoner"). As an aid to mariners, Waghenaer depicts the rugged terrain not just from the traditional perspective—as it would appear from above—but also in profile, as it would appear from the sea. This map covers a roughly 50-mile (80 km) stretch of Spain's northern coastline.

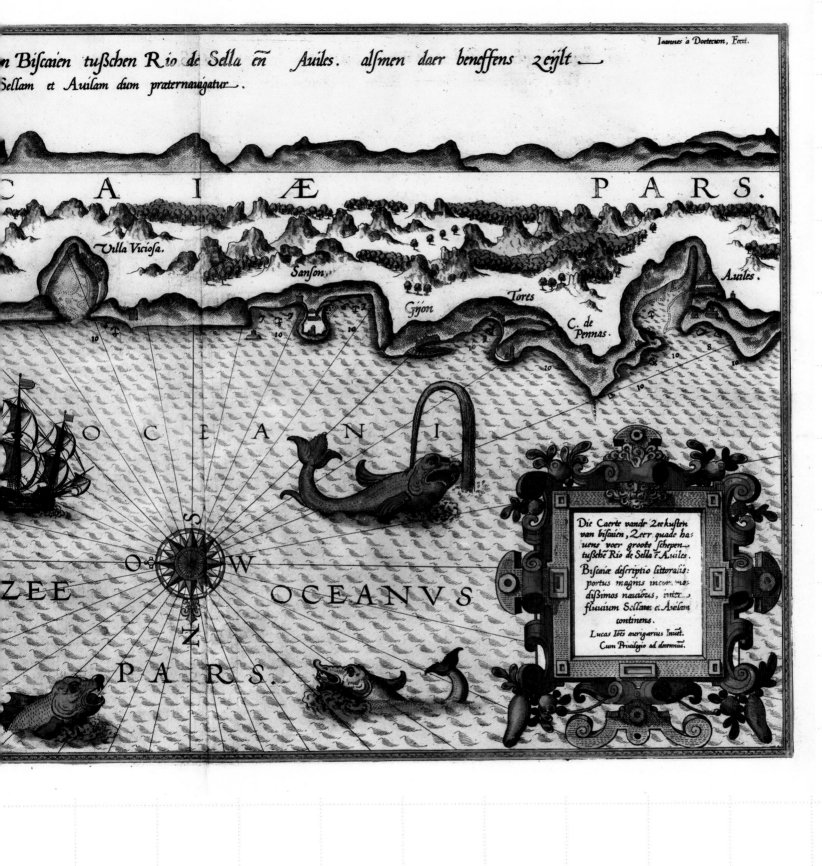

Biscaien tuſſchen Rio de Sella ēn Auiles. alſmen daer beneffens zeijlt.

Sellam et Auilam dum praternauigatur.

Ioannes à Doetecum, Fecit.

CAIÆ PARS.

Villa Viciosa.

Sanſon

Gijon

Tores

C. de Pennas

Auiles.

OCEANI

ZEE

OCEANVS

PARS.

Die Caerte vande Zeekuſten van biſcaien, Zeer quade hauens voer groote ſchepen tuſſchē Rio de Sella ē Auiles.

Biſcaie deſcriptio littoralis: portus magnis incommodiſsimos nauioribus, inter fluuium Sellam et Auilam continens.

Lucas Ioēs aurigarius Inuēt.

Cum Priuilegio ad decennium.

Ol' Man River's Restless Past

CHARTING THE MISSISSIPPI'S MANY PATHS

CREATED *1944*
SOURCE *U.S. Army Corps of Engineers*

The Mississippi River flooded in dramatic and deadly fashion in 1927, inundating more than 26,000 square miles (67,000 sq km) of land with up to 30 feet (9 m) of water. The deluge, which displaced more than a million people and killed hundreds, remains one of the worst natural disasters in U.S. history.

There's an argument to be made, however, that this disaster wasn't entirely natural. For 200 years, a patchwork of levees had gradually been built up to protect towns and farmland from flooding. Before that, the Mississippi had been free to change course for thousands of years, meandering back and forth across the valley, perpetually abandoning old channels and creating new ones. As one U.S. Army engineer put it in 1932, "It writhes like an imprisoned snake." In 1927, that snake broke through the levees in several places.

Nowhere is this history of movement demonstrated more clearly and convincingly than on a set of maps made by geologist Harold Fisk in 1944. His previous work on the geology of Louisiana included a map of some old Mississippi River channels that caught the notice of the U.S. Army Corps of Engineers, which had been authorized in 1928 to control the unruly river. In 1941, they contracted Fisk, then a young professor at Louisiana State University, to help them better understand, and therefore tame, the river known as the Big Muddy.

Tasked with conducting a study of the geologic history of the entire Lower Mississippi River Valley from Cairo, Illinois, to the Gulf of Mexico, Fisk and his team of four geologists spent more than two years traversing the valley, studying the landscape and poring over aerial photos and old topographic maps to find evidence of abandoned river channels. They also drilled more than 300 holes into ancient river sediments and collected data from existing

Geologist Harold Fisk's colorful 1944 maps of the Mississippi River's former channels reveal the river's propensity to change course. The maps are celebrated by cartographers today as exceptional examples of the craft.

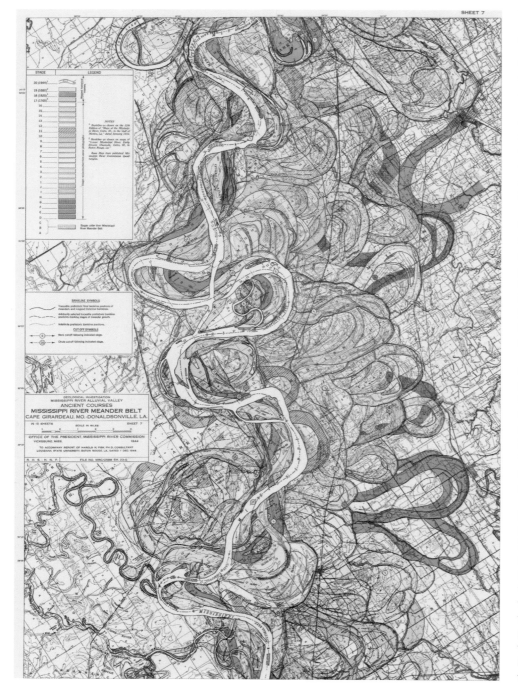

LEFT This map of old Mississippi River channels is one of 15 in Fisk's 1944 report that cover the Lower Mississippi River Valley from Cairo, Illinois, to the Gulf of Mexico. The active channel at the time of Fisk's research is shown in white.

water and oil wells, amassing information from around 16,000 holes in the earth.

The geologists carefully pieced the data together to trace 27 different channels the river had occupied during the previous 6,000 years. A skilled draftsman named Billy Dement plotted the channels onto maps at a scale of 1 mile per inch (0.6 km/cm), representing each one with a different color. The result, published as part of Fisk's full report in 1944, is an improbably beautiful collection of highly technical scientific maps inconspicuously named "plate 22."

The maps dramatically reveal how much the river can wander—up to 50 miles (80 km) from side to side—and hint at how it does this. As water flows through a curve in the river, the water on the outside of the bend flows faster, slowly eroding the bank and deepening the curve. As the curve grows, sometimes the river takes a shortcut by carving a new channel across the neck of the curve, which is happening to two curves (in white) near the center of the map above. Abandoned curves form crescent-shaped lakes known as oxbows (like

the one in the satellite image comparison), which over time is filled with sediment when the river periodically overtops its banks and floods the surrounding plains. The same process is constantly repeating up and down the length of any meandering river.

Fisk's maps lay bare the fact that many of the towns dotting the landscape adjacent to the Mississippi sit directly in the path of former channels. All of the flatland flanking the river is part of the territory the Mississippi is wont to roam. Though his maps very effectively portray the river as perpetually restless, Fisk argued that it was actually settling down, becoming what he called a "poised" river. He perceived a gradual straightening in the mass of twists and loops.

This idea fit with the Army Corps' efforts to straighten the river by building channels to cut off bends, shoring up levees, and trying to hold the river in place. According to Fisk, they were just hastening what the river was doing on its own. The policy appeared to be working, holding back high water in 1944, 1945, and 1950. But more recent flooding, in 1973, 1993, and 2011, has led the Army Corps to constantly reevaluate its strategy as it battles the river.

Though not all of Fisk's ideas have been borne out, his maps have withstood the test of time, and some have even enjoyed a second life in recent years. Because multicolor maps of this size—each one measures 28 by 40 inches (71 by 102 cm)—were very expensive to produce in 1944, only 1,000 original copies of the report were printed. Persistent demand from scientists and engineers for the out-of-print maps prompted the Army Corps to digitize them in the 1990s and make them freely available online. Eventually the maps caught the attention of cartographers and designers, who have hailed them as exemplars of the craft. They've appeared in magazines, on album covers, and in poster shops.

"They just do such a wonderful job of showing an overall pattern, an overall dynamic process unfolding over thousands of years, at the same time that they show us the details of the evidence for that pattern," says cartographer and historian Bill Rankin of Yale University.

Rankin says it's interesting that these maps that are now seen as "an icon of gorgeous cartography" weren't part of the canon until long after they were made. "There might be countless other gorgeous maps buried in government reports that we don't know about," he says. ✷

16 | All Over the Map

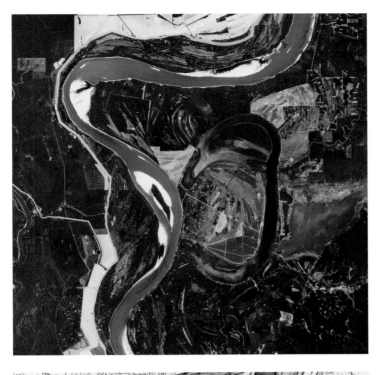

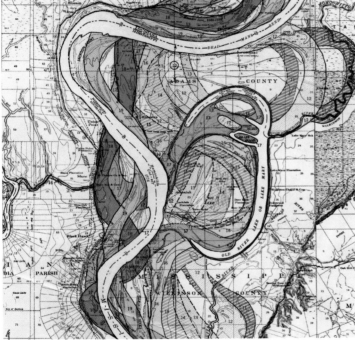

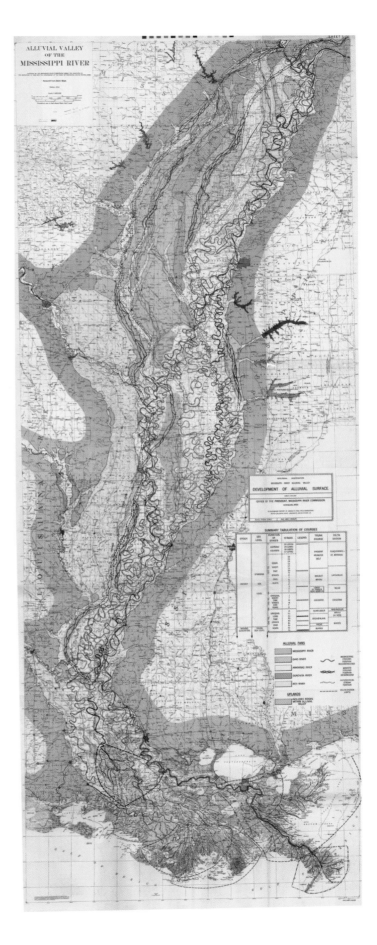

ABOVE A comparison of Fisk's 1944 map (bottom) with a satellite image from 1999 (top) shows a Mississippi River meander that has been cut off by a new channel to form an oxbow lake. The traces of even older abandoned channels can be seen on the surrounding plain.

RIGHT The extent of Fisk's investigation of the Lower Mississippi River Valley is shown on this map from his 1944 report with the river's historical courses simplified into several groups. The solid blue line represents the most recent channels (since 1765) that Fisk's team mapped in the field.

A Pirate's Pilfered Atlas

A 17TH-CENTURY ENGLISH BUCCANEER BOUGHT HIS FREEDOM WITH A COPY OF A STOLEN SPANISH ATLAS

CREATED *1669–1685*
SOURCE *National Maritime Museum; British Library; Huntington Library*

In 1680, English pirate Bartholomew Sharpe and 300 men crossed the Central American isthmus at Panama, captured a Spanish ship, the *Trinity,* and used it to raid Spanish vessels up and down the Pacific coast of Central and South America. Their exploits became famous, in large part because they were a remarkably literate band of buccaneers: Five of the men, including Sharpe, kept detailed journals.

From these accounts, we know that one of the most valuable treasures they seized was not gold or silver, but an atlas of Spanish sailing charts. Sharpe later commissioned a colorfully illustrated English copy of the stolen atlas and presented it to the king of England—a gift that likely saved his freedom, if not his life.

The daring theft occurred off the coast of Ecuador. Early on the morning of July 29, 1681, one of Sharpe's men spotted the sails of a Spanish ship. The pirates gave chase, killed the Spanish captain in a volley of gunfire, and took the ship, the *Rosario.* Onboard, they found hundreds of jars of wine and brandy, some fruit, and a small amount of money. They transferred this prize to the *Trinity* before cutting down the *Rosario*'s mast and setting her adrift with her crew of 40 still onboard. The pirates also abandoned 700 slabs of a dull gray metal they believed to be tin. To their great regret, they later discovered it had actually been unrefined silver—a fortune that would have been "the richest Booty we had gotten in the whole Voyage," one crew member wrote.

They did not, however, mistake the value of another item they found on the *Rosario.* Sharpe described it in his journal as "a Spanish manuscript of prodigious value." One of his men wrote that it was "a great Book full of Sea Charts and Maps, containing a very accurate and exact description of all the Ports, Soundings, Creeks, Rivers, Capes and Coasts belonging to the South Sea, and all the Navigations usually performed by the *Spaniards* in that Ocean."

By "South Sea," he meant the Pacific Ocean. Vasco Núñez de Balboa, the first European to reach the Pacific via the New World, had crossed the narrow neck of land separating the Atlantic and Pacific at Panama in 1513, much as Sharpe and company had done. Because the overland route goes from north to south, Balboa called it the South Sea.

A century and a half later, the Spanish still controlled those waters, and the English desperately wanted a piece of the action. That's why the Spanish maritime atlas, or *derrotero,* was so valuable. The crew of the *Rosario* had tried to throw the book overboard during the scuffle, but Sharpe somehow managed to save it (in his journal, he doesn't say how, but he claims the Spanish cried when he got his hands on it).

The map (on page 21) is from a Spanish *derrotero* that historians once thought was the one captured from the *Rosario.* Its navigation directions and views of harbors as they would appear from out at sea would have been incredibly valuable to sailors at the time. More recent

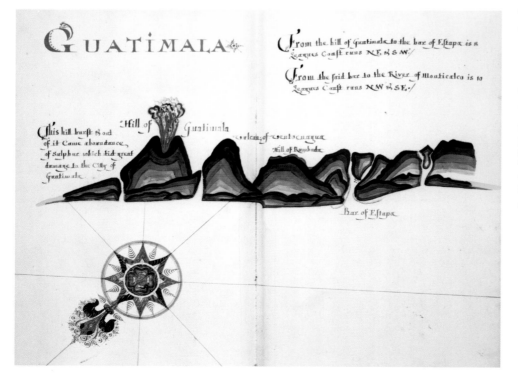

OPPOSITE The pirate Bartholomew Sharpe hired London mapmaker William Hack to create an atlas based on a stolen Spanish *derrotero*. This map, added by Hack to show the route sailed by Sharpe and his men around South America, comes from a 1684 version of the atlas that was presented to King Charles II.

LEFT This page from Hack's atlas, from a 1685 version presented to King James II after the death of Charles II, shows a volcano visible from Guatemala's Pacific coast. "This hill burst & out of it came abundance of sulphur which did great damage to the City of Guatimala," Hack wrote.

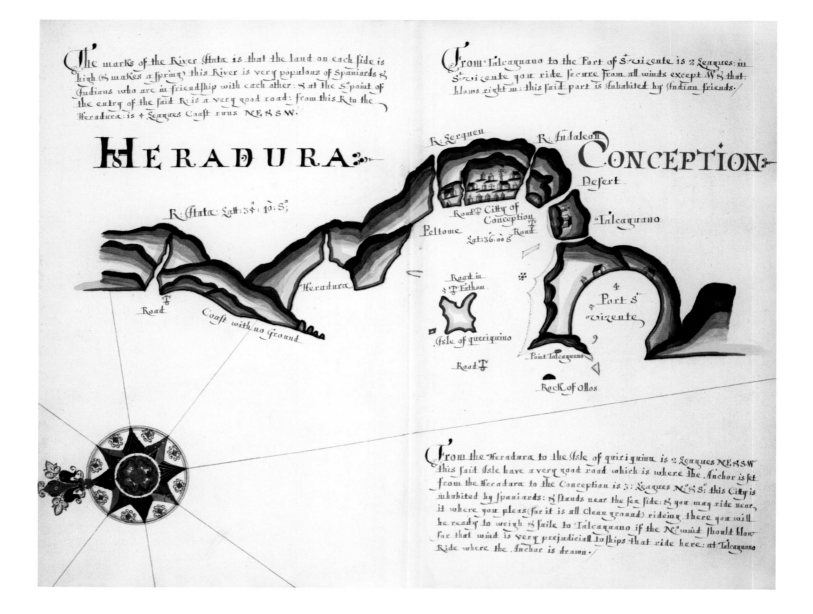

The marks of the River Itata is that the land on each side is high & makes a spring this River is very populous of Spaniards & Indians who are in friendship with each other: & at the S point of the entry of the said R is a very good road: from this R to the Heradura is 4 Leagues Coast runs NE & SW.

From Talcaquano to the Port of S vizente is 2 Leagues: in S vizente you ride secure from all winds except W & that blows right in: this said part is inhabited by Indian friends.

HERADURA:

R. Serquen

R. Andaleon

CONCEPTION:

Desert

R. Itata Latt: 35° 40 S

Road To Citty of Conception Lat: 36: 00 S

Road

Peltome

Talcaquano

Heradura

Road in S T Eatham

Part S vizente

Road

Coast with no Ground

Isle of queriquino

Road T

Point Talcaquano

Rock of Ollos

From the Heradura to the Isle of quiriquina is 2 Leagues NE & SW this said Isle have a very good road which is where the Anchor is set from the Heradura to the Conception is 3: Leagues N & S: this City is inhabited by Spaniards: & stands near the sea side: & you may ride near it where you pleas (for it is all clean ground) rideing there you will be ready to weigh & saile to Talcaquano if the N wind should blow for that wind is very prejudiciall to ships that ride here: at Talcaquano Ride where the Anchor is drawn.

ABOVE A page from the 1685 copy of Hack's atlas showing the coastline of South America around Concepción, in what is now Chile. Hack notes that the Itata River (on the left side of the map) "is very populous of Spaniards & Indians who are in friendship with each other."

research suggests that this derrotero was actually captured a decade earlier by the famous pirate Henry Morgan. If the *Rosario* derrotero still exists, its whereabouts are unknown.

After their encounter with the *Rosario*, Sharpe's men continued to raid ships along the Pacific coast, causing huge financial losses for the Spanish, destroying 25 ships, and killing more than 200 men. When they eventually turned for home, they sailed to the south and rounded the tip of South America, becoming the first Englishmen to do so from the west.

On his return to London in 1682, Sharpe found trouble waiting. The Spanish ambassador was fuming over the death of the *Rosario*'s

captain and demanded that Sharpe be tried and hanged for piracy. Two witnesses gave compelling testimony against him at trial, and yet, surprisingly, he was acquitted.

The reason may have been the derrotero. Sharpe knew from the beginning that it would be of great interest to King Charles II. By the time the trial rolled around, the king had already seen it, and arrangements had been made to have an English copy made.

The cartographer hired to redraw the maps was William Hack, a former sailor who may or may not have once been a pirate himself. According to an essay by Edward Lynam, a former map curator at the British Library, Hack had

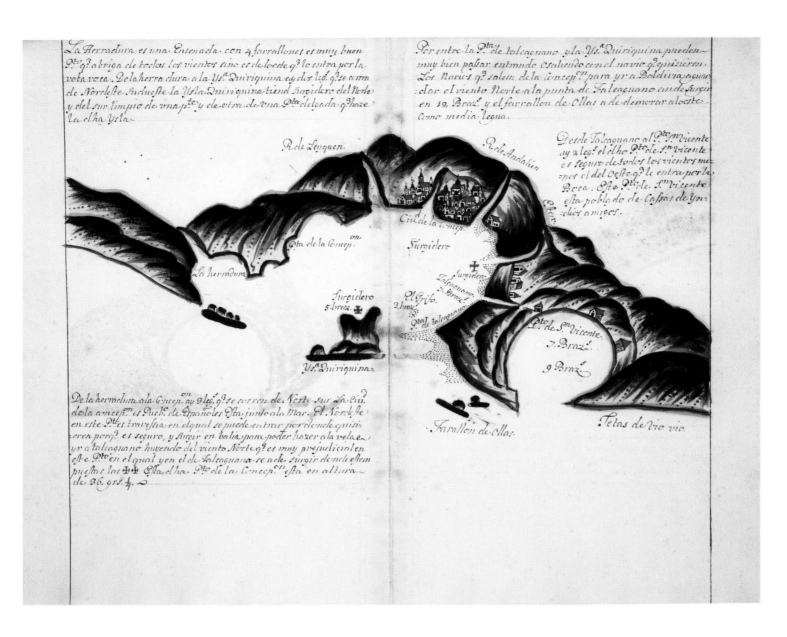

The handwritten map text appears as:

La Herradura es una Ensenada con 4 farrallones es muy buen Pto qe abriga de todos los vientos sino es del oeste qe le entra por la vela vela. De la herra dura a la Ysa Quiriquina ay dos leg qe se corren de Noreste Sudueste la Ysla Quiriquina tiene Surgidero del Norte y del sur limpio de vna pte y de otra de vna Pta delgada qe haze la dha Ysla.

Por entre la Pta de Talcaguano yla Ysa Quiriquina pueden muy bien pasar entrando esaliendo con el navio qe quisieren. Los Navios qe salen de la Concepn para yr a Boldivia aguar dar el viento Norte a la punta de Talcaguano en de surgir en 19 Braz y el farrallon de Ellas a de demorar al oeste como media legua.

Desde Talcaguano al Pto Sn Vicente ay 2 leg el dho Pto de Sn Vicente es seguro de todos los vientos me nos el del Oeste qe le entra por la Boca. Este Pto de Sn Vicente esta poblado de Casas de Yn dios amigos.

R. de Leyquen · R. de Andalien · Ciu. de la Concep. · Sta. de la Concep. · Surgidero · La herradura · Surgidero 5 brez. · Surgidero · Talcaguano 7 Braz. · El Grifo 3 braz. · Pta Talcaguano · Ysa Quiriquina · Pto. de Sn Vicente 7 Braz. · 9 Braz. · Farallon de Ellas. · Tetas de Vio vio.

De la herradura a la Concepn ay 3 leg qe se corren de Norte sur La Ciu. de la Concepn es Pueb. de Españoles Sta junto a la Mar. El Noreste en este Pto es travessia en elqual se puede entrar por donde quisi eren perqe es seguro, y surgir en bahia para poder hazer a la vela y a Talcaguano huyendo del viento Norte qe es muy prejudicial en este Pto en el qual y en el de Talcaguana se ade surgir donde esten puesto las Estrellas. Pto de la Concepn esta en altura de 36 grs. ½

ABOVE This map, which covers roughly the same area as the one from Hack's atlas opposite, comes from a 1669 Spanish derrotero that Hack may have had access to (although it wasn't his primary source). Handwritten navigational notes describe the terrain as it appears from sea.

evidently decided it was safer to make a living by "collecting, over a bottle of brandy in the local tavern, secret and exciting information from unemployed buccaneers and selling it to members of the Government and the aristocracy."

Hack made several copies of a South Sea atlas based on the *Rosario* derrotero (to a lesser extent, he also appears to have used the derrotero that Morgan stole). Hack's colorful drawings are endearingly childlike, yet his handwritten descriptions of prevailing winds, safe anchorages, and local landmarks as they appear from sea would have been very useful for navigation. He depicts dozens of harbors along the coast of the Americas (see the map

on the previous page of Concepción, in what's now Chile). Verdant hills dotted with trees and houses are a common feature, along with the occasional erupting volcano (see the map of Guatemala on page 18).

The first copy, naturally, was given to the king, with a dedication written by Sharpe. It was a savvy move: Instead of being hanged, Sharpe was given a captain's commission in the Royal Navy and command of a ship assigned to find a sunken Spanish treasure ship in the Bahamas. It was a plum assignment, but perhaps too tame for Sharpe. He made his own way to the West Indies instead and resumed an on-and-off life of crime, a pirate at heart to the end of his days. ✴

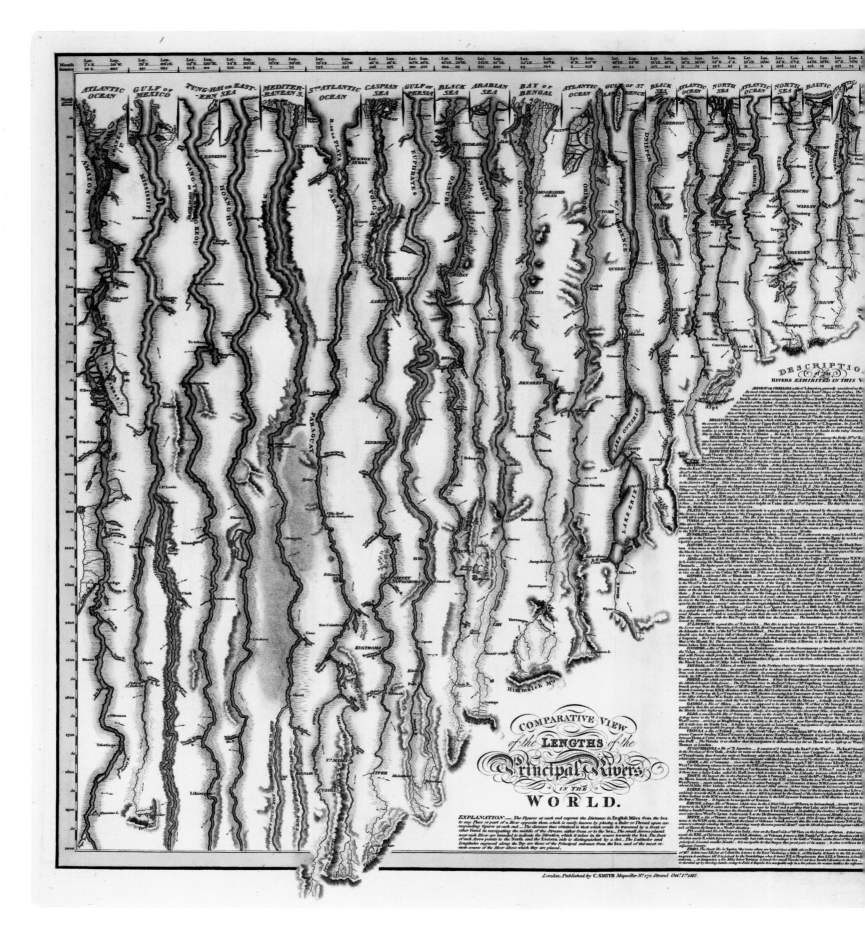

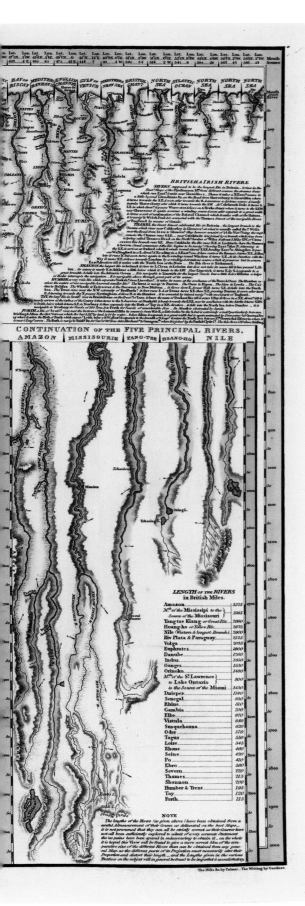

The World's Rivers at a Glance

19TH-CENTURY COMPARATIVE CHARTS OFFERED A GLOBAL PERSPECTIVE ON NATURE

CREATED *1817*

SOURCE *David Rumsey Map Collection, Stanford Libraries*

In the early 19th century, the tables of geographic facts often found in atlases began to morph into something far more interesting: visualizations. It started with charts comparing the heights of several mountains on different continents, growing to include dozens, or even hundreds, of the world's tallest peaks. The mountains were usually depicted in a sort of pile, the tallest mountains rising up on one side of the page with progressively lesser peaks lining their flanks in the foreground. It was the first time people could readily compare the relative sizes of global geographic features in a visual way.

Soon mapmakers applied the technique to the world's rivers, straightening them out and hanging them from their mouths across the top of the page according to length. Charles Smith's "Comparative View of the Lengths of the Principal Rivers of the World," published in London in 1817, was one of the earliest of these comparative visualizations. They became quite popular in Europe and North America, often as a combination chart with the longest rivers on the left and the tallest mountains on the right in a diagonal configuration.

Smith's chart came with a lengthy "description of the rivers exhibited in this view" that reflects the state of geographical knowledge at the time. The description notes that the source of the Yang Tse Kiang "appears to be in Thibet" and that "the Natives in their Canoes" navigate the Amazon and its tributaries "tho' many parts are rapid & dangerous." The Saint Lawrence contains "an immense Volume of Water," and

the course of the Mississippi is "extremely winding." Smith also notes that the "notion of the Ganges running through a Cavern beneath the Himmaleh Mts" appears to have been disproved.

Though discussion of the lengths of some of the world's longest rivers continues today, 19th-century comparative charts varied wildly on some of these statistics. For example, Smith's 1817 chart lists the Nile as 2,600 miles (4,184 km) long, but on an 1852 chart it had grown to 3,200 miles (5,150 km) long, and today it's considered to be around 4,200 miles (6,759 km) long. Mountains were no different. Over the course of the century, Mount Elbrus in Russia was listed anywhere between 16,411 and 18,526 feet (5,002 and 5,647 m).

As explorers, geographers, and scientists learned more about the world's rivers and mountains and how to accurately measure them, the numbers in these charts moved closer to the truth. But greater knowledge about the physical world in general may also have contributed to the decline in the popularity of comparative charts toward the end of the 19th century: As the blank places on the maps were filled in and the mysteries of geography were solved, maps became more accurate and the charts lost their appeal.

"We can lament their passing," John Wolter, a former chief of the Geography and Maps Division at the Library of Congress, wrote in 1972. "For they are certainly fascinating to peruse and a pleasure to view—perhaps the next best thing to viewing the mountains and rivers themselves." ✳

Charts, like this one from 1817, that compiled geographical features such as mountains and rivers were popular in Europe and North America in the 19th century. Here, the world's major rivers are straightened and laid out according to length for comparison.

The Epic Quest for a Northwest Passage

FOR CENTURIES, MAPMAKERS HAVE CHARTED ROUTES THROUGH ARCTIC WATERS THEY BARELY KNEW

CREATED *1558–1875*
SOURCE *Osher Map Library*

I t had to be there: an ocean at the top of the world. The ancient Greeks drew it on their maps, and for centuries, the rest of Europe did too. From the 1500s onward, countless men died trying to find it, hoping for a maritime shortcut across the Arctic that would open up new trade routes to Asia. Now, thanks to a warming planet, the long-sought Northwest Passage actually exists . . . at least for part of the year.

The idea of a northern ocean passage dates back to at least the second century A.D. Mathematician Claudius Ptolemy and the ancient Greeks believed that Earth had four habitable zones balanced by two uninhabitable, frigid ones—often thought to be made up of water—at the top and bottom of the globe. But it wasn't until the early 16th century, after the voyages of Italian explorer Christopher Columbus, that the idea of a Northwest Passage took hold in the popular European imagination. After all, when Columbus sailed west looking for a sea route to the East, he found a continent blocking the way. The Northwest Passage would be a way around this impasse.

"After the Spanish and Portuguese took control of the trade routes in the south along the coasts of Africa and South America, it once again becomes a very popular idea as a way for the Dutch and the French and the English to get access to the East and the riches they believed to be there," says Ian Fowler, former director of the Osher Map Library at the University of Southern Maine.

Maps from this period are filled with the wild imaginings of mapmakers. The famous 1633 map by Gerard Mercator to the right depicts the North Pole as it was described in legends: a massive rock surrounded by water and four large islands. Nonexistent bays and islands were common on these maps, as were sea monsters (see below). Gamesmanship and outright deception were common too. The map at the top of page 26 comes from a book published in 1558 to describe voyages the Venetian Zeno brothers made in 1380. The story is almost certainly bogus, Fowler says, made up in an attempt to retroactively claim the discovery of the New World for Venice. Even so, the map was widely copied and may have led some expeditions astray. "It's dangerous," Fowler says. "It shows Greenland connected to Europe, which is obviously not true. South of Iceland, there's a number of fictitious islands. And to the west of Greenland there's a nice open sea, which at this time would have been unnavigable because of pack ice."

Early explorers occasionally played fast and loose with the facts. Englishman Martin Frobisher didn't find the Northwest Passage on any of his three voyages in the late 1500s, but that didn't stop him from making grandiose claims. "He discovered some straits, pretended to find a lot more," Fowler says. On one trip, he returned to England with tons of what he said was gold-containing ore. It was enough to convince his backers to

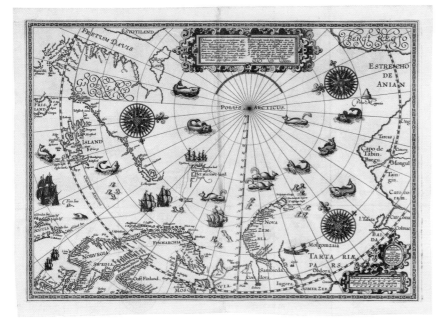

RIGHT This 1633 map by Gerard Mercator depicts the North Pole as a massive rock surrounded by water. It also includes the nonexistent island of Frisland, shown in an inset at top left and on the map itself near the bottom.

LEFT Sea creatures abound in this 1598 map by Dutch explorer Willem Barents, who drew it while stuck in sea ice on his third trip to the Arctic.

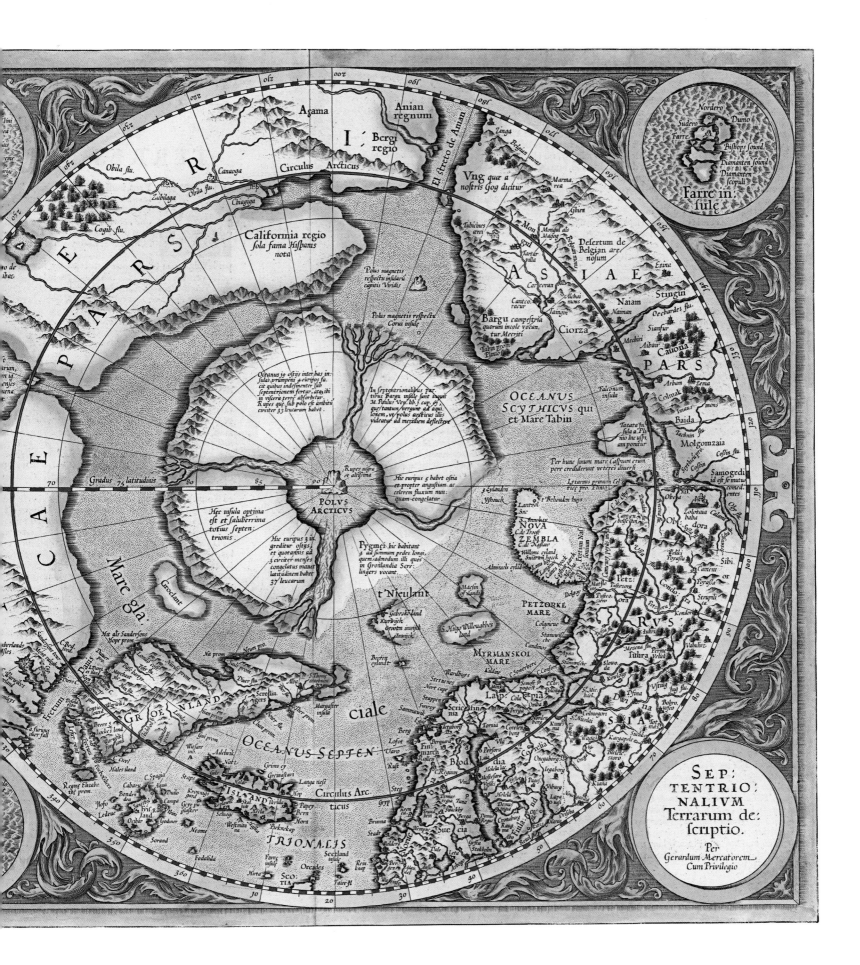

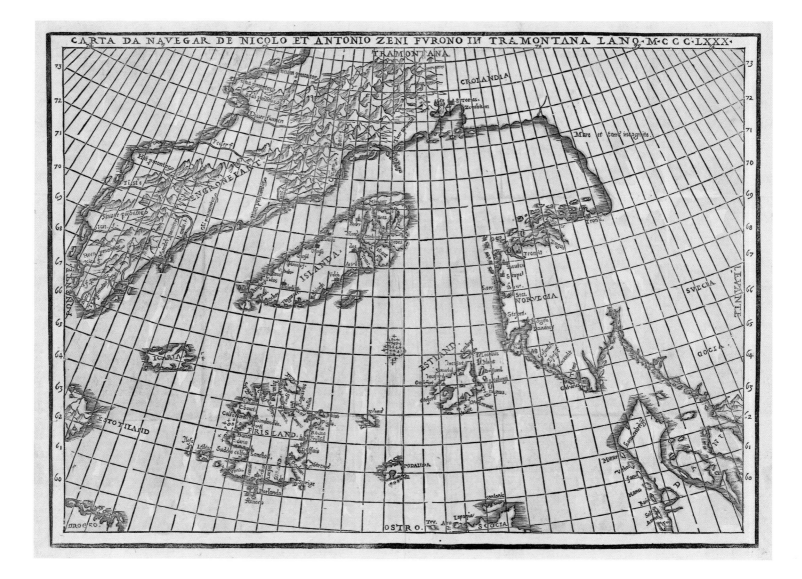

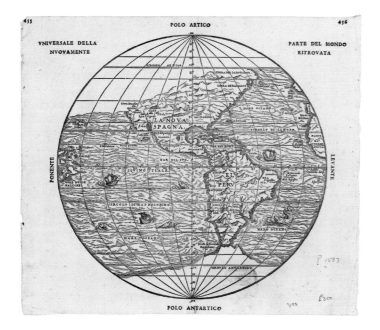

LEFT This 1563 map by Giovanni Ramusio and Giacomo Gastaldi was the first accurate map of the Americas sold commercially, but the blank areas at the poles reflect the lack of geographic knowledge at the time.

ABOVE This 1558 map of the Arctic, supposedly based on the travels of the Venetian Zeno brothers, wrongly depicts Greenland as connected to Europe. The open sea to the west would have been packed with ice.

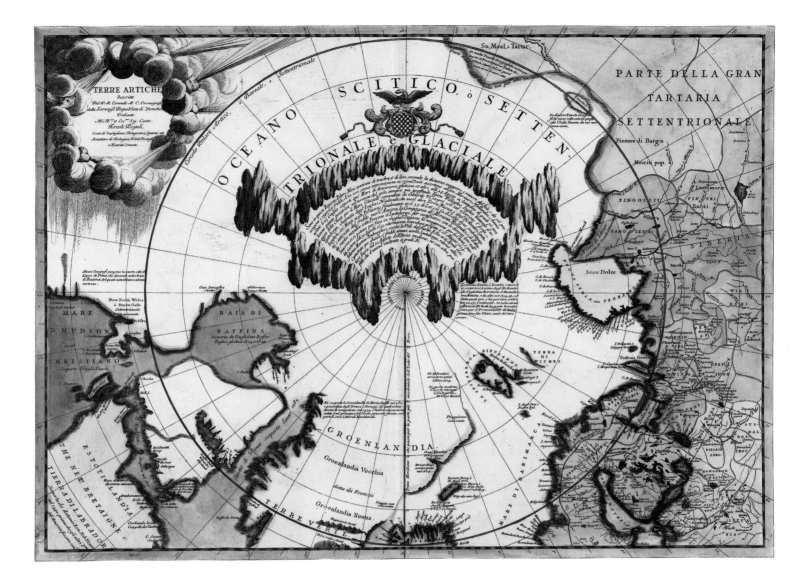

ABOVE Colored clouds represent the northern lights on this 1709 map by Jacques Peeters. Peeters attributed features on the map to the explorers who discovered them, and he used a dotted line to indicate an unmapped region of Greenland's coast (at bottom center).

fund another trip, but it ultimately turned out to be pyrite—fool's gold.

With time and additional exploration, the maps got better. The map on page 28, published in Russia in 1784, was the first to show details gleaned from a large and highly organized survey of the Arctic coast of Siberia. It depicts a possible Northwest Passage. On the far right side, "R. de l'Ouest" connects Hudson Bay to the Pacific Ocean. Notice the level of detail on the Asian side of the Pacific compared to the North American side; the situation is reversed in a map published the same year based on Captain James Cook's exploration of the coast of Alaska.

Perhaps the most famous attempt to find the Northwest Passage was the expedition led by Sir John Franklin in 1845. Franklin was an officer in the British navy who had led two previous expeditions to the Arctic, but this time the expedition didn't return on schedule.

Franklin's wife, Lady Jane, pressed the British government to send a search party, which they did in 1848. The search grew to include more ships over the coming years, and newspaper reports on the hunt for the missing expedition gripped the British public.

Ultimately, all the searchers found were several graves of men who'd died early on in the voyage and a few scattered notes and other relics. What they didn't know at the time was that both of Franklin's ships had become trapped in ice and all 129 men, including Franklin, had perished. Both ships have been found in the past few years. Researchers discovered the H.M.S. *Terror* in surprisingly good condition at the bottom of an Arctic bay in 2016: The large glass windows on the stern cabin were unbroken after nearly 170 years.

Unbeknownst to Franklin and other explorers of his day, their expeditions coincided with what scientists call the Little Ice Age—a period

On the map (selected labels):

NOUVELLE CARTE
DES DECOUVERTES FAITES PAR DES VAISSEAUX RUSSIENS AUX
CÔTES INCONNUES DE L'AMERIQUE SEPTENTRIONALE AVEC
LES PAIS ADIACENTS.
Dreſsée ſur des memoires authentiques de ceux qui
ont aſsiſté a ces decouvertes, et ſur d'autres
Connoiſsances.
A S.t Petersbourg a l'Academie Imperiale
des Sciences 1784

MER GLACIALE

AMERIQUE SEPTENTRIONALE

KAMTSCHATKA

ISLES DES KURILES

ISLE DE NIPHON

MER DU SUD

BAFFINS BAY

of several centuries of unusual cold in the Arctic. As temperatures began to climb toward the end of the 19th century, the Northwest Passage finally began to open up. Norwegian explorer Roald Amundsen completed the first journey made entirely by boat through the passage in 1906. It took three years, including two winters on the ice.

Sailing the Arctic has been getting easier of late. As polar ice has melted, the route has become more accessible. In September 2016, a cruise ship carrying 1,700 people became the first passenger liner to complete it. The melting of Arctic sea ice has raised the possibility of new trade routes and development for energy production, as well as the potential for territorial conflicts and environmental damage to a relatively untouched part of the Earth.

For better or worse, a new chapter in the storied history of the Arctic is just beginning, and cartographers' dreams of a Northwest Passage may be on the verge of coming true. ✳

ABOVE This 1784 map based on Russia's Great Northern Expedition is far more detailed on the Asian side of the Pacific, but it includes a possible water route through North America: "R. de l'Ouest" (lower right) connects Hudson Bay to the Pacific Ocean.

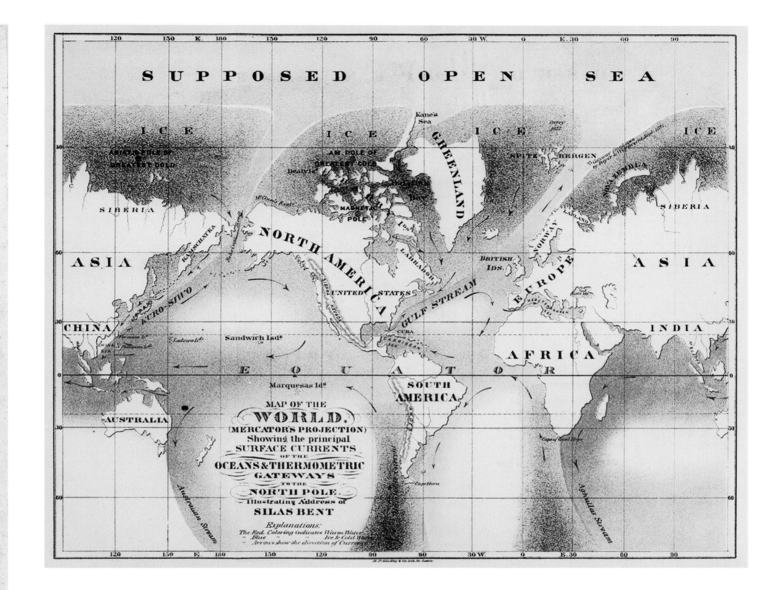

MAP OF THE
WORLD.
(MERCATOR'S PROJECTION)
Showing the principal
SURFACE CURRENTS
OF THE
OCEANS & THERMOMETRIC
GATEWAYS
TO THE
NORTH POLE.
Illustrating Address of
SILAS BENT

Explanations:
The Red. Coloring indicates Warm Water.
" Blue " " Ice & Cold Water.
" Arrows show the direction of Currents.

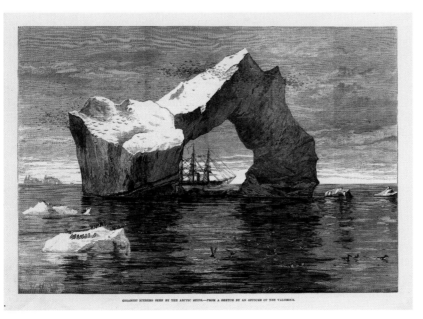

ABOVE Dubious ideas about a Northwest Passage persisted well into the 19th century. U.S. Navy officer Silas Bent used this 1872 map to claim that the Gulf Stream and other warm currents fed an open sea around the North Pole.

LEFT The British public was enthralled by stories of Arctic exploration. This 1875 image from the *Illustrated London News* shows a giant iceberg seen by a British expedition.

Ode to an Ocean

A HAND-PAINTED MAP MURAL TEEMING WITH WILDLIFE CELEBRATES THE PACIFIC

CREATED *1940*
SOURCE *David Rumsey Map Collection*

In 1936 and 1937, the U.S. Army Corps of Engineers created an artificial island in San Francisco Bay to be the site for the 1939 Golden Gate International Exposition. The Pacific-themed fair staged on the new 400-acre (160 ha) Treasure Island was an eclectic display of architecture, art, and entertainment including an 80-foot (24 m) statue of the goddess Pacifica, and Sally Rand's Nude Ranch, a show featuring scantily clad "ranch hands."

An exhibit hall called Pacific House was filled with a collection of bespoke artwork, much of it map themed, for which celebrated Mexican artist Miguel Covarrubias was invited to paint a series of enormous murals. Best known for his distinctive caricatures of famous people that appeared in the *New Yorker* and *Vanity Fair* magazines and for his circle of famous friends that included Eugene O'Neill, Zora Neale Hurston, Langston Hughes, and Diego Rivera, Covarrubias painted six maps of the Pacific Ocean that are unlike anything else he created in his career. The most striking was the 24-foot (7.3 m)-wide "Fauna and Flora of the Pacific," using colors to represent climate and vegetation zones and featuring everything from a sloth to a cypress tree. The description in a printed atlas of the collection touts "famous and often lurid" tropical animals in the green zone, the "so-called Marco Polo mountain sheep" of the white zone in Siberia, and the kiwi in New Zealand's light olive green zone, "a strange bird that seems designed by an American comic-strip artist."

After the fair, the murals spent time on display in the American Museum of Natural History in New York City and then hung in San Francisco's Ferry Building for more than four decades. When that building was renovated in 2001, the murals were removed and put into storage for years before being cleaned and restored and sent on a brief tour in Mexico. In 2008, they returned to Treasure Island to be stored again, and were largely forgotten. Four of the murals are there still. The other two met very different fates. "Art Forms of the Pacific Area" disappeared somewhere between New York and San Francisco in the 1950s and was never seen again. But "Fauna and Flora," now valued at $1.5 million, hangs in San Francisco's acclaimed de Young Museum, where thousands of visitors can appreciate it every year. ✳

Miguel Covarrubias's *Pageant of the Pacific* atlas contains prints of six enormous, themed maps that he painted as murals for the 1939 San Francisco World's Fair, including this one of plants and animals found in the Pacific region.

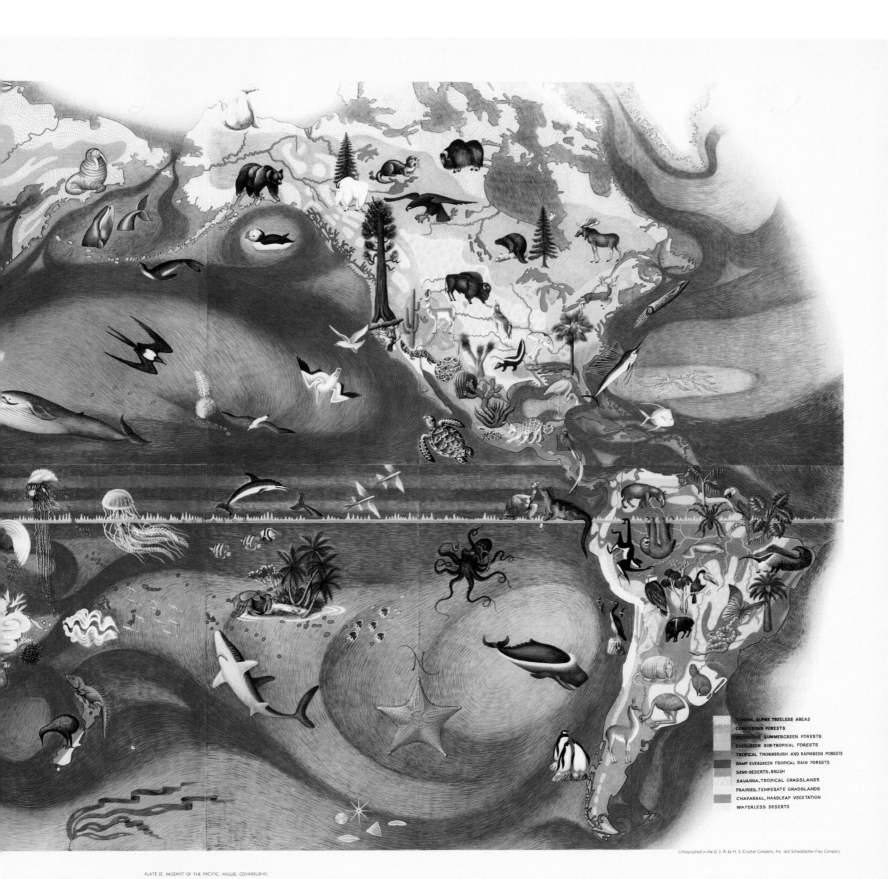

TUNDRA, ALPINE TREELESS AREAS
CONIFEROUS FORESTS
DECIDUOUS SUMMERGREEN FORESTS
EVERGREEN SUB-TROPICAL FORESTS
TROPICAL THORNBRUSH AND RAINGREEN FORESTS
DAMP EVERGREEN TROPICAL RAIN FORESTS
SEMI-DESERTS, BRUSH
SAVANNA, TROPICAL GRASSLANDS
PRAIRIES, TEMPERATE GRASSLANDS
CHAPARRAL, HARDLEAF VEGETATION
WATERLESS DESERTS

Lithographed in the U. S. A. by H. S. Crocker Company, Inc. and Schwabacher-Frey Company

PLATE II: PAGEANT OF THE PACIFIC: MIGUEL COVARRUBIAS

Published by Pacific House, San Francisco, California

A Sea Atlas Full of Beauty and Heartbreak

INNOVATION DIDN'T AUTOMATICALLY BRING SUCCESS IN THE CUTTHROAT WORLD OF 17TH-CENTURY MAPMAKING

CREATED *1658*
SOURCE *Osher Map Library*

The mapmaking business in 17th-century Amsterdam was brutally competitive. The Dutch East India Company had a lock on the spice trade, sending hundreds of ships to the Far East to procure black pepper, cinnamon, nutmeg, and other exotic ingredients. All of those ship captains—not to mention the many others plying trade routes closer to home—needed maps and charts to guide them, and a handful of skillful map publishers competed for their business, including a talented, but largely unappreciated, cartographer named Arnold Colom.

The big players in this tough cartographic world were the Blaeus. Willem Blaeu, and then his son Joan, were the official cartographers for the Dutch East India Company, giving them unrivaled access to the latest geographic information and a lucrative inside track on the company's business. It helped that they also did beautiful work; they are by far the most famous cartographers from this great era of Dutch cartography.

But they weren't the only ones making beautiful maps. Little is known about Arnold Colom, but he seems to have been something of an underdog in the world of mapmaking. He produced only two major works, but this one, his 1658 *Zee-atlas, ofte, Water-wereldt (Sea Atlas, or, Water World),* was an innovative publication, unlike anything else on the market at the time.

The "pilot books" the Blaeus were making were practical guides for working seamen, packed with up to 200 pages of detailed notes and instructions on sailing and navigation. The maps in these books were often beautiful, but they were meant to be functional and focused mostly on important Dutch trade routes in the North Sea and Mediterranean. Colom's atlas was something different. For one thing, it was big. Its pages were more than 2 feet (0.6 m) tall and nearly as wide—four times the size of those in the Blaeus' pilot books, which were about the size of the book you're currently reading.

"It would be an insult to call it a coffee table book, but that was the idea," says Jason Hubbard, a map collector and researcher who has studied Colom. Unlike a coffee table book, a 17th-century Dutch sea atlas can fetch well over $100,000 at auction; collectors treat them as works of art.

Perhaps feeling squeezed by the Blaeus' grip on the map market, Colom was trying to reach a new audience: merchants and other relatively wealthy citizens who had an interest in the maritime trade but were unlikely to ever take the helm of a ship themselves. Colom left out all of the sailing instructions, limiting his text to a two-page introduction. This was a crafty move, Hubbard says. The audience he was trying to reach didn't need such technical information, and leaving it out saved Colom a small fortune on printing costs. These savings allowed him to sell his atlas at a lower, more affordable price, despite the larger pages.

Colom knew better than to skimp on the maps themselves. Unlike his competitors, he included charts of far-flung regions in addition to the local waters. Colom's was the first sea atlas to include a chart of New Netherland (soon to be seized by the English and renamed New York) and the first with charts of both the West and East Indies (see page 34). Maps of these areas would have been hard to come by in Amsterdam in those days, but Colom made them available to anyone with enough money to buy his atlas. As was typical at the time, the atlas was printed in black and white from copper plates and hand-colored according to the taste and budget of the purchaser.

Colom's atlas doesn't appear to have been the big

This map from Arnold Colom's 1658 *Zee-atlas* shows the North Sea coasts of England, the Netherlands, and Norway. It contains far more detail, including spot depths and the locations of shoals, than do the maps in the atlas of distant parts of the world that the Dutch had only begun to explore.

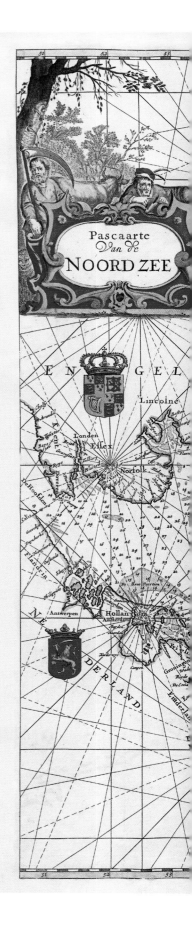

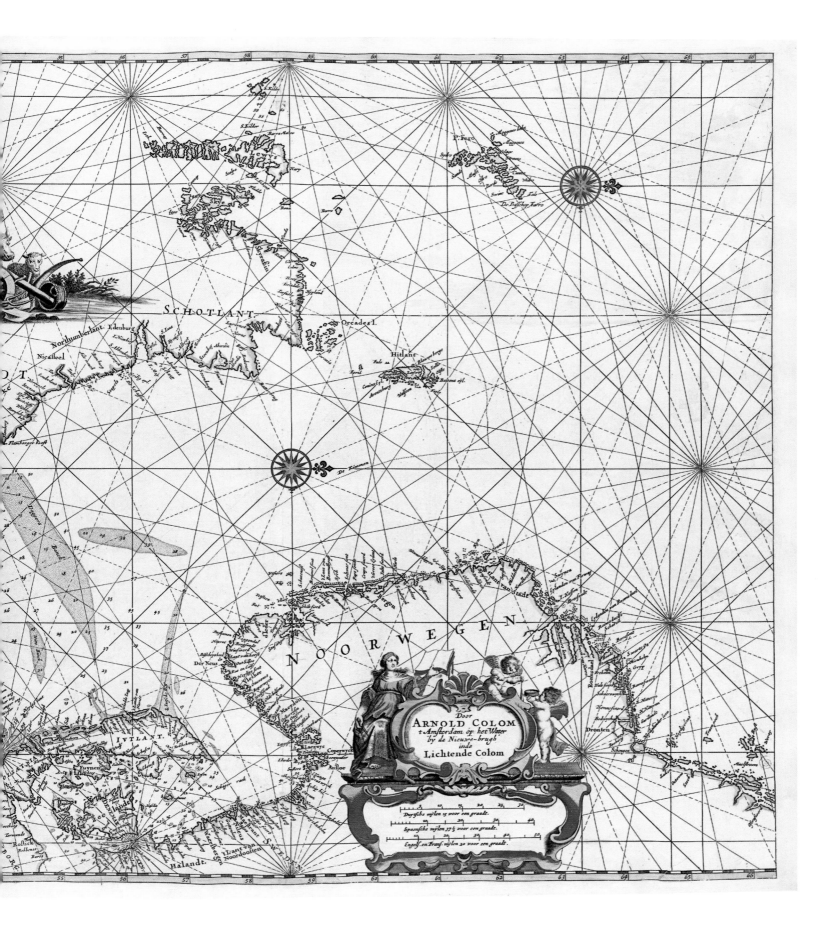

Door
ARNOLD COLOM
t'Amsterdam op' het Water
by de Nieuwe-brugh
inde
Lichtende Colom

Duytsche mylen 15 voor een graadt.

Spaensche mylen 17½ voor een graadt.

Engelf. en Franf. mylen 20 voor een graadt.

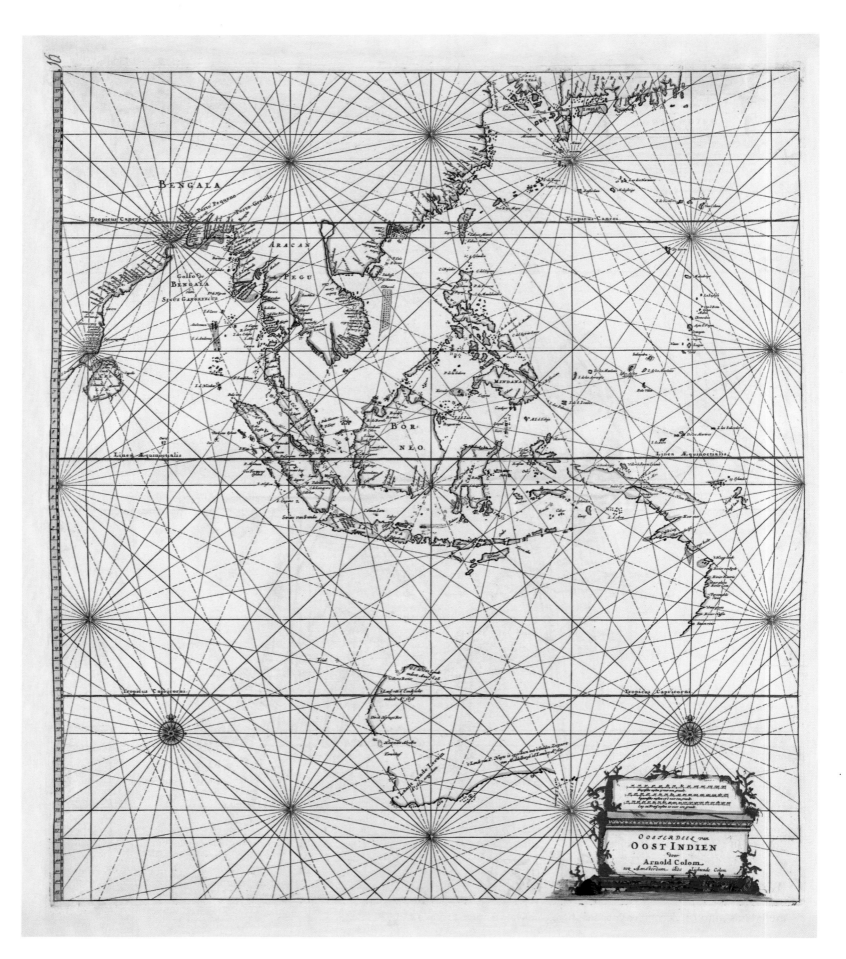

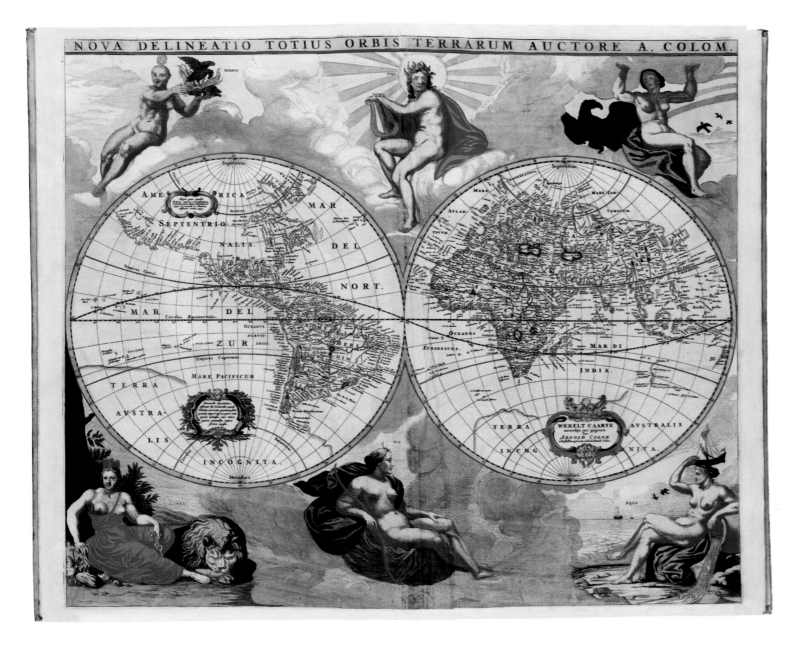

NOVA DELINEATIO TOTIUS ORBIS TERRARUM AUCTORE A. COLOM.

commercial success he'd hoped for. Records indicate that he got behind on his rent and gave up the copper plates used to print the *Zee-atlas* to settle a debt with his landlord in 1663. "That's the last act of desperation," Hubbard says. "The copper plates are the most valuable thing you have." Colom died a few years later, in his mid-forties.

If Colom didn't profit from his pioneering atlas, others certainly did. Mapmaker Hendrick Doncker acquired Colom's copper plates and used them to create his own *Zee-atlas,* adding exotic birds and other decorative flourishes here and there and replacing Colom's name with his own. Doncker issued atlas after atlas in the years after Colom's death, and competing mapmakers followed suit. The style of large sea atlas Colom had invented was suddenly a best-selling item.

Colom's plates passed on to another mapmaker, and then another. They were in use for at least 100 years. The clean lines on Colom's charts and his artful frontispiece, above, remain a testament to his skill as a mapmaker and engraver—and a cruel reminder that skill isn't always enough to make it big. ✳

OPPOSITE Along with its unusually large size, the inclusion of far-flung regions like the East Indies distinguished Colom's atlas from those made by his competitors.

ABOVE The statuesque figures on the frontispiece of Colom's atlas represent Day and Night, as well as the four classical elements: Fire, Air, Earth, and Water.

The Shape of Water

MAPPING ALL THE WATERWAYS IN THE CONTIGUOUS UNITED STATES

CREATED *2016*
SOURCE *Muir Way*

This map of the contiguous 48 states shows every stream, river, and lake—and nothing else. Though it looks a lot like a shaded-relief map, it's simply the pattern of rivers that creates the appearance of mountains and valleys.

The map is based on radar data collected from the space shuttle as it orbited Earth, bouncing radar signals off the surface and recording how long it took the signals to arrive back at the spacecraft. The shorter the distance is between the shuttle and that spot on Earth, the less time a signal takes to return; the shortest times indicate the highest points of elevation. NASA translated all of those bounce backs into a digital elevation model that covers 80 percent of the planet's surface, and most of its land mass, at around 100-foot (30 m) resolution—the most detailed global topographic map ever made.

For the map, a series of algorithms was applied to the topography data to identify the waterways, from small seasonal streams all the way up to the Mississippi River and the Great Salt Lake. The width of the rivers on the map reflects their place in the watershed hierarchy, known as the Strahler number. The streams at the headwaters of a river are considered first-order streams and are drawn with thin lines. Where two first-order streams meet, their combined route is a second-order segment, indicated with a thicker line. Two second-order segments join to become an even thicker third-order line, and so on. "Instead of showing the actual size of the rivers, it represents their interconnectivity and flow," says designer Jared Prince, who produced the map for his company, Muir Way. "It reminds me of the human vascular system and how rivers and streams support our country's ecosystems in a similar way."

By leaving out everything but waterways, the map highlights how they interact with topography. Mountainous areas are dominated by shorter rivers that are often roughly parallel, while flatter regions have longer rivers with more winding paths. The flow of water slowly erodes the landscape, carving valleys and canyons into mountains and hills and creating flat plains. ✳

Only rivers, streams, and lakes are shown on this map of the contiguous United States. The map was made using algorithms and elevation data collected by NASA's space shuttle program.

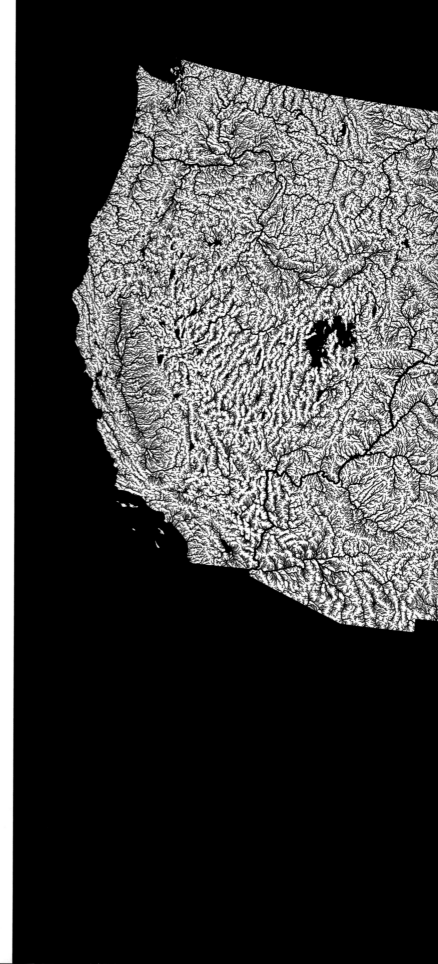

The Curse of the Nicaragua Canal

A TANTALIZING MARITIME SHORTCUT THAT HAS CONTINUED TO DEFY ALL EFFORTS TO BUILD IT

CREATED *1858–1899*
SOURCE *David Rumsey Map Collection, Stanford Libraries; ProQuest; PJ Mode Collection of Persuasive Cartography, Cornell*

The idea of digging a canal across the Central American isthmus dates back to the 16th century and the Spanish conquistadores, but they didn't have the technology to make it happen. It took the invention of the steam shovel 300 years later to breathe life into these aspirations.

In 1858, a flamboyant French journalist named Félix Belly traveled to Central America to pursue construction of a canal that would connect the Atlantic and Pacific Oceans. Whether Belly was acting in an official capacity for the French government or acting of his own accord remains murky. Regardless, he managed to negotiate a treaty resolving a border dispute between Nicaragua and Costa Rica and to secure a concession that would allow a canal to be built.

The canal would follow the San Juan River inland from the Atlantic port of San Juan del Norte, using a series of seven locks to raise ships up to the giant Lake Nicaragua about 100 feet (30 m) above sea level over a course of about 100 miles (160 km). Another six locks would lower ships back down to Salinas Bay on the Pacific side. But Belly was better at promoting big ideas than financing them, and the venture ran out of money within a few years.

Belly wasn't the only one chasing the dream. The discovery of gold in California in 1848 showed how valuable such a maritime shortcut would be to an increasingly westward-looking United States. A canal could cut 8,000 miles (13,000 km) or more off the trip from the East Coast down around the tip of South America and back up to Pacific ports. The U.S. government sent surveyors and engineers to check out the options, and a consensus was reached: The canal should be built not in Panama, where it is today, but 400 miles (650 km) northwest—in Nicaragua.

Nicaragua was closer to American ports, and the large, navigable Lake Nicaragua in the middle of the route meant that just two short canal segments would need to be dug on either side. In addition, the lake's low elevation meant that relatively few locks would be needed.

Panama had higher mountain passes and a reputation as a disease-ravaged hellhole. A railroad had been built in the 1850s to shuttle

Frenchman Félix Belly hoped to build a canal across Nicaragua to connect the Atlantic and Pacific Oceans. This 1858 map, created by Belly's engineer, Thomé de Gamond, shows the proposed route. It was published in a book that also included a copy of the treaty Belly had negotiated between Nicaragua and Costa Rica.

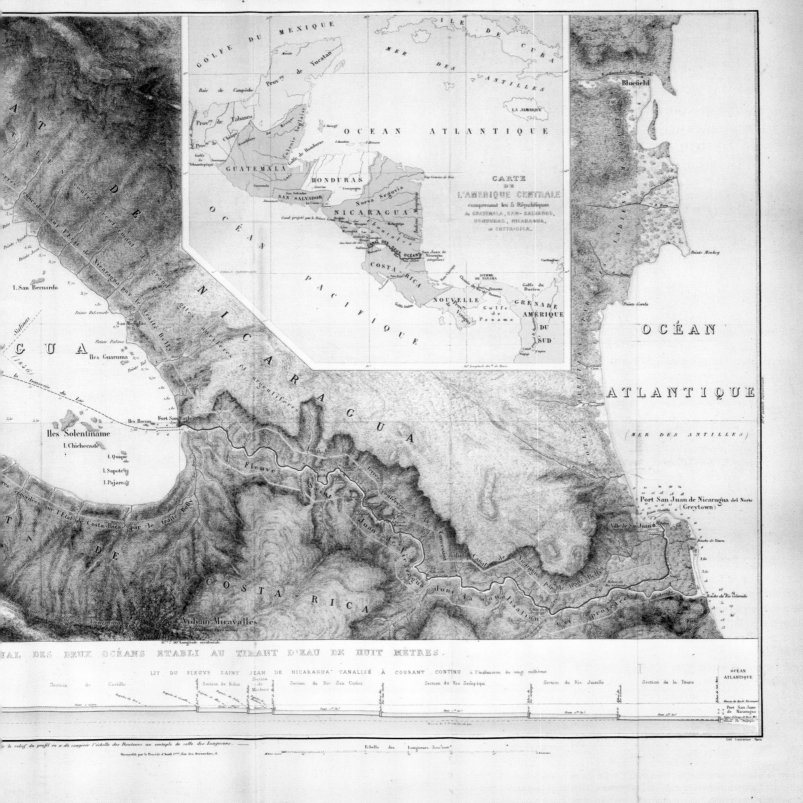

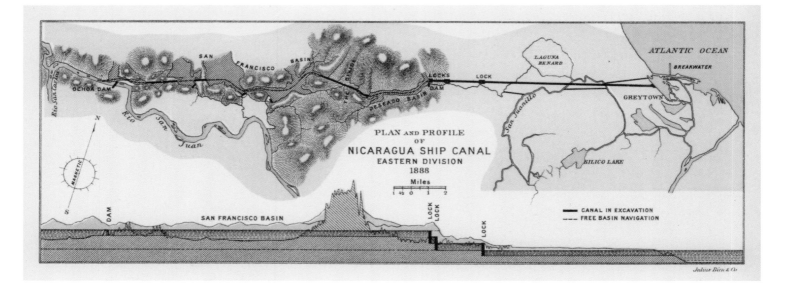

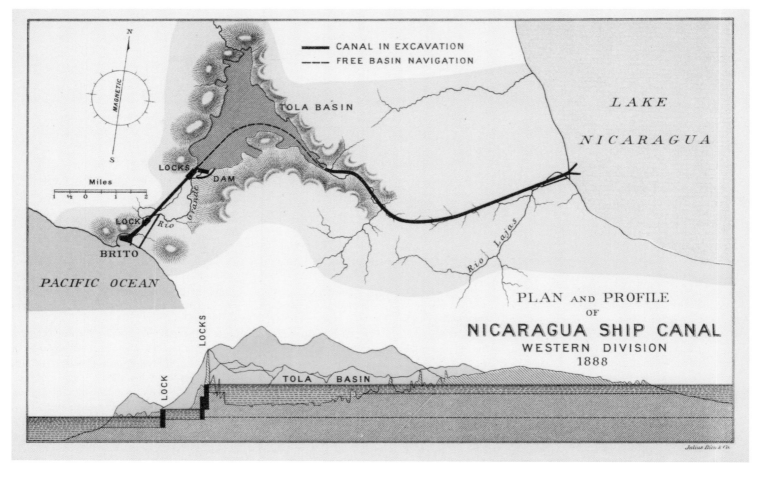

ABOVE These maps from the reports of the Maritime Canal Company of Nicaragua show slightly different routes from the ones Belly proposed, taking a straighter course inland on the Atlantic side instead of following the San Juan River (top) and then a more northerly route from the lake to the Pacific (bottom). This route is more direct and requires fewer locks.

OPPOSITE In this 1899 editorial cartoon published in *Judge* magazine, President William McKinley stands astride a map of Central America, holding a pick and rolling up his sleeves as he eyes a banner marking the "proposed Nicaragua canal." Ships laden with American goods for foreign markets appear to be lining up to cross, while Uncle Sam brings picks and shovels from Washington, D.C.

A THING WELL BEGUN IS HALF DONE.

Uncle Sam—"Finish the canal, McKinley, and make our national expansion complete in your first administration."

people and cargo across the isthmus to Panama City. During construction, thousands died of cholera, dysentery, and other tropical scourges. "The horrors of the road in the rainy season are beyond description," wrote Ulysses S. Grant, then a young Army officer, after making the trip in 1852.

The maps opposite come from the reports of the Maritime Canal Company of Nicaragua, which was incorporated by the U.S. government in 1889. The following year, the company reported to Congress that great progress was being made. A breakwater had been built and a channel dug to improve the harbor at San Juan del Norte (also called Greytown). Several streams had been cleared of debris and prepared for dredging. Barracks, machine shops, warehouses, and other buildings had been erected, and a railroad was being built to carry workers and machines inland from the port. The venture was short-lived, however. An economic crisis, the panic of 1893, put an end to the company.

Subsequent attempts to revive the project came and went. Meanwhile, the canal the French

had begun digging in Panama in 1880 was faring even worse. Malaria and yellow fever were taking a horrific toll on the workers, and the engineers had underestimated the challenges. Landslides kept ruining the work at a crucial cut across the Continental Divide. By the turn of the century, the first French company in charge had gone bankrupt and its successor was in dire straits.

To some American politicians, a half-built canal in Panama that could be bought on the cheap began to look like an attractive proposition, and the Nicaragua route suddenly faced serious competition. A few days before a crucial Senate vote in 1902, a proponent of the Panama plan made sure every senator received a small gift: a Nicaraguan postage stamp depicting an erupting volcano—a menacing reminder of the region's seismic volatility. In a close vote, the Senate decided to move toward purchasing the Panama Canal from the French.

The United States bought the project in 1904, including all the equipment and the work done to date, for the bargain price of

$40 million. Ten years later, the Panama Canal opened to ship traffic, and it has been a vital shipping route ever since.

But the dream of a canal across Nicaragua wasn't dead. In 2013 a mysterious Chinese telecom tycoon cut a deal with the Nicaraguan government to build a canal that would be big enough to accommodate supersized container ships. From the start, the plan was controversial. Local landowners and indigenous groups objected to the possibility of their land being taken away. Conservationists raised concerns about the threat to wetlands, rain forests, and other vulnerable areas, as well as to water quality in Lake Nicaragua, the country's largest reservoir of drinking water.

A groundbreaking ceremony was held in 2014, and then the project fizzled out. The tycoon reportedly lost his fortune in the stock market, and apart from widening a few roads, construction never got under way. The plan to build a canal across Nicaragua looks to be truly dead—at least for now. ✳

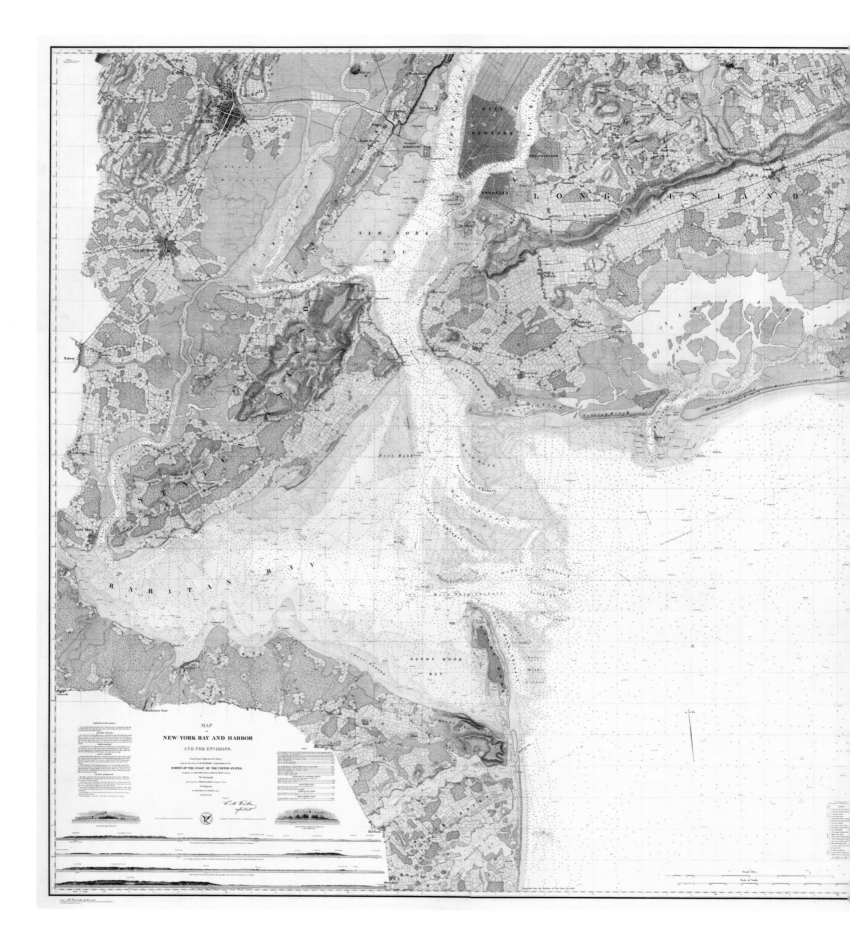

Sounding New York Harbor

THE U.S. COAST SURVEY GETS OFF TO AN AUSPICIOUS START

CREATED *1844*
SOURCE *David Rumsey Map Collection, Stanford Libraries*

The first map published by the U.S. Coast Survey was a long time coming, but it was well worth the wait. Congress authorized a survey of the coast in 1807, but it would be another 37 years before this chart of "New-York Bay and Harbor and the Environs" was engraved and printed for the public. It pushed the upper bounds of accuracy for the time, comparable to maps made more than a century later. And it contains details of an important discovery made while surveying the entrance to the harbor—one that, if discovered earlier, might have changed U.S. history.

One reason publication took so long was the meticulous nature of the Survey's first superintendent, Ferdinand Hassler. He came to the United States from Switzerland in 1805, hauling a library of more than 3,000 scientific and technical books, as well as some standard weights and measures, including an iron bar marked with the exact length of a French meter. Hassler insisted on a methodical scientific approach. Before even beginning to map the seafloor, he built a geographical framework on

coastal land by using astronomical observations to fix the locations of points and triangulating between them. This involved a lot of intense bushwhacking up steep slopes, careful measurement, and advanced trigonometry.

Once a network of triangles in the New York area was established, they began charting the underwater landscape. Boats traversed the area to be mapped, stopping at regular intervals to lower a lead weight on a line to the seafloor to measure depth. They used sextants and spyglasses at each stop to measure the angle between two fixed stations on land. The same thing was done from each of the land stations, measuring the angle between the boat and the other station. The location of the boat was calculated from those angles and a sounding depth marked at each point (see below).

Hassler was particularly interested in finding another route for ships to pass over the shallow area that stretched across most of the mouth of the harbor between Long Island and Sandy Hook. At the time, ships had to hug the coast near Sandy Hook to access the harbor through the main ship channel. Hassler sent Thomas Gedney

to look for a new deepwater channel to the north.

Gedney was a naval lieutenant whose career with the Survey included tackling an armed man trying to assassinate President Andrew Jackson in 1835 and capturing the famous slave-bearing ship *Amistad* in 1839. In 1835, Gedney found the new channel Hassler had hoped for. It was 2 feet (0.6 m) deeper than the main channel, allowing larger ships to enter the harbor at low tide and providing a more direct route in. Had Gedney's Channel been known during the Revolutionary War, the British blockade of New York Harbor and the occupation of New York would have been much more difficult.

The Survey had already delivered some preliminary charts of important ports at the request of Congress, but Hassler was determined that no official maps would be published before they were ready. Engraving of the copper plates for the New York chart didn't begin until 1842, eight years after Gedney began his work in the harbor. Sadly, Hassler died before the chart was published in 1844, but his careful work ensured the soundness of the Survey's foundation and its legacy as the country's first federal scientific agency. ✳

OPPOSITE This 1844 map of New York Harbor was the first official map published by the U.S. Coast Survey (which was renamed the Coast and Geodetic Survey in 1878 and incorporated into the National Oceanic and Atmospheric Administration in 1970). It includes hundreds of depth measurements, or soundings, made by lowering a lead weight on a line into the water until it hit bottom.

BELOW The Main Ship Channel into New York Harbor is shown on the left side of this section of the map. Gedney's Channel, which was discovered during the making of the map, is on the right. The numbers represent depth measurements.

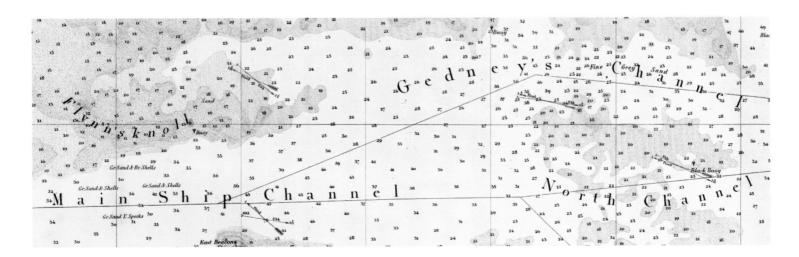

CITIES

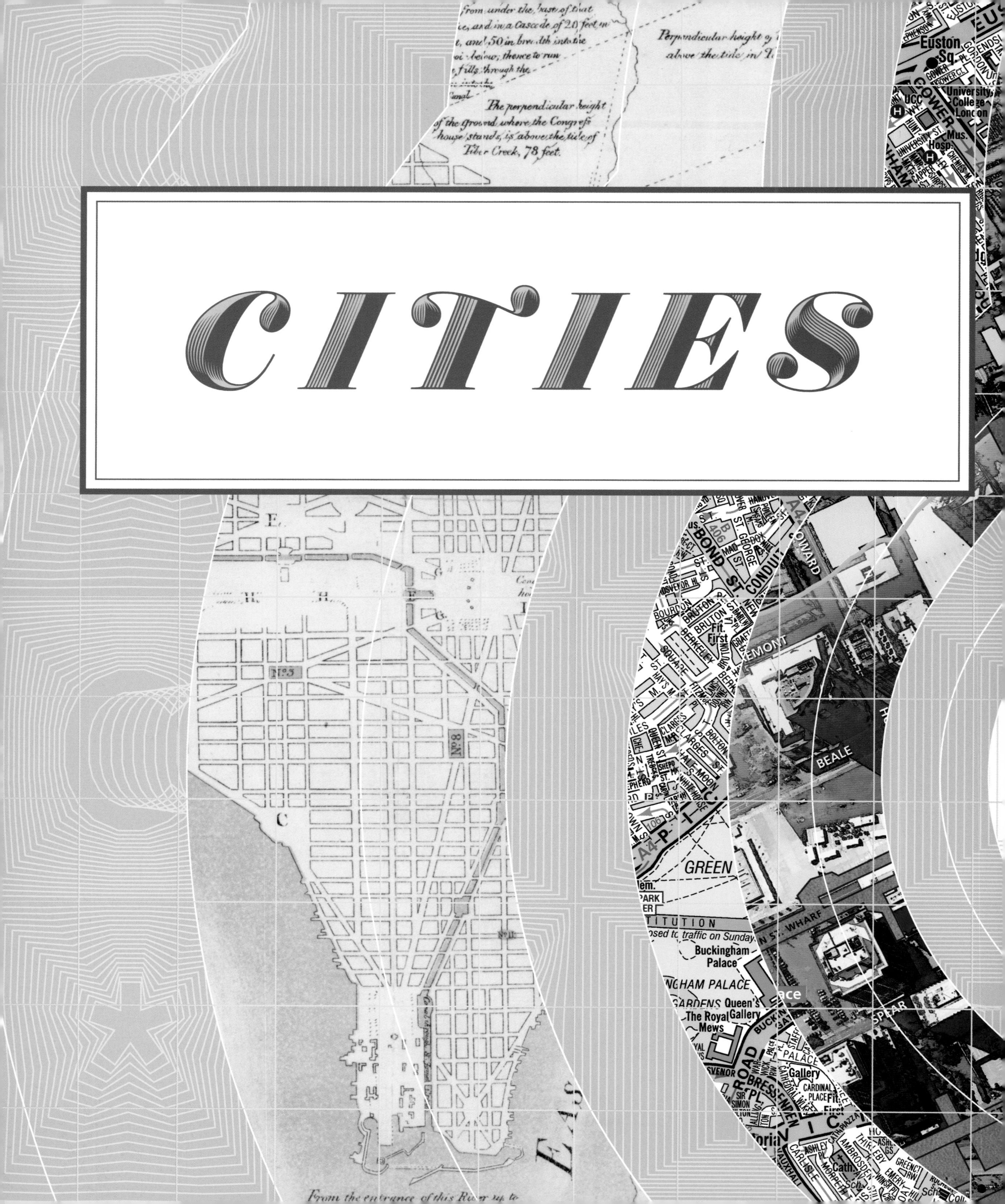

The perpendicular height of the Ground where the Congress house stands, is above the tide of Tiber Creek, 78 feet.
Perpendicular height
above the tide in
No.5
No.8
C
E.
From the entrance of this River up to
Euston Sq.
University College London
UCC
Mus. Hosp.
BOND ST.
ST. GEORGE
CONDUIT
BRUTON
BERKELEY SQUARE
Fit First
BOLTON
HALF MOON
GREEN
Buckingham Palace
closed to traffic on Sunday
The Royal Mews
Queen's Gallery
Gallery
CARDINAL PLACE
PALACE
BRESSENDEN PL
ROAD
CARLISLE
ASHLEY
AMBROSDEN
FREMONT
BEALE
ST. WHARF
SPEAR
HOWARD

THE EMBARCADERO

PIER 1

Mapping Urban Environments

Maps of cities are among the most familiar, practical, and intriguing maps there are. Street plans of well-known metropolises like Washington, D.C., London, and New York City are instantly recognizable and can evoke the places themselves in the minds of their viewers. People often feel an emotional connection to the spatial pattern of their hometown, childhood stomping grounds, or the place where they first struck out on their own.

This connection to the graphic representation of cities also makes them effective records of the past. They provide a stable foundation on which to track change and capture the ephemeral aspects of city life, as the maps in this chapter demonstrate. The inexorable rise of the Ottoman Empire in the 16th century is brought to life in colorful bird's-eye views of conquered cities (see page 60). A map of the buried bones of ships abandoned in San Francisco during the gold rush era reveals where landfill has expanded the city's coastline (see page 56). The explosion of digital data has given cartographers endless ways to explore the world today, such as tracking where photos are taken in New York City to show where tourists spend their time and where New Yorkers themselves hang out (see page 64).

A familiar lattice of roads offers something viewers can relate to: a concrete framework for understanding the intangible aspects of cities and the life within them. At a time when urbanites and travelers alike use digital maps to navigate the streets, the city plan is as close to a universal cartographic language as it gets. ➤➤

HISTORIC MEXICO CITY
(1794, Library of Congress)

This map of Mexico City is more than two centuries old, but to people who know Mexico's capital today, the pattern of streets is unmistakable. The city's historical center is dominated by the Zócalo, one of the largest plazas in Latin America, which is flanked by buildings depicted on the map that are still standing today. The map was part of an effort to clean up the city and crack down on corruption. The colors indicate where improvements had been made (red) and where they were still needed (yellow).

The Ages of Amsterdam

VISUALIZING THE CITY'S RICH HISTORY THROUGH ITS BUILDINGS

CREATED *2013*
SOURCE *Bert Spaan for Waag Society*

Amsterdam has one of the most recognizable city plans in Europe. It's also a prime example of the typical evolution of cities on the Continent, with an old center surrounded by swaths of increasingly newer construction, as you can see in this map of color-coded building ages.

The orderly pattern of Amsterdam's center is the result of 17th-century city planning, carefully structured around a system of concentric semicircular canals. Today there are more than 60 miles (100 km) of waterways throughout the city that create around 90 islands and require more than 1,500 bridges. The historic canal district, known as the Grachtengordel, was added to UNESCO's World Heritage List in 2010.

The innermost ring is the Singel canal, which marked the edge of the city and served as a defensive moat in the late 15th and 16th centuries. Most of the buildings between the Singel and the outermost ring, the Singelracht, were built in the 17th century during the Dutch Golden Age. But scattered among the pre-1800 buildings, colored red, is a sprinkling of blue post-1960 buildings.

The largest of these newer buildings is the Stopera, a combined *stadhuis* (city hall) and opera house, which stands out in light blue where the Amstel River enters the city center from the south. Several other locations were considered for either the opera or the city hall, but in 1979 the city decided to combine the

buildings into one facility, which opened in 1986. It was built on the Vlooienburg, originally an artificial island built in the early 17th century as an industrial site. In 1882 a bordering canal was filled in, and Vlooienburg became a Jewish quarter that was once home to the great Dutch painter Rembrandt and the Dutch philosopher Benedict de Spinoza. A public market still exists where the canal used to be.

A bit north and west of the Stopera near the center of town, the single red-colored building resembling a number eight floating in an open square is what may be the oldest nonreligious building in Amsterdam. Known as the Waag (weigh house), it was built in the late 15th century as a gate in the walls around the oldest part of the city. The Waag has served many purposes since then, including as a fire station and a surgical theater. Today it is home to the Waag Society, a foundation for artistic, technological, and social innovation, which also made this map of Amsterdam building ages.

The map, based on data from the Dutch government, is representative of a trend of interactive web maps of building ages that started in 2013 in the United States. The maps were inspired by the increasing number of city governments there that began making these sorts of data publicly accessible in digital form for the first time. European cities have also been working to make data easier to explore and use, smoothing the way for maps like this one. ✳

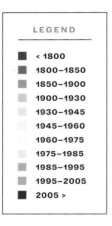

LEGEND

■ < 1800
■ 1800–1850
■ 1850–1900
  1900–1930
  1930–1945
  1945–1960
  1960–1975
  1975–1985
■ 1985–1995
■ 1995–2005
■ 2005 >

Amsterdam's buildings are color-coded by date on this map made in 2013. The pattern reveals the growth of the city from the old canal-ringed center, filled primarily with red-colored buildings built before 1800, to the outskirts dominated by buildings built after 1960, colored in shades of blue.

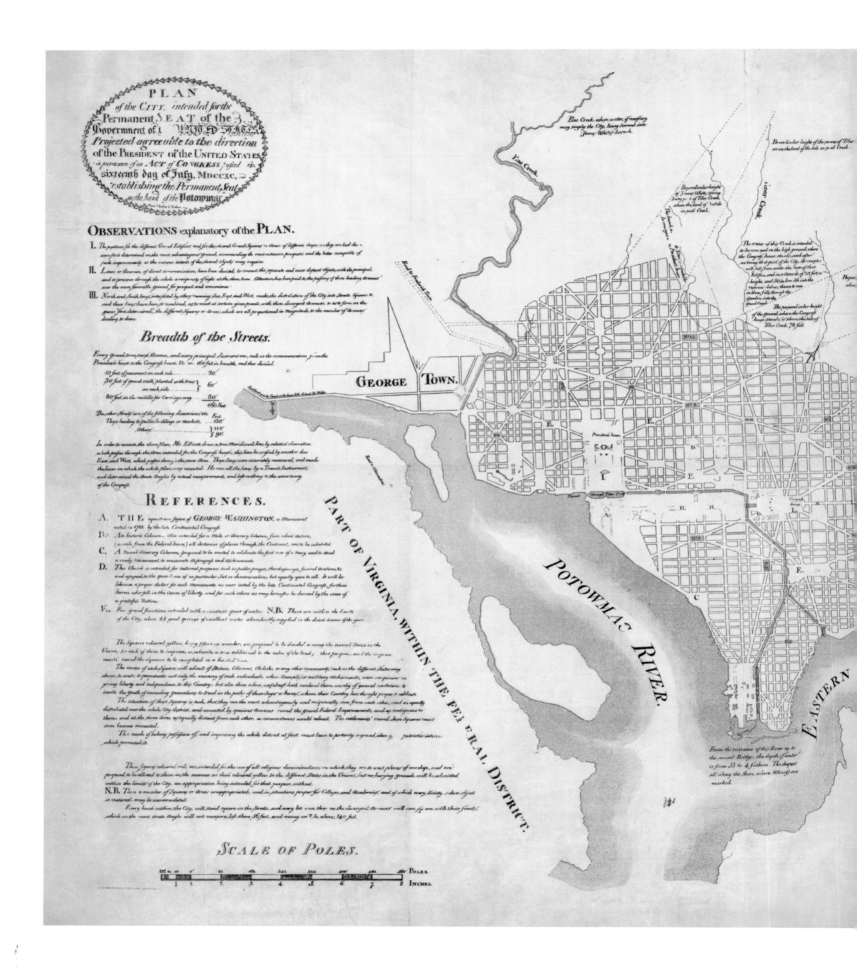

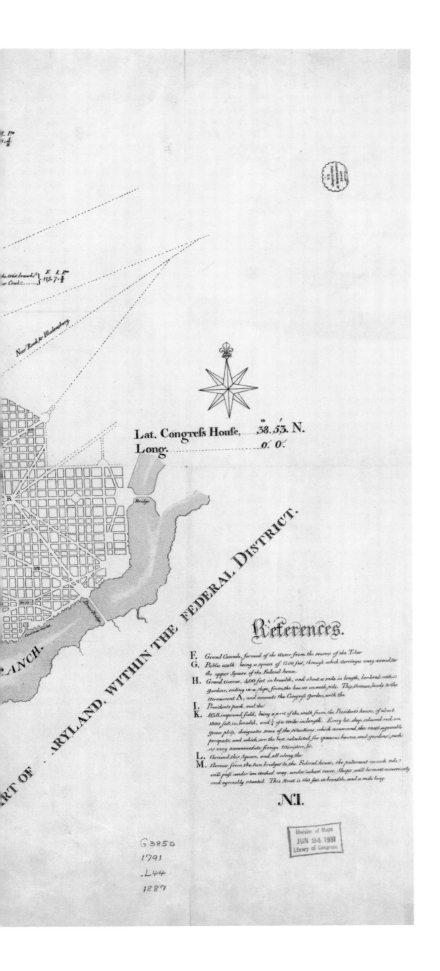

Planning the Capital

THE VISIONARY FRENCHMAN WHO DESIGNED WASHINGTON, D.C., AND DIED IN OBSCURITY

CREATED *1791*
CREATOR *Pierre Charles L'Enfant*

Locked deep in the bowels of the Library of Congress, a darkened, nearly illegible map sits in a 100-pound (45 kg) case filled with pressurized argon gas. Its contents have been mostly obscured by years of neglect and misguided attempts at preservation, but it's still possible to make out the words at the top: "Plan of the City intended for the Permanent Seat of the Government of the United States." The story of the unlikely man behind the first map of the nation's capital was also obscured for more than a century.

Pierre Charles L'Enfant left Paris for America in 1776 at the age of 22. Like many of his fellow countrymen, including the Marquis de Lafayette, he came to fight with the American army during the Revolutionary War. L'Enfant may have been hoping for military glory, but his most important wartime accomplishment was networking. He curried favor with an impressive roster of men that included Alexander Hamilton, James Monroe, and George Washington. He had trained as an artist at France's prestigious Royal Academy, and even painted Washington's portrait during the war.

But he also had an aptitude for architecture and engineering. After the war, Hamilton helped steer his career in that direction by recommending him for high-profile jobs. By 1788 L'Enfant had landed the plum assignment of renovating and expanding the city hall building in New York to serve as the seat of the new federal government. In less than six months, he had transformed the building into what one local reporter called "by far the most extensive and elegant of any in America." And so, three years later, the 36-year-old Frenchman was able to persuade President Washington to let him plan the nation's permanent capital city.

Secretary of State Thomas Jefferson instructed L'Enfant to select a location within a 100-square-mile (260 sq km) federal territory along the Potomac River for a modest collection of government buildings. But by the time L'Enfant arrived at the site on March 9, 1791, he already had a grand vision for an expansive city

This copy of Pierre Charles L'Enfant's map of Washington, D.C., was produced in 1887 by the U.S. Coast and Geodetic Survey. L'Enfant's original 1791 manuscript map has darkened with age and mistreatment, to the point of illegibility.

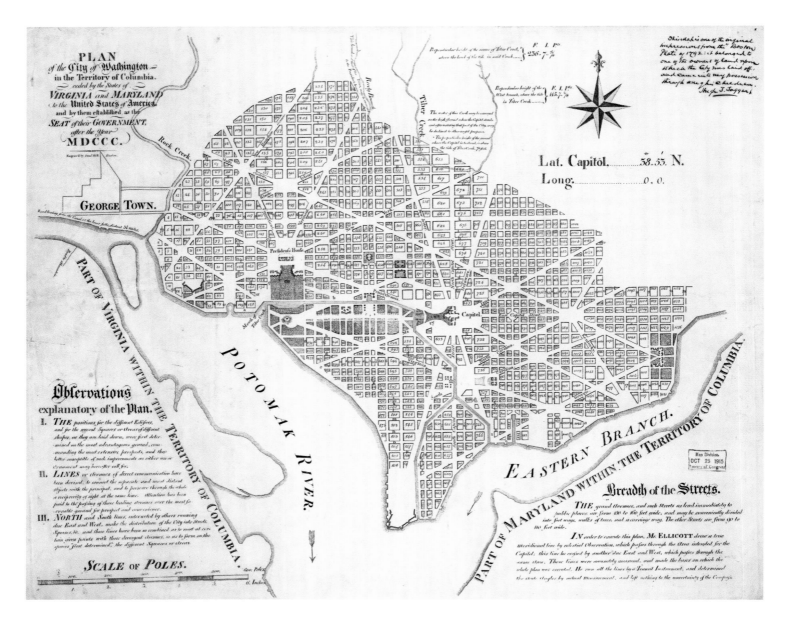

worthy of the president and representative of the ideals of the new republic.

Washington had asked him to come up with a preliminary plan in three weeks, and he spent most of those days on horseback, rain or shine, taking stock of sparsely populated forest, marsh, and farmland. L'Enfant hewed his plan to the topography, placing the "Congress house" atop the highest hill near the center of the territory, with the rest of the city radiating from it like spokes. A grand, wide avenue meant to be a democratic "people's park" extended from the hill to the Potomac. The president's house was to sit on a smaller rise with a magnificent view of the river, its grounds meeting the avenue at a right angle (see map at top right).

The network of long diagonal avenues and public squares extending away from the two federal houses set the design apart from the uniform street grids of American cities like Philadelphia, which L'Enfant described as "tired and insipid." Instead, his plan was an American take on the European baroque style of cities like Rome. He envisioned a city on a much grander scale, one that would eventually be home to a million people—larger than all of America's major cities at the time combined.

When Washington arrived at the site at the end of March, he immediately bought into L'Enfant's dramatic, soaring idea for the city. The president gave him just five months to complete the final plan, and L'Enfant worked feverishly to meet the ambitious deadline. By August he had created what biographer Scott Berg would call "the first great artistic achievement that could be truly called American." And that's when things started to fall apart.

L'Enfant disagreed with others involved in the project, including Thomas Jefferson, about how to execute the plan and finance construction of the city. Jefferson preferred to auction off lots and slowly build the city from the proceeds. L'Enfant believed the government should grant property around some of the public squares to each of the 14 states and let the city grow organically from these outposts, eventually knitting together into a cohesive city. He feared that Jefferson's plan would lead to speculation and empty lots, stunting the city's growth.

The disagreement slowly festered until it blew up and caused L'Enfant to be pushed out of the project altogether. The lead surveyor on the project, Andrew Ellicott, drafted a subtly revised version of the plan at Jefferson's behest (above). He straightened a few streets and removed some public squares. Though the

OPPOSITE At Thomas Jefferson's request, surveyor Andrew Ellicott altered L'Enfant's plan in 1792. He straightened a few roads, eliminated a few public squares, and removed L'Enfant's name as the author of the map. Ellicott also enlarged and capitalized his own name where L'Enfant had given him credit for his surveying work (lower right under "Breadth of the Streets").

RIGHT L'Enfant's vision for the capital included a canal connecting the Potomac River and the Anacostia River (called Eastern Branch on L'Enfant's map). The canal was completed in 1815, but fell out of use and was largely covered up by the end of the century. This map of L'Enfant's original design for the Mall was created in 1901 for the McMillan commission by the U.S. Army Corps of Engineers.

BELOW The McMillan Plan for the Mall was inspired in part by L'Enfant's original design (right) and bears many similarities. But this 1902 map of the plan includes 700 acres (280 ha) of land made in the 1870s by dredging sediment from the Potomac River and depositing it on the bank. This landfill now underlies the Lincoln Memorial and the Reflecting Pool.

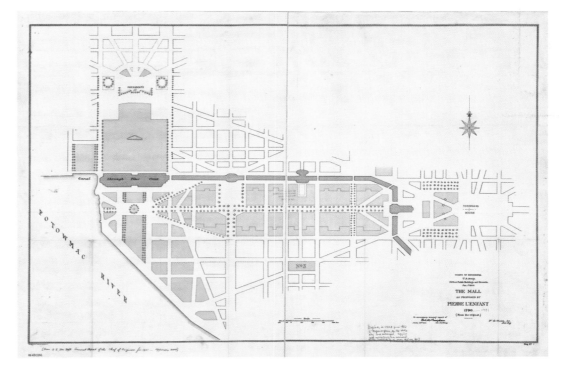

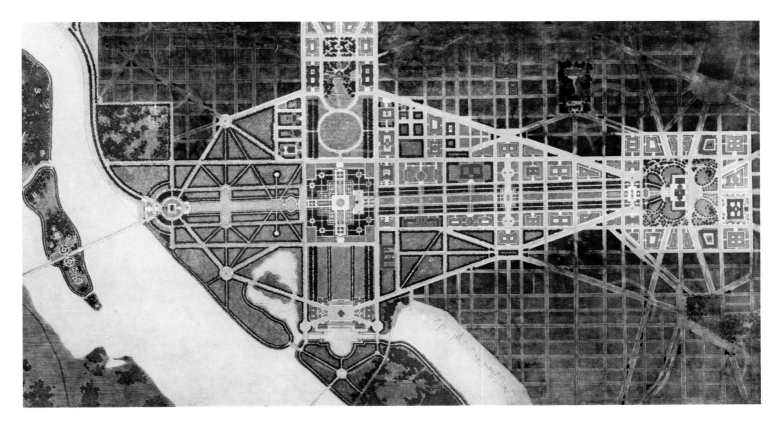

work was still essentially L'Enfant's, the map was stripped of his name.

Time would prove L'Enfant's concerns were valid. Growth of the city was slow and halting, and it would be more than a century before key aspects of his vision were borne out. In 1900, a group of 75 of the nation's preeminent architects met in the capital. Their intent was to come up with a plan to revitalize the city, which they felt had grown haphazardly and not met its promise. The National Mall in particular was in an unacceptable state—a patchwork of mis-

matched gardens, fences, and railroad tracks. Their trained eyes saw no discernible meaning, no unity of design.

Frederick Law Olmsted, Jr., son and namesake of the famous landscape artist (see page 136), proposed that they revisit L'Enfant's vision for the public space he had intended as the democratic heart of the city. The idea gained momentum and eventually won the support of the federal government thanks to the backing of Michigan Senator James McMillan.

Olmsted Jr. and architects Daniel Burnham

and Charles Kim were charged with developing a plan. They studied the way L'Enfant's design emphasized the importance of the Capitol building, but they were also strongly influenced by the growing City Beautiful movement that aimed to bring splendor to cities that would inspire civic engagement and moral consciousness. When maps and scale models of the resulting McMillan Plan were displayed at the Corcoran Gallery of Art in January 1902, thousands of people waited in line, eager to see the capital's future. President Theodore Roosevelt came to see it and

commented on the "greatness of the conception." L'Enfant's grand avenue was back, unifying the houses of government and expertly melding with the landscaping and monuments planned for the new land that had been created by filling the Potomac's tidal flats. The McMillan Plan was implemented bit by bit over the ensuing decades and continues to inform city planners today.

L'Enfant's vision wasn't the only thing the plan resurrected. He had died poor, taken in as a charity case by descendants of one of his admirers and buried alongside servants and slaves on their property just outside the federal district. But his remains were exhumed in 1909, and the city's original planner became the first immigrant to lay in state in the Capitol rotunda.

Finally recognized for his work, he was reburied in Arlington National Cemetery. At the ceremony, President Howard Taft aptly conveyed what the moment signified for L'Enfant: "There are not many who have to wait one hundred years to receive the reward to which they are entitled until the world shall make progress which enables it to pay the just reward." ✳

A public exhibition in 1902 of the McMillan Plan to redesign the Mall included a map (see page 53, bottom), a 3-D model, and this gorgeous oblique bird's-eye view of Washington, D.C., painted by Francis Hoppin, who also famously designed a home for the writer Edith Wharton. This painting would become the iconic image of the new design for the capital.

San Francisco's Buried Shipwrecks

DOZENS OF 19TH-CENTURY VESSELS STILL LIE BENEATH THE CITY'S STREETS

CREATED *1852–2017*
SOURCE *San Francisco Maritime National Historical Park and others*

Every day, thousands of passengers on San Francisco's underground streetcars pass through the hull of a 19th-century ship without knowing it. Scores of pedestrians walk unaware over dozens of ships buried beneath the streets of the city's financial district. These vessels brought eager prospectors to San Francisco during the California gold rush only to be mostly abandoned and later covered up by landfill as the city grew in the late 1800s.

As news of the gold rush began spreading in 1848, people were so desperate to get to California that all sorts of dubious vessels were pressed into service. On arrival, ship captains found no waiting cargo or passengers to justify a return journey; besides, they and their crew were eager to try their own luck in the goldfields. The ships weren't necessarily abandoned—often someone was hired to keep an eye on them—but they languished and began to deteriorate. The daguerreotype on pages 58–59, part of a remarkable panorama taken in 1852, shows what historians have described as a "forest of masts" in Yerba Buena Cove.

Sometimes the ships were put to other uses. The most famous example is the whaling ship *Niantic,* intentionally run aground in 1849 and used as a warehouse, saloon, and hotel before it burned down in a huge fire in 1851 that claimed many other ships in the cove. A hotel was later built atop the remnants of the *Niantic* at the corner of Clay and Sansome Streets, about six blocks from the current shoreline.

Some ships were sunk by their owners. Real estate was a hot commodity, but the property laws had loopholes. "You could sink a ship and claim the land under it," says Richard Everett, the San Francisco Maritime National Historical Park's curator of exhibits. You could even pay someone to tow your ship into position and sink it for you. As landfill covered the cove, you'd eventually end up with a piece of prime real estate. All this maneuvering, and the competition for space, led to a few skirmishes and gunfights.

In the 1800s, San Francisco's shoreline was several blocks inland from where it is today. At least 50 ships remain buried in this area, which runs north along the waterfront from where the Bay Bridge now stands (in the bottom left corner).

COIT TOWER

Telegraph Hill

TRANSAMERICA
PYRAMID BUILDING

Sydney Town

MONTGOMERY

MONTGOMERY

BROADWAY

THE FILBERT STEPS

Niantic

SANSOME

SANSOME

SANSOME

GREENWICH

LeBa

General
Harrison

VALLEJO

GREEN

UNION

FILBERT

NORT
DO

Tecumseh

Apollo

Georgian

CLARK'S
POINT

Wm.Gray I

2 Unknown

Palmyra

A Brig

Louisa

BATTERY

UNION

GRIFFING'S WHARF

GREENWIC
DOCK

Hoff St. Harbormaster

Arkansas

A Brig

Philip Hone

BATTERY

Dryade

INDIA DOCK

Thomas
Bennett

Francis
Ann

Ricardo

Fortuna

Dalmatia

Japan

FILBERT

Fort Vigilance

Fame

FRONT

Balance

FRONT

FRONT

CUNNINGHAM'S WHARF

BUCKELEW'S WHARF

LAW'S WHARF

COWELL'S WHARF

Envoy

GREENWICH

Callao

Salem

Stieglitz

Alida

Brilliant

Almandralina

Rhone

GREEN

Autumn

DAVIS

Globe

Magnolia

Cordova

Garnet

DAVIS

Henry Lee

Noble

Elmira

BROADWAY WHARF

THE EMBARCADERO

DRUMM

Hardie

Inez

VALLEJO WHARF

Othello

Bethel

DRUMM

Exploratorium

Elizabeth

DRUMM

PIER 5

PIER 19

CALIFORNIA STREET WHARF

SACRAMENTO ST. WHARF

LONG WHARF or CENTRAL WHARF

CLAY STREET WHARF

WASHINGTON STREET WHARF

JACKSON STREET

PACIFIC STREET WHARF

PIER 17

Rome

PIER 9

PIER 15

MARKET STREET WHARF

REET WHARF

FERRY
BUILDING

THE EMBARCADERO

PIER 1

PIER 3

PIER 7

PIE

W

S

N

E

San Francisco's Buried Shipwrecks | **57**

One of these intentionally scuttled ships was the *Rome*, which was rediscovered in the 1990s when the city dug a tunnel to extend a streetcar line, the N-Judah, south of Market Street. Today the line (along with two others, the T and the K) passes through the forward hull of the ship on the way from downtown to the city's western neighborhoods (see sketch on page 59).

The San Francisco Maritime National Historical Park first made a map of sunken ships in 1963 after studying reports from historians and archaeologists. The orange circles on the 2017 map represent sites that have been discovered and studied more recently. One of the most interesting is a ship-breaking yard at Rincon Point, at the southern end of Yerba Buena Cove near the current anchorage point for the San Francisco–Oakland Bay Bridge. A man named Charles Hare ran a lucrative salvage operation there, employing at least 100 Chinese laborers to take old ships apart. Hare sold off brass and bronze fixtures for use in new ships and buildings, as well as scrap

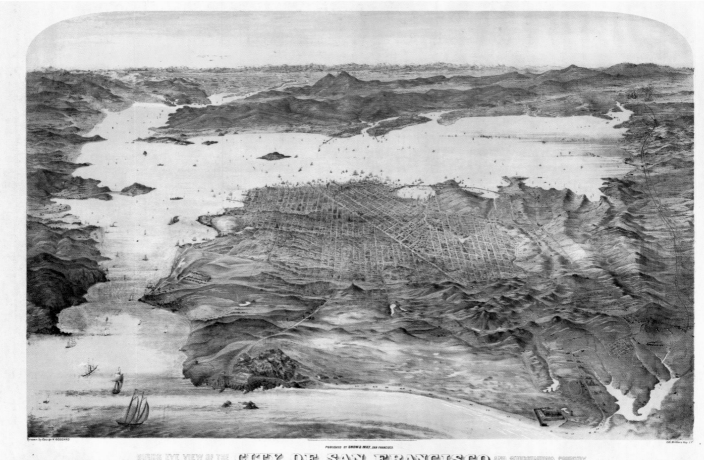

BIRDS EYE VIEW OF THE **CITY OF SAN FRANCISCO** AND SURROUNDING COUNTRY

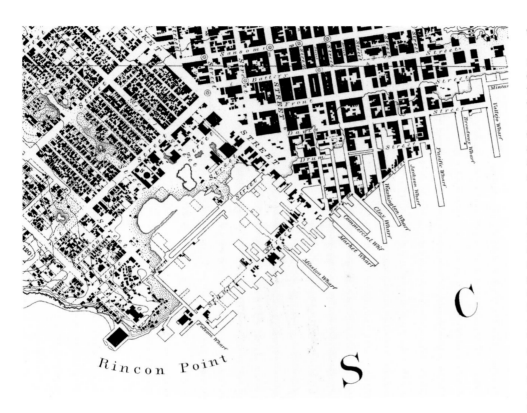

Rincon Point

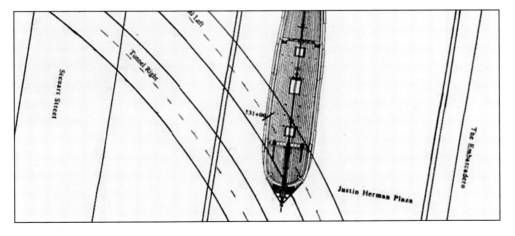

Justin Herman Plaza

TOP This detail from an 1857 map published by the U.S. Coast Survey shows structures extending into Yerba Buena Cove as it was being filled in.

ABOVE A sketch by marine archaeologist James Allan shows the underground streetcar track passing through the hull of the *Rome* just south of Market Street.

---

wood, a valuable commodity in those days.

The massive fire in 1851 killed Hare's business. Archaeologists have found the remnants of six ships at the site that were presumably in the process of being salvaged at the time of the fire. One, the *Candace*, was another whaling vessel pressed into service to bring gold-crazed prospectors to San Francisco. They also found a small, flat-bottomed boat called a lighter used to shuttle goods from moored ships to shore.

In 2006, a development project near Broadway and Front Streets turned up bones that archaeologists suspect came from Galápagos tortoises (the site is marked by an asterisk on the map on page 57). After passing around Cape Horn at the tip of South America on their journey from the East Coast, many ships stopped in the Galápagos Islands and threw a few of the hardy reptiles in the hold— providing a source of fresh meat for the long voyage north to California. Menus from the era show that turtle soup was a common offering at restaurants and lodging houses around the cove. Everett says: "They got to San Francisco, and lo and behold—they had more turtle than they could eat."

Eventually Yerba Buena Cove was filled in. People built piers out into it to reach ships moored in deeper water, Everett says: "The wharves are constantly growing like fingers out from the shore." Then people began dumping debris and sand into the cove, which was only a few feet deep in many places to begin with. "By having guys with carts and horses dump sand off your pier," Everett says, "you could create land that you could own." A map published by the U.S. Coast Survey in 1857 (above and to the left) shows the cove in the process of being filled in.

It was a land-grab strategy with lasting ramifications, as evidenced by the ongoing controversy over Millennium Tower, a 58-story skyscraper completed in 2009. The building, filled with multimillion-dollar apartments, is slowly tilting as it sinks into the soft ground near what was once the southern edge of Yerba Buena Cove. ✳

Mapping the Ottoman Empire

A 16TH-CENTURY POLYMATH'S INNOVATIVE CITY VIEWS

CREATED *1537–1564*
CREATOR *Matrakçı Nasuh*

Matrakçı Nasuh had an almost impossibly broad range of skills. A famous statesman in the Ottoman Empire, he excelled in everything from math to swordsmanship to calligraphy. Nasuh was an elite military officer and an adept military strategist. He invented a war game called Matrak that was used to train soldiers, which is how he came by his name. But Nasuh's crowning achievement would add three new occupations to his lengthy résumé—historian, geographer, and artist—and has inspired historians to compare him to his multitalented contemporary Leonardo da Vinci.

With the empire ascending toward its peak in the mid-16th century, Suleiman the Magnificent asked Nasuh to write a history of the Ottoman sultans and their conquests. Nasuh spent more than two decades chronicling their military exploits, including the events of Suleiman's reign that Nasuh witnessed as they unfolded. He worked on at least nine volumes, several of them illustrated with beautiful overhead views of conquered cities. These illustrations are essentially maps made in an innovative new style. They are clearly influenced by the European bird's-eye views that were in vogue at the time, and they are strongly related to Persian miniatures: small, colorful paintings in books that illustrated poetry and literature. Nasuh's city views reflect the Ottoman monarchy's taste for celebratory depictions of their accomplishments, tempered by an interest in historical accuracy.

His best-known map is this two-page city view of Istanbul on the right that has become an important source for historians. It is incredibly detailed and includes the city's important Muslim landmarks. On the right half of the map is the famous Hagia Sophia, which was built as an Eastern

---

Profiles of famous landmarks like the Hagia Sophia are recognizable on this groundbreaking 16th-century map of Istanbul by Matrakçı Nasuh. The painting was a two-page illustration in a written history of the Ottoman Empire. The two halves of the map have different bird's-eye view orientations.

Orthodox cathedral in the sixth century and had been converted to a mosque by the time the map was made. The Topkapi Palace where the sultans lived is also visible. Interestingly, the left half of the map, which shows the Golden Horn waterway and the 14th-century Galata Tower, is oriented to a different visual perspective so that readers need to rotate the book clockwise to see it right-side up.

It's likely that Nasuh didn't paint the maps himself. The standard practice at the time was for several specialists to each paint one aspect of a piece, such as buildings, landscapes, or foliage. But Nasuh was almost surely responsible for the maps' major innovation, which was basing them on contemporary sketches from the field instead of relying exclusively on information from second-hand reports and previous depictions. The maps' level of accuracy and detail has led historians to conclude that someone involved

in their making—perhaps Nasuh himself—must have been in each city as it was sketched.

As a military strategist for Suleiman during his conquest of Iraq and Iran from 1534 to 1535, Nasuh certainly could have made the sketches himself for that campaign. The volume covering the expansion of the empire during this period is perhaps his most ambitiously illustrated work. Suleiman's campaign culminated in the capture of Baghdad, which is depicted on a double-page

OPPOSITE Unlike most of the other cities Nasuh illustrated, Aleppo was not at the frontier of the growing Ottoman Empire. Its inclusion in his history book likely reflects the city's regional economic and political importance at the time.

LEFT Nasuh's two-page illustration of Baghdad is divided in two by the Tigris River. The two sides of the map have opposing oblique bird's-eye perspectives, and the surrounding area is dotted with desert shrubs and animals.

BELOW The Ottoman navy is shown during an attempt to occupy the French city of Nice on the Mediterranean coast in 1543. The assault on Nice was unsuccessful, but the navy succeeded in occupying the French port city of Toulon.

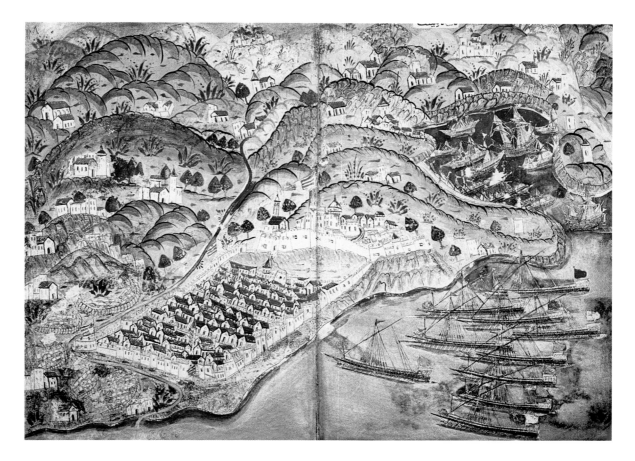

spread with opposing orientations separated by the Tigris River (above center). The map shows the east side of the city fortified with walls and includes three large mosques. Nasuh illustrated virtually every stopping point and important city the army passed through on the way to and from Baghdad, including Aleppo. The map of Aleppo (above left) is stylistically quite different from the others in its volume, further evidence that the maps may have been painted by multiple artists. The illustration is dominated by the walled fortress of the Citadel, which survives to this day but sustained heavy damage during the Syrian civil war that began in 2011.

Another of Nasuh's volumes covers an Ottoman naval expedition to France in 1543 and includes views of several coastal French cities. France had invited the expedition in hopes of forging an alliance but soon regretted it. The Ottoman navy saw the invitation as an opportunity to pillage European cities on the Mediterranean coast. They occupied the French port of Toulon and made attempts at other cities, including Nice (above right).

Nasuh's idea to illustrate the military campaigns and boundaries of the Ottoman Empire with city maps was completely new at the time. His approach was clearly effective, because many historians during his time (and after it) imitated it in their own work. ✳

Two Tales of a City

DIGITAL PHOTOS REVEAL WHERE LOCALS AND TOURISTS HANG OUT

CREATED *2010*
CREATOR *Eric Fischer*

Where are the most interesting places in a city? It depends who you ask. Every person has his or her own individual taste, of course, but one of the traits that most influences the answer to this question is whether a person is a local or a tourist.

Cartographer Eric Fischer was pondering this question, mapping his own tracks through the San Francisco Bay Area, when he discovered that the photo-sharing site Flickr had public data on where its contributors' photos were taken. Fischer realized that with time-stamped Flickr photos, he could see other people's tracks as well. "It was kind of this life-changing moment of not just being able to look at my own data, but to figure out what places in the world other people were interested in," he says.

He downloaded the data and traced people's paths in different cities. He color-coded them by the mode of transportation people were probably using, based on their speed between shots: Around 3 miles an hour (5 km/h) indicates walking; around 30 miles an hour (50 km/h) is car travel; around 10 miles an hour (16 km/h) is bikes or ferries.

When he posted the maps online, his viewers were fascinated. But they wondered whether the maps reflected anything about real life in these cities or just showed where tourists go. To find out, Fischer looked at people's behavior over time. Somebody who posts pictures from the city over the course of a year probably lives there, he reasoned. Someone who posts photos for just a week is probably a tourist, especially if that person usually posts photos from a hometown somewhere else.

On his map of New York City (opposite), Fischer found clear separations between locals (blue) and tourists (red). Tracks in yellow are unclear, usually because they are the only photos in a person's account, so there's no way to tell if that person was visiting or just taking photos of a scenic ferry ride on the way to work. Unsurprisingly, Times Square is the most photographed place in the city. Other typical tourist spots like the Statue of Liberty also inspire a lot of shots. Interestingly, the Brooklyn Bridge is shot more often by tourists, whereas the neighboring Manhattan Bridge is shot more by New Yorkers. "I think it's based on how well known the bridge is," Fischer says.

A few cities, like Rome (below right) and Las Vegas, are dominated by tight clusters of tourist photos. Others, like Taipei (below left) and Toronto, have a majority of local residents' photos in a more diffuse pattern. Most have a mix, with some spots that are heavily photographed by residents and rarely by tourists. "If you're only in a place for a week, there's just a limit to how many places you can go," Fischer says. "You're probably not going to discover these other, more hidden treasures." ✳

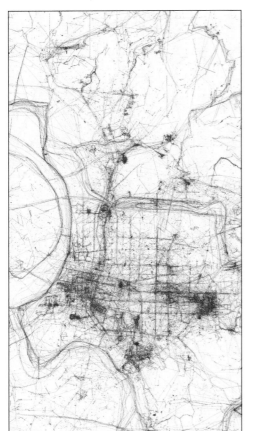

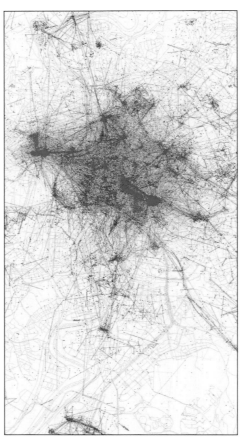

OPPOSITE In this map of New York City, the paths New Yorkers and tourists take are revealed by the photos they uploaded to Flickr from 2010 to 2014. New Yorkers are designated by blue lines; red lines show where tourists spent their time. Yellow lines designate the routes of people who could be either locals or tourists.

FAR LEFT In Taipei, Taiwan, photos posted to Flickr by local residents (shown in blue) are in a more diffuse pattern, with a few small clusters of photos taken by tourists (shown in red).

LEFT Most of the photos shot in Rome and posted to Flickr are taken by tourists (shown in red) and concentrated in areas such as the west side of town around Saint Peter's Basilica and on the southeast part of town near the Colosseum.

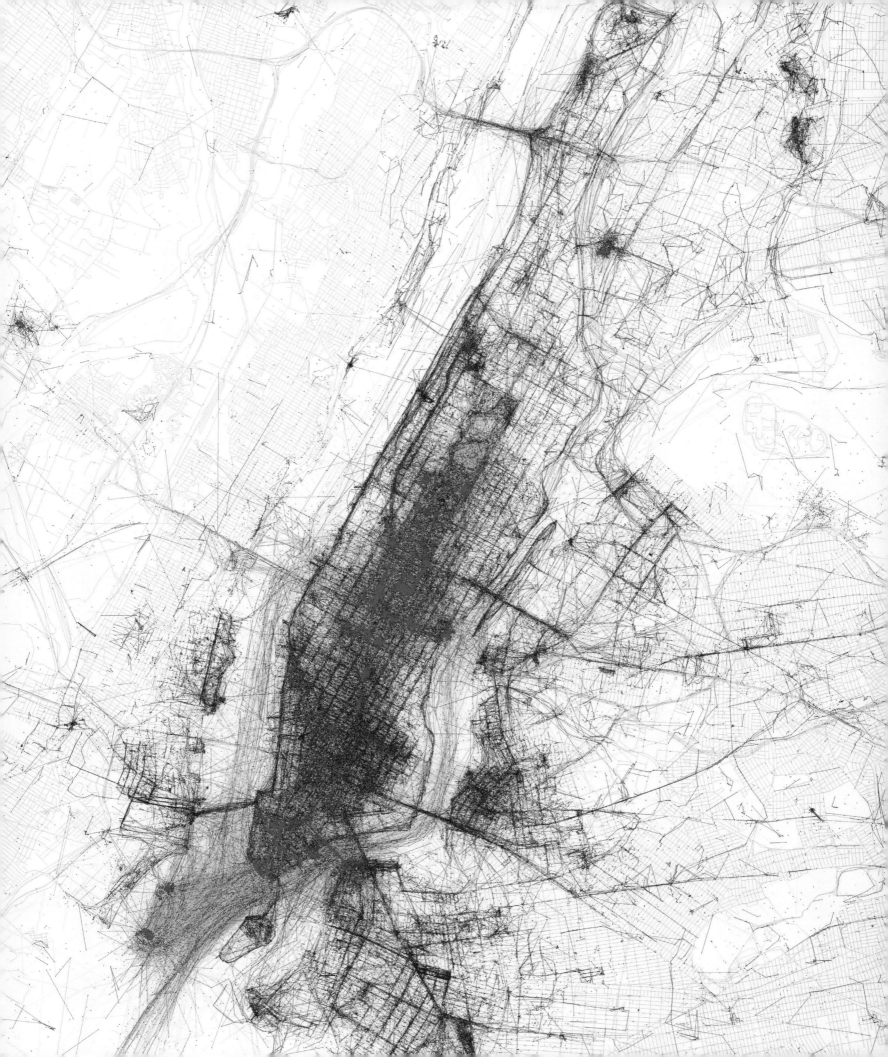

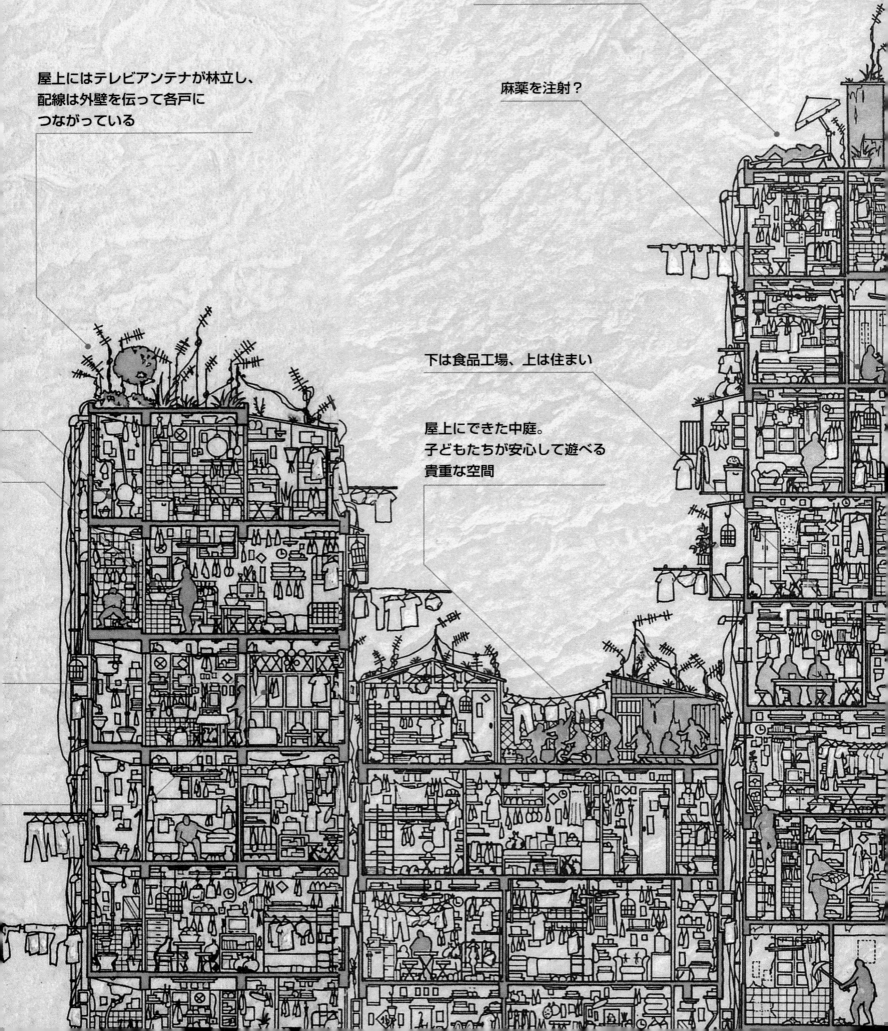

ひなたぼっこで極楽気分だ

屋上にはテレビアンテナが林立し、
配線は外壁を伝って各戸に
つながっている

麻薬を注射？

下は食品工場、上は住まい

屋上にできた中庭。
子どもたちが安心して遊べる
貴重な空間

ついたてだけで[
トイレと台所

台所で行水

手術室もあ･

下まで捨てに行
めんどうだ、ホ

水運び屋

腸詰め工場

Hong Kong's Notorious City Within a City

A METICULOUS, HAND-DRAWN MAP CAPTURES LIFE INSIDE THE DENSEST HUMAN SETTLEMENT THAT HAS EVER EXISTED

CREATED *1997*
CREATOR *Hitomi Terasawa*

Kowloon Walled City started as a squatters' camp inside an old Chinese fort in Hong Kong. In the years following World War II, its population swelled with refugees fleeing the civil war in mainland China. Residents built the place up piece by piece, doing the construction off the books as city planners and building inspectors turned a blind eye.

By the early 1990s, tens of thousands of people lived, worked, and played inside this 7-acre (2.8 ha) complex of midrise buildings. How dense was it? Picture Manhattan, the densest urban area in the United States. Now picture 50 times as many people packed into the same space. Conditions inside the complex were squalid. Gangs sold drugs to residents seeking an escape. Heroin overdoses were common. So was prostitution.

Eventually Hong Kong officials decided enough was enough, and in 1993 the city began demolishing Kowloon Walled City—but not before a team of Japanese architects took it upon themselves to explore the warren of rooms and corridors and map it for posterity. They called themselves the Kowloon Walled City Expedition.

The group arrived in Hong Kong just a few months before demolition was scheduled to start. A construction supervisor on the demolition crew agreed to let them explore the abandoned compound on a few conditions: They were given only eight days to do it, they were not to bother any of the construction workers, no more than six of them could enter at a time, and the city of Hong Kong would not be responsible for any accidents or injuries.

On a roof bristling with TV antennas, children find a rare opportunity to play outdoors (center) in this detail from Hitomi Terasawa's illustrated cross-section of Kowloon Walled City.

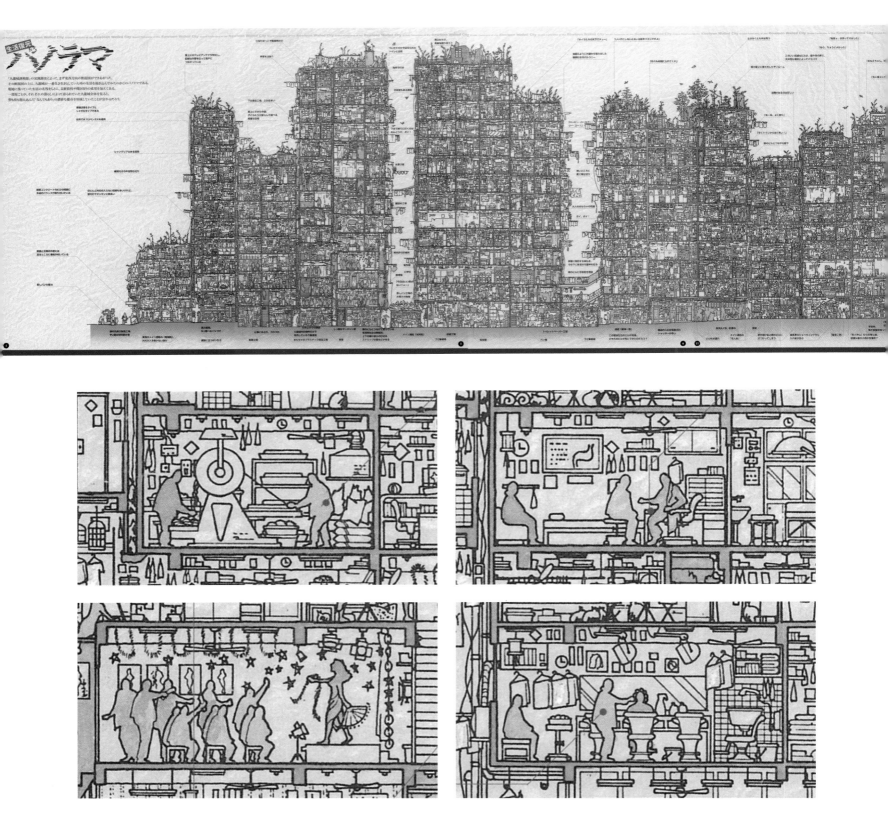

ABOVE Rooms inside the complex were put to many uses legitimate and otherwise. They include (clockwise from top left) a sausage factory, doctor's office, hair dresser, and what appears to be a strip club.

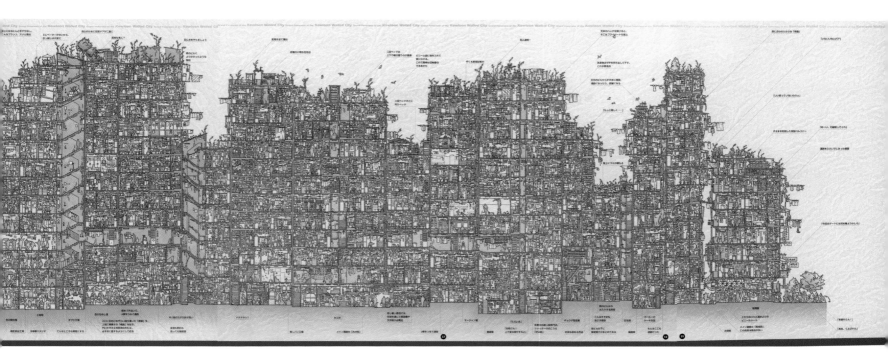

ABOVE Terasawa's map of Kowloon Walled City covered eight pages of a Japanese book published in 1997. Her drawings depict hundreds of rooms, hidden passageways, and vignettes of residents going about their daily lives.

RIGHT An aerial photo taken in 1989 reveals the dense cluster of some 500 buildings that made up Kowloon Walled City. The flight path of planes landing at the nearby Kai Tak Airport limited their height to 14 stories.

The expedition immediately divided into teams. One team worked on a floor plan, while another took measurements and photographs to re-create a cross-section of the compound. Back in their hotel at night, they used their notes and photographs to figure out what each room had been used for based on the furniture, trash, and other clues that had been left behind.

These maps were created a few years later by Hitomi Terasawa, an illustrator who worked from the material collected by the expedition to re-create a cross-sectional view of the walled city as it might have looked in its heyday. Terasawa captured evidence of vice, to be sure— like the room where a young woman dances in front of an audience of men (see the bottom left detail on page 68). But she also recorded signs of life that can be found in any city: laundry hung out to dry on balconies, pots boiling on stoves, and children jumping rope.

This was a city within a city with its own schools, temples, and economy. It was famous throughout Hong Kong for its cut-rate dentists, who didn't have a license to operate in other parts of the city. Small shops fabricated things out of metal and plastic, and tiny mom-and-pop factories made everything from candy to noodles. Rumor had it that 80 percent of the fish balls floating in bowls of noodle soup around Hong Kong were made inside the walled city.

The infrastructure was shaky at best. Questionably potable water came from about 70 wells dug by residents. Electricity often came from illegal connections to the city grid. In a 2014 documentary produced by the *Wall Street Journal,* a former mailman recalls getting shocked because an uninsulated wire had come in contact with a metal mailbox. He also remembers the rats. "I've never seen rats so big that their bellies dragged on the ground," he says.

The walled city has long inspired writers, video game designers, and other creative types. The dilapidated Narrows neighborhood in Gotham City in the 2005 movie *Batman Begins* is modeled on it, as is an enormous video arcade outside Tokyo, Japan; even the trash and graffiti are faithfully reproduced.

A park now occupies the site where the walled city once stood, but the true legacy of the place is its enduring pull on the imagination. ✳

Boston's Soft Side

HOW LANDFILL SHAPED THE CITY FOR BETTER OR FOR WORSE

CREATED *1630–2018*
SOURCE *Boston Public Library and others*

The smell of rotting garbage and sewage was what convinced the city of Boston to undertake one of its first major landfill projects. The year was 1800 and the miasmatic theory of disease—the idea that foul odors were the source of outbreaks—had taken hold. Bostonians feared the stench emanating from the waste collecting in a shallow cove on the north end of town. So they decided to cover it up.

The problem had started more than 150 years earlier when the cove was dammed off for tidal power to run some gristmills. In addition to powering mills, the newly formed Mill Pond (opposite) became a favorite dumping ground for household trash and dead animals. Local residents were draining their privies directly into the pond as well. At first, tidewater washed much of the refuse out of the pond. But in 1800, the proprietors shut some of the mills down and closed half of the floodgates, which stopped the flow of water. The filth began to accumulate. And stink.

It's unclear whether this unpleasant result was all part of their plan, but the proprietors soon began lobbying the city to let them fill Mill Pond in and sell the resulting land. The prospect of more taxable land was appealing to the city, and residents were concerned that the pestilent odors were a dangerous source of disease. In 1807 the filling began.

The fill came from nearby Beacon Hill, which would end up losing around 60 feet (18 m) of elevation to various land-making projects over the years. Today the 50 acres (20 ha) of new land created by filling Mill Pond is known as Bulfinch Triangle, after architect Charles Bulfinch's triangle-shaped plan for the new streets as shown on an 1841 map (see page 72, right). Later, more land was extended outward from the triangle to support railroad depots.

When the Puritans established the city in 1630, much of the land that underlies the heart of Boston today didn't exist. The Boston peninsula, called Shawmut by the local Native Americans, covered less than 500 acres (200 ha). It was dotted with hills and connected to the mainland by a narrow neck that was submerged during high tides. But over the next three and a half centuries, Boston would gain more than 5,000 acres (2,000 ha) of man-made land.

One of the most extensive areas of landfill in Boston is its Back Bay neighborhood. Back Bay encompassed the large area of tidal flats on the north side of the neck. Like Mill Pond, the bay was dammed off for mill power in 1821. Once that dam was built, it was probably inevitable that Back Bay would eventually be filled.

Small pieces of land began growing soon after, including the Boston Public Garden just west of the Boston Common. In the 1830s, the bay was further partitioned by railroad lines (see the 1841 map on page 72) that reduced circulation and hampered the already underwhelming tide power that never kept more than just a few mills running.

Once again, partitioning soon led to a sewage-fueled stench that had residents decrying the unhealthy miasma

---

LEFT This map from around 1775 shows the city of Boston, a century and a half after its founding, filling most of the Shawmut Peninsula. The dam enclosing Mill Pond is near the north end of the peninsula. Long Wharf was built on the cove on the east side, and the narrow Boston Neck connects the peninsula to the mainland.

....

BELOW In 1630, the year Boston was founded, the city had little more than a few roads, some bare hills, and a dam enclosing Mill Pond near the north end of the Shawmut Peninsula. This map is oriented with west at the top.

wafting into the city. The historian Nancy Seasholes found the situation vividly described in an 1849 city report: "Back Bay at this hour is nothing less than a great cesspool into which is daily deposited all the filth of a large and constantly increasing population . . . A greenish scum, many yards wide, stretches along the shores of the Western Avenue [Mill Dam], whilst the surface of the water beyond is seen bubbling like a cauldron with the noxious gases that are exploding from the corrupting mass below."

In 1850, this bubbling cauldron began being filled in earnest. On an 1878 map (opposite, top left), part of the bay had been filled, including the beginning of Commonwealth Avenue. The street was envisioned as a grand boulevard with a beautiful public walk full of greenery down its center, all aimed at increasing the value of the land. Another unstated aim was likely to create an attractive place for New Englanders to buy homes, which would entice them to settle in Boston and counter the rapid influx of Irish immigrants. By the end of the century, the bay was completely filled.

Today Back Bay is one of the city's most desirable neighborhoods. But it's also among those most vulnerable to an unfortunate legacy of man-made land: foundation rot. Structures built on the landfill are supported by dozens of 30- to 40-foot (9 to 12 m)-long wood pilings, similar to telephone poles, that reach down through the fill to a hard layer of clay. These pilings sit entirely below the water table, which protects them from microbes that would attack them in dry air, causing rot.

But water leaking from the fill into sewers or tunnels can cause the water table to drop below the pilings. This is what happened in 1929, when leaks into a sewer pipe in the heart of Back Bay exposed some of the pilings holding up the Boston Public Library, causing cracks in the building's grand entryway. The repair cost was $200,000, the equivalent of almost $3 million today. Since then, around 200 other buildings have had their pilings repaired. Today the typical cost of underpinning a home with rotted pilings can reach $400,000 or more.

In 1986 the city established the Boston Groundwater Trust, which tracks water levels in the city through a network of monitoring wells on public property. But with more man-made land than any other American city (with the possible exception of San Francisco; see page 56), Bostonians will be living with this problem for the foreseeable future. ✳

ABOVE These maps, which move through time from 1806 to today (from left to right: 1806, 1841, 1878, and 2018), show the gradual growth of Boston as more and more land was made. In 1806, Mill Pond had been enclosed at the north end of the city, but it still existed. By 1841, it had been filled in, along with much of the cove around Long Wharf and some of the land around the Boston Neck connecting the peninsula to the mainland. In 1878, Back Bay was partially filled on the city's southwestern side. Today, Back Bay is entirely filled, as is South Bay.

OPPOSITE BOTTOM Boston's modern shoreline (in light green) compared to the 1630 shoreline (dark green) shows how much Boston and the surrounding area has grown. All of the land in light green between the two shorelines was made by filling in shallow parts of the harbor.

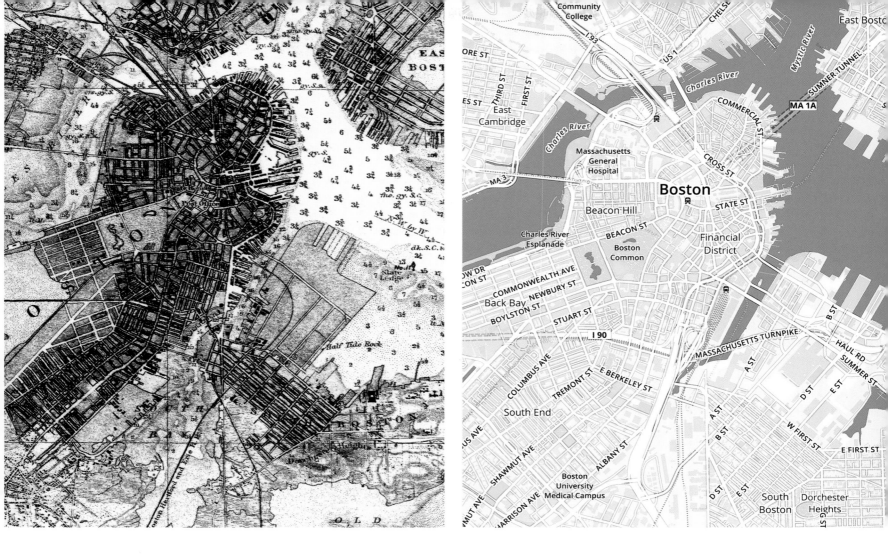

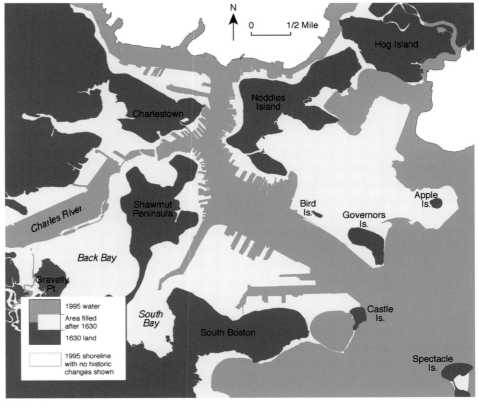

1995 water

Area filled after 1630

1630 land

1995 shoreline with no historic changes shown

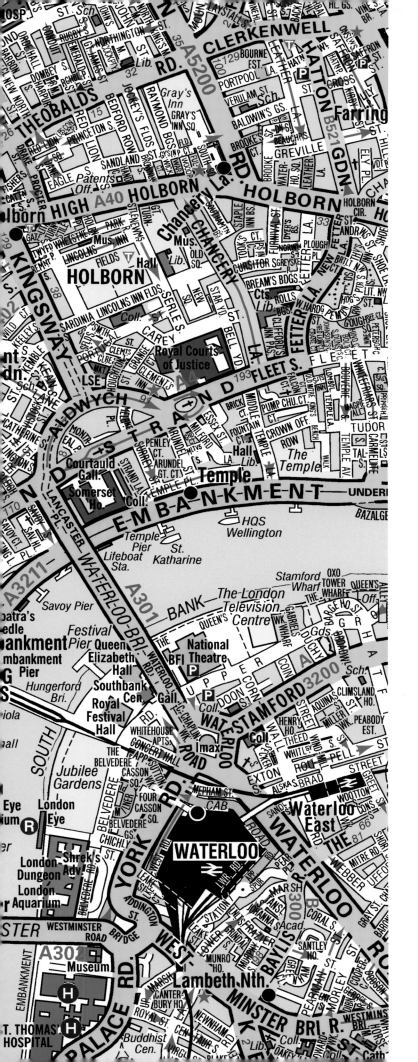

Demystifying London

THE MAPS TAXI DRIVERS USE TO MASTER ONE OF THE WORLD'S MOST CONFUSING CITIES

CREATED *2018*
SOURCE *Geographers' A-Z Map Company*

Within a 6-mile (9.7 km) radius of Charing Cross, the famous intersection in the center of London, are some 25,000 streets. It's a bewildering network of roads and lanes that have an infuriating tendency to change names or direction of travel from one block to the next. A taxi driver needs to know them all.

To earn the right to operate one of London's iconic black cabs, aspiring drivers face one of the hardest tests in the world, known as The Knowledge, during which an applicant must be prepared to recite an efficient route between any two points the examiner chooses. These can be drawn from more than 125,000 points of interest, ranging from obvious landmarks like Buckingham Palace to an obscure back alley pub.

The maps most taxi students use are made by Geographers' A-Z Map Company, known to the British as "A to Zed," an 82-year-old map publisher with a history as colorful as its maps.

The company was started in 1936 by Phyllis Pearsall, the daughter of a Hungarian cartographer. According to her own telling, Pearsall got lost going to a party one rainy night and resolved to create a better map. She claimed to have walked the streets of London by herself, often starting at dawn, logging more than 3,000 miles (4,800 km) over the course of a year to produce her first atlas.

Charming as the story is, it has its skeptics. Among them is Peter Barber, the head of maps at the British Library, who has argued it's more likely that Pearsall updated and improved on one of the many atlases in circulation at the time, such as the similar-looking ones her father made.

Whether Pearsall's story is true or a clever bit of marketing, A-Z maps are widely admired for their clarity, even as they pack a remarkable amount of information into a small space. "They're a work of art, really," says Peter Allen, a taxi driver and teacher at Knowledge Point School in London. He says that students studying for The Knowledge often refer to major and minor roadways as "oranges" and "lemons," a nod to the distinctive orange and yellow color scheme A-Z uses to indicate the hierarchy of roads. Smaller streets are white, which allows students to easily highlight favored shortcuts.

On the streets of London, it's common to spot taxi students on scooters driving their routes with an A-Z atlas mounted on the handlebars. Those who pass The Knowledge study for an average of four years. By that time, one would think, they're seeing oranges and lemons in their sleep. ✳

The street names on A-Z maps of London were originally lettered by hand so they could capture the twists and turns of London's streets and still remain legible. This section shows an area of central London, with Charing Cross near the center.

FLICT

AND

CRISIS

3 | CONFLICT AND CRISIS

The Cartography of War and Strife

Maps made during wartime have especially rich stories to tell. They show that military strategy is always rooted in geography: It's important to know not just the location of the enemy but also the resources and supply lines they depend on.

One elegant example is John Badger Bachelder's panoramic map of the Battle of Gettysburg (see page 80). Based on Bachelder's sketches and interviews with troops, this map has shaped the historical account of how the fighting played out during this turning point in the American Civil War. A starker example is the German map that plots the devastation caused by U-boats in World War I (see page 98). The seas surrounding the British Isles are covered in a cloud of red dots, each one representing a sunken ship, many of them civilian cargo or passenger ships—a chilling illustration of the deadly effects of these new war machines.

Other maps in this chapter have stories to tell about wars that nations prepared for but never ended up fighting. They're part of a long tradition of nations stealing maps from each other and sending secret expeditions to map potential adversaries, a conspiracy of mapmakers and spies.

These maps reveal the drama of wars and other conflicts, but their stories aren't just about military strategy and geopolitical scheming. They also harbor stories about the terrible human cost of these conflicts. ➤➤

THE TENTACLES OF EMPIRE
(1944, Cornell University— PJ Mode Collection of Persuasive Cartography)

Maps have long been used in the war for public opinion. This map was commissioned by the Dutch government, in exile in London during World War II. The octopus is a common symbol on propaganda maps, and this one, which represents Japan, is especially menacing. Its long, yellow tentacles wrap around the islands of the Dutch East Indies (now Indonesia). The text reads: "The Indies Must Be Free! Work and Fight for It!" Indeed, when Japan finally surrendered in 1945, the Indonesian people immediately declared themselves independent of the Dutch as well.

Bachelder's Gettysburg

HOW ONE MAN SHAPED THE COUNTRY'S MEMORY OF A CRITICAL CIVIL WAR BATTLE

CREATED *1864*
SOURCE *Library of Congress, Geography and Map Division*

The bodies were still being buried when John Badger Bachelder arrived at the Gettysburg battlefield in July 1863. He was on a mission to capture, with both pen and paint, what had transpired during the three-day battle.

The following year, he published a striking panoramic map of the battlefield that detailed the positions of every Union and Confederate regiment during each day of battle. It helped turn Bachelder, a landscape painter with no military background and no formal training in either cartography or history, into the most influential Gettysburg historian of all time. Bachelder left an outsize footprint on both the land and the legacy of this famous clash, helping to secure its place in the country's collective memory as the turning point of the American Civil War.

"He had a much greater impact than anybody else on the story we know today," says Gettysburg historian Tom Desjardin. That includes every historian who came after him, as well as everyone who was in the battle, right up to the commanders of the two armies.

Bachelder had waited a long time for Gettysburg. He'd spent years trying to make a grand painting of another major event in American history, the Battle of Bunker Hill in 1775, but he couldn't find the detail he needed to properly illustrate the nearly century-old battle. When the Civil War broke out, he set his sights on a fresh conflict.

In 1862, he embedded himself with Union forces with a plan to "wait for the great battle which would naturally decide the contest; study its topography on the field and learn its details from the actors themselves, and eventually prepare its written and illustrated history." Bachelder hadn't yet seen any worthy action when he fell ill and was forced to head home. But before he left the field, he asked army officers to send a message if it looked like the great battle he was hoping for was imminent. In 1863, word of Gettysburg reached him.

Bachelder got to work as soon as he arrived on the scene.

John Badger Bachelder wasn't a historian or a cartographer before he arrived at Gettysburg shortly after the fighting had ceased. But his map of the battlefield helped him become the most renowned authority on the event and have a major influence on how this Civil War battle is remembered to this day.

ABOVE The famous "Copse of Trees," which Bachelder said was the landmark used to direct the final Confederate charge, stands at the center of the action in this section of the map. A few years after the battle, Bachelder saved the trees from being cut down by the farmer whose land they stood on.

RIGHT The Union Army regiments, shown in white (second day of the battle) and blue (third day), used Culp's Hill as part of its defensive line against the Confederates, shown in black (second day) and orange (third day).

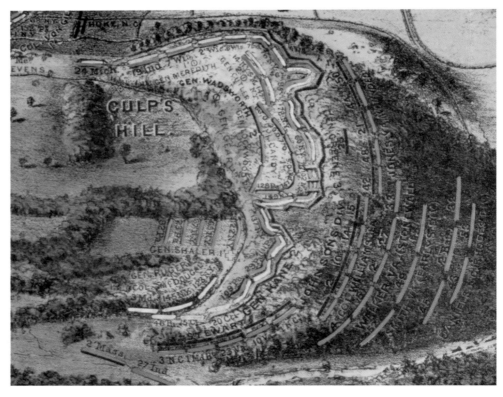

LEFT Bachelder stands on the Gettysburg battlefield with his wife, Elizabeth, in 1888. His written history of the battle was never published, but the many firsthand accounts he gathered have become a valuable resource for historians.

ABOVE Union Army commanders signed Bachelder's map beneath the endorsement: "The positions of the troops of our respective commands represented upon this picture have been arranged under our immediate direction and may be relied upon as substantially correct."

First, he sketched the topography by horseback and on foot. Next, he sought the details of the battle from eyewitnesses. He took his map to hospitals and interviewed wounded soldiers, even taking some of them back to the field so they could point out their positions and recount what they'd witnessed. After 84 days in the Gettysburg area, Bachelder put everything he had learned onto the map and headed out to talk to the Union regiments that had moved on.

As he later recalled, "I spent the entire winter of 1863 and 1864, visiting every Regiment, holding conversations with its officers and with privates in many cases, submitted to them the drawings I had made of the Field and had them corroborate and complete the position of the troops upon it." Still not satisfied, he mailed copies of the map to all of the relevant Union commanders, asking them to mark the locations and movements of their units.

When the map was finally finished and published in spring 1864, it bore signatures of approval from most of the Union Army commanders (above right). The endorsement of Maj. Gen. George Meade, who had led the Union victory at Gettysburg, was written boldly in his hand across the bottom border of the map: "I am perfectly satisfied with the accuracy

with which the topography is delineated and the position of the troops laid down."

And with that, Bachelder had established himself as the most authoritative documentarian of Gettysburg and was well on his way toward cementing its place as the decisive battle of the war. The map itself seemed to lend credibility to its inexperienced author as a historian, according to Desjardin. One Union Army general who saw the map before the war's end said, "Your drawing, in addition to its present interest to all who were engaged in the battle and its artistic beauty will have a future historic value which can hardly now be appreciated."

In 1880, on the strength of his work and reputation, Bachelder persuaded Congress to award him the almost unbelievably huge sum of $50,000 (somewhere in the neighborhood of $1 million today) to write the definitive history of Gettysburg.

Though he toiled for years and gathered hundreds, if not thousands of accounts from both sides, he never compiled them into a published history. Still, Bachelder's narrative of the events at Gettysburg would come to dominate the collective memory of the battle, and indeed the war. He's responsible for establishing the famous "Copse of Trees" as the landmark that guided the final unsuccessful Confederate charge. He also

was the one who dubbed the point of farthest penetration by that charge as the "High Water Mark" of the Confederacy. His interviews and notes amount to one of the largest collections of data on any event in American history and have been an incredible boon to historians.

Bachelder also put his physical imprint on the battle's legacy. As the superintendent of tablets and legends for the Gettysburg Battlefield Memorial Association from 1883 to 1887, he had the final word on placing and inscribing the vast majority of the more than 1,300 tablets, markers, and monuments that pepper what is now Gettysburg National Military Park.

His influence was not without controversy, however. Some soldiers challenged his placement of monuments meant to mark the locations of regiments during the battle. One regiment took their case all the way to the Pennsylvania Supreme Court (where they prevailed). Today's historians have deduced that the battle narrative Bachelder favored probably influenced the accounts of the soldiers he interviewed, whose memories were often shaky.

Even so, by getting to the Gettysburg battlefield so quickly and sticking with his research for decades, Bachelder may have gotten as close to the truth as anyone could. ✱

Communist Plotting

DURING THE COLD WAR, THE SOVIET MILITARY SECRETLY MAPPED THE ENTIRE WORLD

CREATED *1940s–1980s*
SOURCE *East View Geospatial and the collection of John Davies*

After September 11, 2001, as the United States prepared to invade Afghanistan, military planners realized they were missing something crucial: detailed modern maps of the country they were about to attack.

Initially, the best maps at their disposal were based on aerial surveys from the late 1950s. They had satellite imagery too, of course, but that lacked some essential details, says Thom Kaye, a cartographer who worked as a contractor for the National Intelligence Mapping Agency at the time. Soon Kaye and his colleagues came to rely on another, seemingly unlikely, source: Soviet military maps made during their occupation of Afghanistan in the 1980s.

"We relied on the Russian maps because they had incredible detail about things you could only have known if you had people on the ground," Kaye says. The Soviet maps pinpointed the locations of schools, hospitals, mosques, and other landmarks, all of which would be invaluable to troops trying to get their bearings in a foreign land.

The Russians had annotated their maps thoroughly—very thoroughly. Kaye was fascinated to find notes on mountain passes that included the dates when they were free from ice and snow and passable for travel. Water wells, an important feature in an arid land, are barely discernible on satellite imagery, but the Russian maps included their locations, notes on how salty the water was, and whether it was safe to drink.

Naturally, the Soviets also mapped their Cold War adversaries. Their maps of American cities are remarkably detailed, including some military facilities that don't appear on American-made maps of the same era. The same was true of their maps of Europe. It was, in fact, one of the greatest mapping efforts the world has ever known.

The Pentagon, U.S. Capitol, and White House, among other Washington, D.C.-area landmarks, are visible in this Soviet military map from 1975, a product of one of the largest covert mapping operations of all time.

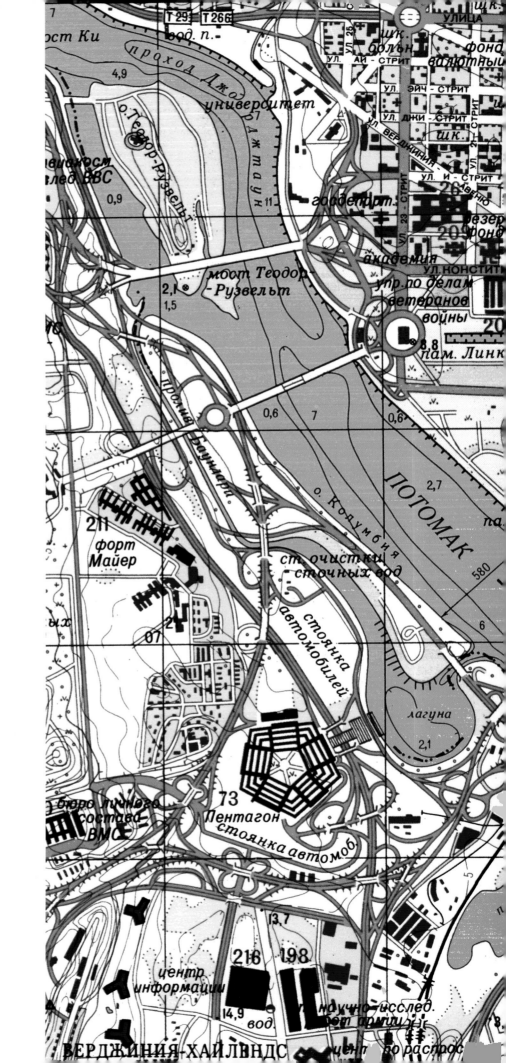

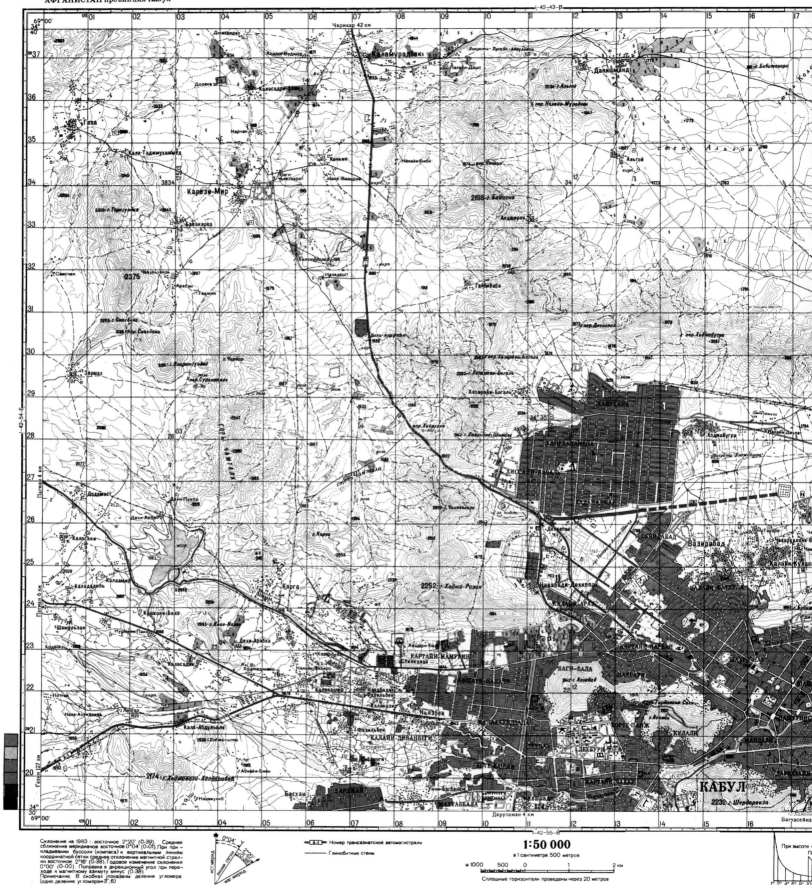

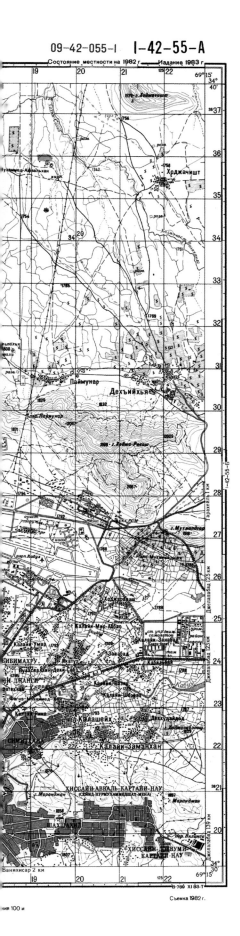

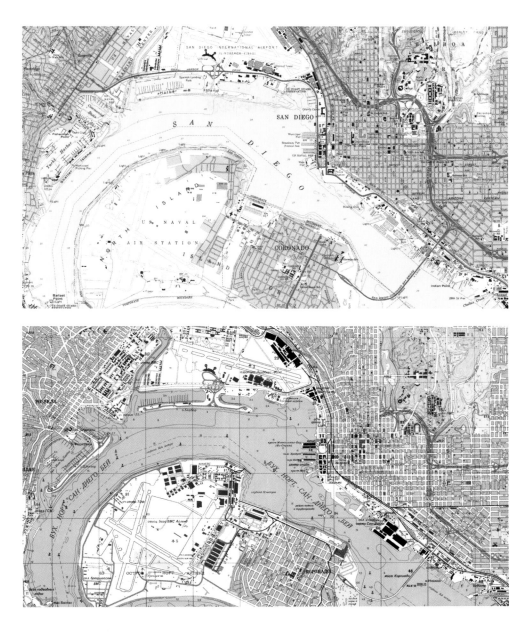

LEFT This 1982 Soviet map shows the area around Kabul, Afghanistan. The U.S. military used maps like this one in planning the invasion of that country after the terrorist attacks of 9/11.

ABOVE A 1980 Soviet map of San Diego (above) shows more buildings (dark green) at the Naval Training Center and Marine Recruit Depot than does a map of the same area (at top) produced by the U.S. Geological Survey in 1978.

Beginning in the 1940s, the Soviets mapped the world at seven scales that ranged from a series of maps that covered the globe in 1,100 chunks the size of a smallish U.S. state to a series of city maps so detailed you can see transit stops and the outlines of individual buildings. It's impossible to say how many people took part in this massive cartographic enterprise, but it would have been well into the thousands, including surveyors, cartographers, and possibly spies. All in all, they produced hundreds of thousands of individual maps.

Most of these maps were classified, their use carefully restricted to military officers. Behind the Iron Curtain, most people did not have access to accurate maps—quite the contrary. The government intentionally distorted maps made for public consumption,

УСЛОВНЫЕ ЗНАКИ ТОПОГРАФИЧЕСКИХ КАРТ
МЕСТНЫЕ ПРЕДМЕТЫ

ОБРАЗЕЦ ИЗОБРАЖЕНИЯ МЕСТНЫХ ПРЕДМЕТОВ НА КАРТАХ

OPPOSITE A magenta line indicates the Berlin Wall in this 1983 Soviet map of the divided German city.

LEFT The ultraspecific symbols used on military maps are superimposed on drawings of the objects they represent on this Soviet training poster.

introducing random variations that rendered them nearly useless for navigation and stripping them of any details that might benefit an enemy should they fall into the wrong hands.

Much of what's known about this secret Soviet military project—and much remains unknown—is outlined in a 2017 book, *The Red Atlas,* by John Davies, a British map enthusiast who has spent more than a decade studying these maps, and Alexander Kent, a geographer at Canterbury Christ Church University.

Davies and Kent argue that the Russian maps were a predigital Wikipedia, a repository of everything the Soviets knew about a place. That sets them apart from the maps made by U.S. and British military and intelligence agencies during the Cold War, which tended to focus on areas of strategic interest. The Russian maps do contain loads of strategic information, from the condition of roadways to the load-bearing capacity of bridges, but they also document seemingly unrelated things: what construction materials were used to build houses in a given area and what kind of trees grow in the surrounding forest.

The Russians were obsessed with infrastructure—things like transportation networks, power grids, and factories—all of which are noted on the maps and often described in exhaustive detail. For that reason, Davies sees the maps not so much as invasion maps but as a guide to taking over the world. "There's an assumption that communism will prevail, and naturally the U.S.S.R. will be in charge," he says.

Very little is known about how the Russian military made these maps, but it appears they used whatever material they could get their hands on. In the United States, for example, they would have had access to the topographic maps made by the U.S. Geological Survey (USGS). But they didn't just copy them, according to Davies, who has spent the better part of a decade cataloging subtle differences between the Soviet maps and maps that would have been publicly available around the same time. Often the Soviet maps contain details that don't appear on contemporary maps from the United States or the United Kingdom. A Russian map of San Diego from 1980 (see page 87) shows more detail on the buildings at the Naval Air Station on Coronado Island and other military facilities in the area than does the USGS map of the same area published in 1979.

In this case, the added detail may have come from satellite imagery, which the Russians had access to after the launch of their first spy satellite in 1962. In other cases, it's difficult to imagine how they could have gotten certain details without people on the ground. According to one account, the Russians augmented their maps of Sweden with details obtained by diplomats working at the Soviet Embassy, who had a tendency to picnic near sites of strategic interest and strike up friendly conversations with local construction workers. One such conversation, on a beach near Stockholm in 1982, supposedly yielded information about Swedish defensive minefields—and led to the Soviet spy's deportation after a Swedish counterintelligence agent lurking nearby overheard.

For anyone who lived through the Cold War, there's something chilling about seeing a familiar landscape mapped through the eyes of a potential enemy, familiar landmarks labeled in unfamiliar Cyrillic script. Yet the Soviet maps remain strangely appealing. They're remarkably well made, even by modern standards. "I continue to be in awe of the people who did this," Davies says.

As the Soviet Union broke up in the late 1980s, the maps began appearing in map dealers' catalogs. Telecommunications and oil companies were eager customers, buying up Russian maps of Central Asia, Africa, and other parts of the developing world for which no good alternatives existed. Aid groups and scientists working in remote regions used them, too.

Exactly how these maps came to be available in the West is a touchy subject. They were never meant to leave the motherland, and they have never been formally declassified. In 2012, a retired Russian colonel was convicted of espionage, stripped of his rank, and sentenced to 12 years in prison for smuggling maps out of the country.

"That's the murky side of the story," Davies says. "No one wants to talk about that." ✳

The 18th-Century War for Europe

ANNA BEEK'S LOVELY MAPS BELIE THE BLOODSHED OF THE WAR OF THE SPANISH SUCCESSION

CREATED *1684–1709*
SOURCE *Library of Congress, Geography and Map Division*

The early years of the 18th century were a turbulent time in Europe. The king of Spain had just died, and his designated successor turned out to be the 17-year-old grandson of King Louis XIV of France. This turn of events gave the mighty House of Bourbon even more power and influence on the Continent, which didn't sit well with England, Austria, and the Holy Roman Empire, which formed an alliance to fight the young king. For more than a decade, Europe was consumed by the War of the Spanish Succession.

These maps, which portray some of the conflict's key sites and battles, are the work of Dutch mapmaker Anna Beek. She ran a publishing house in The Hague, which was then the capital of the Dutch Republic.

It wasn't uncommon for women to be involved in map publishing in the Low Countries at the time, says Carlyn Osborn, a map specialist at the Library of Congress. She notes that publishing houses were often run by an extended family, with wives and daughters involved in all stages of map creation and printing. In some cases, wives took over the business when their husbands died.

Beek's husband didn't die: He ran off, leaving her with seven children and—thanks to the local court that granted her divorce—his business. Osborn's research suggests that Beek ran the publishing house with aplomb, applying for several patents and suing a competitor who ripped off her work.

Three hundred years later, we can only speculate who would have bought Beek's maps and how they would have used them. "Some of them appear to be news maps that would have been put up in a public space where people could come by and read about a recent battle," Osborn says. "The literacy rates in the Low Countries were incredibly high at the time, so they would have been readable by a large majority of people." Some have descriptions of the fighting in both French and Dutch.

Because The Hague was a prominent European trading center, Beek's atelier would have had access to news of the war from passing merchants and other sailors, allowing them to make maps that were remarkably up-to-date by the standards of the time and publish them within a few months of the event.

Some of Beek's maps are more ornate, suggesting they may have been treated as souvenirs meant to be hung in public or perhaps someone's home. One such map (on page 93), for example, provides an especially ornate view of one of the major battles of the War of the Spanish Succession: the Battle of Malplaquet fought in northern France in 1709. The brutal winter that year had depleted the French army, and the alliance was on the attack, led by the Duke of Marlborough, the great British commander. Marlborough's force of 100,000 encountered a slightly smaller French force near the small village of Malplaquet. The French had taken up a strong defensive position in the woods, and the ensuing combat—tree-to-tree fighting with muskets, cavalry attacks and counterattacks, and cannon fire—took a horrible toll. In a single day of fighting, the alliance suffered 22,000 casualties and the French suffered 12,000. It was one of the deadliest

This map published in 1708 shows fortifications in and around the city of Strasbourg on the Rhine River, which now forms the border between France and Germany. It includes several smaller forts that were demolished in the fighting.

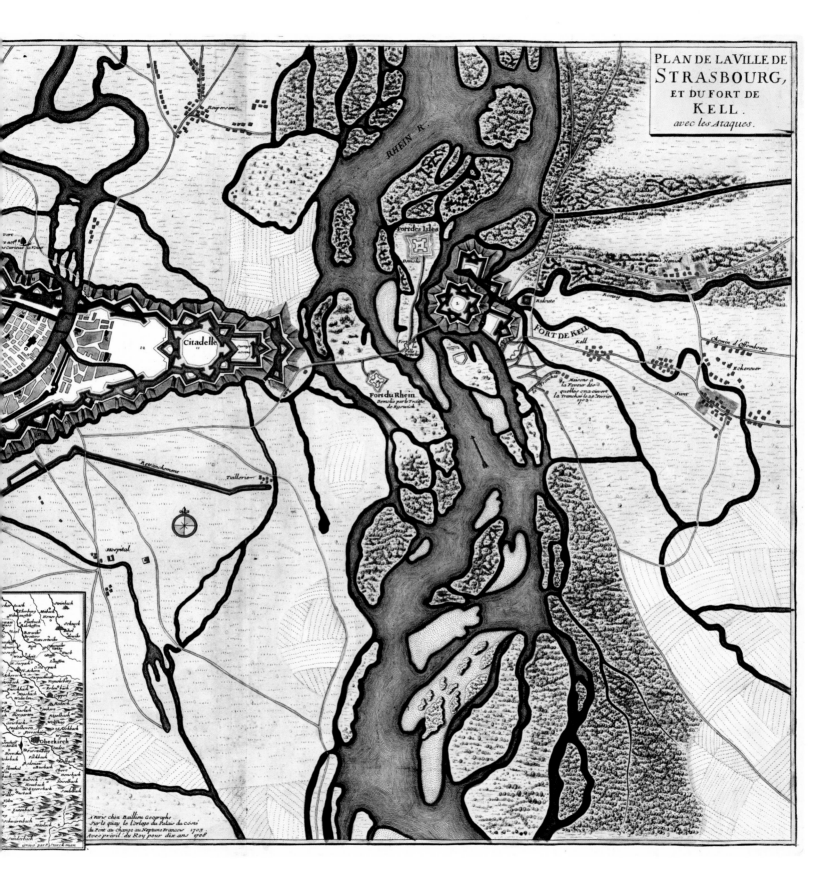

PLAN DE LA VILLE DE
STRASBOURG,
ET DU FORT DE
KELL.
avec les Ataques.

RHEIN R.

Fort des Isles

Citadelle

Fort du Rhein

FORT DE KELL

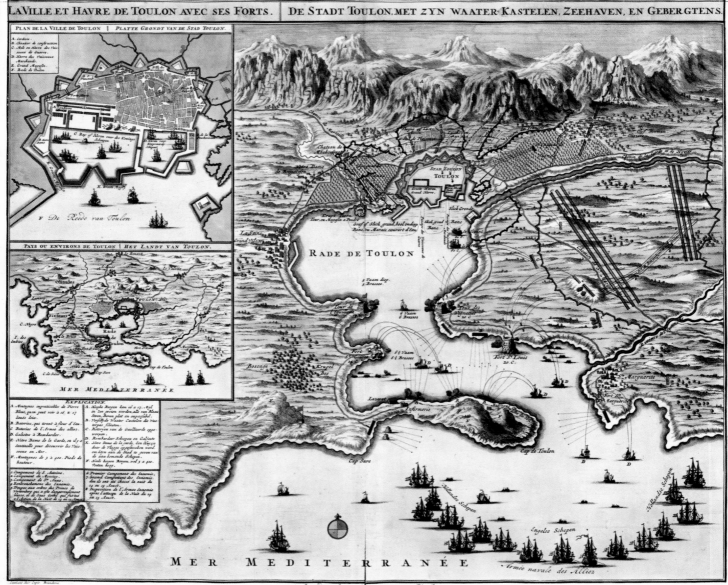

PLAN DE LA VILLE DE TOULON. | PLATTE GRONDT VAN DE STAD TOULON.

F De Reede van Toulon.

PAYS OU ENVIRONS DE TOULON | HET LANDT VAN TOULON.

MER MÉDITERRANÉE.

EXPLICATION.

RADE DE TOULON

MER MÉDITERRANÉE

à Amsteldam chez Nicolas Visscher avec Privilege.

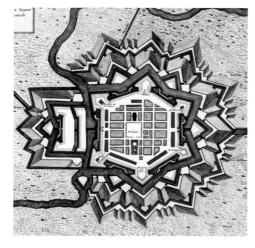

ABOVE At the Battle of Toulon in 1707, French and Spanish forces repelled an attempt by the British and their allies to take the city—the site of a major French naval base—on the Mediterranean coast.

LEFT Star-shaped fortifications are a common feature on Anna Beek's maps. The sharp angles and sloping walls repelled cannon fire, and the bastions provided a clear view—and a clear shot—for a fort's defenders.

OPPOSITE At the bottom of her map of the bloody Battle of Malplaquet, Beek lists the commanding officers for each regiment. Colored bars indicate how the forces were arrayed on the battlefield.

battles of the 18th century. Beek's red and green lines dispassionately lay out how the forces were arrayed on the field of battle, but the bodies piled up in the decoration in the lower right corner hint at the carnage.

A rumor that Marlborough had perished in the fray led to a song memorializing him, set to the tune we now know as "For He's a Jolly Good Fellow." Marlborough did survive, however, and his Pyrrhic victory at Malplaquet helped keep the French on the ropes. When the war finally ended, the terms of the treaties favored the allies, marking the rise of Britain as Europe's great power at the expense of France and Spain. Beek's maps beautifully capture the battles that led to that momentous change. ✳

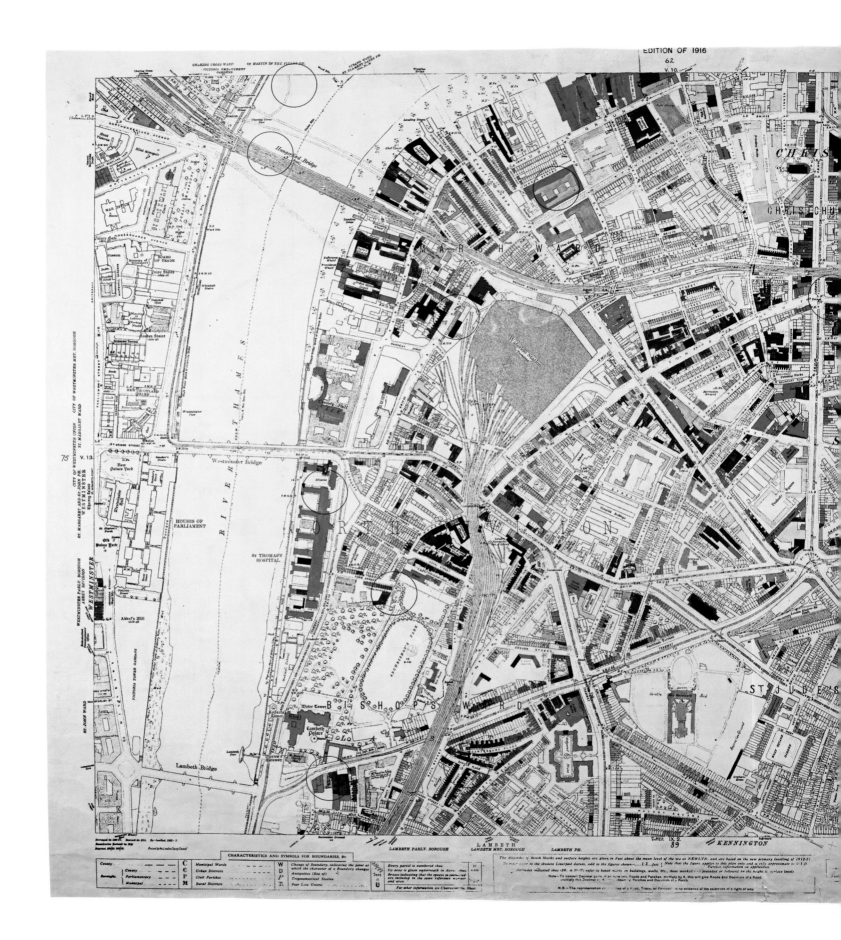

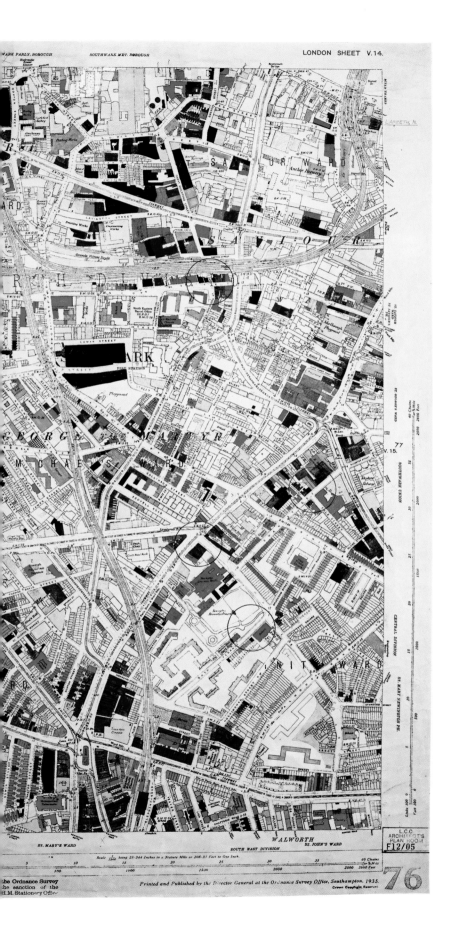

The Colors of Destruction

MAPPING WORLD WAR II DAMAGE IN LONDON AS THE BOMBS FELL

CREATED *1940–1945*
SOURCE *London Metropolitan Archives*

The German Luftwaffe dropped tens of thousands of bombs on London from 1940 to 1945, killing around 30,000 people. More than 70,000 buildings were completely demolished, another 1.7 million damaged. The degree of damage to every one of these buildings was logged and mapped in near real time by surveyors, architects, engineers, and construction workers. The result is an incredible set of 110 maps, color-coded by hand, that reveal the devastating extent of the destruction in exacting detail. Today the maps provide a unique window into this harrowing time in London's history.

As soon as the bombs started falling, data collection for the maps began. The London County Council, the central administrative authority for roughly the area known today as Inner London, tasked its Architect's Department with responding to bomb damage as it occurred. Surveyors, who before the war were responsible for making sure construction regulations were followed and buildings were up to code, suddenly found themselves in charge of rescue operations. They worked with local rescue services made up of people from the construction fields, like engineers and bricklayers.

"Their primary aim was to pull people out of rubble and destroyed buildings and try to save lives," says Laurence Ward, principal archivist at London Metropolitan Archives, which holds the original maps. "They were set up as the rescue service because they had an understanding of how buildings worked."

LEGEND

■ **Total Destruction**

■ **Damaged Beyond Repair**

■ **Seriously Damaged**
Doubtful if Repairable

■ **Seriously Damaged**
Repairable at Cost

■ **General Blast Damage**
Not Structural

□ **Blast Damage**
Minor in Nature

■ **Clearance Areas**

London's Waterloo and Elephant and Castle neighborhoods suffered a lot of damage from German bombs during World War II, as shown on this map that was hand-colored to indicate the severity of the destruction as damage reports came in.

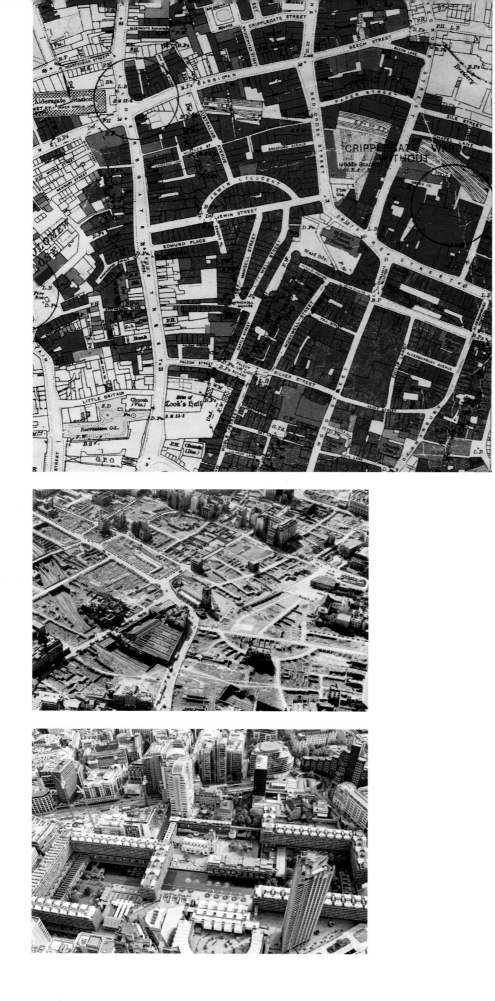

These men were the ones deciding how much time was left to try to save people before a damaged building might collapse. In all, the rescue services responded to 16,396 incidents and saved 22,238 people. They lost 54 of their own men during these efforts.

Once a rescue operation was finished, the mapping began. The surveyors and rescue workers worked together to classify the damage, building by building, into six categories ranging from "Minor in Nature" to "Total Destruction." Their reports were recorded onto maps of the city made in 1916 by the Ordnance Survey, Britain's national mapping service, and updated to 1940. Each damage category was given a color, and the status of every affected building was colored by hand.

A diary entry from April 20, 1941, written by an architect in the rescue service, gives a vivid description of what the work was like: "For the block I have started on—eight floors high with two flats on each floor—has had its whole face ripped off . . . I found it possible to stand on part of the roof. So, clutching a broken chimney, I surveyed the damage there. My notebook became very messy. What with the dust and soot, wet filth and the perspiration of fluster on my hands, it was difficult to read what I wrote. The notes served their purpose however when, after drying the book, I had to transcribe them into a report."

Visually, the maps are striking. The apparent randomness of the colors stands in contrast to the more orderly pattern of streets and buildings.

In some places, whole swaths containing several blocks and dozens of buildings are colored black (Total Destruction) and purple (Damaged Beyond Repair). In other places, the severity of damage varies widely, with areas colored yellow (Minor in Nature) peppered with black, purple, and red (Seriously Damaged).

Circles denote strikes from V-1 and V-2 rockets, known as flying bombs, which caused tremendous damage. Beginning in June 1944, Germany added the V-1 to its attacks, which up to that point had mostly consisted of aircraft dropping incendiary bombs. The V-1 was a pilotless aircraft that carried a 1,870-pound (850 kg) warhead and could navigate by autopilot and crash into a target. Though the rockets hit their targets only about a quarter of the time,

more than 2,000 landed in the London region, killing 2,329 people. In September 1944, a V-2 rocket, the world's first ballistic missile, hit London. By the war's end, 517 had detonated in London, killing 2,511 people.

"I just find it staggering that they managed to just carry on. London just carried on working," Ward says. "It must have been an extraordinary time."

Immediately after the war, the maps were used for insurance claims and for city planning as reconstruction of bomb sites began. The damage transformed London into the architecturally diverse city it is today. The maps help explain how it came to be that rows of grand old Victorian buildings are interspersed with more modern, functional low-rise housing typical of the 1960s.

A stark example of juxtaposed architecture is St Giles-without-Cripplegate, a Gothic church built in the 14th century. The Cripplegate area was heavily bombed; two V-1 flying bombs struck within blocks of the church. On the damage map on the opposite page, St Giles is colored pink (Seriously Damaged) and surrounded by a sea of buildings colored purple (Damaged Beyond Repair). Virtually every structure around the church had to be torn down (opposite middle), but St Giles was repaired and still stands today: a sole survivor surrounded by modern buildings (opposite bottom).

"There are just so many stories which these maps provide the starting point for," Ward says. "They're a great source in the sense that they make you want to go on and find out more." ✳

U-Boats Strike Terror at Sea

A GERMAN MAP DOCUMENTS DEADLY SUBMARINE ATTACKS DURING WORLD WAR I

CREATED *1918*
SOURCE *Library of Congress, Geography and Map Division*

It was a type of combat the world had never seen. In February 1915, Germany declared unrestricted submarine warfare in the Atlantic Ocean, vowing to attack not just the British warships enforcing a crippling blockade of its ports but also merchant ships—including ones from neutral countries. No longer would Germany follow the gentlemanly rules of sea combat, which required that attacking ships ensure the safety of a ship's crew before seizing its cargo or sending it to the watery depths. There would be no more warning shots. This was total war.

The map to the right depicts the devastating toll over the course of a single year. Each red dot represents a ship sunk between February 1, 1917, and February 1, 1918. The map is also a snapshot of the war in progress. The light blue areas correspond to the restricted zones, where German U-boats prevented the transit of other ships. Brown areas off Germany's North Sea and Baltic coasts show the region blockaded by the British, and tiny red pairs of crossed swords point to sites of naval skirmishes.

"The submarine was the first man-made weapon to go about its war-making business in the third dimension," writes naval historian Jan Breemer. For that reason, submarines defied countermeasures. As long as they stayed underwater, U-boats were invisible. Even if a warship detected one, hitting a moving target with the freedom to move up and down was a significant challenge. Unarmed merchant ships could only hope the U-boat torpedoes missed.

The results were deadly. German U-boats torpedoed more than 5,000 merchant ships and 100 warships during World War I. Tens of thousands of lives were lost. So, too, were millions of tons of cargo. The attacks were concentrated off the coast of the British Isles and in the Mediterranean Sea as the Germans sought to cut off the trade routes that brought food and other essential supplies to Britain, although they ranged from the Black Sea to the Cape Verde islands off Africa.

Not shown on the map is perhaps the most infamous U-boat attack: the 1915 sinking of the passenger liner RMS *Lusitania* off the coast of Ireland. Nearly 1,200 people died, including 128 Americans, and the ensuing public outcry created pressure for the United States to enter the war it had tried to avoid. ✳

RIGHT This detail from a 1918 map, produced by a German publishing house for the general public, shows ships sunk by U-boats between February 1, 1917, and February 1, 1918.

BELOW These cross-sectional diagrams of deadly German U-boats come from a map published several years after the war.

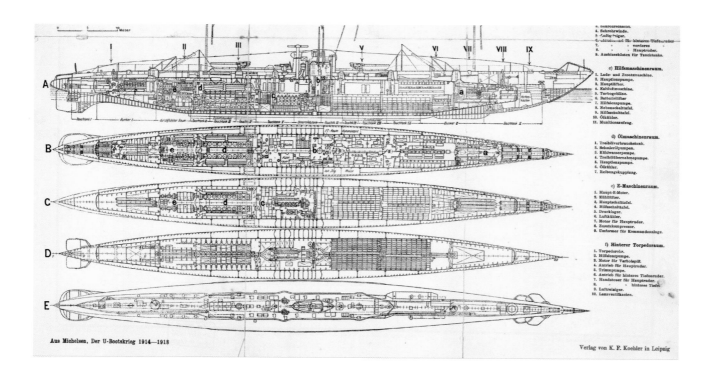

Aus Michelsen, Der U-Bootskrieg 1914—1918

Verlag von K. F. Koehler in Leipzig

World War II in 3-D

THE PAINSTAKINGLY CRAFTED TERRAIN MODELS THAT HELPED THE ALLIES WIN

CREATED *1944*
SOURCE *Library of Congress, Geography and Map Division*

Many of the key Allied operations carried out during World War II were planned and prepared for in secret—and in miniature. Unbeknownst to most of the world, a small detachment of British and American men and women built scale models of hundreds of potential targets, and had an outsize impact on the war.

The models, such as this one of Utah Beach in Normandy, France, were made at various scales to be used for strategic planning and for briefing troops before sending them into unfamiliar territory. They were based on whatever maps were available, supplemented by fresh aerial photos acquired at great risk to the pilots, many of whom died in the process. The model makers' work was extremely accurate, down to the color of buildings and the height of hedges. The result was three-dimensional representations that were far easier to understand, especially for troops who weren't skilled in reading maps or interpreting aerial photos. They were credited with saving countless lives.

The Royal Air Force (RAF) created the model-making unit, known as V-Section, in 1940, and the United States joined the effort in 1942. Both countries scoured their ranks for men with relevant skills, including architecture, industrial design, mapmaking, sculpture, and painting. They recruited outside the armed forces as well, even hiring several people from Hollywood and a set designer for New York City's Radio City Music Hall. With demands for models increasing, and having exhausted all available men, they began hiring female students from British art schools. The motley crew was based at Medmenham, an RAF station east of London.

To make the models, they began by cutting hardboard (similar to particle board) to follow contour lines traced from an enlarged map. The cutouts were then stacked and nailed down to create the topography. They used a plaster of paris mixture to fill in and sculpt the intervening topography. Model builders constantly referred to stereoscopic aerial photos to make sure every swale and hillock was accurate.

Next, precisely scaled photographs were draped over the top of the model, dampened, and stretched where needed. Paint was applied to add realistic color, in thin coats to let the texture from the photographs show through. Each road was hand-painted at the correct width. Buildings were cut to size out of linoleum, their height often gleaned from shadows on aerial photos. Hedgerows and trees were applied with a homemade contraption similar

This 3-D terrain model of Utah Beach in Normandy, France, was made to help the Allies plan their D-Day assault in June 1944. It is made of two 4-foot (1.2 m)-square pieces that were meticulously built with attention paid to the accuracy of every detail, so that commanders and troops would know exactly what to expect. In the close-up (right), you can see buildings and the hedgerows that are common in the French countryside. Models like this one were made in secret by a specialized unit and were credited with saving many lives.

LEFT A model maker uses a homemade tool, similar to what bakers might use to decorate a cake, to apply hedgerows to a terrain model used by Allied forces. The models were a well-kept secret, but just in case there were leaks, sometimes the model unit was assigned to make decoys of places that were not actual targets.

BELOW A U.S. Navy lieutenant uses a terrain model to brief officers and men who participated in landing operations during the invasion of southern France on June 5, 1944, the day before D-Day.

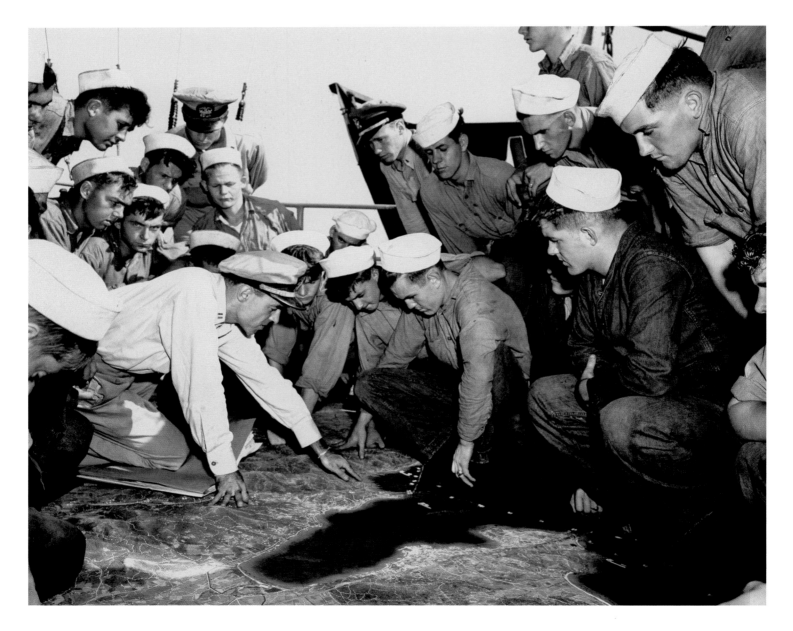

to an applicator used to decorate cakes. No detail was too insignificant; there were even tiny boats scattered in harbors, sometimes featuring a single clipped beard hair as a mast.

Models made for Air Force bombing raids were often photographed, and sometimes filmed, with lighting set up to match the time of day of the planned operation so that pilots could see exactly what the scene would look like.

Every possible effort was made to ensure those scenes were accurate, as mistakes could cost lives. In a rare instance recounted by U.S. Army corporal Leonard Abrams in a memoir about his time as a model maker in V-Section, a sea wall was made too tall on a model of the German-occupied port of Dieppe, France, leaving Allied tanks exposed to artillery fire where they thought they would be shielded during battle. It was the only error on a model that was otherwise indispensable and likely saved hundreds of lives, but it showed how high the stakes for accuracy were.

One of the largest, most important, and most secret model-making projects was for the D-Day assault on Normandy on June 6, 1944. The entire Normandy coast was modeled at a scale of 1:5,000, about 1 mile per foot (5 km/m). The Germans had placed many obstacles on the gentle slope of Utah Beach designed to damage or destroy approaching vessels, all of which would be hidden at high tide. So the D-Day operation required a low tide just before dawn under a bright moon. The assault was originally planned for June 5, but bad weather was forecast. Twenty-seven-year-old Navy intelligence officer Charles Lee Burwell, whose specialty was tides and beach obstacles, used the Utah Beach model to explain what would happen if the Allies delayed the operation by a day or two, or several days. According to Burwell, among those attending the briefing was Gen. Dwight D. Eisenhower, who ultimately made the decision to proceed on June 6. Burwell held on to the model after the war and gave it to the Library of Congress in 2003.

The models proved critical to the Allies' success. According to a letter to Abrams from Gen. Mark Clark in 1964, "They were employed extensively in every major amphibious or airborne operation. Probably the most outstanding and at the same time most important to the success of an operation were those for the landings in Normandy, France," he wrote. "Many will attest to the fact that success or failure depended to a large extent upon these models." ✳

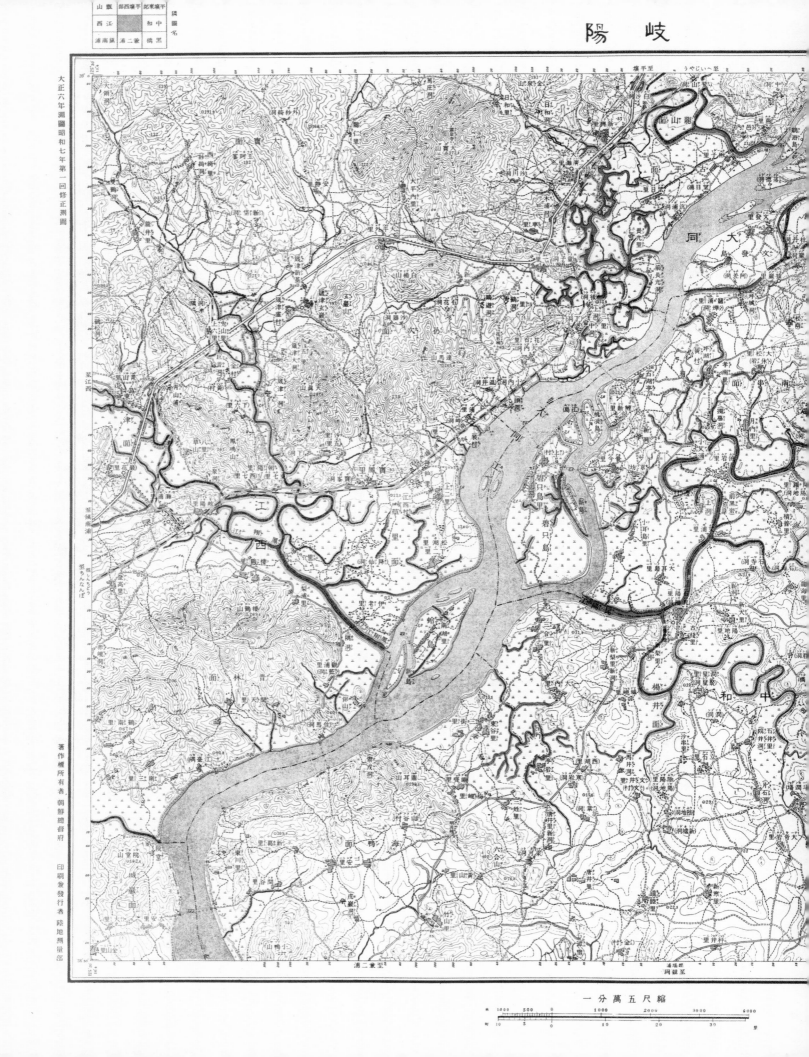

岐陽

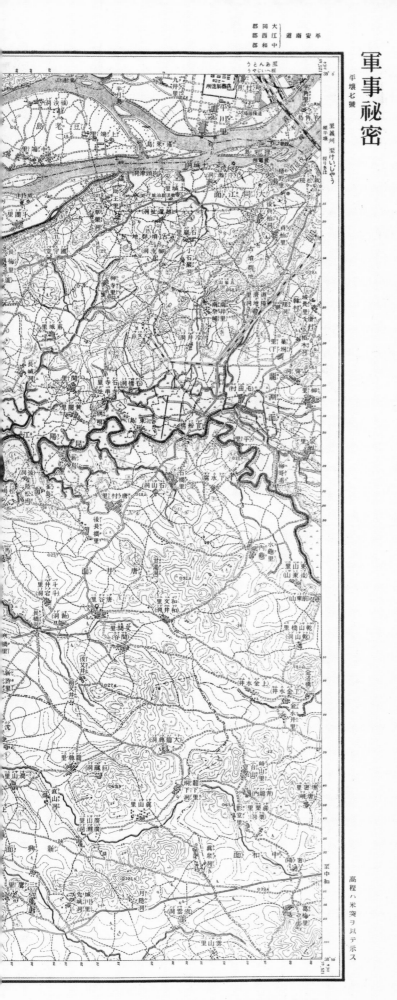

Japan's Secret Maps of Outer Lands

MAPS CAPTURED BY THE U.S. ARMY AT THE END OF WORLD WAR II SHOW ASIA IN EXACTING DETAIL

CREATED *1870s–1940s*
SOURCE *Stanford University Libraries*

In the waning days of World War II, American soldiers confiscated thousands of secret Japanese military maps, along with the plates used to print them, and shipped them to the United States for safekeeping. The maps, which cover much of Asia, depict far more than just the local topography. Some focus on transportation systems, others on the ethnicity of the local people and the prevalence of disease. The Japanese know these maps as *gaihōzu*—maps of outer lands. To the Americans, they were a valuable source of intelligence on a recently defeated foe, but also on a newly emerging one: the Soviet Union.

The Army Map Service considered it unwise to hold such a valuable strategic resource at a single location that could be destroyed in a nuclear strike, so it distributed the maps to dozens of libraries and institutions around the country. And there they remained, virtually forgotten, for decades.

Around 2008, Meiyu Hsieh, a Stanford University graduate student, decided to investigate some rumors she'd heard about mysterious stacks of old Asian maps amid the archives of the Hoover Institution, a think tank on campus. Hsieh's dissertation research focused on why the ancient Han dynasty was able to build the first large, enduring empire in China more than 2,000 years ago. But many of the relevant archaeological remains don't appear on modern maps and satellite imagery because they've either eroded away over time or been covered up in the process of China's industrialization. Older maps, Hsieh reasoned, might hold some important clues.

Eventually her inquiry led her to a dark room lined with drawers in the basement of Stanford's earth sciences library. Hsieh spent an entire afternoon trying to

This 1947 Japanese military map shows the area around Pyongyang, the current capital of North Korea.

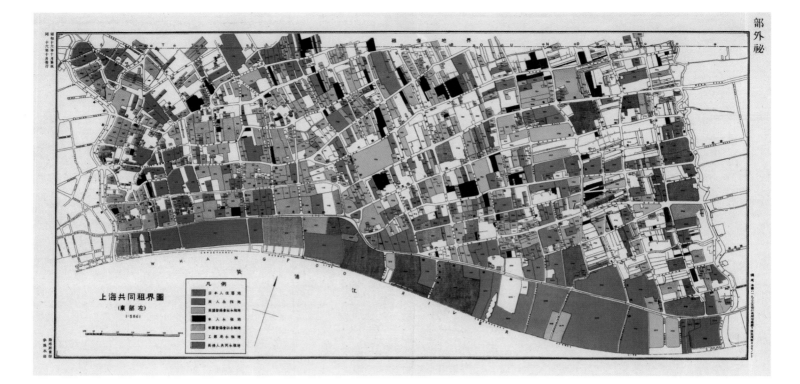

ABOVE This Japanese map of Shanghai is color-coded to indicate who lived and worked there. Green indicates Japanese residential districts, for example, and light blue indicates areas with American-registered companies.

BELOW This is a detail from a map of Keijo, as the Japanese called what's now Seoul, South Korea, during their rule from 1926 to 1945. The white area to the left is a large public space, originally the grounds of a 14th-century palace.

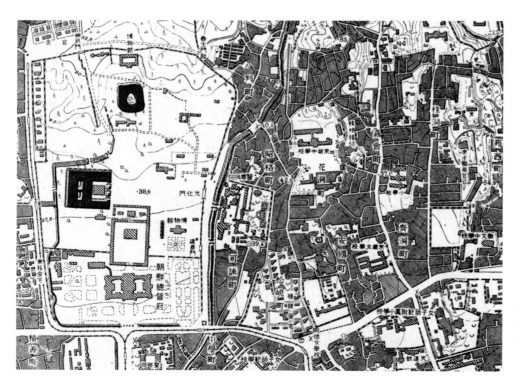

figure out what was inside them. She'd found the university's cache of Japanese military maps, which had been moved to the library's basement years earlier from the dusty attic of Hoover Tower. The university, it turns out, had roughly 8,000 of them.

According to Shigeru Kobayashi, a retired professor in Osaka and the foremost expert on gaihōzu, the Japanese military started making these maps around 1870, long before World War II. It was a fraught period in Japan's history. Elsewhere in the world, the imperial powers of Europe were busily carving up Africa. Japanese leaders thought they had two choices: become a colonial power or get taken over by one. They didn't want to be somebody else's colony, and so a kind of defensive imperialism was born.

At first, the military copied any maps they could get their hands on from neighboring countries. But army officers soon realized they needed more detailed maps, and so they began sending teams to survey the coastlines and, later, inland areas of China and Korea.

Not surprisingly, Japanese surveyors weren't always welcome in other countries. According to Kobayashi, in 1895 angry Koreans killed several assistants on a Japanese survey team (Japan annexed Korea in 1910 and held it until the end of World War II). Beginning in 1913, Japan sent secret survey teams into China. These men disguised themselves as traveling merchants and made their maps, equipped with only a compass, by counting their steps to mark distance.

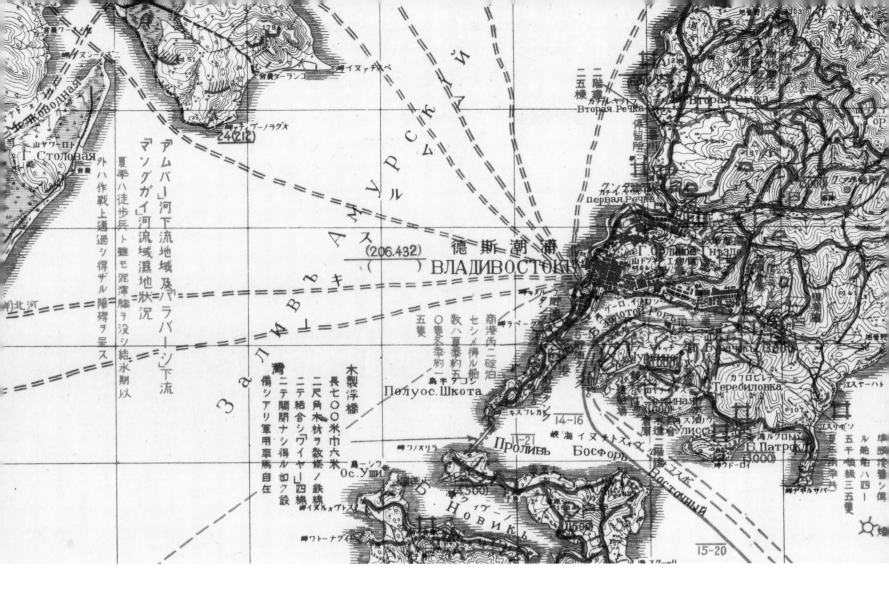

In the age-old tradition of cartographic copying, the Japanese often built on maps they'd captured from their foes, adding their own notes and details on top of the original, as seen on the Cyrillic script visible on the Japanese map above of Vladivostok, Russia. Naturally, their enemies did the same thing. The U.S. Army used captured Japanese maps at the Battle of Okinawa and elsewhere.

In addition to topographic maps showing the terrain of other countries, the Japanese military made everything from aeronautical charts to city maps showing who lived and worked in different neighborhoods (as with the map of Shanghai on the opposite page). Many of these maps contain detailed notes in Japanese on features that might be of strategic value, such as the suitability of a coastline for landing boats or the locations of factories used to make weapons. One map of a South Pacific island includes notes on the local diet and the location of the island's only ice machine.

The area covered by the gaihōzu extends as far north as Alaska and Siberia, as far west as India and Madagascar, and as far south as Australia. No one knows how many maps were made, mostly because the Japanese military kept its mapping program secret and ordered the maps destroyed as the U.S. Army closed in at the end of World War II. Many of the maps that survive today were apparently saved by the Japanese cartographers who'd devoted their careers to making them. They defied orders to destroy their work, preferring to see it confiscated by the enemy instead.

The gaihōzu have lost their strategic value, but researchers like Kobayashi and Hsieh still see them as a unique window into Asia's past. While Hsieh, now a historian at Ohio State University, is hunting for clues to an ancient civilization, Kobayashi is interested in using the maps to study deforestation and other types of environmental degradation in Southeast Asia and China. Both hope these maps, created with military goals in mind, will have a second life in the peaceful pursuit of knowledge. ✳

Refugees on the Move

MAPPING THE MOVEMENTS OF MILLIONS OF PEOPLE DISPLACED BY CONFLICT

CREATED *2014*
CREATOR *Hyperakt and Ekene Ijeoma*

In 2016, more than 22.5 million people left their home countries seeking refuge from persecution, violence, or war—the largest number since the United Nations began keeping count in 1950. Syria, in the midst of a deadly civil war, was the largest producer of refugees that year. Five and a half million people fled the country.

The map is part of an attempt to show the recent history of refugee crises around the world. It comes from an interactive website created by a New York social impact design agency, Hyperakt, based on more than 40 years of refugee data. According to the UN definition, people become refugees only once they leave their home country. Nearly twice as many people fled their homes without crossing an international border in 2016.

"I'm a refugee myself," says Deroy Peraza, one of the firm's founding partners. "It's part of my identity." Peraza was born in Cuba and came to the United States as a young boy. He realized many people shared his experience, but he wanted to find out more. "I had no sense of how big these migrations are and how long they've been happening and where they've been happening," Peraza says.

The online version of the map plays like a movie, with red circles popping up wherever large numbers of people flee to another country as the years tick by. Iraq pops up in the early 1990s, then Rwanda, then Bosnia. The big red circle over Afghanistan is virtually a permanent fixture. There's almost always something happening in central Africa, too. Hover over one of the circles and a burst of lines appears showing where all the refugees went—often to neighboring countries that are poorly equipped to handle the influx. As of 2016, the United States ranked 18th among asylum countries, with 268,513 refugees from 158 countries residing here. "That shows how important we are as a safe haven for people who are being persecuted," Peraza says. ✳

In 2016 more than five million refugees fled Syria—more than any other country. The neighboring countries of Turkey, Lebanon, and Jordan took in most of them.

2016 | Syria
Aleppo Falls to Regime Force

VIEWING

ORIGINATING FROM
SYRIA
5,524,333

POPULATION
18,502,000

REFUGEES / POPULATION
1 of 3

TOP 3 OF 110 ASYLUMS
TURKEY
2,823,987

LEBANON
1,005,503

JORDAN
648,836

75 76 77 78 79 80 81 82 83 84 85 86 87 88 89

5,524,333
refugees from Syria
(1st of 149 origins)

LAND

SCAPES

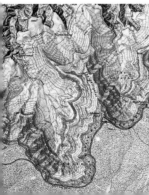

The Challenge of Mapping Terrain

Some of the most beautiful maps ever made are those that attempt to convey an accurate sense of the land. This is no easy task. Throughout the history of cartography, the problem of portraying a three-dimensional landscape in two dimensions has challenged mapmakers and pushed their artistry to new heights.

The maps in this chapter showcase all sorts of methods for portraying landscapes on the page. One of the greatest innovators was Eduard Imhof, a Swiss cartographer who pioneered techniques of shaded relief that simulate the shadows cast by mountains (see page 132). Imhof helped put the Swiss at the forefront of topographical representation in the 20th century, which is why the American explorer and mapmaker Bradford Washburn hired top Swiss cartographers to draw the cliff faces on his iconic 1978 map of the Grand Canyon (see page 118). It was the finishing touch on a map that Washburn spent years measuring the canyon in order to make.

Austrian artist Heinrich Berann developed another way to illustrate mountains. His 1991 panoramic painting of Yellowstone National Park (see page 114) uses creative distortions to produce an effect that is arguably more beautiful than any view of the park that exists in reality. His work has inspired others like Jim Niehues, who makes gorgeous, and effective, ski trail maps by subtly repositioning the slopes into one view (see page 139).

Today's cartographers are still emulating, tweaking, and building on these methods, using ever more sophisticated digital tools to map the landscapes around us. ➤➤

TOWERING TOPOGRAPHY
(1857, Boston Rare Maps)

This intriguing bird's-eye view of India was published in London by Mary Read, one of the rare independent female publishers of the 19th century. Read was likely hoping to capitalize on a spike in interest in India after a rebellion against British rule erupted there in May 1857, four months before the map was published. The map includes hundreds of cities drawn in profile, but the most striking feature is the vertically exaggerated Himalayan mountain range that dominates the horizon and looms over the subcontinent.

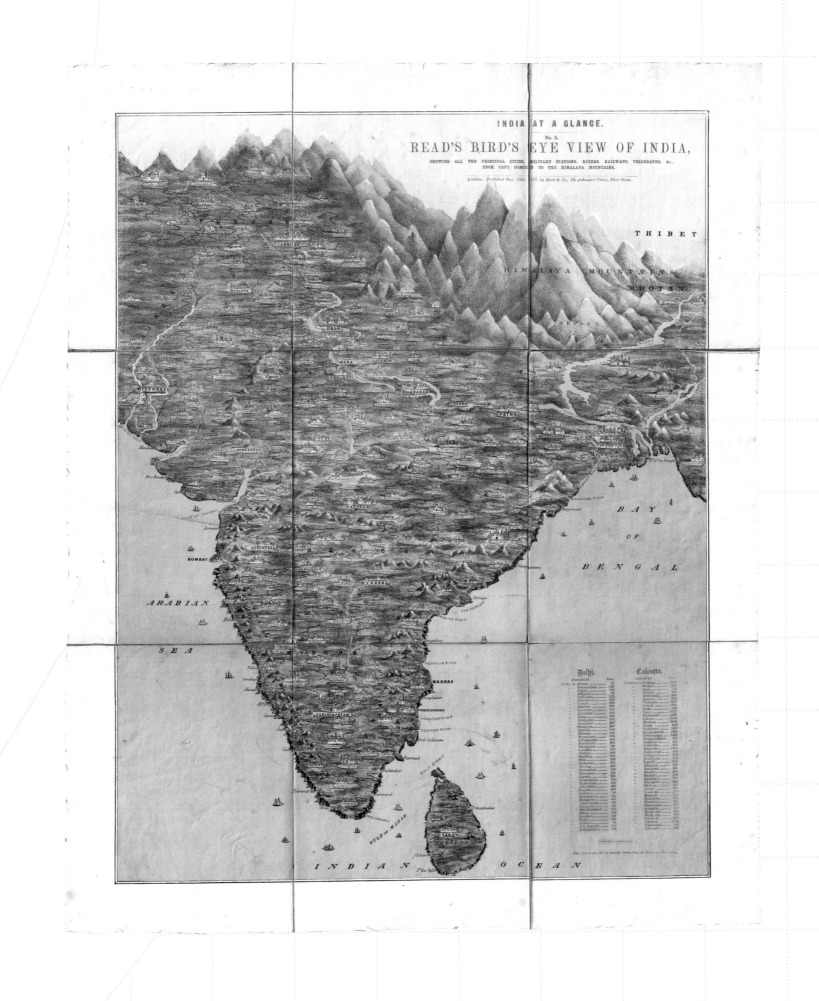

INDIA AT A GLANCE.

No. 2.

READ'S BIRD'S EYE VIEW OF INDIA,

SHOWING ALL THE PRINCIPAL CITIES, MILITARY STATIONS, RIVERS, RAILWAYS, TELEGRAPHS, &c.,
FROM CAPE COMORIN TO THE HIMALAYA MOUNTAINS.

London: Published Sept. 12th, 1857, by Read & Co., 10, Johnson's Court, Fleet Street.

Cartographic Panorama

HEINRICH BERANN PIONEERED NEW TECHNIQUES FOR DRAMATIC VIEWS OF GRAND LANDSCAPES

CREATED *1991*
SOURCE *U.S. National Park Service*

Heinrich Berann mastered the ability to include the same amount of detail in the valleys of his cartographic panoramas as at the peaks, unlike the view from a plane. He also accentuated important features, such as Old Faithful Lodge in the upper right part of this 1991 painting of Yellowstone National Park. As depicted, it would be three-fourths of a mile (1.2 km) long in real life.

Heinrich Berann's painting of Yellowstone National Park is in many ways a better view than any to be found in real life. It's a classic example of a cartographic panorama: a hybrid of map and art that Berann pioneered and mastered.

At the height of his artistic genius, Berann painted four exceptional panoramas for National Park Service posters. His work has stood the test of time so well that in 2018, the Park Service released new digital images of his original paintings, including this one of Yellowstone from 1991.

Born into a family of artists in Austria in 1915, Berann was trained in design, sculpture, and anatomical art. His considerable painting skills were self-taught and he never studied cartography, but he had a talent for both. In 1934, his first panorama of a new mountain pass road in the Austrian Alps won first prize in an art contest, setting Berann on the path to becoming an innovator of the craft.

In 1963, his work caught the attention of *National Geographic* magazine, which commissioned two panoramas of Mount Everest. He also worked with Marie Tharp and Bruce Heezen to create the first realistic views of the ocean floor for a series of supplements for the magazine. In 1977 the trio teamed up to produce their iconic World Ocean Floor map that revealed the nature of the seafloor as never before (see page 188).

Over his 60-year career Berann painted hundreds of panoramas, mostly of the Alps, slowly developing and perfecting his style. His work is based primarily on topographic maps and aerial photos, but his panoramas are selectively distorted to showcase the most important aspects of a landscape. For example, at the top of the Yellowstone panorama, Berann rotated the north-south trending Teton Range about 55 degrees to the east to reveal its iconic east-facing profile rather than a more geographically correct but unrecognizable end-on view. He also increased the size of some landmarks, including Old Faithful Lodge on the right side of the image, the Grand Canyon of the Yellowstone near the center, and several of the park's major geysers.

Cartographers making 3-D digital maps today try to re-create some of Berann's techniques, such as a gradual change of perspective: The land is tilted toward the viewer on the bottom half of the panorama and rolls back to appear flatter near the

top, evoking the view from an airplane window.

Though they bend geographic reality, all of these choices help create a more beautiful and understandable landscape. "And that's really where the magic of his work comes into play," says Tom Patterson, a senior cartographer for the National Park Service. "The whole idea was to provide to the public a marvelous view of these parks that they wouldn't see themselves," he says. "If you were flying over these parks in an aircraft, the view that you would see would not be as compelling as a Berann panorama because of all the artistic techniques that he used." ✳

The Burning Mountain

200 YEARS OF LAVA FLOWS ON MOUNT VESUVIUS PAINT A BEAUTIFUL PORTRAIT OF DESTRUCTION

CREATED *1832*
SOURCE *Houghton Library, Harvard University*

This 19th-century map of lava flows from 28 eruptions at Italy's Mount Vesuvius, each designated with a different color, is an intriguing portrait of the volcano that shows how precarious it was, and is, to live on its flanks.

The map was made by a British amateur geologist living in Naples named John Auldjo, who was the first British citizen to climb Mont Blanc in 1827. His published account of the ascent, with accompanying sketches, became the most popular mountaineering narrative of the time. Looking for more adventure, Auldjo headed to Vesuvius in 1831 during an eruptive phase.

Auldjo's aim was to produce a book of sketches of the volcano, which he paired with a sort of traveler's guide to hiking Vesuvius, and a history and map of its eruptions. The text begins: "Among the enchanting features of the far-famed scenery around the Bay of Naples, the favoured region of poets, none is more attractive than Vesuvius, 'the burning mountain,' which has allured the curious and learned in all ages, and from all countries."

Mount Vesuvius is best known for the catastrophic eruption that buried most of the Roman city of Pompeii beneath as much as 20 feet (6 m) of ash in A.D. 79. An eyewitness account written by Pliny the Younger was so detailed and accurate that the type of explosive eruption he described is now known as a Plinian eruption.

Though Vesuvius hasn't erupted with as much ferocity since then, in 1631 the volcano sent major lava flows streaming down its flanks, killing thousands of people. This event began a new phase for Vesuvius, with similar but smaller eruptions threatening nearby cities and towns.

In 1831 when Auldjo arrived, the mountain was becoming a tourist destination. His *Sketches of Vesuvius,* published in 1832, begins with detailed descriptions directing visitors to trails with the best scenic overlooks, the most unusual rock formations, and the gentlest grades. His drawings are of dramatic scenes with bright red lava flows, many including men in white pantaloons, top hats, and canes casually looking on as the volcano erupts in the background (below).

Auldjo goes on to describe everything that is known about 43 historical eruptions beginning with the Pompeii catastrophe in A.D. 79. "There has not been a period of a hundred years, in which some part of the lands around the base of Vesuvius has not been ruined by earthquakes, destroyed by currents of lava, or covered with ashes," he wrote.

Evidence of the older events had largely been obscured by later eruptions, so Auldjo's map starts with the sizable flows of 1631, which he colored pink. "The torrent of lava divided itself into seven principal streams," he wrote, "destroying gardens, vineyards, towns, everything that lay in its way." The subsequent eruptions through 1831 that he mapped were all smaller, but many still did damage, including two that reached all the way to the bayside town of Torre del Greco. Collectively, the 28 lava flows snaking down the sides of Vesuvius on the map reveal the volcano's violent past in a single view and act as a warning for the future. Nearly a dozen more eruptions have occurred since Auldjo's map was published, the most recent in 1944. Today around 600,000 people live in the volcano's line of fire. ✳

The small cone, from the S. E. summit of the great cone.

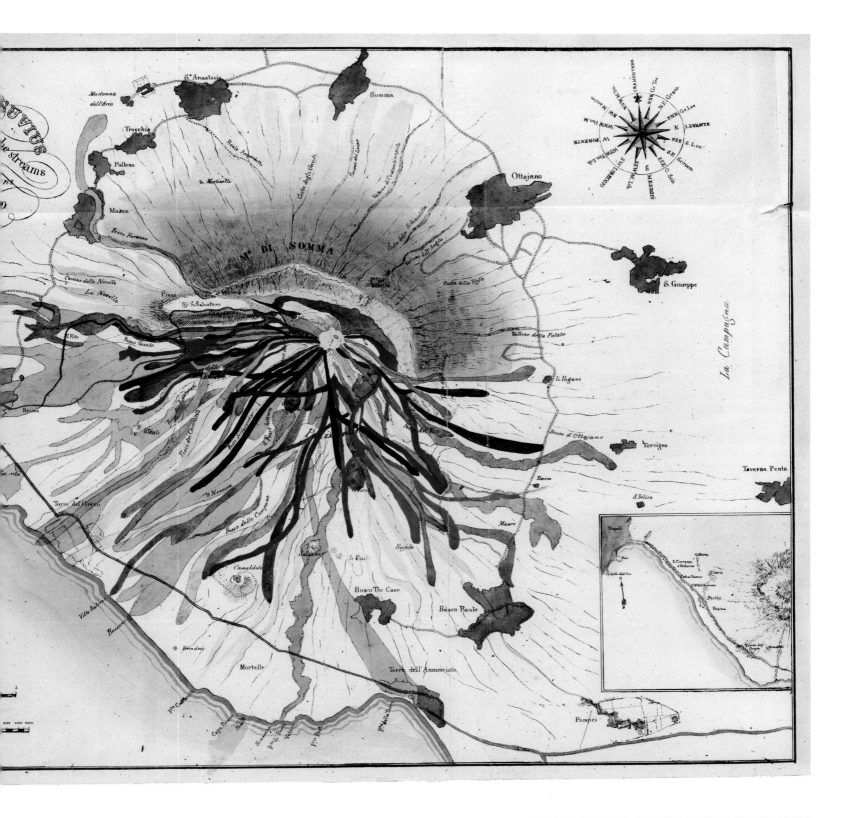

OPPOSITE Mount Vesuvius had become a tourist attraction when John Auldjo visited it in 1831. Many of the sketches he made of the eruption that was ongoing at the time include men in fancy clothes and top hats enjoying the show.

ABOVE The lava that flowed from 28 eruptions of Mount Vesuvius between 1631 and 1831 is recorded on this map, with the flows from each eruption marked in a different color. The oldest eruption recorded on the map (colored pink) was also the largest.

The Heart of the Grand Canyon

THE EPIC EIGHT-YEAR ADVENTURE TO MAP ONE OF THE MOST BELOVED NATURAL WONDERS ON EARTH

CREATED *1978*
SOURCE *National Geographic*

In 1970, Bradford Washburn undertook a cartographic endeavor that would be unheard of in today's digital world. It took eight years of planning, fieldwork, analysis, drafting, painting, and negotiating to create his map of the Grand Canyon. The result, "The Heart of the Grand Canyon," published by National Geographic in 1978, is still considered by many to be the most beautiful map of the area ever created.

"Maps are simply not made like this anymore," writes cartographer Ken Field. "It's the epitome of dedication and commitment to the craft of making a map."

It all started when Washburn and his wife, Barbara, visited the Grand Canyon in 1969. They had come to acquire a boulder from the bottom of the canyon to display in front of Boston's Museum of Science, where Washburn was the director. "We were astonished that no good large-scale map was available anywhere," he recalled. He decided to make one himself.

At age 60, Washburn was a world-renowned explorer, mountaineer, and photographer with an impressive and unusual résumé. He was the first to ascend more than a dozen peaks in Alaska; he gave Amelia Earhart advice that might have kept her from getting lost had she heeded it; and a book of his mountain photography would one day include a preface written by Ansel Adams. He had led dozens of mountain expeditions, all without any major injuries to his teams—he even once risked his life to rescue three sled dogs from a crevasse. Barbara accompanied him on many of his expeditions and became the first woman to climb the tallest mountain in North America, Alaska's Mount McKinley (now officially called Denali).

Several of these expeditions were backed by National Geographic, and one resulted in a gorgeous relief map of part of the St. Elias Mountains on the Alaska-Canada border. In 1939 he became director of the Museum of Science, which provided a small annual research fund of $10,000. In 1970, he used that money to get started on what would become an epic project to map one of the world's greatest natural wonders.

The first order of business was to get an aerial view of the canyon. He ordered complete coverage from around 26,000 feet (8,000 m) and then again from around 16,000 feet (5,000 m). Photos in hand, he and Barbara headed into the canyon for the next step: setting up a survey network in the canyon and along the rim, starting with Yaki Point, which had a known elevation, latitude, and longitude recorded on a U.S. Geological Survey brass benchmark hammered into the rock.

Many of the points in their survey were extremely difficult or impossible to reach on foot, so Washburn hired helicopters to get them there. The Washburns and their assistants may have been the first people to ever set foot on some of the canyon's most remote points.

Often Washburn was dropped off on top of a pinnacle or small butte (see page 121) along with surveying equipment, such as a state-of-the-art laser range finder device still under development, on loan from the company that made it. Using a built-in telescope, Washburn would aim the helium-neon laser at a reflecting prism

RIGHT "The Heart of the Grand Canyon" map took eight years of fieldwork, drafting, and painting to complete. It was published by National Geographic in 1978 as a stand-alone map and as a supplement to the July magazine issue.

LEFT Bradford Washburn and his wife, Barbara, plot their position on an aerial photo as they measure the length of the North Kaibab Trail in the Grand Canyon in 1973. The Washburns measured nearly every trail in the canyon with a surveyor's wheel.

THE HEART OF THE
GRAND CANYON
Grand Canyon National Park, Arizona
Produced by the Cartographic Division
National Geographic Society
GILBERT M. GROSVENOR, PRESIDENT AND CHAIRMAN
NATIONAL GEOGRAPHIC MAGAZINE
JOHN B. GARVER, JR., CHIEF CARTOGRAPHER
Museum of Science, Boston, Massachusetts
BRADFORD WASHBURN, HONORARY DIRECTOR

positioned on another point miles away. The laser beam would be reflected back to the range finder, which measured how long the beam's round-trip took and translated that into distances that were accurate to within 6/100 of an inch per mile (1 cm/km). Washburn used a 40-pound (18 kg) surveying instrument called a theodolite to measure the angles between each of the control points, providing him with the relative position and height of each set of points.

After a few weeks in the canyon, Washburn was convinced of the potential for "a map of really superlative beauty as well as topographic quality." Knowing exactly where to find the expertise, and the funds, needed to realize that potential, he asked the National Geographic Society to join the project.

The society's archives contain hundreds of pages of correspondence about the project that reveal Washburn's boundless enthusiasm, penchant for effusive prose, and stubborn commitment to make a map of the highest possible caliber. "The resulting map, if produced with sparkling quality, could be an exciting addition to world cartography," he wrote in a funding proposal, "and depict one of the world's most magnificent cartographic challenges."

In 1971, Washburn got the $30,000 he'd asked for, and in return he promised, "You can count on me leaving no stone unturned to see to it that this job is beautifully executed."

He wasn't kidding. Over the next seven years, Washburn sweated every detail, from instructing his team on how to coax helicopter pilots into early morning flights, to how to make the canyon's cliffs look jagged enough on the map. Along the way, the project doubled in size, from 84 square miles (218 sq km) of the South Rim, the most heavily visited area in the canyon, to a 165-square-mile (427 sq km) area that included both rims and around 90 percent of the most popular trails.

Every measurement on the ground was double- or triple-checked, with particular attention paid to trails. The Washburns measured nearly every foot of every trail at least once, if not twice, using a wheel with a circumference exactly one-thousandth of a mile (see page 118).

By pushing the wheel along the ground and marking their progress on a special set of aerial photos taken along each trail from around 12,000 feet (3,700 m), they determined the trails' precise lengths. Not satisfied with just his own measurements, Washburn sent assistants and volunteers into the canyon to retrace his steps with very specific instructions. "If you make a bad mistake, never back up, as the

OPPOSITE A portion of Washburn's Grand Canyon map shows Dana Butte (also in photo above) at center left and the popular Bright Angel Trail leading up to the park headquarters at the bottom left. The locations of rapids are marked with V shapes on the Colorado River.

ABOVE Bradford Washburn stands atop Dana Butte as he uses a surveying instrument called a theodolite to measure the horizontal and vertical angles between two points in the Grand Canyon. His wife, Barbara, sits next to him recording the data. Some of the surveying points used for the map could only be reached by helicopter.

wheel won't reverse," he wrote to one volunteer surveyor. "Just stop and cuss a reasonable amount. Then go back to where you know you made your last reliable measurement."

By 1974, the fieldwork had entailed around a dozen trips by the Washburns that amounted to 147 days in the canyon, almost 700 helicopter landings, thousands of measured distances and angles, and around 100 miles (160 km) of triple-checked trail measurements. The costs, split between National Geographic and the Museum of Science, had topped $100,000, equivalent to nearly half a million dollars today. But the hardest part was yet to come.

Turning all of this fieldwork into a map would turn out to be just as laborious and twice as complicated as gathering the data. Washburn's goal was to produce a masterpiece, which meant putting together an all-star team to make the map. "Nothing quite like this has ever been done before," he wrote to the president of the National Geographic Society.

To translate all the aerial surveys and field measurements into contour lines on a base map, Washburn hired a New York mapping

company that he deemed "extraordinarily expert in this intricate work." For what he considered "the most complex and challenging shaded-relief project ever attempted," he insisted on engaging the universally acclaimed Swiss Federal Office of Topography (also known as Swisstopo). The rest would be in the hands of National Geographic's own world-class cartography shop.

Washburn directed every aspect of the map's creation and had his say on each detail. He corrected contour lines so that the sharp corners of trails lined up precisely with creek crossings, worried about what sort of line should represent ephemeral streams, and debated how much blue shading should be used in the shadows. He was particularly concerned that the canyon's distinctive colors be captured faithfully, so he ordered yet another aerial survey, this time in color, "in order to give the cartographers a very accurate understanding, not only of the color of the rock, but also the exact extent of trees and other vegetation."

Even then, Washburn wasn't satisfied. He arranged for a cartographer from Switzerland

and another from National Geographic to be flown to the canyon to see the colors for themselves. Internal National Geographic memos about the project reveal a sort of admiring exasperation with his determination in comments such as, "Bradford Washburn will not take no for an answer!" and "Bradford Washburn never gives up!"

The Swiss cartographers were, and still are, unrivaled in their ability to give mountains and cliff faces the illusion of three dimensions with a technique known as hachuring, which involves drawing short, precise lines in the direction of the slope. According to Washburn, it would sometimes take them "more than a day of intense labor to produce a few square centimeters of cliffs." To date, cartographers have been unable to top the handiwork of the Swiss.

"I think everyone would agree that the manual rock hachuring that you see on Washburn's map and other maps made by Swisstopo is just wonderful," says Tom Patterson, a cartographer for the National Park Service whose own work mapping the canyon has been inspired by Washburn's map. "It's basically state-of-the-

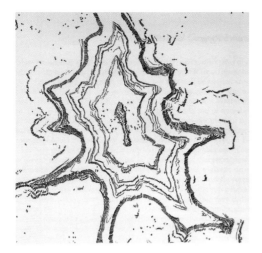

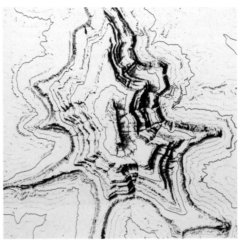

art and hasn't been replicated by digital tools."

National Geographic's own Swiss-trained cartographer, Tibor Tóth, painted the relief shading onto the map. The Grand Canyon map was the largest and most time-consuming relief map Tóth worked on during his 22 years at National Geographic. By his account, it took 1,074.5 hours to paint it.

In the end, all that work paid off exactly as Washburn hoped: The map is exceptional, both technically and aesthetically. National Geographic produced two versions of "The Heart of the Grand Canyon" map, one at the full 33-by-34-inch (84 by 86 cm) size, and another covering slightly less territory as a supplement to the July 1978 issue of *National Geographic* magazine, putting it in the hands of more than 10 million readers around the world.

Today, this sort of arduous, time-intensive data collection has been largely supplanted by GPS technology. But the artistry of the map has arguably not been surpassed. "Washburn's Heart of the Grand Canyon map is still the gold standard for Grand Canyon mapping today," Patterson says. ✳

The Beauty of Hand-Drawn Landforms

ERWIN RAISZ CREATED INCREDIBLY DETAILED PORTRAITS OF THE EARTH'S SURFACE

CREATED *1967*
SOURCE *David Rumsey Map Collection*

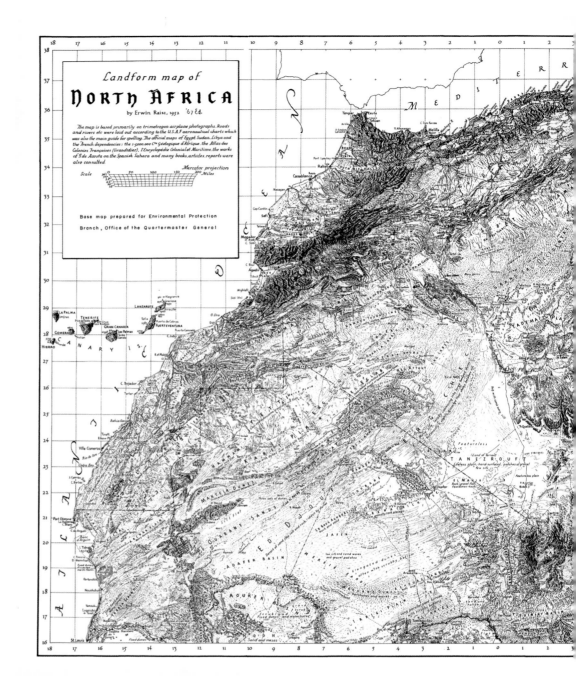

A diminutive, soft-spoken Hungarian immigrant, Erwin Raisz had a huge impact on American cartography. He was one of the best pen-and-ink mapmakers of the 20th century, perfecting manual techniques even as the digital age began to encroach on cartography.

Raisz helped develop and popularize a technique for depicting the physical landscape, known as a physiographic diagram or landform map, using three-dimensional representations of terrain on a two-dimensional map base. With this method, he was able to impart a sense of what the scenery actually looks like in an immediately recognizable way. The Rockies on Raisz's landform maps look like mountains, the Sahara is filled with sand dunes, and the Everglades appear swampy. These maps can't convey relative elevation as precisely as topographic-contour maps can, but Raisz was more interested in accurately portraying the Earth's surface.

"The map appeals immediately to the average man," he wrote in 1931. "It suggests actual country and enables him to see the land instead of reading an abstract location diagram. It works on the imagination."

Some of his landform maps, including this 1967 edition of his 1952 map of North Africa, are between 3 and 4 feet (around 1 m) wide and filled with an almost unfathomable amount of hand-drawn detail and hand lettering. They are based on the best maps and aerial photographs available at the time and were undoubtedly the best source for information on the terrain in areas of the world that were still poorly mapped, like North Africa. In fact, as late as 2005, geographers working on a new digital landform map of the area based on satellite images used Raisz's map as their reference, noting that "this hand-drawn product remains the most detailed landform map of the Sahara in existence."

Raisz developed his drawing ability by constantly sketching the landscape wherever he was. He had a lot of opportunity to practice while accompanying his wife, Marie, on trips all over the world to acquire exotic goods for her antique store. He even invented a system of "geographic stenography" to record landscapes as he traveled through them by car, train, bus, or plane, says Joseph Garver, a retired research librarian at the Harvard Map Collection.

Raisz codified his mapping method in a system of graphic symbols that cartographers could use to represent 40 different landforms (see page 127) based on oblique views of actual terrain—everything from tundra to coral reefs to canyons. He suggested three different types of sand dunes, eight different mountain forms, and more than a dozen types of flatlands and plains. He also created different symbols to indicate types of geology, water, and vegeta-

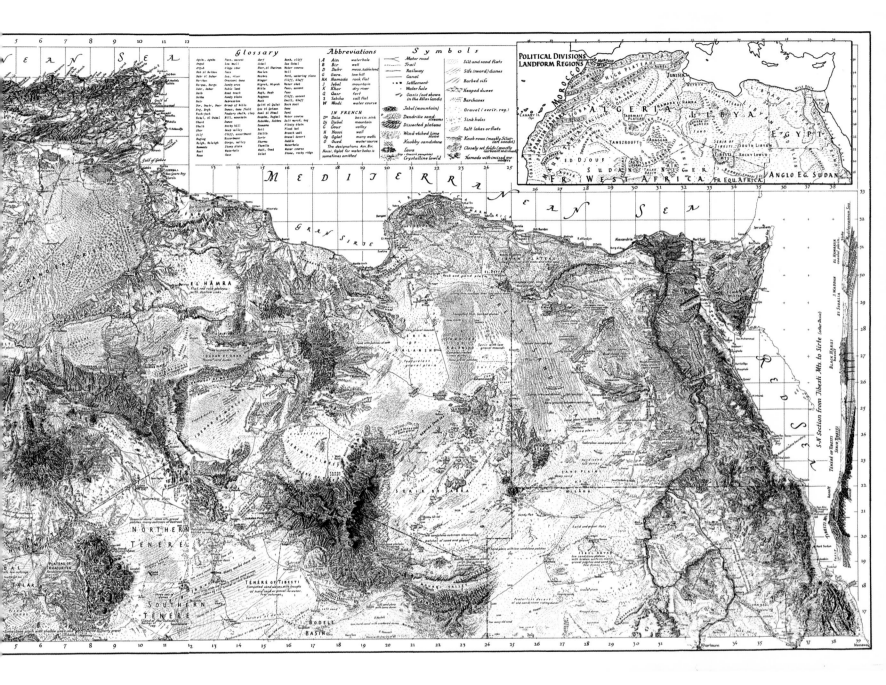

tion, as well as for distance, altitude, and color.

Though Raisz is best known for his beautiful maps, he also had a hand in shaping a generation of American cartographers. Cartography wasn't even considered an academic discipline when Raisz arrived in the United States in 1923, but he helped change that. While he was a graduate student in geology at Columbia University, he taught the school's first cartography class in 1927. Harvard University hired him in 1931 to teach cartography at its Institute of Geographical Exploration.

He wrote the first cartography textbook in English in 1938. His *General Cartography*

Erwin Raisz depicted 18 types of landforms on his 1952 hand-drawn map of North Africa (this one is the 1967 edition), including four kinds of sand dunes. More than four decades after he created it, scientists working on a new landform map based on satellite images used Raisz's map to guide them, saying the 47-by-13-inch (119 by 34 cm) landform map was still the most accurate in existence at the time.

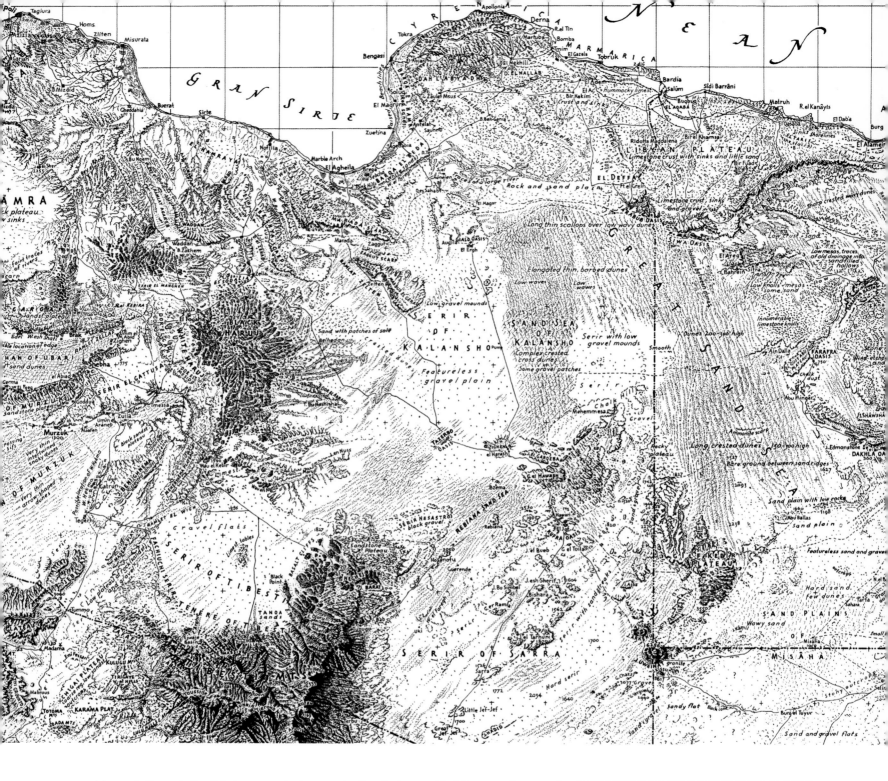

would remain the only English-language textbook for another 15 years, becoming the field's most important reference for both students and cartographers in the United States. In it, Raisz sought to forge an academic discipline by teaching not just the techniques of making maps but also the scientific basis for cartography and the history of the craft. He was largely responsible for establishing cartography as a component of the study of geography. In 1943, with the goal of inspiring more experimentation with map projections, he invented a new projection that resembled the curved armor of an armadillo (see page 267).

His doctorate in geology gave Raisz a deeper understanding of the structure of the Earth's crust, and he was a firm believer that "the cartographer must be a student of the land." Of course, it was Raisz's considerable artistic skill that allowed him to convey that understanding so appealingly. But he believed his system of landform symbols would help budding mapmakers portray the land regardless of artistic talent.

ABOVE This close-up of the northeast corner of Raisz's map of North Africa reveals the incredible amount of detail he included on the map. He did all the lettering by hand.

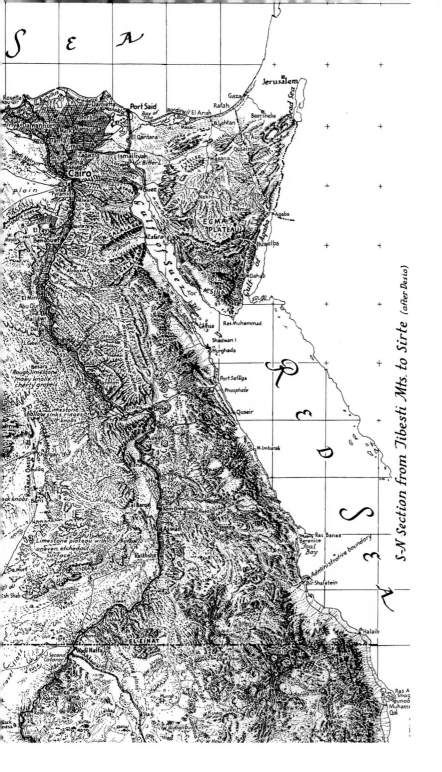

S E A

Jerusalem

Port Said

Cairo

EGMA PLATEAU

M SINAI

S-N Section from Tibesti Mts. to Sirte *(after Desio)*

RED SEA

9. **Plateau with advanced dissection in arid regions** (Badlands) *(South Dakota)*

10. **Plateau with more advanced dissection in arid regions** (Mesaland) *(Raton Mesa region)*

11. **Folded mountains** (peneplaned and redissected) *(Newer Appalachians)*

12. **Dome mountains** " " " *(Black Hills, S.D.)*

13. **Block mountains** *(Great Basin)*

14. **Complex mountains, high** *(Big Smoky Range)*

15. " " " **glaciated** (Alpine mts) *(Grand Teton)*

16. " " **medium** *(Adirondacks)*

17. " " **low** (Matureland) *(S.E. New England)*

18. " " **rejuvenated** *(Klamath Mts)*

19. **Peneplane** *(Finland)*

20. **Peneplane rejuvenated** *(Piedmont)*

21. **Lava plateau, young** *(Snake R. Plateau)*

22. " " **dissected** *(Columbia Plateau)*

23. **Volcanoes** *(Java)*

"He was always telling his students cartography is as much an art as it is a science," Garver says.

Garver interviewed some of Raisz's students, who said he could be difficult to understand due to his soft voice and heavy accent, but he still managed to inspire them with his enthusiasm and incredible drawing skill. He often sketched panoramic cross-sections of continents from memory across the chalkboard, which the students were always reluctant to erase afterward. Garver thinks his students may have been the ones who

convinced him to put some of these sketches onto long rolls of brown wrapping paper with multicolored chalk. Several of these impressive drawings survive in the Harvard Map Collection.

After the Institute for Geographical Exploration was shuttered in 1950, Raisz taught at several other schools and continued to produce his hand-drawn landform maps until he died in 1968 at age 75. While the world of cartography took its first steps toward automation, he pressed on with pen and ink, carefully crafting each mountain range, shoreline terrace, and fjord. ✳

ABOVE Raisz developed a system of graphic symbols to represent 40 types of landforms on maps, including five kinds of plateaus and eight forms of mountains. Fifteen of his landform symbols are shown here.

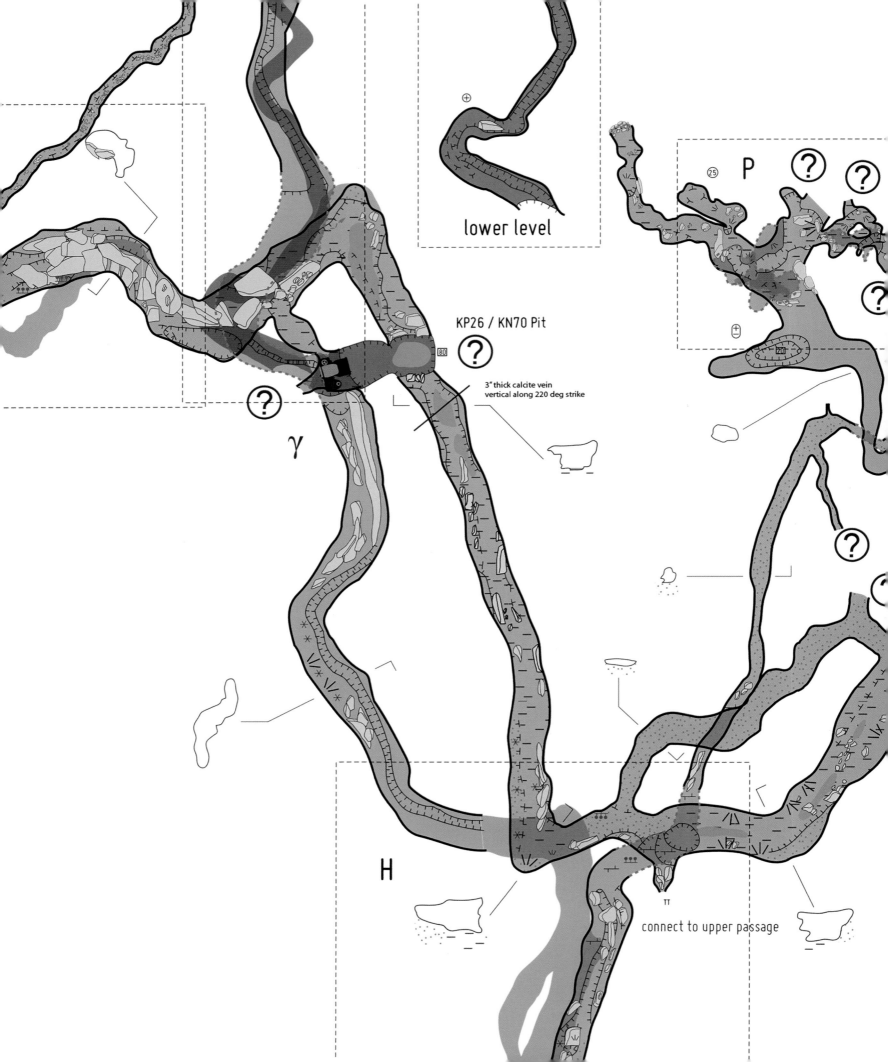

lower level

KP26 / KN70 Pit

(?)

3" thick calcite vein
vertical along 220 deg strike

γ

(?)

P

(?) (?)

(?)

(?)

(?)

H

connect to upper passage

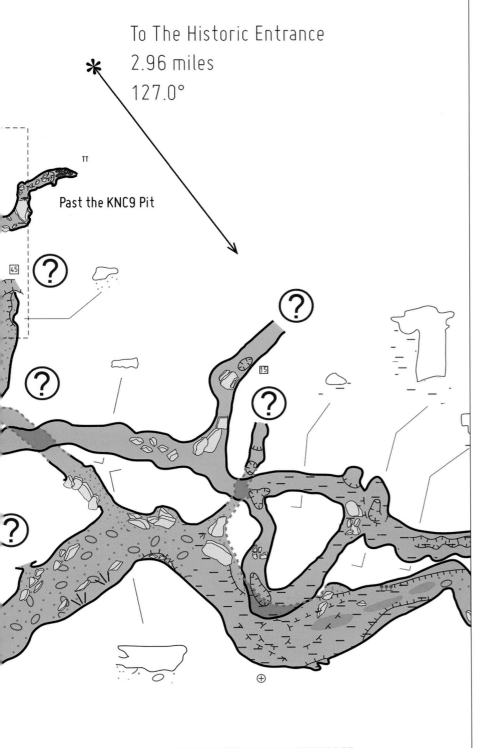

To The Historic Entrance
2.96 miles
127.0°

Past the KNC9 Pit

Mapping an Underground Labyrinth

CAVERS HAVE SPENT DECADES SURVEYING ONE OF THE WORLD'S LONGEST CAVES

CREATED *2014*
CREATOR *Stephen Gladieux*

Hike through a certain cow pasture in Kentucky and across a field of waist-high grass and you'll hit the edge of the forest. Just a few minutes more and—if you know where to look—you'll find a sinkhole and, at the bottom of that, a metal hatch. This hatch leads to the Fisher Ridge Cave System, one of the longest caves in the world.

The nearby Mammoth Cave National Park is home to the world's longest cave system, with more than 400 miles (650 km) of underground passages. Mammoth has been a tourist attraction since the late 1800s. Fisher Ridge, by contrast, was discovered only in 1981 by a team of cavers who call themselves the Detroit Urban Grotto. They have been exploring and mapping it ever since, so far charting more than 128 miles (206 km) of underground passageways.

The cave is known for its abundance of sparkling white gypsum crystals, which sometimes form delicate white "flowers," says the Grotto's chairman, Stephen Gladieux, a metallurgical engineer who has been exploring the cave for more than a decade and made these maps of their depths. There are other interesting rock formations in places, like stalactites and stalagmites, but they aren't the main draw for most cavers. Rather, it's the chance to go somewhere nobody else has ever gone, Gladieux says. "It's one of the few places left in the world where every weekend without fail you can go somewhere no human has ever been, and not only that, but the light from your helmet is the first ray of light to hit that surface or rock—ever!"

Mapping the cave is a crucial part of this endeavor. Without a map, cavers would waste time covering ground that's already been covered, possibly harming the cave's delicate ecosystems in the process.

Different colors indicate passages at different depths in this detail of a tiny part of the so-called KN Canyon section of the Fisher Ridge Cave System. Question marks indicate potential passages that have yet to be explored. Oddly shaped outlines show what the cross section looks like at that point.

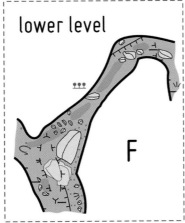

lower level

F

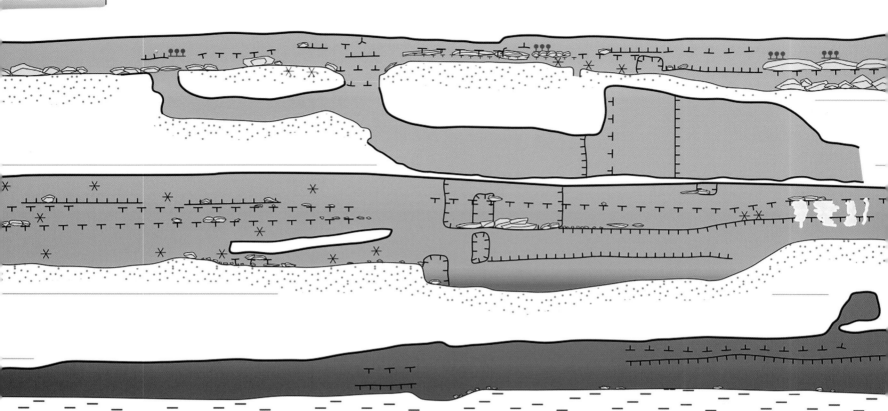

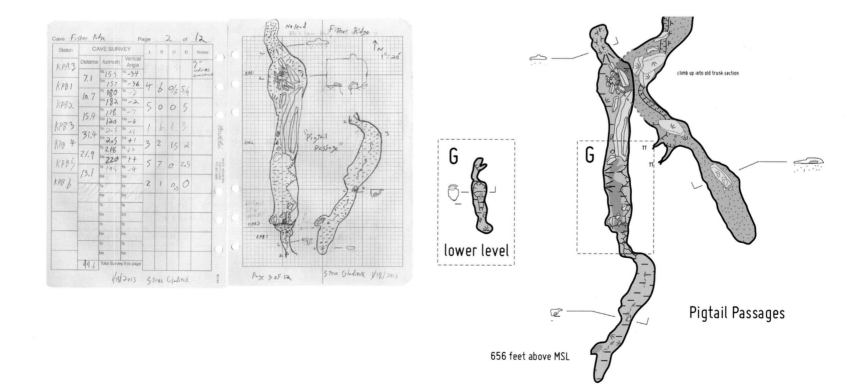

Pigtail Passages

climb up into old trunk section

G
lower level

656 feet above MSL

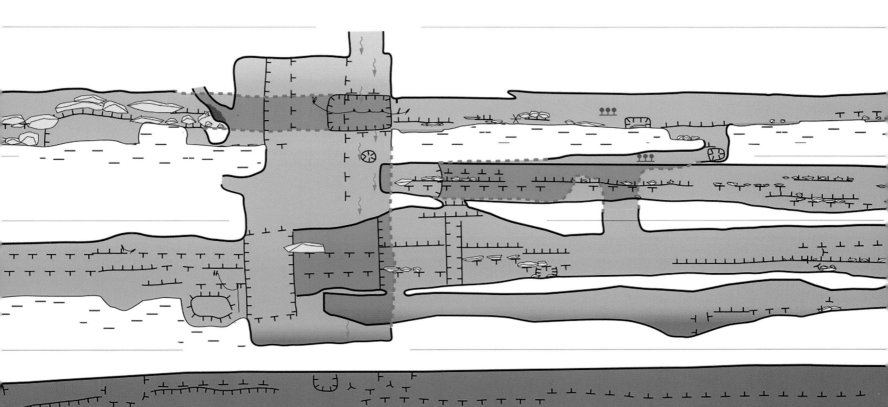

Cave surveyors typically work in teams of four. One person scouts ahead. The second and third position themselves at two survey stations, which could be any two points with a clear view of each other, and use a measuring tape, clinometer, and compass to measure the distance, slope, and direction between the two points. Getting good readings isn't always easy. "You might be lying on your chest in four inches of freezing water in a spot where you have to exhale to squeeze forward," Gladieux says. The fourth person records all these numbers in a waterproof notebook and sketches the passage (see the sketch opposite).

Survey trips are all-day affairs and average about 3 miles (5 km) round-trip, depending on the difficulty of travel. There's a lot of "canyon hopping" in this section of the cave, Gladieux says. "You walk on a ledge that's two or three feet wide and next to you is a 60-foot drop, and then your ledge runs out and you have to step across a gap to a ledge on the other side," he says. "Some people really struggle with that."

In other places the cave mappers use a highline to cross an open pit, clipping onto a rope strung across the gap and pulling them-

selves to the other side in a classic mountaineering maneuver known as a Tyrolean traverse. "You have the sensation that you're hanging in space," Gladieux says. "You're very aware that there's nothing under you."

Gladieux describes his cartographic training as "whatever I learned as an Eagle Scout," but his map has won recognition from both cavers and cartographers. The major challenge, he says, was representing depth, which he decided to do with color, using purple for the deepest passages of the cave, green for mid-depths, and tan for regions close to the surface (see above).

The map details you see here cover just a tiny fraction of the known and mapped parts of the Fisher Ridge Cave System. There may be much more of it yet to be discovered. Question marks inside circles on the map indicate places where surveyors found a promising lead, which could be anything from a tiny opening with a bit of breeze blowing out to a more obvious passage that the cavers ran out of time to investigate. Many of those question marks will turn out to be dead ends, Gladieux says, but almost any one of them could open up miles of new passageways for exploration. ✳

OPPOSITE LEFT These pages from Gladieux's notebook record survey measurements and his sketch for a part of the cave known as the "Pigtail Passages." Dashed lines indicate that the floor is silt or clay; dots represent sand.

OPPOSITE RIGHT In this part of the finished map, the tan section to the left corresponds with Gladieux's notebook sketch of the Pigtail Passages. The inset image marked "G" shows a close-up of a small passage below the main one.

ABOVE This view shows how Gladieux used color to indicate depth inside the cave. Tan is closest to the top, but still about 135 feet (40 m) below the surface. The deepest indigo passage is nearly twice as deep.

Mountain Masterpieces

A PIONEERING SWISS CARTOGRAPHER MADE THE ALPS POP OFF THE PAGE

CREATED *1930s–1970s*
SOURCE *Swiss Alpine Museum and ETH Library*

It's no easy feat to make mountains jump off a map's flat surface. The mapmakers who do it best seem to work a kind of magic, creating the illusion of depth where it doesn't exist and giving viewers the sensation of soaring over the landscape like a bird.

The Swiss cartographer Eduard Imhof was a pioneer of this kind of mapmaking. He made the painting to the right in 1938, and many cartographers consider it a masterpiece for its naturalistic depiction of the landscape around Walensee, a large lake in the Swiss Alps. Its size is impressive too—6.5 feet (2 m) tall and just over 15 feet (4.5 m) wide.

Imhof loved to draw and paint from an early age. As a young boy, he took a sketchbook and paints on hikes with his father near their home in Zurich. He aspired to be a mountaineer, but eventually settled on studying surveying and mapmaking at the Swiss Federal Institute of Technology in Zurich, where, at age 25, he became the youngest professor ever hired and worked for the next 40 years (Imhof died in 1986 at age 91).

Mapmakers and artists have used shading to simulate the shadows cast by hills and mountains for at least 500 years, but this technique, which cartographers call shaded relief, became an art form in Imhof's hands. His book on the technique, *Cartographic Relief Presentation*, originally published in German in 1965, is still essential reading for mapmakers.

One of Imhof's greatest contributions sprang from the realization that when you stand on a mountaintop looking toward the horizon, closer peaks appear sharper than distant peaks due to atmospheric haze, says Bernhard Jenny, a cartographer at Monash University in Melbourne, Australia. Imhof mimicked that effect by giving viewers an aerial perspective, as if looking down on the terrain from an airplane. "The high-est peaks are closest to the viewer, so they're depicted with the highest contrast, while the lowest valleys are farthest away, so they're depicted with the lowest contrast," Jenny says. You can see this at work in the Walensee painting: The sharp ridgelines of the highest hills seem to pop out more than the less distinct undulations of the land in the valleys below.

Lighting and color enhanced the illusion of depth in Imhof's work. He didn't invent shaded relief, but he refined the method by exaggerating the difference between light and dark areas and using color to heighten the effect. In the Walensee painting, for example, he used yellow, ocher, and other warm tones to suggest the rays of the sun reflecting off the steep mountainsides rising up around the lake and deep red-violet for the shadows.

Imhof saw his Walensee painting as an experiment in what artistic techniques might bring to mapmaking rather than as a map. "I tried to make

ABOVE Faint lines reveal the three panels of cartographer Eduard Imhof's enormous Walensee map painting, which now resides at the Swiss Alpine Museum in Bern.

RIGHT The true size of Imhof's map painting is evident in this photo, taken around 1955. It shows the map in its original home at the Swiss Federal Institute of Technology in Zurich, where Imhof worked for 40 years.

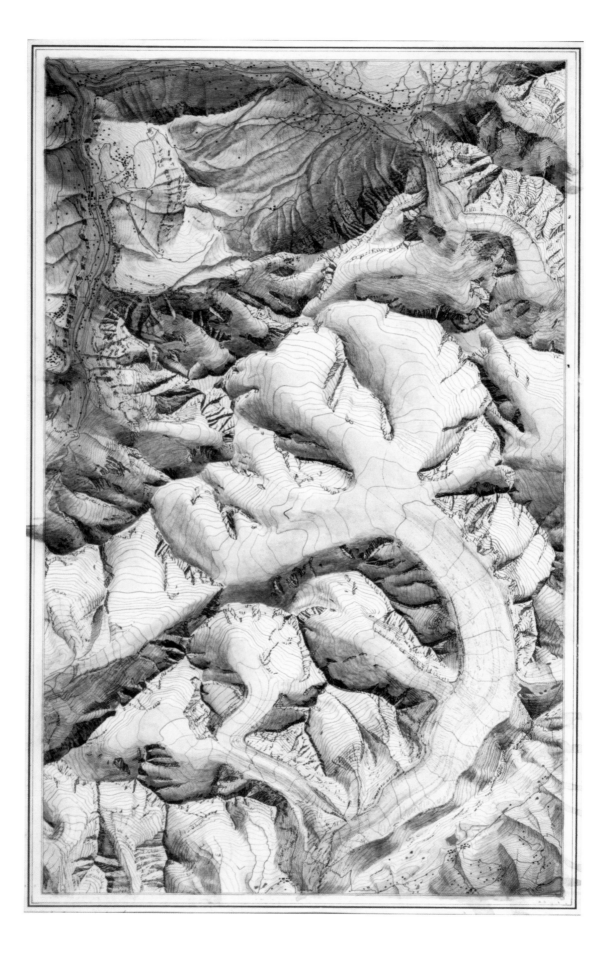

OPPOSITE The Aletsch Glacier is the largest in the Alps. In this map of the region around the glacier, made for a Swiss middle school atlas, Imhof manipulated the color and light to enhance the illusion of depth.

LEFT Eduard Imhof works on a relief model in this photo taken in 1938 at the Swiss Federal Institute of Technology in Zurich, where he worked his entire professional life.

BELOW Closer peaks appear in sharp contrast, and distant peaks fade into the evening mist in Imhof's 1978 watercolor painting of the view from Säntis, a peak in northeastern Switzerland.

a landscape painting by intentionally not following classical cartographic rules," he says in a 1983 Swiss television documentary. He points to a topographic map of the same area, noting that it contains far more information—symbols to indicate churches and different kinds of roads, for example, and numbers to indicate the elevation at certain spots. The painting contains none of this but gives a more pictorial, more immediate sense of the landscape.

In making it, Imhof did not refer to aerial photographs. Rather, he writes in *Cartographic Relief Presentation*, the painting represents "the free artistic interpretation of visual impressions gained during long walks through the mountains."

From the late 1920s through the mid-1970s, Imhof oversaw the production of the atlases used in Swiss primary and high schools. He created the watercolor painting opposite to serve as the base for a map of the enormous Aletsch Glacier in the Bernese Alps. Contour lines have been added to indicate elevation, and symbols indicate roads and buildings. Labels were added later to create a finished version that was unmistakably a map. But Imhof's skilled use of shaded relief, illumination, and color are on full display, exemplifying his beautiful marriage of art and cartography. ✳

A Public Space for Brooklyn

FREDERICK LAW OLMSTED DESIGNED MANY FAMOUS CITY PARKS, BUT HE WAS ESPECIALLY PROUD OF THIS ONE

CREATED *1871*
SOURCE *Brooklyn Historical Society*

He had a profound and lasting effect on public spaces in cities across the United States, but few of the countless people who enjoy his work have ever heard of Frederick Law Olmsted. Many of those who do know his name identify him as the man who designed Central Park in New York City. But Olmsted also designed hundreds of other American parks, college and high school campuses, institutional grounds, residential communities, and cemeteries, as well as the grounds of the 1893 Chicago World's Fair.

Olmsted is considered the father of the field of landscape architecture; to this day, students and practitioners study the principles he espoused. His first designed landscape, Central Park, is a masterpiece that has become one of the best-known and most visited parks in the world. It has even been called the most important American work of art of the 19th century. But Olmsted's second park is in some ways the fullest realization of his vision of public spaces designed to bring people together in scenic, natural settings that would benefit their health.

In 1865, Brooklyn officials decided that their city, then the third largest in the United States, should also have a grand public park. British architect Calvert Vaux, who had teamed up with Olmsted to win the Central Park design competition, again convinced Olmsted to join him in creating a public park for Brooklyn. With a hefty budget and strong buy-in from the city's park commission, the pair created Prospect Park, a 526-acre (213 ha) master class in landscape architecture.

As with many of the other parks Olmsted would design in his lifetime, his goal for Prospect Park was to create a mentally and physically restorative landscape that would counteract the negative health impacts of living in a crowded city. He intended his parks to be democratic places that would benefit all elements of society, especially the poorest and weakest citizens.

This 1871 plan for Prospect Park shows how Olmsted carefully designed a series of contrasting spaces that would feel natural and provide an antidote to the artificial cityscape. On one end of the park, the Long Meadow stretches for a mile, creating an open, pastoral space that feels larger than it is. Olmsted designated specific locations for hundreds of individual trees of more than 80 species to be planted on the meadow's edges. On the other end of the park is a sculpted

Frederick Law Olmsted and Calvert Vaux drew up plans for Prospect Park that convinced Brooklyn city officials to abandon a plan for a small park straddling Flatbush Avenue in favor of a much larger area on the road's east side. Their design required the purchase of $4 million worth of land (in the neighborhood of $60 million today), but park commissioners were convinced that the plan "ought not be changed in any manner."

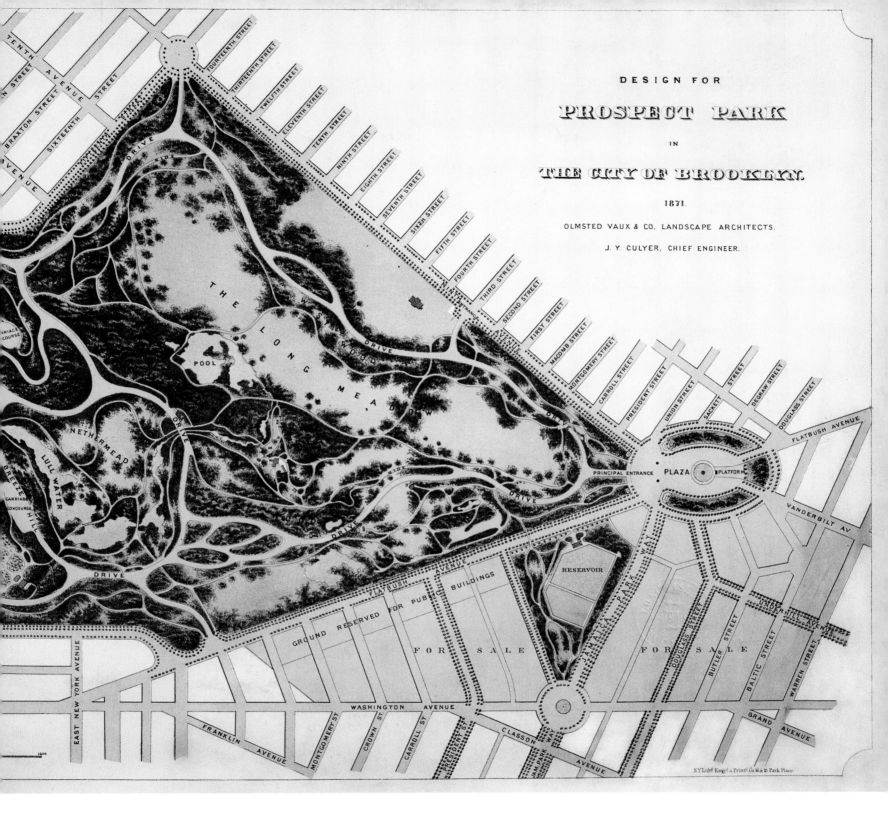

DESIGN FOR

PROSPECT PARK

IN

THE CITY OF BROOKLYN.

1871.

OLMSTED VAUX & CO, LANDSCAPE ARCHITECTS.

J. Y. CULYER, CHIEF ENGINEER.

lake, large enough for boating, that includes a shoreline music pavilion with a stage set on a small island and separate spaces for viewers to sit, stand, or watch from their carriages. In between, paths wind through wooded areas and alongside a picturesque ravine with a stream flowing through it, tumbling over several waterfalls. There is also a children's area with a pond for toy boats, a Quaker cemetery,

several more pools of water, a field for archery, and a parade ground meant to be used for military exercises and sports.

While it was being built, Olmsted wrote to the park board president that Prospect was "thoroughly delightful and I am prouder of it than anything that I have had to do with."

Inspired by the success of the two New York parks, cities across the country began planning

their own public parks. Olmsted designed many of them, including entire park systems for Boston, Buffalo, and Chicago. And in the process, he made public parks an integral part of the American experience.

Though it's not the tourist attraction that Central Park has become, Prospect Park is still an escape for Brooklynites, exactly the respite that Olmsted intended it to be. ✳

Peak 10
13,639 ft

Peak 9
13,639 ft

Peak 8
12,998 ft

Lake Chutes

Snow White

The Back 9

Twin Chutes

Imperial Bowl

George's Thumb

Whale's Tail

Horseshoe Bowl

Contest Bowl

Cucumber Bowl

Peak 7
12,655 ft

Peak 6
12,573 ft

Six Senses

Serenity
Bowl

Beyond
Bowl

Peak 7
Bowl

The
Dunes

Wonderland

Art's
Bowl

JAMES
NIEHUES

Interpreting the Slopes

HAND-PAINTED SKI TRAIL MAPS SHOW RESORTS IN THEIR BEST LIGHT

CREATED *2016*
SOURCE *Jim Niehues*

If you've used a map to navigate your way downhill at a North American ski resort, there's a good chance you've been the beneficiary of the unique skill set of Jim Niehues. He has spent 30 years honing his ability to translate the experience of being on the slopes onto a two-dimensional trail map. He has painted the lifts, runs, trees, and moguls of 194 ski resorts, most of them in the United States. For decades, Niehues has been the go-to guy in this country when it comes to hand-painted ski trail cartography.

Creating a trail map has some interesting challenges, the primary one being how to depict slopes that face all different directions in one view that can be easily understood. For Niehues, that involves a combination of cartography and artistry. "It's the interpretation of the mountain," Niehues says. "It's not measurements; it's how it's perceived."

Niehues credits good timing for some of his success. In 1988, at age 40, he was ready to move on from his career in graphic design and remembered his childhood dream of being a landscape artist. Surrounded by ski resorts in his Colorado home, he saw painting them as a natural fit. A fellow Coloradan, Hal Shelton, had pioneered the technique of combining cartography with artistry to depict resorts in the 1960s and was followed by Bill Brown, also from Colorado, who did similar hand-painted work in the 1980s.

As luck would have it, Niehues reached out just as Brown was looking for a career change.

The landscape of Colorado's Breckenridge Ski Resort has been subtly altered on this map by artist Jim Niehues to let skiers see all the slopes in one easily understandable view.

TOP LEFT Niehues first works out the details of his ski resort maps in a sketch that he expands to a full-size drawing, like this one of Breckenridge, by using a projector to trace the sketch onto an illustration board.

LEFT Sky, snow, and shadows are added to the Breckenridge map with an airbrush. Niehues uses bluer tones for areas that are farther away and warmer tones for the parts that are closer.

BOTTOM LEFT Niehues paints countless individual trees on the slopes of Breckenridge. He'll also add rocks, cliff faces, lodges, parking lots, and cars. The client will later add trail names and difficulty designations.

Brown let Niehues try his hand at a small inset map of the backside of Mary Jane Mountain for one of Brown's maps of Colorado's Winter Park Resort. Niehues was hooked, and the torch was passed.

To create something that will both help guide skiers and reflect their experience of being on the mountain, Niehues starts with aerial photography. Shooting from a helicopter, he captures every angle he'll need to map a resort. Then he uses some creative distortion to put all of that information into a single view. "Basically, what I need to do is move the summits of different lifts and swing the mountain around so that all the slopes are visible," Niehues says, "and do it in a way that is credible."

Keeping the summits close to where they should be vertically on the page and making sure lift and trail lengths are accurate relative to each other is important for maintaining a degree of reality. Niehues works out all the angles and details in a sketch, which he then projects onto a

Mt Timpanogos
11,750 ft
Empire 9,570 ft
Heber City
Flagstaff Mtn 9,100 ft
Bald Mtn 9,400 ft
8,300 ft
nelle Res
8,100 ft
Bald Eagle Mtn
8,400 ft
Little Baldy Pk 7,900 ft
7,200 ft
JAMES NIEHUES
6,750 ft
Park City

30-by-40-inch (76 by 102 cm) illustration board to trace out the base for the painting.

Then he uses an airbrush to paint the sky and the snow, using bluer tones to convey areas that are farther away and warmer colors to show closer ones. Next, he uses brushes to paint in the details: trees, rocks, cliffs, and lodges. He even paints rows of individual cars in the parking lots. Once the painting is done, Niehues sends a digital image of it to the resort to add labels and symbols for the runs.

Some ski areas are more complicated than others, especially those with trails heading down the backside of the main mountain. In these cases, Niehues often adopts a perspective closer to a top-down satellite view in order to capture multiple sides of the same peak. The trick here is to make sure the lifts appear to move up the page and the runs head down it so that skiers understand the terrain at a glance. The above map of Deer Valley Resort in Park City, Utah, is an example of his satellite view technique.

It all adds up to something that Niehues hopes is both beautiful and useful. "I really take a great deal of pride that my art is used to get an awful lot of skiers around mountains, and they depend on it," he says.

Though some resorts use maps made with computer graphics, Niehues insists the hand-painted touch is critical to getting the right feel. And digitally built maps don't look nearly as good when they're scaled up to be printed on signs on the mountain. At that size, he says, you can't get away with using simple triangles for trees, for example.

Niehues has his eye on retirement and worries that hand-painted trail maps could become a lost art. But an up-and-coming ski resort cartographer has asked if Niehues would be willing to help him make the switch from computer graphics to painting.

"It was good timing," he says. "I'm kind of excited that he's picking it up and going to continue doing them by hand." ✷

The terrain of Utah's Deer Valley Resort requires a perspective that is closer to a satellite view in order to include slopes on all sides of the mountain on a single map.

Pinnacle of the Presidential Range

A UNIQUE MAP PROMOTES A PRECIPITOUS TRAIN RIDE

CREATED *circa 1908*
SOURCE *Cornell University—PJ Mode Collection of Persuasive Cartography*

At the dawn of the 20th century, as Ford's first mass-produced automobile, the Model T, was about to hit the market, the Boston and Maine Railroad published a promotional map to entice people to take a train ride to the summit of the Northeast's highest peak.

The prose on the back of the map reads: "To give an adequate description of the view to be enjoyed from the summit of Mount Washington would be impossible here. Some idea of its comprehensiveness and of the principal features of the landscape may be gained from the map herewith presented, and which gives a bird's-eye glimpse of the vast aggregation of mountain peaks, lakes, ponds, river, ravines and forest stretches that meet the eye in this great cycloramic sweep of more than one hundred miles." Many rail companies published such promotional brochures, often with maps, but this one is as unique as the railway it was advertising.

The map's title suggests it gives a bird's-eye view, a style borrowed from Europe that became a popular format for maps of North American cities in the late 19th and early 20th centuries. Those maps were usually drawn as if being viewed at an oblique angle from somewhere around 2,500 feet (750 m) above the ground and were often created by city governments to attract business and visitors. The Mount Washington map is really more of a distorted fish-eye perspective, centered on the train station at the peak with the horizon extending in every direction and 189 other numbered landmarks in the surrounding region.

Mount Washington is the tallest peak in the Presidential Range of the White Mountains, which contains eight or nine other summits named for presidents (depending on whether you recognize New Hampshire's decision to take Henry Clay's peak and give it to Ronald Reagan in 2003). Though George Washington himself never visited the summit of his mountain namesake, President Ulysses S. Grant rode the train to the top in 1869, the year the track was completed.

Passengers rode uphill for 70 minutes in a 40-person car pushed for more than 3 miles (around 5 km) by a steam locomotive on the world's first rack-and-pinion railway, a type of rail system that uses cog wheels and a toothed track to climb up a steep grade. The brochure touts the Mount Washington track as among the steepest cog railways in the world (see below). It included a 300-foot (90 m)-long trestle with a 37 percent grade known as Jacob's Ladder. Riders were greeted at the top of the 6,288-foot (1,917 m) peak by a hotel and restaurant that "boasts of a table that few hotels below the clouds can improve upon."

The railway is still in operation today, and riders can choose to make the trip in an "efficient new biodiesel locomotive" or, for six dollars more, a "classic steam engine." ✳

RIGHT Around 1908, when this promotional map was printed, the White Mountains region of New Hampshire was a major tourist destination. Rail was still the only way for most people to reach the top of Mount Washington aside from hiking.

....

BELOW The trestle pictured here, known as Jacob's Ladder, was the steepest stretch of any cog railway in the world, according to the promotional brochure. The steam train ascended 1 foot (0.3 m) for every 2.67 feet (0.8 m) of track.

Jacob's Ladder, Mt. Washington Railway.

Birds-Eye View from Summit of Mt. Washington; White Mountains, New-Hampshire.

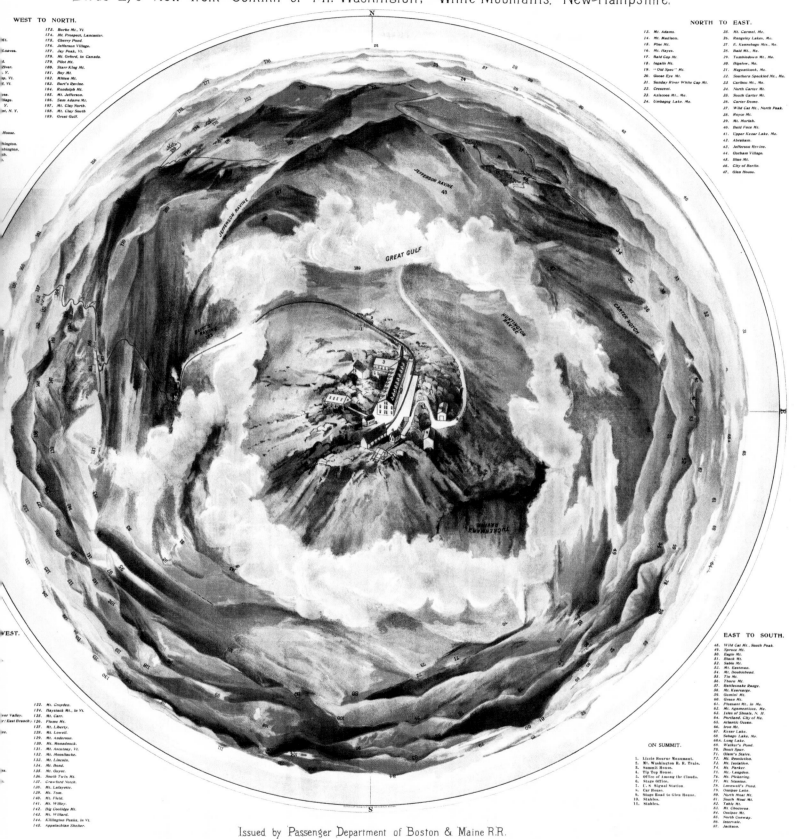

Issued by Passenger Department of Boston & Maine R.R.

MIES

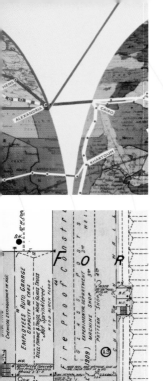

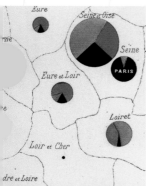

Mapping Money, Industry, and Trade

From farming to fracking, many industries are tied to a particular place. Maps can reveal just why that is. The ones in this chapter tell stories about industries and markets around the globe, pinpointing natural resources like soil and water and tracing the flow of commodities like cotton and meat. These maps are informative, to be sure, but many of them are also surprisingly beautiful.

Several of them capture a thriving industry at a particular moment in time. It's hard to imagine the days when men mined silver by lamplight and brought ore to the surface with an elevator powered by horses, but a map of an early 18th-century Hungarian mine (on page 162) documents that time in remarkable detail. Similarly, maps made at the dawn of the 20th century by fire insurance companies (see page 164) provide a unique look inside the factories of the American Midwest just as they were turning the nation into an industrial powerhouse.

Some maps try to sell something, and entire industries have used maps to boost their business. The whimsical map of all things tea (see page 174) is a prime example. Packed with trivia about tea, it was part of an effort by the British tea industry to revive its fortunes after the Great Depression by expanding into Africa.

Economies can be local or global, fleeting or long-lived. But in every case, if you want to follow the money, a map is a good place to start. ➤➤

CARTOGRAPHIC ADVERTISEMENT
(1897, Cornell University —PJ Mode Collection of Persuasive Cartography)

This late 19th-century map was made for a company that claimed to be the largest dealer of horses in the world. Two of its famous "blue front" buildings—the "Retail Department" and "Auction Department"—are depicted near the top, along with portraits of the company's president and treasurer. The map adopts the bird's-eye view that was popular at the time, and while the location of the company's stables in midtown Manhattan is visible, artistry takes precedence over geography in this impressive advertising map.

The Virtues of Farming

A GOVERNMENT ATLAS USED SCIENCE AND MAPS TO ENCOURAGE A WAY OF LIFE

CREATED *1936*
CREATOR *U.S. Department of Agriculture*

Oliver Edwin Baker was a rural idealist. Born in Tiffin, Ohio, in 1883, Baker became the leading agricultural geographer of his time. In his 30 years at the U.S. Department of Agriculture (USDA), Baker was driven by a deep desire to advance his discipline for the sake of helping farmers, whom he believed were the key not just to American prosperity, but to civilization itself.

One of Baker's signature achievements was the *Atlas of American Agriculture,* published in 1936, which compiled decades of field research on the nation's topography, climate, natural vegetation, and soils. Most of this work had already been published in bits and pieces in various government reports, but by bringing the latest maps and science together in one place, Baker hoped to help farmers make better decisions about how to use their land.

Soil has rarely looked as beautiful as it does in Oliver Edwin Baker's *Atlas of American Agriculture,* from the profiles of soil types that look like abstract art (below) to this digital composite of Curtis Marbut's map showing their distribution across the country.

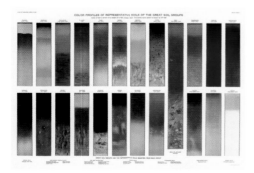

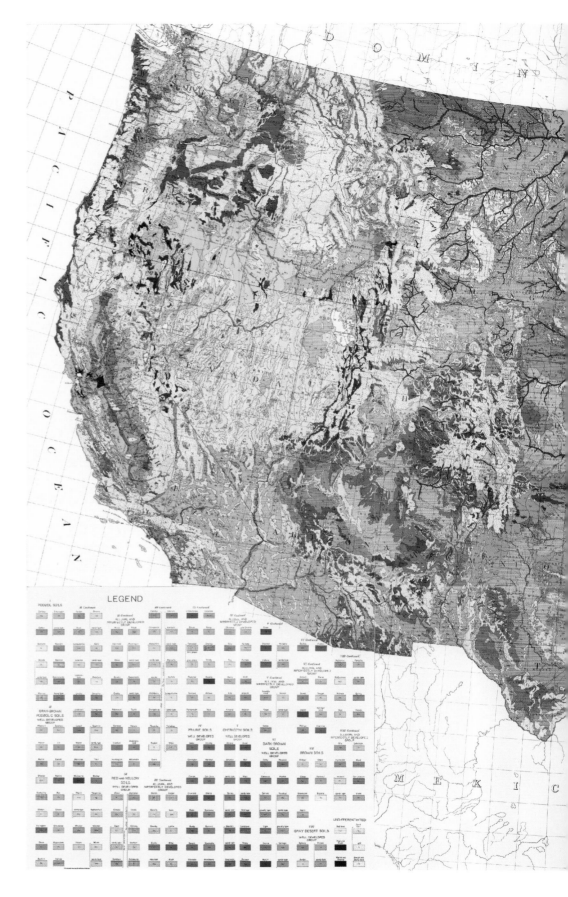

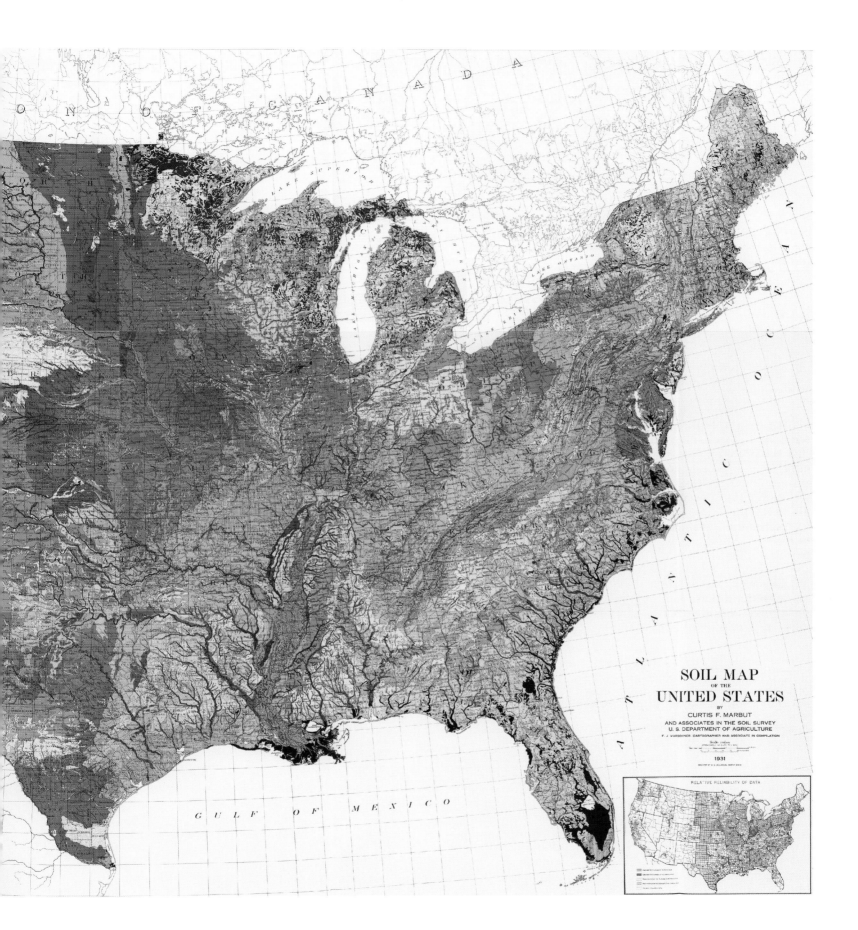

SOIL MAP
OF THE
UNITED STATES
BY
CURTIS F. MARBUT
AND ASSOCIATES IN THE SOIL SURVEY
U. S. DEPARTMENT OF AGRICULTURE
F. J. MARSCHNER, CARTOGRAPHER AND ASSOCIATE IN COMPILATION

1931

UNITED STATES DEPARTMENT OF AGRICULTURE
BUREAU OF PLANT INDUSTRY, W. A. TAYLOR, CHIEF
AND
FOREST SERVICE, W. B. GREELEY, FORESTER

NATURAL VEGETATION
GRASSLAND AND DESERT SHRUB · By H. L. SHANTZ
FOREST VEGETATION · · · · · · By RAPHAEL ZON

WASHINGTON, D.C.
1923

FOREST VEGETATION (WESTERN)

SPRUCE—FIR (NORTHERN CONIFEROUS FOREST) - - -   S

CEDAR—HEMLOCK (NORTHWESTERN CONIFEROUS FOREST):
WESTERN LARCH—WESTERN WHITE PINE - - - - -   WP
PACIFIC DOUGLAS FIR - - - - - - - - - - - -   DF
REDWOOD - - - - - - - - - - - - - - - - - -   R

YELLOW PINE—DOUGLAS FIR (WESTERN PINE FOREST):
YELLOW PINE—SUGAR PINE - - - - - - - - - - -   SP
YELLOW PINE—DOUGLAS FIR - - - - - - - - - -   P
LODGEPOLE PINE - - - - - - - - - - - - - - -   LP
PIÑON—JUNIPER (S. W. CONIFEROUS WOODLAND) - -   J
CHAPARRAL (S. W. BROAD-LEAVED WOODLAND) - - -   C

DESERT SHRUB VEGETATION

SAGEBRUSH (NORTHERN DESERT SHRUB) - - - - -   SB
CREOSOTE BUSH - - - - - - - - - - - - - -   CB
(SOUTHERN DESERT SHRUB)
GREASEWOOD (SALT DESERT SHRUB) - - - - - -   G

GRASS VEGETAT

TALL GRASS (PRAIRIE GRASSLAND)
SHORT GRASS (PLAINS GRASSLAND)
MESQUITE GRASS (DESERT GRASSLAND)
MESQUITE AND DESERT GRASS SAV
(DESERT SAVANNA)
BUNCH GRASS (PACIFIC GRASSLAND)
ALPINE MEADOW (ALPINE GRASSLAND)
MARSH GRASS (MARSH GRASSLAND)

PROFILE
SHOWING CHARACTER OF VEGETATION ALONG PARALLEL 39 N.

Figure 2.— Distribution of the main types of natural vegetation in the United States. The three major natural divisions of vegetation in the United States are forest, grassland, and desert shrub. The forest falls into two clearly marked regions, western and eastern. The western region comprises seven large forest subdivisions and tw subdivisions there are many smaller distinct types not indicated on the map. Four-fifths of the forest was originally in the east. Of this original forest there remains now only about 10 per cent in virgin condition, 50 per cent having been cleared for farm land, 30 per cent cut over and now grown up to trees of sufficient size for saw logs or c

At the time, the farmers needed all the help they could get. Bankruptcies during the Great Depression and the unprecedented Dust Bowl drought had pushed tens of thousands of families to abandon their farms. Desperation was forcing people to farm land that was poorly suited for it, from the nutrient-poor soil in large parts of the South to the short growing seasons in the Upper Midwest, and the arid climate of New Mexico and Arizona.

The crown jewel of the atlas is the accompanying soil map by Curtis Marbut (see page 148), based on the work of the national soil survey Marbut oversaw for the USDA. Armed with augers, Marbut's men swept across large swaths of the country, collecting soil samples and making detailed notes and sketches of what they found. "It was boring, hard, thankless work," says Alex Checkovich, a historian of American science at the University of Richmond.

"Unless, of course, it gave your life meaning."

For Marbut, a widower, it did just that. He was the rare scientist who transformed his field, changing the way American scientists thought about soil by showing that its composition depended on more than just the underlying geology. Through his fieldwork and by translating the work of an important Russian scientist whose ideas hadn't yet made it to the West, Marbut demonstrated the role of climate,

FAR LEFT The relationship between topography and vegetation—especially the vast yellow grasslands of the central plains—is evident in this colorful map from the atlas. The profile at the bottom shows the elevation of the land from coast to coast along the 39th parallel.

LEFT The climate chapters of Baker's atlas provide multiple perspectives on historical weather data. This series of maps focuses on frost, showing (from top to bottom) the average number of days without killing frost, the average date of the last frost in spring, the frequency of unusually short frost-free seasons, and the odds of an unusually late spring frost. Colder areas are blue, while warmer areas are red.

In the introduction, Oliver Baker sounds almost wistful as he explains that the atlas was supposed to contain additional chapters on the social and economic aspects of farming. He doesn't explain why these were ultimately left out, but they were topics that preoccupied him in the years after the atlas was published.

He advocated "rurban" living, in which urbanites grew some of their own food, thereby achieving a measure of the rural virtue of self-sufficiency. It's an idea that was ahead of its time but has become fashionable in some cities today. Baker, his wife, and their four children lived on a large suburban plot in Maryland, where the family raised chickens and cultivated a garden. Toward the end of his life, he bought a farm in the Shenandoah Valley, pursuing to the very last a rural dream that was slipping increasingly out of reach. ✳

native vegetation, and other factors in soil composition. Tragically, he died of pneumonia just weeks after the soil section of the atlas was first published in 1935.

No other part of the atlas rivals the detail of Marbut's soil chapter, but the climate sections are impressive for the way they drill down into the data. They include not just the usual maps of average temperatures, but also maps showing the average date of the first frost in spring and last frost in fall throughout the country. One of the maps, for example, shows when the chance of spring frost dips below 10 percent; another shows how often the frost-free part of the year turns out to be significantly shorter than usual (above). Each iteration was presumably meant to aid farmers trying to decide when to sow their fields and weighing the chances of being early to market against the risks of losing the entire crop.

Mapping Economic Flow

THE INNOVATIVE VISUALIZATIONS OF CHARLES MINARD

CREATED *1858–1869*
CREATOR *Charles Joseph Minard*

There's a remarkable graphic from 1869 that depicts Napoleon's invasion of Russia in 1812 and subsequent retreat the following year. An ever thinning line shows both the army's route and the horrific loss of life suffered by the troops as they were whittled from more than 400,000 down to just 10,000. This stark, compelling depiction is famous among students and scholars of data visualization. It's been called the best statistical graphic ever drawn.

The man who created it, Charles Joseph Minard, is commonly mentioned by academics alongside other data-visualization greats such as John Snow, Florence Nightingale, and William Playfair. But unlike them, Minard's legacy has been almost completely dominated by that one 1869 graphic. Many fans of the Napoleon graphic have likely never even seen the work Minard originally paired it with: a visualization of the huge number of casualties suffered during Hannibal's famous military campaign that crossed the Alps in 218 B.C. (see page 154).

He made scores of other graphics and charts, as well as nearly 50 maps. He pioneered several important thematic mapping techniques and perfected others. For example, though Minard wasn't the first to use flow lines on a map to depict movement, he really raised the bar for doing so. His flow maps were designed to tell a story—to, in his words, "speak to the eyes." Take this series of maps depicting Europe's cotton imports in 1858, 1864, and 1865. By charting the same data over time, Minard was able to show some of the global ripple effects of the American Civil War.

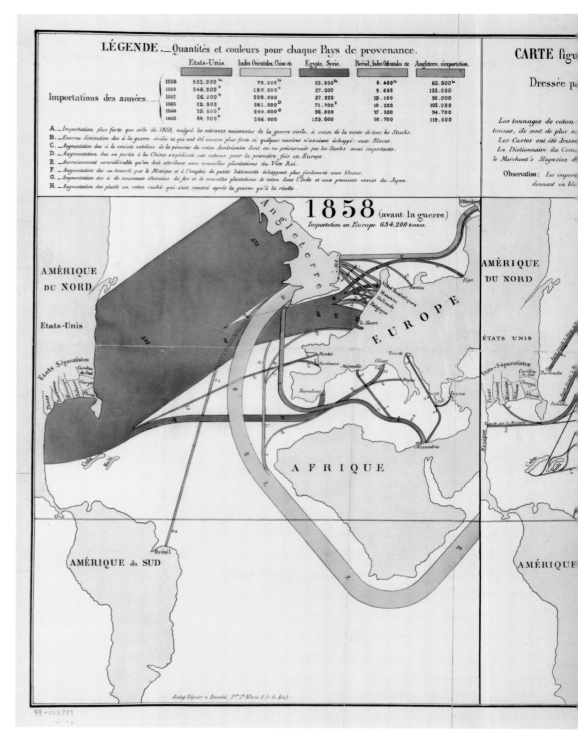

The color of the lines shows what country the cotton came from, and their width indicates the relative amount of cotton that arrived along that route, with each millimeter (.04 in.) of thickness representing 5,000 tonnes of cotton. In the 1858 map, the wide blue line shows how the U.S. cotton industry, built on slave labor, dominated the global market and provided the vast majority of Europe's imports. That all changed in 1861

when the Civil War began. Minard's 1864 map reflects a Union naval blockade that had stopped virtually all exports from the Confederate states except for a few that escaped through Mexico or on smaller blockade-slipping boats. At the same time, it shows that Asia and Egypt had increased their exports to take advantage of the unmet demand. The 1865 map shows that after the war ended, there was a big increase in U.S. exports as

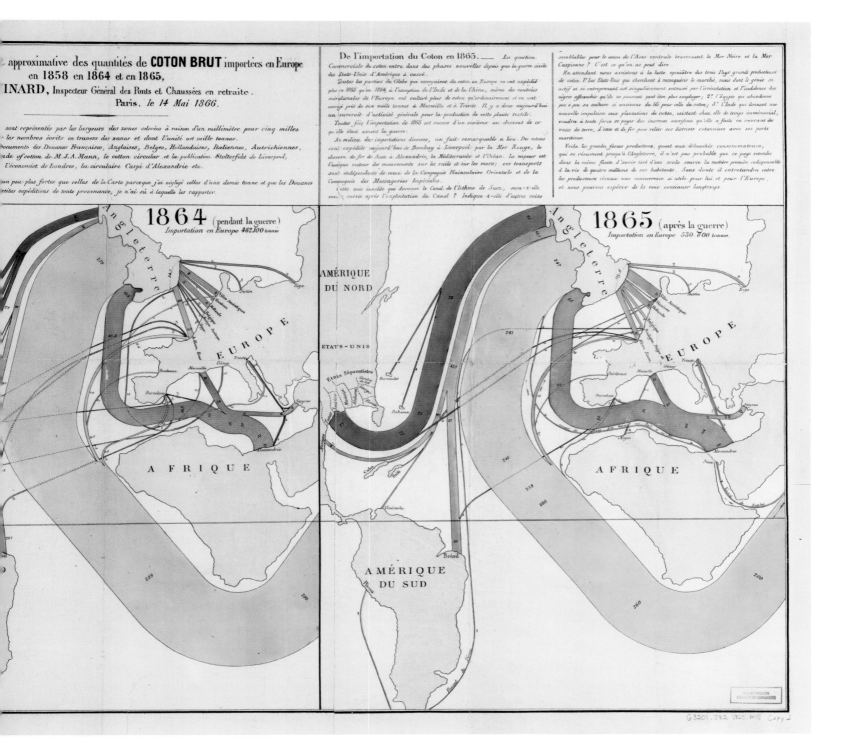

approximative des quantités de **COTON BRUT** importées en Europe en 1858 en 1864 et en 1865,

INARD, Inspecteur Général des Ponts et Chaussées en retraite.

Paris, le 14 Mai 1866.

sont représentés par les largeurs des zones colorées à raison d'un millimètre pour cinq milles les nombres écrits en travers des zones et dont l'unité est mille tonnes.

ocuments des Douanes Françaises, Anglaises, Belges, Hollandaises, Italiennes, Autrichiennes, de of cotton de M.J.A. Mann, le cotton circular, et la publication Stolterfoht de Liverpool, l'économist de Londres, la circulaire Carpi d'Alexandrie etc.

un peu plus fortes que celles de la Carte parceque j'ai négligé celles d'une demie tonne et que les Douanes tites expéditions de toute provenance, je n'ai su à laquelle les rapporter.

De l'importation du Coton en 1865. ___ La question Commerciale du coton entre dans des phases nouvelles depuis que la guerre civile des Etats-Unis d'Amérique a cessé.

Toutes les parties du Globe qui envoyaient du coton en Europe en ont expédié plus en 1865 qu'en 1864, à l'exception de l'Inde et de la Chine, même des contrées méridionales de l'Europe ont cultivé plus de coton qu'ordinairement et en ont envoyé près de six mille tonnes à Marseille et à Trieste. Il y a donc aujourd'hui un surcroît d'activité générale pour la production de cette plante textile.

Toutes fois l'importation de 1865 est encore d'un sixième au-dessous de ce qu'elle était avant la guerre.

Au milieu des importations diverses, un fait remarquable a lieu. Des cotons sont expédiés aujourd'hui de Bombay à Liverpool par la Mer Rouge, le chemin de fer de Suez à Alexandrie, la Méditerranée et l'Océan. La vapeur est l'unique moteur des mouvements sur les rails et sur les mers; ces transports sont indépendants de ceux de la Compagnie Péninsulaire Orientale et de la Compagnie des Messageries Impériales.

Cette voie insolite qui devance le Canal de l'Isthme de Suez, sera-t-elle encore suivie après l'exploitation du Canal ? Indique-t-elle d'autres voies

semblables pour le coton de l'Asie centrale traversant la Mer Noire et la Mer Caspienne ? C'est ce qu'on ne peut dire.

En attendant nous assistons à la lutte opiniâtre des trois Pays grands producteurs de coton. 1.º Les Etats-Unis qui cherchent à reconquérir le marché, mais dont le génie si actif et si entreprenant est singulièrement entravé par l'irrésolution et l'indolence des nègres affranchis qu'ils ne pourront peut être plus employer; 2.º l'Egypte qui abandonne peu à peu sa culture si ancienne du blé pour celle du coton; 3.º l'Inde qui donnant une nouvelle impulsion aux plantations de coton, existant chez elle de temps immémorial, voudra à toute force se payer des énormes sacrifices qu'elle a faits en ouvrant des voies de terre, d'eau et de fer pour relier ses districts cotonniers avec ses ports maritimes.

Voilà, les grandes forces productrices, quant aux débouchés consommateurs, qui se réunissent presqu'à l'Angleterre, il n'est pas probable que ce pays retombe dans la même faute d'avoir tiré d'une seule source la matière première indispensable à la vie de quatre millions de ses habitants. Sans doute il entretiendra entre les producteurs rivaux une concurrence si utile pour lui et pour l'Europe et nous pouvons espérer de la voir continuer longtemps

cotton that had been stockpiled by the Confederate states finally hit the market.

Minard was interested in topics that we'd describe today as "economic geography": mapping the movements of everything from coal to wine to people. He always prioritized the data, often distorting the underlying geography to accommodate it, as on his map of global emigration in 1858 (see page 157).

On it, England's size is exaggerated to fit the thickness of the lines required to represent the number of people leaving for Australia, the United States, and Canada, with 1 millimeter (.04 in.) for every 1,500 people. The English Channel has been widened to make room for the line of emigration from Germany to the United States, and tiny Réunion Island in the Indian Ocean has been enlarged to receive the

Cotton imports from the United States to Europe underwent major changes over the course of the American Civil War, as shown in this series of maps by Charles Minard. The color of the lines on the maps reflects where the cotton came from: blue from the U.S., orange from Asia, and brown from Egypt. Their thickness indicates the quantity delivered, with 1 millimeter (.04 in.) representing 5,000 tonnes.

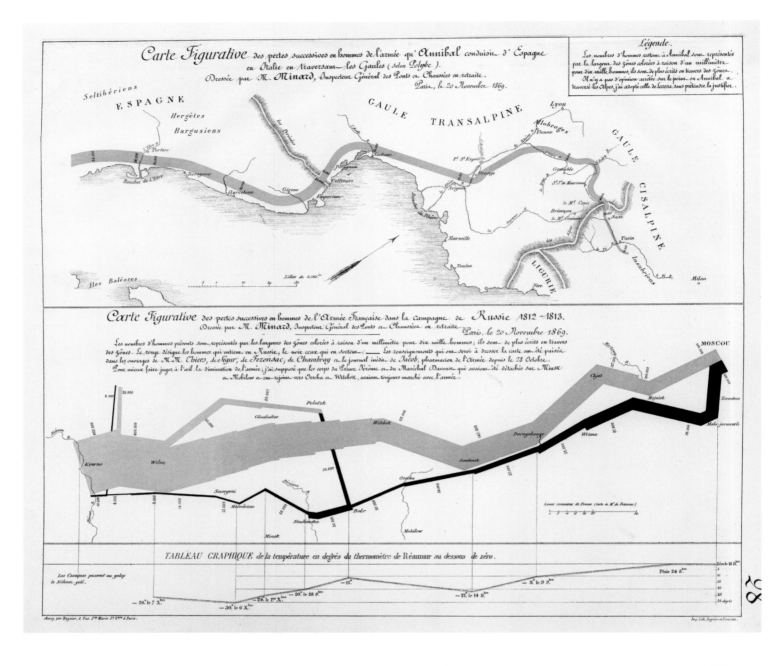

flow line of people moving there from West Africa. All of these geographical tweaks serve to more clearly convey the information that mattered most to Minard.

He also pioneered the use of pie charts as map symbols. Though the invention of the pie chart is credited to Playfair, Minard was the first to use them on a map. He even added his own innovation, turning the pie charts into proportional symbols, as he did on his 1858 map of the origin of butcher's meats supplied to Paris markets (at right). The size of the pies indicates how much meat traveled from each of the country's administrative divisions, called *départements.* The colors within the pies indicate types of meat: black for beef, red for veal,

and green for mutton. All the départements shown in yellow contributed some meat, while the areas that did not supply any meat are tan. A century and a half later, cartographers are still using this technique.

Minard spent his entire career at the École Nationale des Ponts et Chaussées (National School of Bridges and Roads) in a suburb of Paris, working first as a field engineer and then as an instructor. At age 65, he was promoted to inspector general of the school. Though he made some of his maps while there, it wasn't until after his mandatory retirement in 1851, at age 70, that he really dedicated himself to crafting what he called his "graphic tables and figurative maps."

ABOVE Minard's famous 1869 graphic of Napoleon's 1812 march on Moscow (the lower half) is paired with a visualization of Hannibal's military campaign that crossed the Alps in 218 B.C. (the upper half). The casualties suffered are shown by the thinning of the lines—1 millimeter (.04 in.) equals 10,000 men—which chart their routes through space and time.

RIGHT Minard was the first to use pie charts as proportional symbols on a map. On this 1858 map, the size of the pies indicates the relative amount of butcher's meat sent to Paris from each of France's départements. Colors indicate the type of meat (red for veal, black for beef, green for mutton).

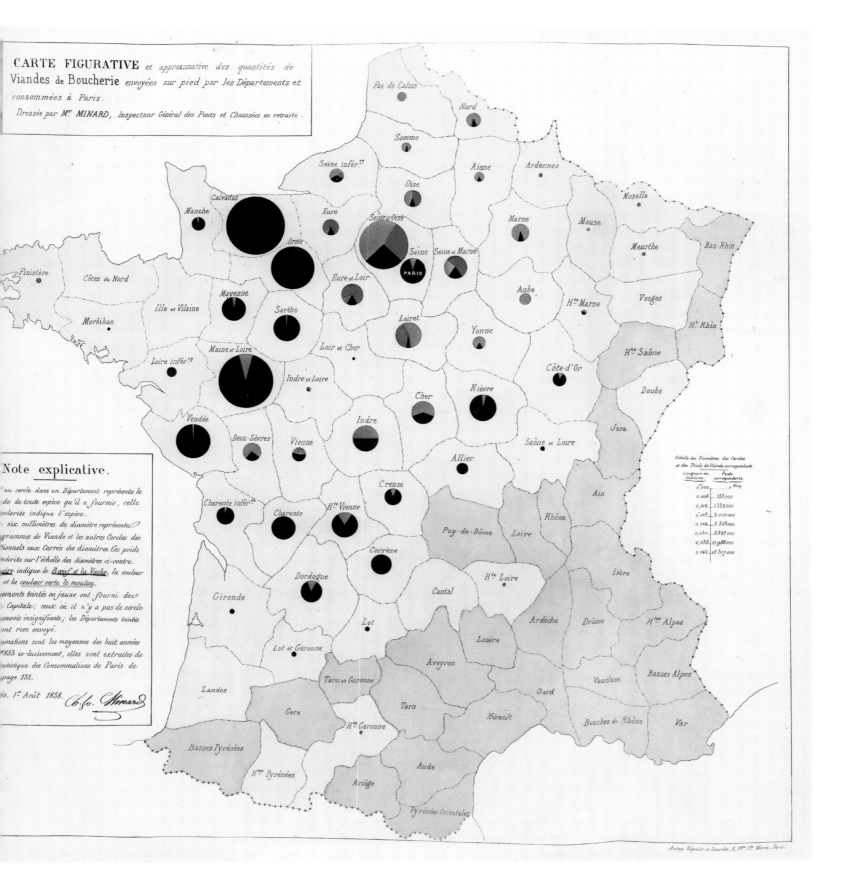

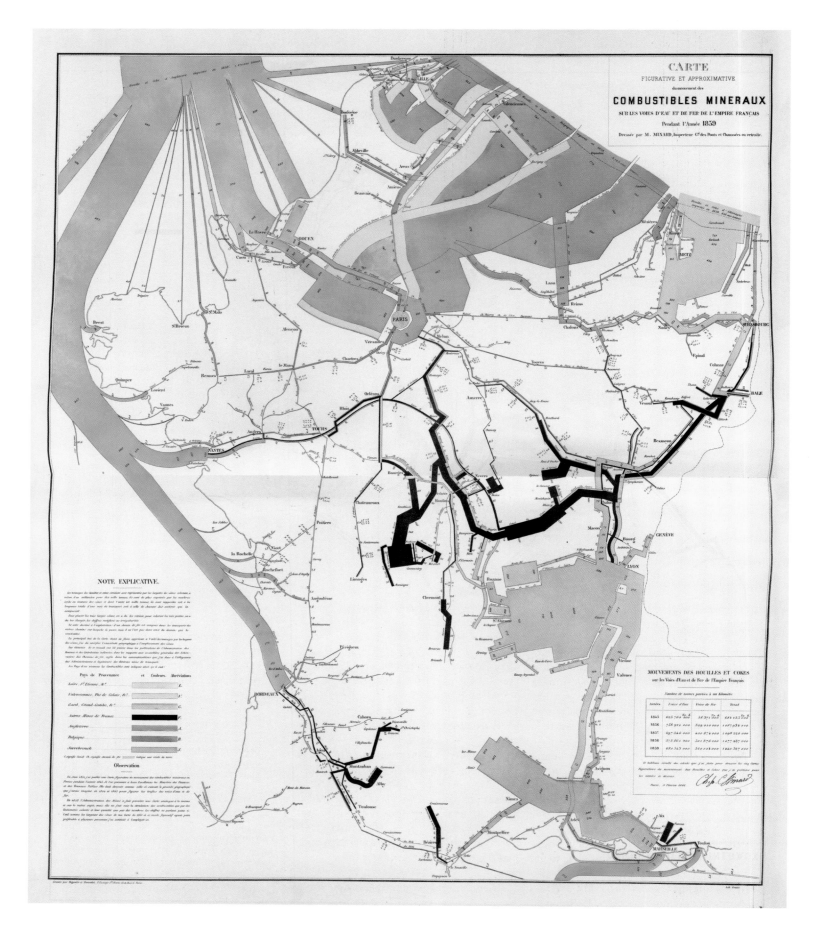

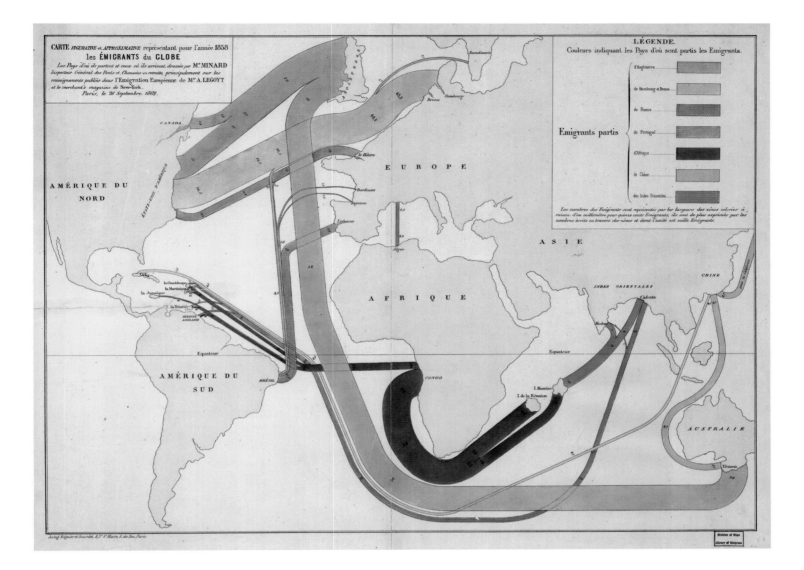

Happy to be freed from his official duties, he essentially began a second career in retirement, making graphics and developing new techniques at a much faster pace than before. He published several maps each year, and they were often widely used by the government and other decision makers and planners. The groundbreaking Napoleon and Hannibal graphics were among the very last he made, less than a year before his death.

By all accounts, Minard had his wits about him until the end. His son-in-law wrote in his obituary, "His surprising memory, his intelligence as alive as always, his regular habits, his sober life, the care with which his family surrounded him, all put at a distance the idea of a coming end." But he had become physically frail in his old age, using crutches to get around, which may be why, with the Prussian army advancing toward Paris, Minard fled for Bordeaux on September 11, 1870, along

with crowds of women, children, and other elderly Parisians. He took only the research he was currently conducting, leaving his books, papers, and "intellectual riches" behind. Perhaps Minard expected he would soon return, but the Siege of Paris began on September 19 and lasted four months. Minard continued to work in Bordeaux, perhaps doing research for his next great map. But on October 24, a brief illness took his life at age 89.

According to his son-in-law, "In the course of his long career as an engineer, he had the good fortune to take part in almost all the great questions of public works which ushered in our century; and during his twenty years of retirement, always au courant of the technical and economic sciences, he endeavored to popularize the most salient results."

It's clear that Minard's greater body of work was well known and appreciated by officials and experts during his lifetime, especially in France.

An 1861 portrait of the French minister of public works features one of Minard's flow maps depicting the movement of goods around France in 1858, draped over a chair in the background. The inclusion is an honor that speaks to his ability to graphically convey information, a skill that data visualization practitioners today still emulate. ✳

OPPOSITE The transport of mineral fuels (coal and coke) into and within France during 1859 is depicted in this map. The thickness of the flow lines indicates quantity of fuel, with 1 millimeter (.04 inches) for every 2,000 tonnes. Colors indicate point of origin.

. . . .

ABOVE The colors of the flow lines on this map of global emigration in 1858 indicate the country migrants left. Thickness of the lines represents the number of migrants, with 1 millimeter (0.4 inches) for every 1,500 people.

The Virgin Waterscape

Lake
Estimated natural shorelines.

Freshwater Marsh
Land inundated annually and populated by tules, cattails, or other hydrophytic vegetation.

Riparian Forest
Broadleaf deciduous forest growing naturally on the sides or banks of rivers and streams, and in bottomlands.

Coastal Brackish Marsh
Land inundated alternately by saline water and fresh water.

Coastal Salt Marsh
Land along the upper intertidal zone of protected shallow bays, estuaries and coastal lagoons. Salt tolerant plants predominate.

Saline and Alkaline Lands
Sinks and basin rim lands characterized by intermittent water high in mineral content.

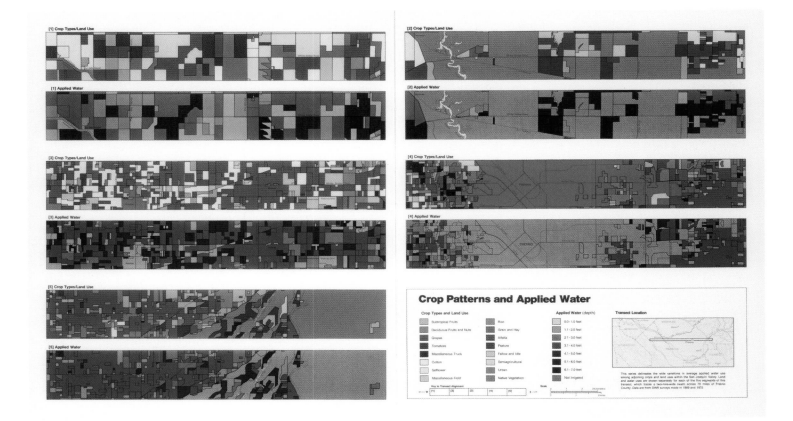

California's Liquid Assets

TRACING THE WATER THAT POWERS THE WORLD'S SIXTH-LARGEST ECONOMY

CREATED *1979*
CREATOR *California Governor's Office of Planning and Research*

"This book sets out to tell the biggest story in the richest, most populous state in the Union." So begins the foreword to a surprisingly ambitious government publication, the *California Water Atlas,* published in 1979 by the state Governor's Office of Planning and Research.

The atlas attempted to distill one of the most complex and contentious issues in the state—water use—into a series of maps and data visualizations that any citizen could understand. The goal of its idealistic creators was to use cutting-edge cartography to better inform the public about the water policy issues confronting the state.

The history and economy of California are inextricably tied to water. Fortunes hinge on where it falls, where it's diverted to, and who decides how it's used. So do many of the state's scenic natural features, from the glacial lakes of the Sierra Nevada to the once thriving wetlands of the great Central Valley.

The idea for the atlas arose from the office of the state's young governor, Jerry Brown. Brown's liberal leanings and tendency to embrace the unconventional had earned him the moniker "Governor Moonbeam" from his more conservative critics. One of Brown's advisors was counterculture hero Stewart Brand, the creator and editor of the *Whole Earth Catalog*, a progressive magazine and guide to political action. Brand was instrumental in getting the water atlas project off the ground.

The goal was to educate people about where the state's water came from and how it was being used, Brand says. He insists there was

OPPOSITE This map of California's waterways as they existed before significant human intervention was based on historical maps made between 1843 and 1878, when most parts of the state were relatively untouched by settlers.

ABOVE These pages from the atlas show five agricultural areas in the state, each represented by two long maps. The top map in each pair shows the type of crops grown there, the bottom one how much irrigation water was applied.

Measured and Unimpaired Streamflows
Water Year 1975

no political agenda. "There were no 'shoulds,'" he says—no prescriptions about what ought to be done. "The book could be used by someone on any side of the issue to get the facts."

The entire project—from wrangling the data from various state and local agencies to creating the maps and graphics—was done in just 15 months. It was an amazing feat, especially in the days before computers.

The atlas begins with the basics of where water falls as rain and snow and includes several maps like the "Virgin Waterscape" map on page 158 that depict the state's lakes, rivers, and wetlands before humans altered them. It goes on to sketch the history of how inhabitants of the state began to alter that picture in the 19th century as they diverted river water, first for mining and later to meet the needs of a burgeoning agricultural economy and fast-growing cities like San Francisco and Los Angeles.

Several chapters explore the economics of water, including which industries are the heaviest users (petroleum and coal mining, by a wide margin) and the relationship between cost and consumption in urban areas. The graphics, with their groovy 1970s color schemes, may look crude compared to modern data visualizations, but the creative displays of

maps and data were groundbreaking in those precomputer days.

The digital age had not quite dawned, but it was getting close. William Bowen, a young geography professor at California State University, Northridge, headed the small team of cartographers. Bowen says one breakthrough came when he happened on a new model calculator from Texas Instruments that could do cube roots. That made it possible to quickly calculate the right dimensions for the many three-dimensional graphics—though someone still had to use a ruler to measure them out and mark them on the page.

The atlas was well received when it came out, winning plaudits from cartographers and water wonks alike. The book originally sold for $20, and the first print run quickly sold out. It was almost too nice for its own good, says Brand. "We wound up with a book that immediately found its way into the rare book rooms of libraries," he says, instead of becoming the continually updated, easily accessible document he had hoped for. If you're lucky enough to find a copy for sale today, it will probably cost a few hundred dollars. As far as Brand is concerned, that's a pity. "We inadvertently created a collector's item instead of a political tool," he says. ✳

ABOVE This graphic represents the water flows of major rivers in California. The yellow figures represent the actual flow measured in a single year, with the peak typically occurring in spring. The corresponding blue figures represent the estimated flow of that river in the absence of dams or other human modifications.

OPPOSITE A massive blue cylinder represents Lake Tahoe on this graphic of California's lakes and reservoirs. The lake, one of the deepest in the world, holds 40 trillion gallons (151 trillion L) of water, dwarfing the state's other lakes and reservoirs.

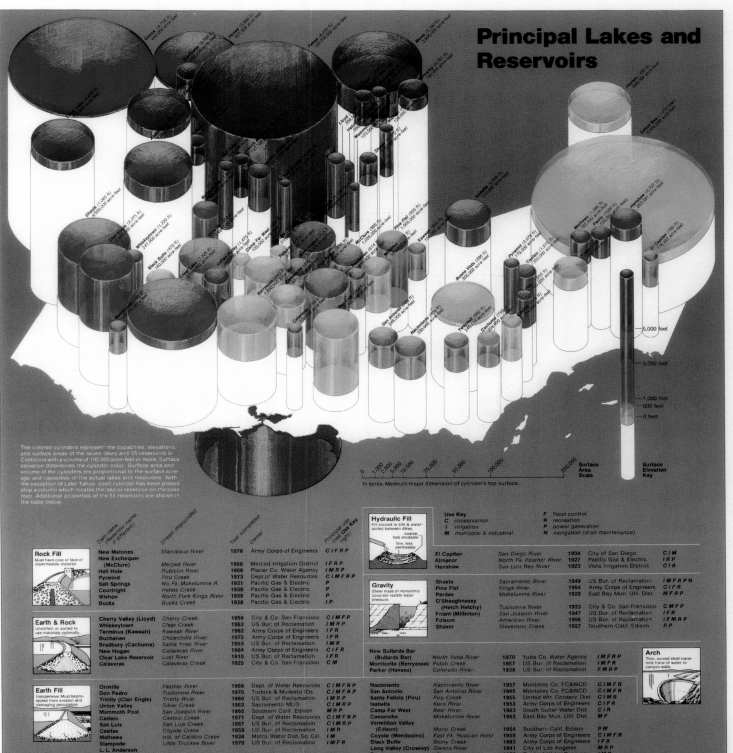

Principal Lakes and Reservoirs

The colored cylinders represent the capacities, elevations, and surface areas of the seven lakes and 55 reservoirs in California with a volume of 100,000 acre-feet or more. Surface elevation determines the cylinder color. Surface area and volume of the cylinders are proportional to the surface acreage and capacities of the actual lakes and reservoirs. With the exception of Lake Tahoe, each cylinder has been placed atop a column which locates the lake or reservoir on the base map. Additional properties of the 55 reservoirs are shown in the table below.

In acres. Measure major dimension of cylinder's top surface.

Surface Area Scale · Surface Elevation Key

5,000 feet · 3,000 feet · 1,000 feet · 600 feet · 0 feet

Use Key (see Use Key right):
- C   conservation
- I   irrigation
- M   municipal & industrial
- F   flood control
- R   recreation
- P   power generation
- N   navigation (draft maintenance)

Rock Fill — Must have core or face of impermeable material.

Dam name	Reservoir name (if different)	Stream impounded	Year completed	Owner	Principal use
New Melones		Stanislaus River	1978	Army Corps of Engineers	C I F R P
New Exchequer	(McClure)	Merced River	1966	Merced Irrigation District	I F R P
Hell Hole		Rubicon River	1966	Placer Co. Water Agency	I M R P
Pyramid		Piru Creek	1973	Dept. of Water Resources	C I M F R P
Salt Springs		No. Fk. Mokelumne R.	1931	Pacific Gas & Electric	P
Courtright		Helms Creek	1958	Pacific Gas & Electric	P
Wishon		North Fork Kings River	1958	Pacific Gas & Electric	P
Bucks		Bucks Creek	1928	Pacific Gas & Electric	I P

Earth & Rock — Unsorted, or sorted to use materials optimally.

Dam name	Reservoir name (if different)	Stream impounded	Year completed	Owner	Principal use
Cherry Valley (Lloyd)		Cherry Creek	1956	City & Co. San Francisco	C I M F P
Whiskeytown		Clear Creek	1963	US Bur. of Reclamation	I M R P
Terminus (Kaweah)		Kaweah River	1962	Army Corps of Engineers	I F R
Buchanan		Chowchilla River	1975	Army Corps of Engineers	I F R
Bradbury (Cachuma)		Santa Ynez River	1953	US Bur. of Reclamation	I M R
New Hogan		Calaveras River	1964	Army Corps of Engineers	C I F R
Clear Lake Reservoir		Lost River	1910	US Bur. of Reclamation	I F R
Calaveras		Calaveras Creek	1925	City & Co. San Francisco	C M

Earth Fill — Inexpensive. Must be protected from erosion and damaging percolation.

Dam name	Reservoir name (if different)	Stream impounded	Year completed	Owner	Principal use
Oroville		Feather River	1968	Dept. of Water Resources	C I M F R
Don Pedro		Tuolumne River	1970	Turlock & Modesto IDs	C I M F R P
Trinity (Clair Engle)		Trinity River	1960	US Bur. of Reclamation	I M R P
Union Valley		Silver Creek	1963	Sacramento MUD	P
Mammoth Pool		San Joaquin River	1960	Southern Calif. Edison	M R P
Castaic		Castaic Creek	1971	Dept. of Water Resources	C I M F R P
San Luis		San Luis Creek	1967	US Bur. of Reclamation	C I M R P
Casitas		Coyote Creek	1959	US Bur. of Reclamation	I M R
Mathews		trib. of Cajalco Creek	1938	Metro. Water Dist. So. Cal.	I M
Stampede		Little Truckee River	1970	US Bur. of Reclamation	I M F R
L. L. Anderson	(French Meadows)	Mid. Fk. American R.	1965	Placer Co. Water Agency	C I M R P
Indian Valley		North Fk. Cache Creek	1975	Yolo Co. FCWCD	I M F R
Twitchell		Cuyama River	1958	US Bur. of Reclamation	I M F R

Hydraulic Fill — Fill sluiced to site & water-sorted between dikes. (coarse / fine, less permeable / erodable)

Dam name	Stream impounded	Year completed	Owner	Principal use
El Capitan	San Diego River	1934	City of San Diego	C I M
Almanor	North Fk. Feather River	1927	Pacific Gas & Electric	I R P
Henshaw	San Luis Rey River	1923	Vista Irrigation District.	C I R

Gravity — Sheer mass of monolithic concrete resists water pressure.

Dam name	Reservoir name	Stream impounded	Year completed	Owner	Principal use
Shasta		Sacramento River	1949	US Bur. of Reclamation	I M F R P N
Pine Flat		Kings River	1954	Army Corps of Engineers	C I F R
Pardee		Mokelumne River	1929	East Bay Mun. Util. Dist.	M F R P
O'Shaughnessy	(Hetch Hetchy)	Tuolumne River	1923	City & Co. San Francisco	C M F P
Friant (Millerton)		San Joaquin River	1947	US Bur. of Reclamation	I F R
Folsom		American River	1956	US Bur. of Reclamation	I F M R P
Shaver		Stevenson Creek	1927	Southern Calif. Edison	R P

Dam name	Reservoir name	Stream impounded	Year completed	Owner	Principal use
New Bullards Bar	(Bullards Bar)	North Yuba River	1970	Yuba Co. Water Agency	I M F R P
Monticello (Berryessa)		Putah Creek	1957	US Bur. of Reclamation	I M F R
Parker (Havasu)		Colorado River	1938	US Bur. of Reclamation	F M R P

Arch — Thin, curved shell transmits force of water to canyon walls.

Dam name	Reservoir name	Stream impounded	Year completed	Owner	Principal use
Nacimiento		Nacimiento River	1957	Monterey Co. FC&WCD	C I M F R
San Antonio		San Antonio River	1965	Monterey Co. FC&WCD	C I M F R
Santa Felicia (Piru)		Piru Creek	1955	United Wtr. Conserv. Dist.	C I M R
Isabella		Kern River	1953	Army Corps of Engineers	C I F R
Camp Far West		Bear River	1963	South Sutter Water Dist.	C I R
Camanche		Mokelumne River	1963	East Bay Mun. Util. Dist.	M F
Vermillion Valley	(Edison)	Mono Creek	1954	Southern Calif. Edison	P M
Coyote (Mendocino)		East Fk. Russian River	1959	Army Corps of Engineers	C I M F R
Black Butte		Stony Creek	1963	Army Corps of Engineers	I F R
Long Valley (Crowley)		Owens River	1941	City of Los Angeles	M R P
Perris		offstream	1973	Dept. of Water Resources	I M R
Prado		Santa Ana	1941	Army Corps of Engineers	F
Buena Vista		Kern River	1890	Boswell Co. & Tenneco W.	I

The Silver Mine Map That Almost Wasn't

A MILITARY DEFEAT NEARLY COST AN OBSESSIVE ITALIAN COUNT THE CHANCE TO PUBLISH HIS LIFE'S WORK

CREATED *1726*
SOURCE *Getty Research Institute*

In 1704, Count Luigi Fernando Marsigli of Italy found himself in hot water. A general in the army of the Holy Roman Emperor, Marsigli (sometimes spelled Marsili) had been sent to defend an important castle on the Rhine River against the French army during the War of the Spanish Succession. Outmanned and undersupplied, the castle surrendered just 13 days after the French attacked. The emperor was severely displeased. Marsigli, who had been second in charge, was dismissed and disgraced in a public ceremony where his sword was broken into pieces. The officer in charge was beheaded.

The incident endangered Marsigli's life's work, which he'd been just about to publish: a massive monograph on the natural and human history of Europe's second longest river and vital commercial corridor, the Danube. For more than 20 years, Marsigli had traveled the region as a military engineer and officer. Driven by an inquisitive mind, he toted around a microscope and other scientific instruments and used them to make extensive notes and detailed sketches of the region's geology, plants, animal life, and settlements. The map here depicts a famous silver mine at Banská Štiavnica in the Kingdom of Hungary (in what is now Slovakia).

Mining began in the area more than 2,000 years ago. By Marsigli's time, the mine was a marvel of technology and an important driver of the region's economy. The well-connected count pulled strings to get the mine boss to allow him inside to sketch the shafts and passages. The result is a uniquely detailed look at the mine's inner workings. Marsigli's map shows the mine extending deep underneath the village. Look closely, and you'll see the miners wielding picks and hammers and holding lanterns to illuminate their work.

After his public shaming, Marsigli kept a low profile. But two decades later, near the end of his life, he persuaded a Dutch publisher to produce the six-volume monograph that includes the mining map. "Would anybody have thought that this work would ever come to light after all the many vicissitudes of my life?" Marsigli wrote in the foreword. Yet, he continued, what had once seemed hopeless had been achieved at last. ✳

Passageways inside this silver mine (shown as roughly horizontal lines) followed veins of ore, which was gathered in leather sacks and carted to several vertical shafts where clever contraptions, driven by horses or men turning a wheel at the surface, hauled up the ore.

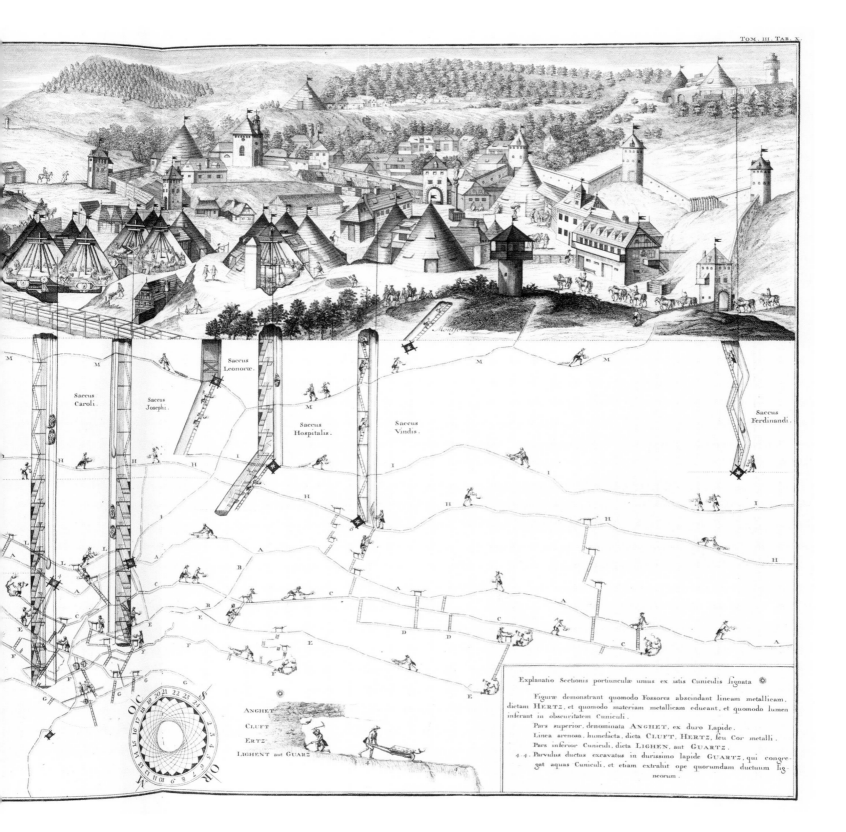

Mapping American Industry

A DETAILED LOOK INSIDE THE FACTORIES THAT DROVE AMERICA'S INDUSTRIAL BOOM IN THE EARLY 20TH CENTURY

CREATED *1894–1950*
CREATOR *Sanborn Map Company*

The Bethlehem Steel Company got its start forging iron for the country's burgeoning rail network in the late 1800s. In subsequent decades, the company became a major contributor to the wave of industrialization and urbanization sweeping America. It built everything from guns and ships for the U.S. Navy to a 45-ton (41 metric ton) axle for the world's first Ferris wheel. Chicago skyscrapers and the Golden Gate Bridge were built with Bethlehem steel.

These early 20th-century maps provide a uniquely detailed look at the inner workings of the Bethlehem Steel plant and other iconic sites of American industry in their heyday. They come from atlases that were made for fire insurance companies, which relied on them to assess the risks—and therefore the rates—of insuring various buildings and facilities.

The 1912 map below shows the massive Bethlehem Steel complex along the banks of the Lehigh River in eastern Pennsylvania. At the time, the plant employed 12,000 people and

operated continuously, according to a note on the map. Railroad tracks brought in raw material and carried finished products away. The dimensions of the blast furnaces and foundries are noted, and colors correspond to the building materials used for the various machine shops, some of which appear to be specialized for making projectiles, armor plates, and bridge parts. With all that fire and molten metal, insurance agents would have been relieved to read that the company employed its own fire department consisting of about 150 men.

The maps were created by the Sanborn Map Company, founded in 1866 by a surveyor named Daniel Alfred Sanborn. The company mapped at least 13,000 U.S. cities and towns, sending surveyors to walk the streets and measure the dimensions of buildings, taking note of their construction materials. Surveyors inspected factories and commercial buildings from the inside, noting any relevant details such as flammable materials and the presence (or lack) of sprinkler systems.

Sanborn surveyors and mapmakers adhered

to a strict code laid out in a closely guarded company manual. They knew exactly what to look for and how things should be drawn and color-coded on the maps. Though they worked anonymously, evidence of their artistry can be seen in flourishes on the ornate title pages like the one on page 167 for an 1894 atlas that covered whiskey warehouses in the mid-Atlantic region.

Major cities had their own sets of Sanborn atlases. A single volume could be 8 inches (20 cm) thick and weigh nearly 30 pounds (14 kg). Insurance companies would lease a set of atlases for their area, and Sanborn employees would periodically visit to update them,

---

Maps from a 1912 fire insurance atlas (below) show the Bethlehem Steel Company as it looked in its heyday. Colors correspond to different construction materials: blue for concrete, red for brick, and yellow for wood frame. The details opposite show several of the blast furnaces used to extract metal from ore (top) and several of the machine shops inside the plant, including the projectile forge shop (bottom).

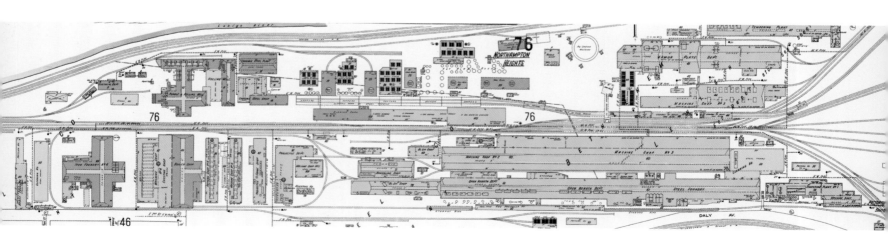

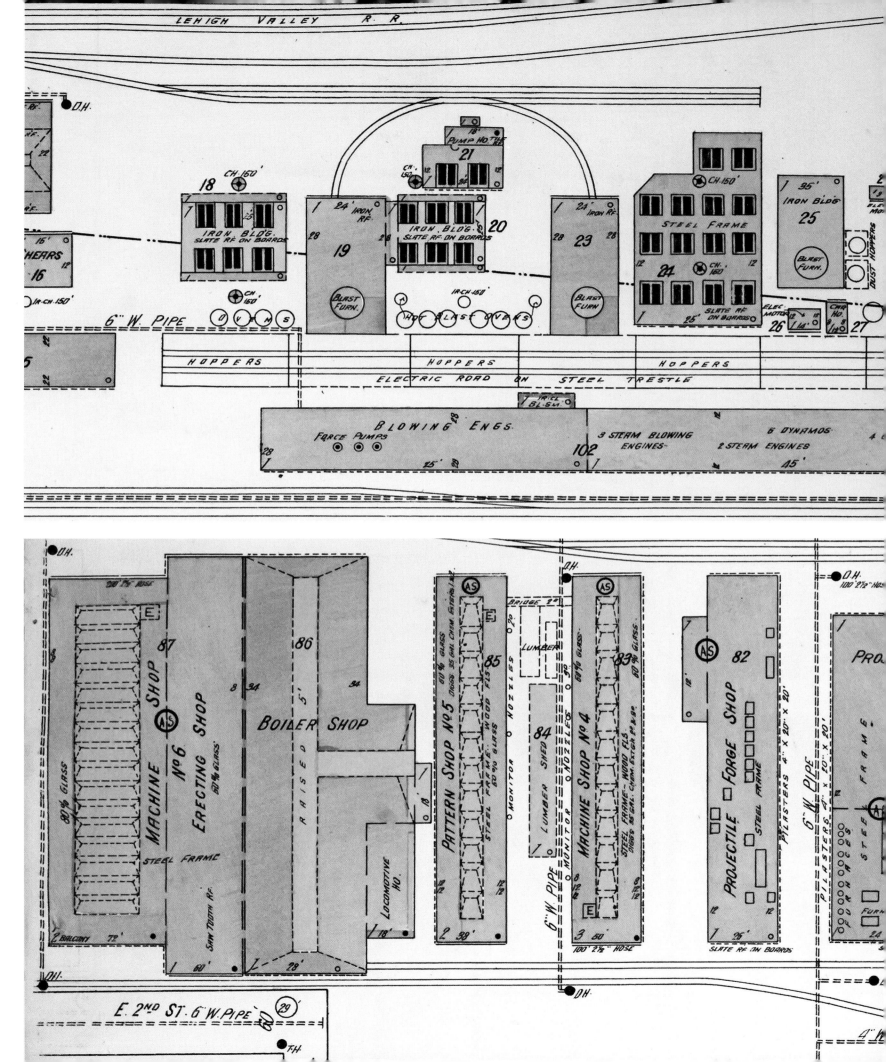

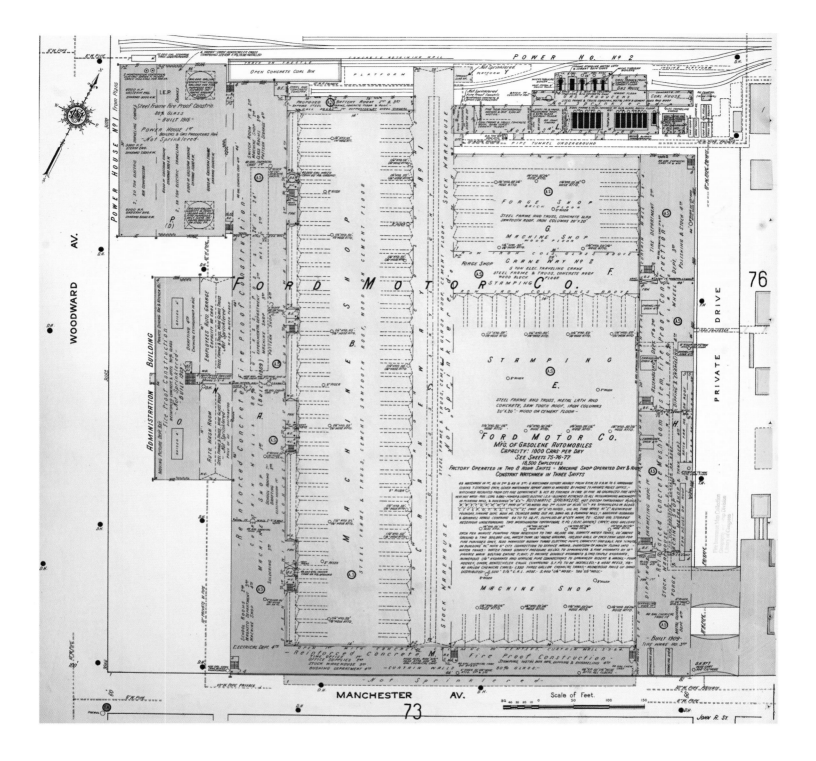

pasting slips of paper onto each map to add a new building or change the description of one. The pasted slips were organized in a specific way: Each came with information about where it went on the map and had tiny marks to help position it on the page (see opposite page).

The fire insurance map business began to falter in the 1950s as insurers turned to using statistical methods to estimate risk instead of detailed evaluations of each property. The older maps still hold interest for urban geographers and historians—or anyone else interested in how a place has changed with time.

The Bethlehem Steel plant closed in 1995, and the company filed for bankruptcy a few years later. Today, the site has been reincarnated as an arts and entertainment venue. Two of the blast furnaces were left in place, and their 230-foot (70 m) chimneys still loom over the site, a reminder of its industrial past. ✷

ABOVE Henry Ford's automobile factory in Highland Park, Michigan, was a marvel of industrial efficiency when it opened in 1910 (it's shown here on a Sanborn map from 1915). Massive windows and an open floor plan provided an abundance of natural light and allowed machines to be packed closely together, reducing wasted motion on the part of the workers.

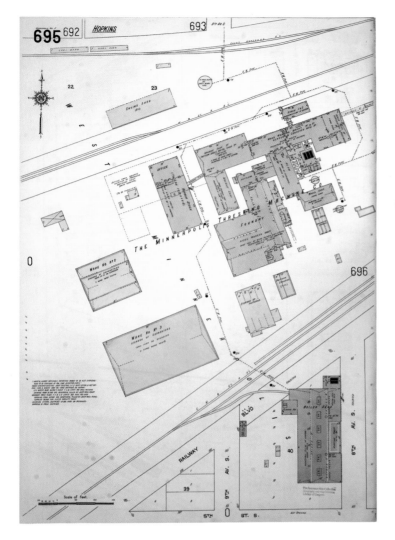

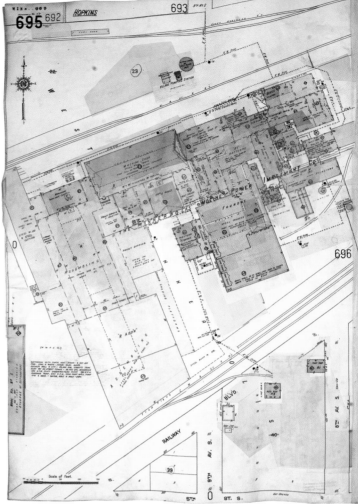

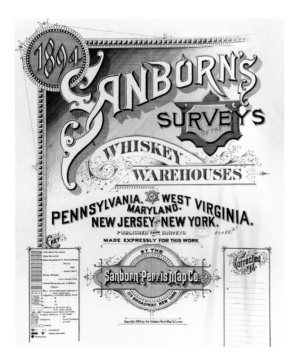

ABOVE The Minneapolis-Moline company in Hopkins, Minnesota, expanded dramatically between 1912 (left) and 1950 (right), supplying tractors and other machinery to American farmers. The dark outlines on the later map show where Sanborn company workers pasted slips of paper onto the map to update it with buildings that had been built or torn down since the previous edition.

LEFT The artistry of the Sanborn draftsmen is evident on the atlases' decorative title pages, like this 1894 atlas covering whiskey warehouses in Pennsylvania, West Virginia, Maryland, New Jersey, and New York. The maps inside the atlases adhered to a strict set of rules for consistency, but no two title pages looked exactly the same.

When Flying Was Fun

VINTAGE MAPS CAPTURE THE ROMANCE AND ADVENTURE OF EARLY COMMERCIAL FLIGHT

CREATED *1920s*
SOURCE *British Airways; Amberly Publishing*

An exciting new mode of travel became possible in the first half of the 20th century for those with enough money: They could take to the skies on a commercial flight. Trips that previously took weeks by sea could be made in days by plane. A Londoner could hop over to Paris for the weekend, for example.

"Aviation was a revolutionary way to travel," says author Paul Jarvis, curator of the British Airways Heritage Collection, the airline's archive of records and artifacts. "There was an air of mystery and adventure about it."

As the fledgling airline industry took off, maps became a vital advertising tool, tantalizing the public with exotic destinations now within their reach and romanticizing this new way of seeing the world.

After World War I ended in 1918, a lot of pilots suddenly found themselves with extra time on their hands, Jarvis says. Some decided to make themselves available for hire, and a number of small private airlines sprang up, using former military aircraft as their fleet. In 1924, the British government bought the best four of these aviation companies and merged them to create Imperial Airways, the first of several precursors to today's British Airways.

Early airline ads emphasized luxury and comfort, drawing parallels to the more familiar passenger compartments of ships (see the bottom of page 170). As on a boat, the kitchen was called a galley, Jarvis writes in his 2016 book *Mapping the Airways.* "In the larger flying boats of the 1930s there were even promenade decks on which passengers could socialise and, literally, watch

This 1938 route map from Imperial Airways includes a cartography lesson: It flattens the globe using a projection inspired by 16th-century mapmaker Martin Waldseemüller.

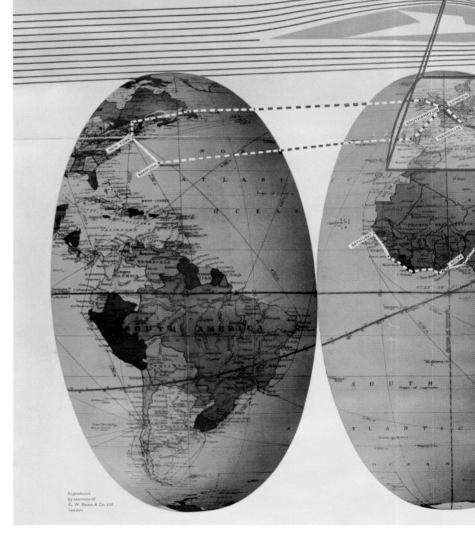

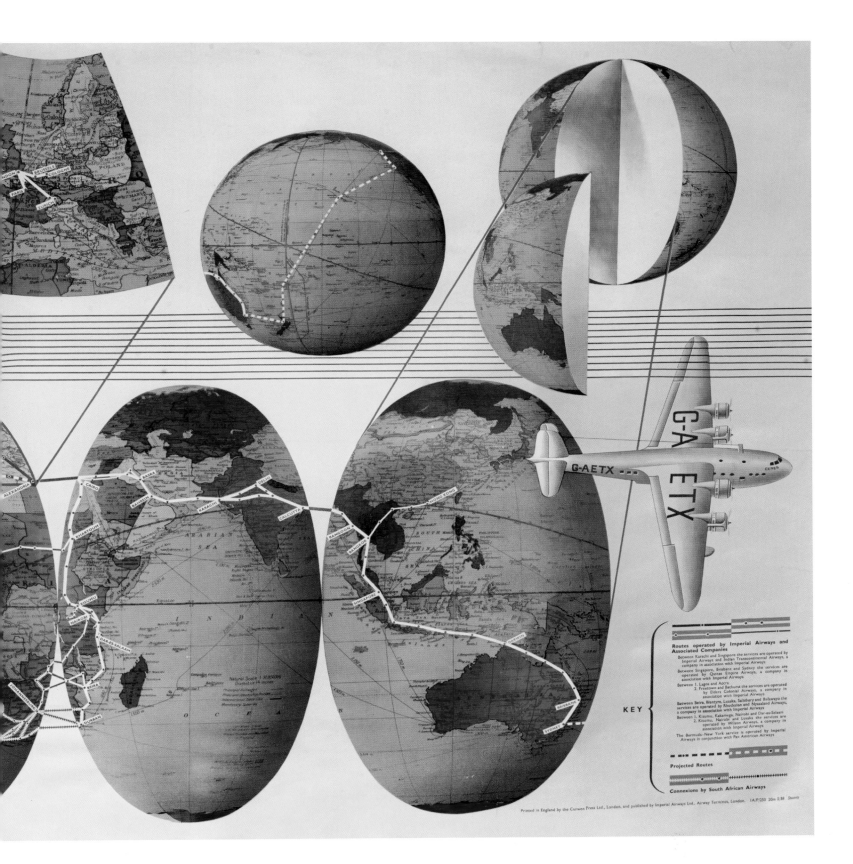

through portholes as the world slid slowly by a few thousand feet below."

At first, "flying was only for the wealthy, or for government servants, the military, and businessmen," Jarvis says. The class of people who flew was used to luxury railcars, and they expected similar amenities when they flew. For example, plane interiors might use mahogany veneers to mimic the solid mahogany furnishings of a Pullman railcar. People dressed for the occasion, too. "Men would wear a suit, collared shirt, and tie," Jarvis says.

The travel times for these early journeys may seem ridiculously slow today, but they would have been mind-blowingly fast for the time. One 1935 Imperial Airways timetable lists nine stops between Brussels and the Congo, with some legs traveled by train. The entire trip is advertised as taking four and a half days, but Jarvis thinks it must have taken at least five. "The airfare would include all hotels, all transfers, all food," he says.

Traveling by air in the 1920s and 1930s was also more perilous. One map Jarvis found in the British Airways collection depicts hills and other landmarks a pilot could use to identify his position if the plane went down in the desert between Cairo and Baghdad. The map also notes the poor condition of some roads. "Very bad going over boulders," it says, an indication that help would be slow to arrive.

During World War II, commercial flights were grounded across Europe. In Britain, airlines were taken over by the military and used for tasks such as flying American and Canadian pilots back home after they'd flown military planes over to aid the Allies in Europe, Jarvis says. The Cold War also had an impact. The Soviets tightly controlled air traffic in and out of Berlin's three airports throughout the 1970s. A map from this era uses narrow strips to illustrate the permitted flight paths. Everything else is blocked out.

Airline maps from the first half of the 20th century include elements of art deco and other artistic movements of their era. Many were made by prominent artists and designers, including László Moholy-Nagy, a leading figure in the Bauhaus art and design school in Germany in the 1920s and early 1930s.

The maps you'll find in the seatback pocket of commercial planes today just aren't as evocative. Even if you're too young to have lived it, it's easy to feel nostalgic for the days before excruciating security lines and embarrassing pat downs, when people put on nice clothes and took five-day flights to the Congo. ✳

OPPOSITE TOP Figures of camels, kangaroos, and people in exotic garb illustrate this 1950s route map. The destinations include British colonial outposts in South Asia, Africa, and Australia.

OPPOSITE BOTTOM Early airline ads, like this one from around 1937, emphasized luxury and comfort and drew parallels to the more familiar passenger compartments of ships.

ABOVE This 1938 poster by artist James Gardner incorporates a stylized route map, likely inspired by Harry Beck's famous 1933 map of the London Underground.

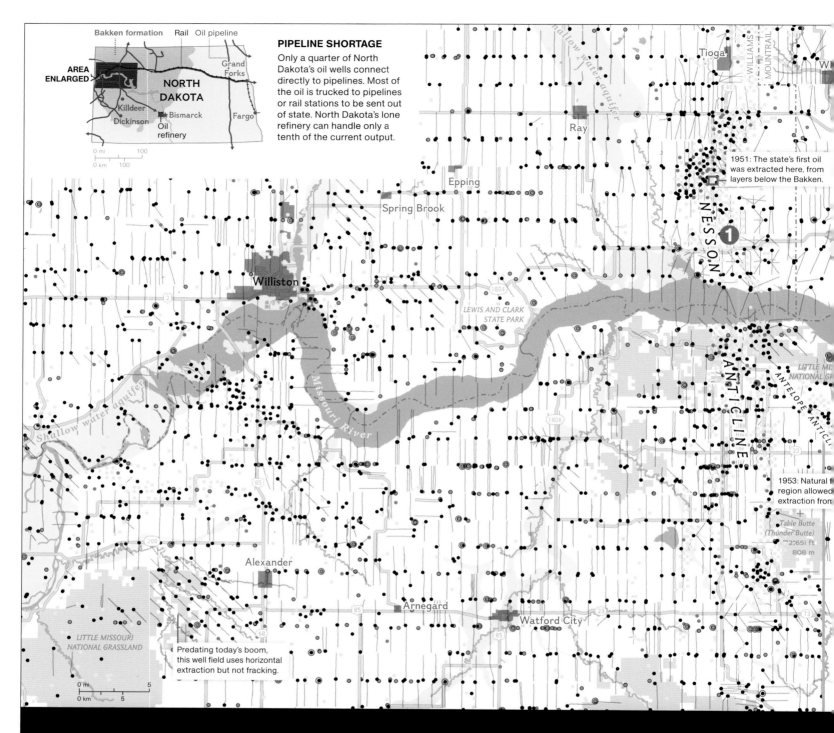

Bakken formation **Rail** **Oil pipeline**

AREA ENLARGED

NORTH DAKOTA

Killdeer
Dickinson
Bismarck
Oil refinery
Grand Forks
Fargo

0 mi 100
0 km 100

PIPELINE SHORTAGE

Only a quarter of North Dakota's oil wells connect directly to pipelines. Most of the oil is trucked to pipelines or rail stations to be sent out of state. North Dakota's lone refinery can handle only a tenth of the current output.

Tioga
WILLIAMS MOUNTRAIL
Ray

1951: The state's first oil was extracted here, from layers below the Bakken.

Epping

NESSON

Spring Brook

1804

LEWIS AND CLARK STATE PARK

Williston

ANTICLINE ANTELOPE ANTIC

LITTLE MI NATIONAL GI

1806

Missouri River

Shallow water aquifer

1953: Natural region allowed extraction from

Table Butte (Thunder Butte)
2,651 ft
808 m

Alexander

Arnegard

Watford City
23

LITTLE MISSOURI NATIONAL GRASSLAND

Predating today's boom, this well field uses horizontal extraction but not fracking.

0 mi 5
0 km 5

Drilling the Prairie

If earth were transparent, you'd see this pattern on a flight over northwest North Dakota. From the more than 3,000 active wells shown here, pipes drop down nearly two miles, then dogleg horizontally for a mile or two through the layer of shale called the Bakken formation. Lines on this map show the horizontal pipes, where fracking for oil occurs.

WELLS

○ Drilling rig

▫ Active oil well

• Status undisclosed

• Inactive, dry, or abandoned well

• Fracturing-fluid disposal well

TOP VIEW (shown in map)

Wellhead ▫——— Horizontal pipe, two miles deep

SIDE VIEW

Ground level

Horizontal pipe, two miles deep

NESSON ANTICLINE Early tra drilling, in the 1950s, focused north-south strip, where rese oil are trapped along an arch geologic structure called an a

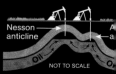

Nesson anticline

OIL

NOT TO SCALE

VIRGINIA W. MASON, NGM STAFF
SOURCES: NORTH DAKOTA DEPARTMEN

Well featured
on pages 48-49

SHELL LAKE
NATIONAL WILDLIFE
REFUGE

Palermo

Stanley

Ross

2006: The
fracking boom
began with
these wells.

New Town

Parshall

FORT BERTHOLD
RESERVATION

Lake
Sakakawea

MOUNTRAIL
McLEAN

MOUNTRAIL

McKENZIE | DUNN

2 **SANISH FIELD** Refinements in
fracking technology let drillers in
this field use longer horizontal
pipes, reducing the number of oil
platforms needed on the surface.

Two-square-mile
lease

3 **PARSHALL FIELD** Shorter horizontal pipes mark this field. The first
large-scale fracking of the Bakken
formation began here, in 2006,
spurring the ongoing boom.

One-square-mile
lease

AQUIFER

NATIONAL GRASSLAND
OR WILDLIFE REFUGE

RESOURCES (WELL DATA AS OF DECEMBER 3, 2012); NORTH DAKOTA GEOLOGICAL SURVEY; NORTH DAKOTA PIPELINE AUTHORITY; IHS ENERGY

Fracking Boom

BRINGING NORTH DAKOTA'S UNDERGROUND ECONOMY TO LIGHT

CREATED *2013*
SOURCE *Ginny Mason, National Geographic*

In 2013, North Dakota was pulling more than 800,000 barrels of oil a day out of the Bakken formation, a 350-million-year-old layer of rock around 2 miles (3 km) below the surface in the state's northwest corner. This map from *National Geographic* magazine's March 2013 issue reveals the impressive level of activity happening underground that isn't visible on the prairie above.

The boom was spawned over a decade ago by advances in a drilling technique known as hydraulic fracturing, or fracking, along with high oil prices and a push to decrease the country's dependence on foreign fossil fuels. This type of extraction has become a significant part of the country's fossil fuels production, even as it has raised concerns about the impact on climate and the local environment. Fracking extracts oil or gas from rock by forcing specialized mixtures of fluids into it under high pressure, causing it to crack. Sand grains in the fluids become lodged in the cracks, propping them open so that oil and gas can flow through.

Oil companies use new directional drilling technology to bore down vertically to the Bakken formation and then make a 90-degree turn to drill horizontally along the rock layer for another mile or two so they can fracture as much of that layer as possible. This helped North Dakota push its daily production to over a million barrels a day in 2015 and 2017. On the map, these horizontal tracks are marked by lines extending from dots that represent every oil well piercing the Bakken in the Williston, North Dakota, area at the time: 3,000 of the state's 8,000 wells. Cartographer Ginny Mason used visible differences in the patterns of the wells to show how the oil field has evolved over time.

The dense cluster of dots near number 1 on the map represents mostly traditional wells from the 1950s that tapped into more easily accessible oil that had pooled beneath an arched rock layer. The wells with short lines near number 3 are early fracking wells from the beginning of the boom around 2006. The tight pattern of long lines near number 2 reflects technological advancements that allowed longer horizontal wells, which lowered costs and left more space on the surface undisturbed by drilling platforms.

The biggest challenge with this map, Mason says, was to take a huge amount of information about a complex and controversial subject and make it clear and approachable, but also correct. ✻

Each dot on this map represents an oil well in northwest North Dakota. The lines extending from the dots depict the tracks of horizontal wells drilled for extracting oil through hydraulic fracturing.

Tea Revives the World

A WITTY MARKETING MAP HELPED REVIVE THE BRITISH TEA INDUSTRY AFTER THE GREAT DEPRESSION

CREATED *1940*
SOURCE *David Rumsey Map Collection*

The British tea industry was in trouble at the end of the Great Depression. Prices had tanked, and demand at home wasn't keeping up. Tea planters needed to expand the market, and to British growers in places like India and Sri Lanka (or Ceylon, as it was known at the time), Africa looked like a golden opportunity: an entire continent of people waiting to be introduced to the joys of tea.

That introduction came in the form of a map made as part of a marketing campaign launched by the International Tea Market Expansion Board, a British trade group. The group hired the graphic artist MacDonald (Max) Gill, who's perhaps best remembered for the very bright and playful map that convinced Londoners to lighten up and stop whining about conditions on the Underground. Gill's tea map, published in 1940, is similarly packed with amusing details.

"TEA is served on passenger liners 1,000 miles up the Amazon," reads a banner over Brazil. "The British Navy drinks two tons of TEA every day," reads another, shouting the name of the beverage, as always, in capital letters. There are quotes from poets and writers on the virtues of tea and statistics on which countries import and export the most. The bright red title says it all: "Tea Revives the World."

"It's a really amazing map," says Erika Rappaport, a historian at the University of California, Santa Barbara. In her 2017 book, *A Thirst for Empire: How Tea Shaped the Modern World,* Rappaport writes that as part of the effort to market tea in Africa, promoters printed out Gill's map as 10-by-20-foot (3 by 6 m) posters. "They'd drive around in vans and set up little stands to educate people about tea and teach them how to make it," she says.

The map includes lots of colorful details in Africa ("Bedouins say that a camel, a gun & TEA are the three essentials of life"), but only a few surprisingly dull anecdotes in China, the birthplace of tea and home to the world's oldest tea culture. That may be more than coincidence, Rappaport says, given that cheap Chinese tea threatened to jeopardize the British share of the world market further. Those seemingly random facts, in other words, may have had everything to do with the price of tea in China. ✳

The detail above from Max Gill's 1940 map for the International Tea Market Expansion Board is packed with fascinating but hard to verify bits of trivia, including "The British Navy drinks two tons of TEA every day" and "TEA is the favourite beverage of the Bantu." The decorative scroll in the bottom left corner of the full map (at right) lists the top tea-growing and -importing countries and claims that 300 billion cups of tea were consumed per year worldwide.

The Beauty of Scientific Maps

Space and time are intrinsic to many fields of science, from evolution to oceanography to particle physics, which makes science fertile territory for mapping. Sometimes scientists use maps to explain their work, occasionally to marvelous effect. Other times, researchers need to make maps to help them find answers. For some studies, the map itself is the science. This chapter contains great examples of scientific mapping that's fascinating, beautiful, or both.

Oceanography got its start with the 19th-century maps of American naval officer Matthew Fontaine Maury, whose charts of winds and currents vastly improved sea travel (see page 207). A century later, Marie Tharp followed in Maury's footsteps, producing gorgeous, detailed maps of the world's ocean floors that changed our understanding of that vast, unexplored region of the planet (see page 184). Modern epidemiology is also rooted in 19th-century maps that traced the spread of disease, pointing the way to possible causes, though not always the right ones (see page 180).

Geology is perhaps the field of science most closely tied to cartography. After the 1906 earthquake in San Francisco, the maps geologists made led to groundbreaking scientific discoveries (see page 194). Maps have also helped scientists decipher the surfaces of other worlds, from the moon to Mars and beyond (see page 204).

Maps made in the name of science show how progress is often spurred by a new understanding of the spatial relationships between things, placing them among the most interesting and enlightening maps there are. ➤➤

THE BIRTH OF A SCIENCE
(1815, Stanford University Libraries)

Near the end of the 18th century, a surveyor named William Smith noticed that different kinds of rock were often layered in the same order in many parts of Britain, and discovered that he could identify specific rock units by the fossils they contained. Smith spent a quarter century making one of the first geologic maps, and the first of an entire country. He used color to show rock units, with darker shades to indicate the bottom of each layer, as seen on this section of his map showing southwest England.

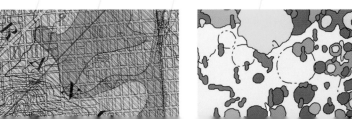
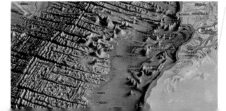

The Topography of Disease

A 19TH-CENTURY DOCTOR MAPPED CHOLERA'S DEADLY TOLL

CREATED *1856*

SOURCE *Princeton University Library*

In 1831, cholera hit the United Kingdom and began killing tens of thousands during successive waves of terrifying outbreaks. The disease was fatal for as many as a quarter of its victims, often within just days of exposure. Many scientists of the day embraced the theory that epidemics were caused by the foul air, or miasma (from open cesspools, raw sewage, and rotting rubbish), that hung over large swaths of most major cities. That is, until a young English doctor named John Snow documented an outbreak of cholera in his London neighborhood in 1854.

As the story goes, Snow carefully mapped the locations of the victims' homes and demonstrated that the deaths were clustered around a public water pump on Broad Street in the Soho district (see page 182, top). By interviewing the victims' families, he was able to trace nearly every case of cholera back to that water pump, bolstering his theory that cholera is a waterborne disease and convincing the local authorities to remove the pump's handle. The story has become legendary, and Snow's map is often portrayed as a breakthrough moment in both cartography and epidemiology. The truth, of course, is much messier.

Snow did indeed do excellent work that helped advance the science, and his map still rightfully stands as a shining example of medical cartography. But it wasn't until long after Snow's death in 1858 that his theory was proved correct and his work was hailed as a turning point. "His map has become an icon and Snow himself an almost mythic figure," writes medical geographer Tom Koch in *Cartographies of Disease*. "Few focus, therefore, on Snow's failure to convince his contemporaries of his argument, the limits of his thesis in the context of his time."

Snow wasn't the only one mapping cholera in England in 1854. The physician Henry Wentworth Acland tracked an outbreak in Oxford that affected 290 people that year. His work, which resulted in the 170-page *Memoir on the Cholera at Oxford* and an accompanying map (at right), was "perhaps the most comprehensive study of an urban disease of its day," according to Koch.

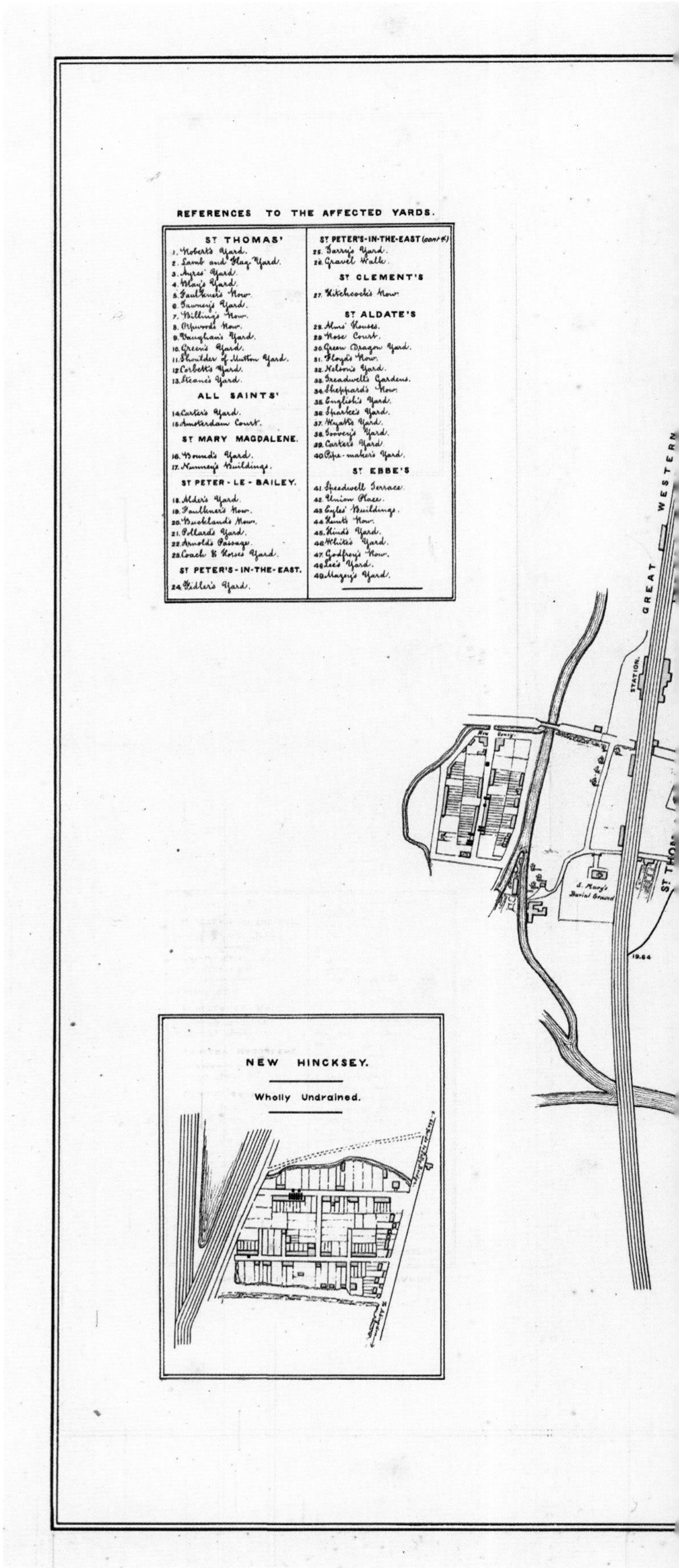

Henry Acland mapped the victims of three cholera outbreaks in Oxford, England, in the mid-19th century and concluded that the disease was connected to foul air that collected in lower elevations.

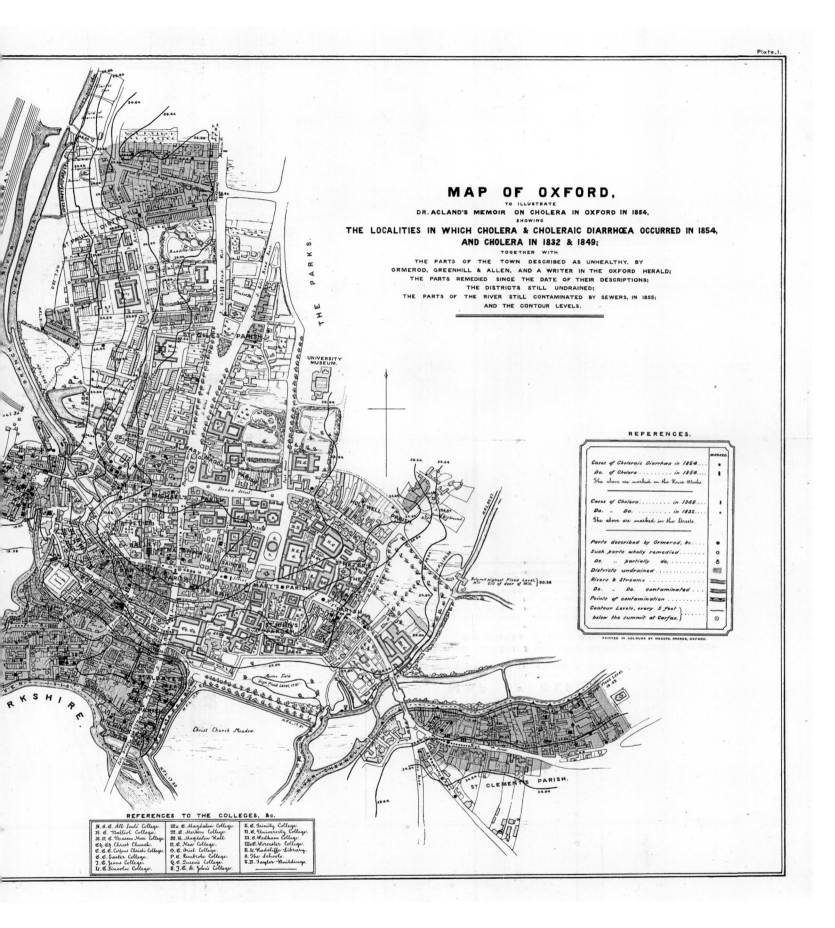

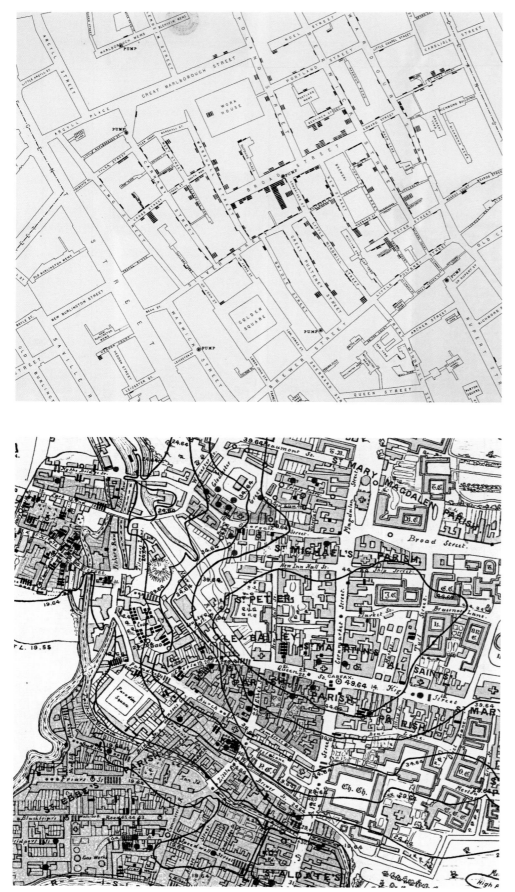

Some experts found Acland's work more convincing than Snow's, partly because of its breadth and thoroughness. But Acland's research had another big advantage: Its conclusions supported the prevailing miasmatic theory of disease, which had been developed over centuries. Snow, on the other hand, was bucking the mainstream with his waterborne disease theory.

While Snow's analysis was focused on one possible explanation for the outbreak and his argument rested on the visual clarity of his map, Acland took a more statistical approach that considered many potential disease factors. In addition to mapping victims, Acland included sites that had previously been deemed unhealthy (brown dots), those that had subsequently been cleaned up (brown circles), streams that were unpolluted, and those that had been contaminated (dashed lines), including point sources of the contamination such as outflows of raw sewage (see close-up at left). Areas with poor drainage were shaded green.

Snow was content to stop mapping the cholera deaths that occurred after he thought his case had already been made. By contrast, Acland mapped the entire list of victims in 1854, as well as those of two previous outbreaks. He used different symbols for the locations of victims' homes from 1832 (blue dots), 1849 (blue bars), and 1854 (black squares and bars). And, most important for his argument, Acland mapped the physical topography of the town with 5-foot (1.5 m) contour lines. His map, together with his statistical analysis, showed a clear correlation between elevation and the disease. In each of the three outbreaks, people in low-lying areas suffered a much higher rate of infection and death. Even the higher spots that had unhealthy brown dots fared better than the lowlands.

Acland's map neatly backed up the miasmatic theory, suggesting that the toxic air would collect and remain in low areas with less

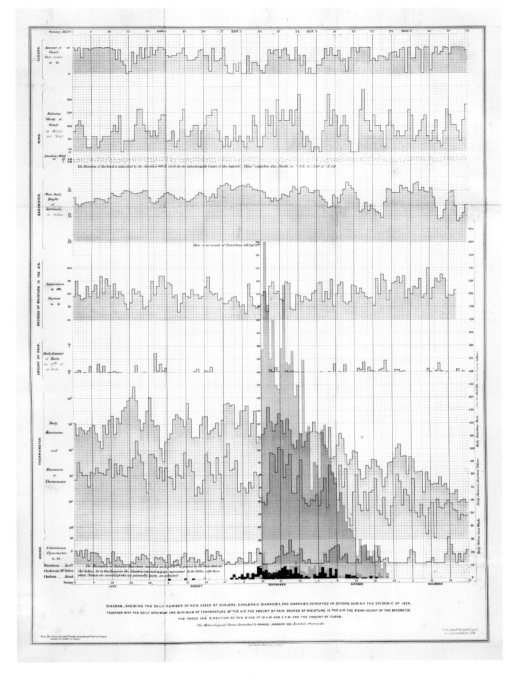

with copious data, is that 1854 was an abnormal year for weather in Oxford. Comparing it with the 25 years prior, he found that rain was abnormally low, as was wind speed. The list of things that were abnormally high included temperature range, pressure, thunder and lightning, days with hail, and appearances of the northern lights.

He couldn't quite put any of these variables together with elevation to form a reasonable explanation, especially considering that the previous outbreaks didn't follow the same pattern. But Acland was still confident that if another epidemic were to occur, "the rapidly advancing science of Meteorology" would be able to use data to clarify which of the abnormalities played a role.

Acland's study was more comprehensive—and at the time, more convincing—than Snow's, but it had one glaring flaw: His conclusion was definitively wrong. "Like much of the science of every era, it missed an intervening vector," Koch writes. What Acland failed to see was that at higher elevations, water typically came from wells or streams, while lower areas mostly relied on rivers that were often polluted with sewage. But, Koch notes, "the mapping—and here, the mapmaking—were clear, consistent, and, if ultimately incorrect, still rigorous."

Snow's theory was largely dismissed during his lifetime, but he ultimately triumphed long after his death. Conversely, Acland enjoyed recognition from his peers for his work on cholera, but lived to see the theory it supported disproved. Still, his work is worth more than a footnote, argues data visualization journalist Alberto Cairo.

"The myth of the hero who singlehandedly wrecked miasmatic theory obscures the fact that those who held onto it were also thoughtful fellows," Cairo writes. "It is unfortunate that we don't study them further, as we humans learn much more from our mistakes—both individual and collective—than from our successes." ✳

wind. "His statistics are showing that he had an excellent argument and evidence," says Este Geraghty, chief medical officer for the mapping software company Esri. But Acland failed to see the whole picture, making his a cautionary tale, she says. "You have to determine what things mean, not just the outcome and the correlation."

Acland saw polluted water as a potential contributor to pestilent air, not a medium for the spread of an invisible agent of disease. Consequently, he hadn't paid attention to sources of drinking water. Instead, like many of his contemporaries, he looked to the weather for clues to

how elevation could be influencing the disease.

"That there is a connection between the state of the Atmosphere, or of the imponderable agents of the globe, and the existence of the Epidemic, is scarcely doubted by those who have carefully attended to its history," he wrote.

Acland meticulously charted the time line of the 1854 outbreak against a host of local climate variables, including temperature, barometric pressure, wind, rain, humidity, cloud cover, and ozone levels (above). But he was unable to find anything that waxed and waned precisely with the number of new cholera cases. What Acland was able to demonstrate,

The Ocean Floor Revealed

MARIE THARP'S GROUNDBREAKING CARTOGRAPHY BROUGHT THE UNDERWATER WORLD INTO FOCUS

CREATED *1961–1977*
CREATORS *Marie Tharp, Bruce Heezen, and Heinrich Berann*

By the halfway mark of the 20th century, explorers had ventured into much of the world's most extreme topography. They had planted their flags at the North and South Poles and on many of the world's tallest, most treacherous peaks; Everest would soon be conquered as well. But the world had yet to get even a glimpse of the planet's greatest unexplored territory of all: the ocean floor.

The nearly three-quarters of the planet's surface that is buried beneath thousands of feet of water was thought to be a relatively flat, featureless plain. But that was about to change. In 1952, geologists Marie Tharp and Bruce Heezen teamed up on a mapping project that would reveal the true nature of the seafloor and help revolutionize our understanding of the Earth.

"I had a blank canvas to fill with extraordinary possibilities, a fascinating jigsaw puzzle to piece together," Tharp wrote in a perspective 50 years later.

At a time when the field of geology was completely dominated by men, Tharp started her career by taking advantage of a rare opportunity. World War II had left the University of Michigan short on manpower for its geology department, so it opened its doors to women for the first time. Tharp was accepted and completed a master's degree in 1945. In 1948 she landed a job at Columbia University's geology department as a drafting assistant for oceanography graduate students, including Heezen.

Tharp arrived at Columbia right at the start of a new era in oceanography. Previously, the only information available about the topography of the seafloor was crude depth measurements made by dropping lead weights attached to ropes from ships. But after World War II, ships began collecting depth data in earnest with echo sounders. The new technology worked by bouncing pulses of sound off the seafloor and measuring how long it took for them to return. Longer times meant deeper ocean, and shorter times indicated higher ground.

Heezen was part of the first wave of scientists plying the seas on research vessels. By 1952, he and scientists at other coastal institutions, private companies, and the military had recorded tens of thousands of soundings of the North Atlantic Ocean. Tharp was assigned to help Heezen make sense of it all by converting the echo times to depths and plotting profiles of the seafloor beneath the ships' tracks. After months of painstaking

ABOVE Marie Tharp and Bruce Heezen work on a physiographic map of the ocean floor using depth soundings recorded along ships' tracks, like the one in the foreground of the photo.

OPPOSITE This Atlantic Ocean floor map was painted by Austrian artist Heinrich Berann based on physiographic maps made by Tharp and Heezen. It was published as a supplement to the June 1968 issue of *National Geographic* magazine.

plotting and drafting, she had pieced together six profiles that crossed the entire North Atlantic at different latitudes.

Though the profiles covered only a tiny fraction of the seafloor, Tharp was already starting to envision the underwater landscape. The work of early oceanographers like Matthew Fontaine Maury (see page 207) had found the vague outline of a rise in the middle of the Atlantic Ocean, but Tharp's profiles revealed there was actually a huge ridge running from north to south right down the center of the ocean.

ATLANTIC OCEAN FLOOR

-12000 Depth in feet below sea level
-9000 Height above sea level
(14000) Height above the 16,000-foot average depth of the abyssal plains

Produced in the Geographic Art Division
National Geographic Society
MELVIN M. PAYNE, PRESIDENT
for THE NATIONAL GEOGRAPHIC MAGAZINE
MELVILLE BELL GROSVENOR, EDITOR-IN-CHIEF; FREDERICK G. VOSBURGH, EDITOR
WILLIAM N. PALMSTROM, CHIEF, GEOGRAPHIC ART DIVISION

Based on bathymetric studies by Bruce C. Heezen and Marie Tharp of the Lamont Geological Observatory
Painted by Heinrich C. Berann, Compiled by Leo J. Bobrofschmidt

HORIZONTAL SCALE 1:30 412,800 OR 490 MILES TO THE INCH AT THE EQUATOR
VERTICAL SCALE EXAGGERATED
Mercator Projection
JUNE 1968

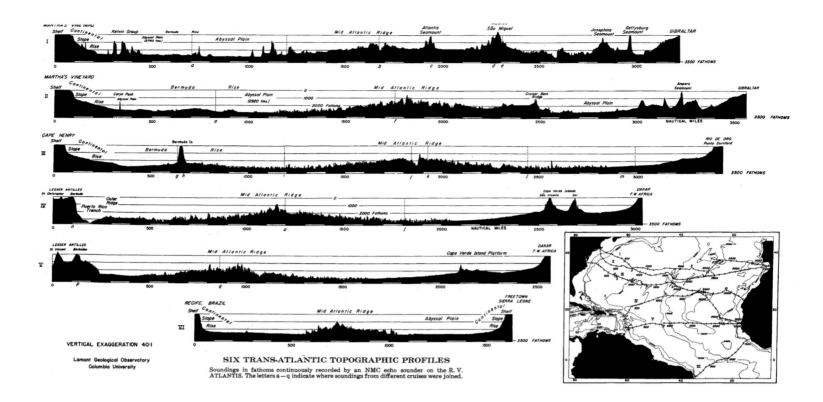

VERTICAL EXAGGERATION 40:1

Lamont Geological Observatory
Columbia University

SIX TRANS-ATLANTIC TOPOGRAPHIC PROFILES

Soundings in fathoms continuously recorded by an NMC echo sounder on the R. V. ATLANTIS. The letters a — q indicate where soundings from different cruises were joined.

The thing that really jumped out at her, however, was a V-shaped cleft at the crest of the ridge that looked very similar in all the profiles. Tharp suspected the cleft might continue along the axis of the entire Mid-Atlantic Ridge. If she was right, her discovery was potentially much more than just a submarine valley. Tharp thought it could be evidence for continental drift—the controversial idea that the continents have moved across the surface of the Earth.

In the 1950s, scientists in the United States were almost unanimous in their disdain for this idea, and Heezen was no exception. No plausible driving force for such movement had been put forth, they argued. But Tharp thought the valley she'd discovered might support the idea. "The valley would form where new material came up from deep inside the Earth, splitting the mid-ocean ridge in two and pushing the sides apart," she wrote.

It took her months to convince Heezen the rift was there, but he eventually came around when unrelated research corroborated Tharp's work. In 1953, he had an assistant plotting the epicenters of undersea earthquakes for a project to help Bell Laboratories choose locations to lay new transatlantic cables. Comparing this map to Tharp's, they found a line of epicenters lined up with the rift valley.

By following the epicenters, Tharp now had a way to locate the ridge in between the sounding profiles. She began making what's known as a physiographic diagram, illustrating the relief of the seafloor with a three-dimensional perspective (see map opposite). This approach illuminated the rift valley in a way that simple contour lines couldn't. "It allowed us to capture the seafloor's many textured variations, contrasting the smoothness of the abyssal plains, for example, with the ruggedness of the mountains along the ridges," she later recalled.

Another major benefit of the technique was that it allowed them to get around the U.S. Navy's decision to classify all detailed contour maps of the ocean floor. The physiographic diagram gave them a way to publish their work without revealing precise depths, so they could share what they had discovered with the world. Their map of the North Atlantic, which first appeared in 1957 in a technical journal, was by far the most comprehensive map ever made of an ocean.

The map wasn't an immediate success. "The reaction in the scientific community ranged from amazement to skepticism to scorn," Tharp recalled. Some scientists thought there was too much speculation about the terrain between the depth profiles, and others weren't convinced the rift existed.

But as new data from other parts of the world began arriving at Columbia, Tharp found more evidence of mid-ocean ridges, complete with rifts and earthquake epicenters. Soon she could see the true scope of what they had discovered: a continuous ridge system running through all the major oceans, encircling the planet. By the late 1960s she had mapped all of Earth's major oceans.

Meanwhile, more and more evidence was accumulating that the continents were in fact on the move.

Heezen and Tharp's work would play a key part in transforming the idea of continental drift into a new model for how the Earth works: plate tectonics. Geologist Harry Hess of Princeton University had posited that instead of the continents plowing through the ocean crust, the seafloor itself was moving. Hess's idea, known as seafloor spreading, suggested Tharp had been right about the rift in the Mid-Atlantic Ridge: This is where the Earth's crust breaks apart and new crust is formed. The new ocean crust slowly and continuously moves away from the rift as more crust is created.

The rift was the physical manifestation of Hess's idea, and Tharp's maps provided the visual evidence. "To get the old-school geologists to believe that this was something that was observable as opposed to theorized, it really was the rift valley that clinched it for them," says Arthur Lerner-Lam, a seismologist and deputy director of the Lamont-Doherty Earth Observatory at Columbia University.

Stubborn scientists weren't the only ones

Tharp's maps spoke to. Her work also caught the attention of National Geographic, which invited Tharp and Heezen to work with Austrian landscape painter Heinrich Berann (see page 114) to transform their map of the Indian Ocean into an illustration for the magazine in 1967. This began a decade of collaboration with Berann that produced some of the most beautiful and intuitive maps of the world's oceans ever created, including the Atlantic Ocean map (page 185).

The culmination was the 1977 world ocean floor map on the following pages, a masterpiece that has never been surpassed in its artistry or ability to clearly convey the nature of the seafloor at a glance. "It was adding the visual stylistic element that I think helped make that map as informative and significant as it ended up being," says Lerner-Lam.

Despite her critical role in their research, Tharp often took a backseat to Heezen when it was presented, published, and cited by other scientists. It wasn't until the decade before Tharp's death in 2006 that the significance of her contributions to both science and cartography were truly recognized. She was celebrated by the Library of Congress, honored by oceanographic institutions, and Columbia's Lamont-Doherty created a fellowship in her name to promote women in science.

"It was a once-in-a-lifetime—a once-in-the-history-of-the-world—opportunity for anyone, but especially for a woman in the 1940s," she wrote. "The nature of the times, the state of the science, and events large and small, logical and illogical, combined to make it all happen." ✳

OPPOSITE Tharp used depth measurements made with echo sounders on boats as they crossed the ocean to draw profiles of the seafloor, like these of the Atlantic Ocean. The Mid-Atlantic Ridge is visible near the center of each profile.

ABOVE Tharp illustrated the ocean floors by drawing the relief as if viewed at an angle from above to make physiographic diagrams like this one from 1961 of the South Atlantic Ocean.

NEXT PAGE The last map that Tharp and Heezen made was an incomparable world ocean floor map, painted by Heinrich Berann. The 6.2-by-3.5-foot (1.9 by 1.1 m) map was published in 1977, shortly after Heezen died, and still hangs in many oceanography departments across the globe.

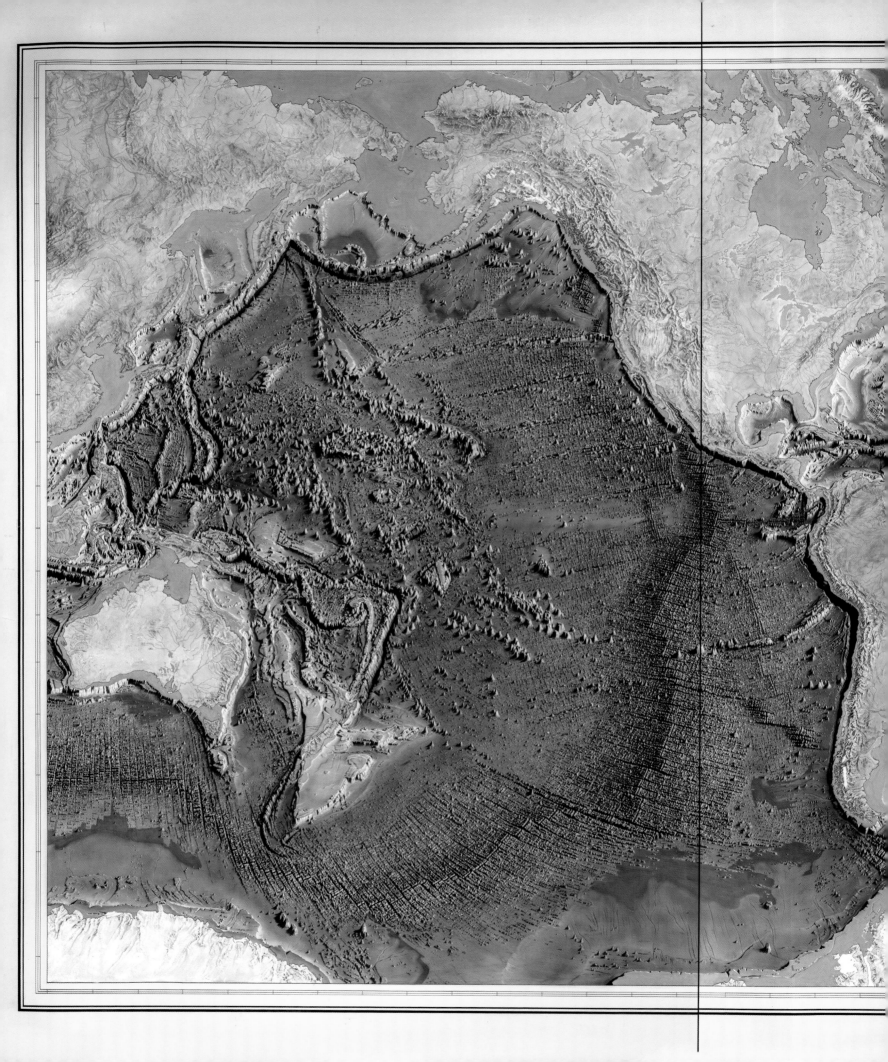

Rome Unearthed

A MAP MADE BY A 19TH-CENTURY ARCHAEOLOGIST CAPTURES THE CITY'S HISTORY IN EXQUISITE DETAIL

CREATED *1901*
SOURCE *MappingRome project and others*

Rodolfo Lanciani's map of Rome is one of the most intriguing maps ever made of one of the most mapped cities in human history. Completed in 1901, Lanciani's map documents the city—from its ancient past through the end of the 19th century—with the meticulous eye of a trained archaeologist.

The map is huge: roughly 17 by 24 feet (5 by 7 m). Lanciani published it as 46 separate sheets over the course of eight years. In what was a notable innovation for the time, he used color to depict what the city looked like in different phases of its history—a strategy modern cartographers have exploited to beautiful effect (see page 48). Imperial and early Christian buildings are shown in black, medieval and early modern buildings are shown in red, and modern construction is shown in blue (from Lanciani's perspective, "modern" meant anything after 1871, when Rome became the capital of a newly unified Italy).

"It's one of the first attempts to show the different periods of historic Rome on a map," says Allan Ceen, an urban historian and collaborator on the MappingRome project, a collaboration of designers and scholars that is digitizing maps and other documents related to the city's history.

Lanciani lived during a pivotal time in Rome's history. Italy, long a collection of separate states, had finally been unified, and a major expansion project was under way to fill in unused spaces inside the walls of the ancient city. All this construction was turning up ruins that had been buried for centuries. Lanciani treated these construction sites as archaeological digs, carefully measuring and sketching these discoveries before they were covered up again by new construction. "Lanciani was dismayed and distraught as parts of the city were being built up on the ruins of ancient Rome and erasing the history of the city," says James Tice, a professor of architecture at the University of Oregon and one of the leaders of the MappingRome project.

Lanciani drew on a wide variety of sources to make his map, which he named "Forma Urbis Romae" after an early third-century map of the same name that was carved in marble. This ancient

This detail from a digital reconstruction of Lanciani's map created by the MappingRome project captures the heart of the ancient city, from the Colosseum (the oval at far right) to the Tiber River. The map is a work in progress, but scholars are working to align it with modern maps of the city and refine Lanciani's color scheme for building ages.

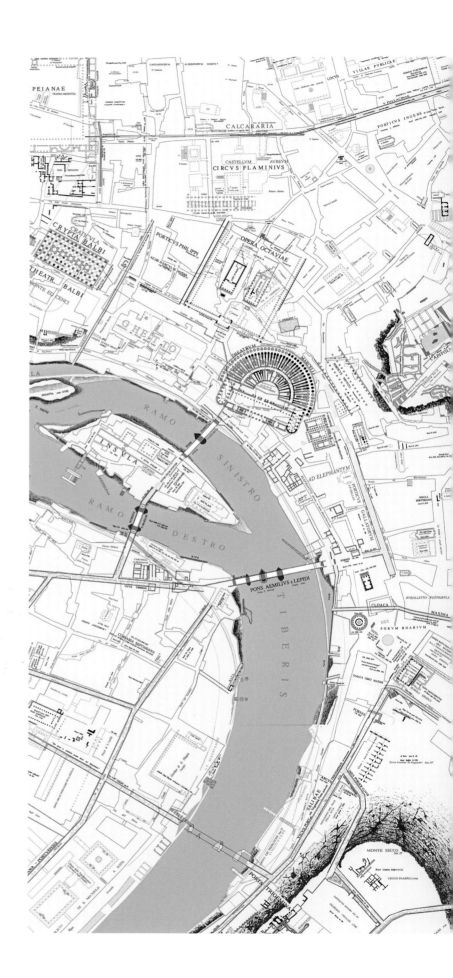

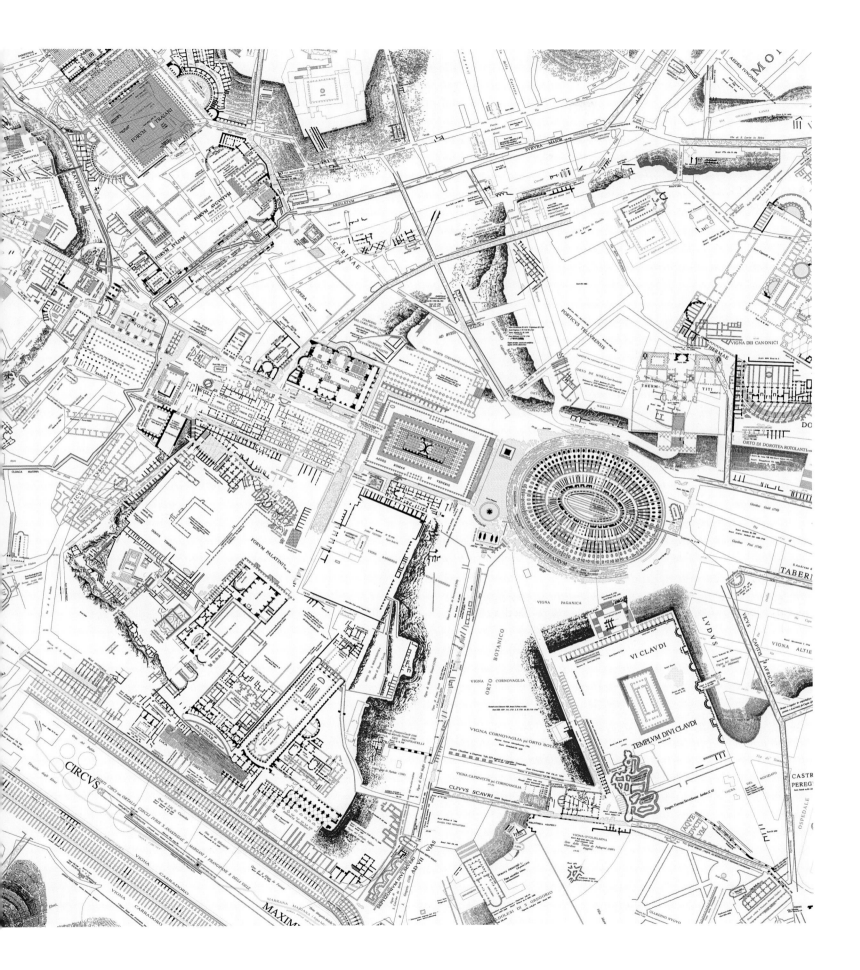

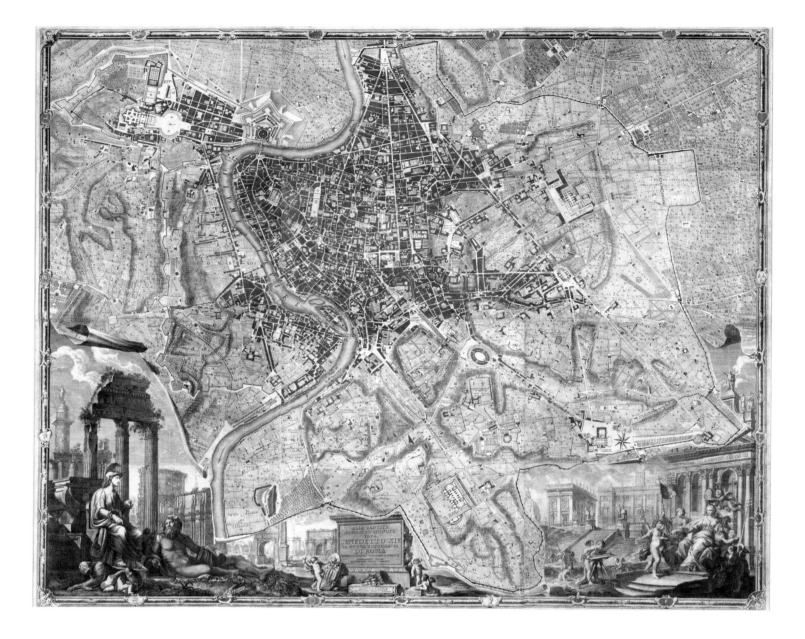

map would have made even Lanciani's map look puny—it was roughly 43 by 60 feet (13 by 18 m). At a remarkable scale of 1:240, the detailed marble map showed even the floor plans of individual buildings. Only fragments—nearly 1,200 of them—have survived, and Lanciani referred to them in creating his map.

Another major source for Lanciani was the beautiful 1748 map created by Giambattista Nolli (see above). This architect and surveyor's map of Rome bucked the cartographic tradition of the time, which favored a slightly elevated bird's-eye perspective, by showing the city from directly above. Buildings are completely flat, with their outlines and basic floor plans visible. The detail is remarkable, and remarkably accurate; centuries later, modern

satellite maps line up well with Nolli's map.

Much had changed in Rome since Nolli's day, so Lanciani turned to tax maps, architectural plans, sketches, drawings, paintings, and photographs to fill in details about the city's development. His archive at the Istituto Nazionale di Archeologia e Storia dell'Arte in Rome contains thousands of these documents, including the sketch opposite of Piazza del Popolo, a large public square that was redesigned in the early 1800s by the architect Giuseppe Valadier.

"The particular problem that Valadier solved brilliantly was to connect the original piazza with the top of the Pincian hill which overlooks it through a system of ramps, suitable for horse carriages to negotiate," says Tice. Today, he adds, those ramps are still used—by people on bicycles.

One of the long-term goals for the Mapping-Rome project is to update and improve the digital version of Lanciani's map. That work includes updating his map with ruins discovered in the past century and eventually creating more finely grained layers—breaking Lanciani's single black layer for ancient buildings into multiple layers corresponding to historians' subdivisions of the ancient period, for example.

Lanciani's map has aged gracefully in the century since it was created, and with a little help it should keep historians and urban designers engaged and inspired well into the future. Its clean, elegant design packs in an astounding amount of detail, making it possible to picture Rome as it once was, as it became, and as it might become. ✳

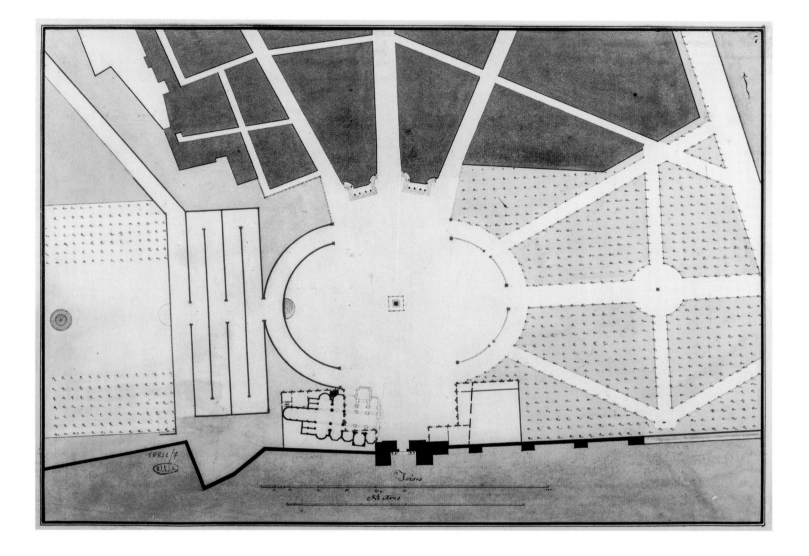

OPPOSITE Giambattista Nolli's 1748 map of Rome was remarkably accurate for its time. It shows the outlines of hundreds of buildings, and even the basic floor plans for some of them.

....

ABOVE This 1813 plan for the Piazza del Popolo (People's Square) was later modified by Giuseppe Valadier, who turned the series of ramps leading up a hill to the left into a more graceful, curving design.

....

RIGHT These fragments from the original marble Forma Urbis Romae, from the Antiquarium Comunale museum in Rome, depict the Ludus Magnus, a training school and arena for gladiators.

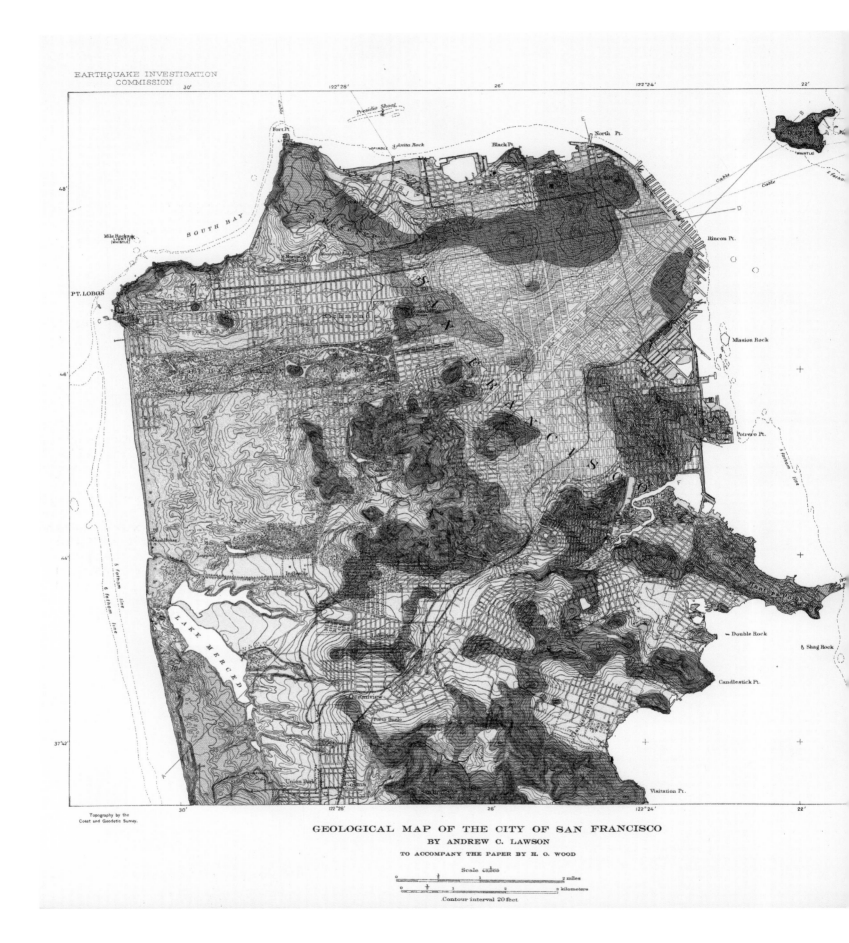

GEOLOGICAL MAP OF THE CITY OF SAN FRANCISCO

BY ANDREW C. LAWSON

TO ACCOMPANY THE PAPER BY H. O. WOOD

Scale 40,000

Contour interval 20 feet

LEGEND

Made land.

Pleistocene and Recent Marine sands, sandstone and alluvium.

Pliocene-Merced Series Sandstone, pebbly conglomerate, sandy shales, clays and one thin ash bed.

Serpentinized peridotite intrusive in the Franciscan.

Spheroidal basalt and diabase chiefly intrusive in the Franciscan.

Sandstone—Stratigraphic position not well determined—probably above the formations listed below.

Upper formation of radiolarian chert.

Middle formation of sandstone.

Lower formation of radiolarian chert.

Lower formation of sandstone.

Franciscan Series

Original shore line of city.

San Francisco's Great Earthquake

HOW 1906 CHANGED THE CITY, AND SCIENCE, FOREVER

CREATED *1908*
SOURCE *David Rumsey Map Collection, Stanford Libraries*

The violent shaking roused San Francisco at 5:12 a.m. on April 18, 1906. Buildings collapsed as the ground beneath them foundered; roads cracked and buckled; gas lines were severed; water mains broke. The ensuing fire nearly erased the city. Just minutes after the quake, gas leaking from busted pipes ignited fires that burned for four days, devouring around 500 blocks and at least 28,000 buildings. More than 200,000 people—over half of the city's population—were left homeless. At least 3,000 people died.

The magnitude 7.8 quake lasted no more than a minute, but it had a huge and lasting impact. Its effects are still being felt today.

Within weeks of the disaster, citizens eager to prove they had not been broken by the devastation began resurrecting their city. A decade later, they had rebuilt everything that had been knocked down or burned.

Geologists all across the Bay Area also quickly got to work. Within hours, dozens of scientists were documenting the damage. Within days, the governor formalized the effort into the State Earthquake Investigation Commission and appointed Andrew C. Lawson, the head of the University of California geology department, to lead it. What these geologists learned would change the science of earthquakes forever. It would also show that in the rush to rebuild, San Franciscans were putting future generations at higher risk.

Lawson's team published a report in 1908 that is one of the most important the earth sciences has ever produced. Known to geologists simply as the Lawson report, it contains at least six major revelations about the nature of earthquakes and their effects. It laid the foundation for all we've learned about them since then and helped set earth science on a path that would lead to the theory of plate tectonics more than 50 years later.

The San Andreas fault that unleashed the massive quake wasn't even on the geologic map of the area Lawson had made just a decade earlier. But after the quake, the team was able to trace the fault for 600 miles (around 960 km)—nearly the entirety of the 800-mile (1,300 km)-long fault—all the way to Los Angeles. In places near the earthquake's epicenter, they found fences and roads that had been cut by the fault and offset by as much as 20 feet (6 m). They were surprised that, unlike most other faults they had studied, this one moved horizontally rather than

LEFT Andrew Lawson made this detailed geologic map of San Francisco after the 1906 quake. Colors represent the different kinds of rock and sediment underlying the city. Red is hard rock like basalt or diabase, green indicates sandstone, and yellow is man-made land.

RIGHT Immediately after the 1906 quake hit San Francisco, gas leaking from severed pipes started a fire. The flames destroyed a huge swath of the city, shown on this map from a scientific report published in 1908.

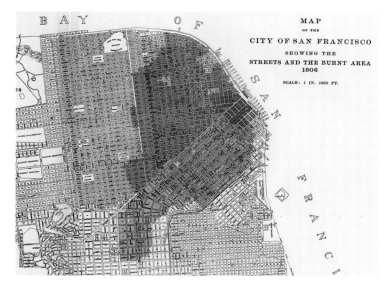

MAP OF THE CITY OF SAN FRANCISCO SHOWING THE STREETS AND THE BURNT AREA 1906

SCALE: 1 IN. 1850 FT.

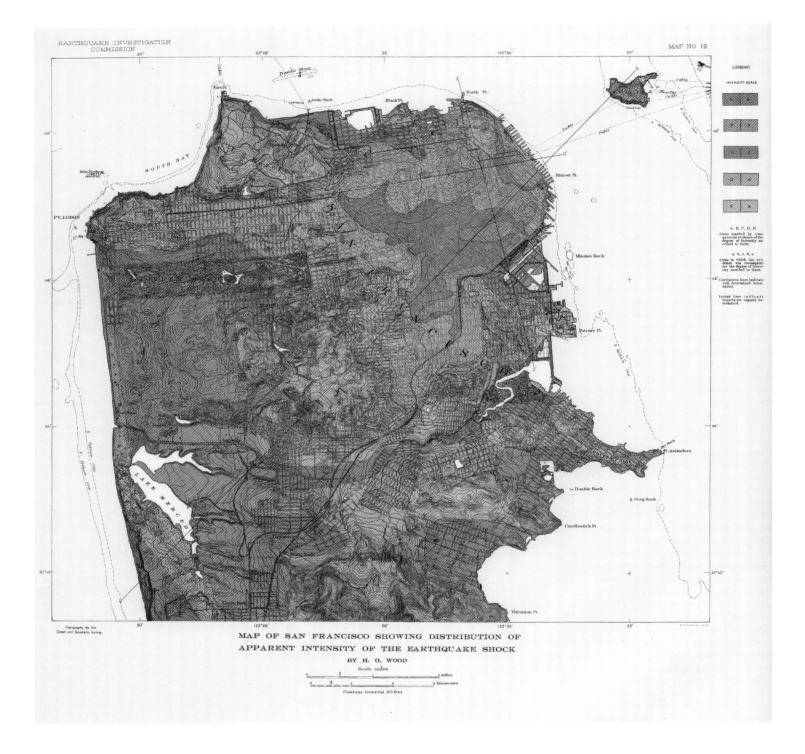

MAP OF SAN FRANCISCO SHOWING DISTRIBUTION OF
APPARENT INTENSITY OF THE EARTHQUAKE SHOCK
BY H. O. WOOD

ABOVE Engineers made this map of apparent shaking intensity in San Francisco during the 1906 quake by assessing the severity of damage to buildings. By comparing this map to the geologic map on page 194, Lawson's team discovered a relationship between the amount of damage suffered by buildings and the geology they were built on. Hard rock like diabase was relatively safe, and man-made land was the most dangerous.

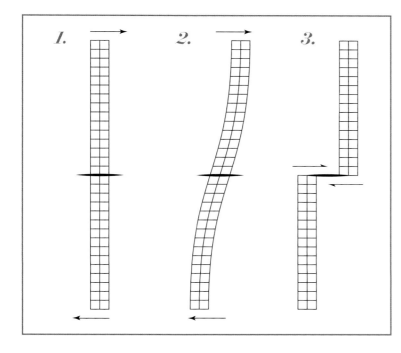

ABOVE The horizontal movement of tectonic plates in opposite directions strains the land along the fault at their border. Eventually the strain causes the two sides to overcome the friction along the fault and suddenly slip, causing an earthquake.

RIGHT Geologist G. K. Gilbert took this photo of a woman near the ruptured San Andreas fault south of San Francisco after the 1906 quake. The fault moved as much as 20 feet (6 m) horizontally in places.

vertically—an early clue that the San Andreas fault is the boundary between two massive tectonic plates slowly grinding past each other along the Earth's surface.

They also deduced that the 1906 quake was not the first major jolt the San Andreas had produced. The way the ground moved during the earthquake tended to accentuate topography, extending ridges and deepening valleys. They saw that those ridges and valleys had been slowly built by repeated earthquakes, which meant more were likely to happen in the future.

An even bigger discovery came from analyzing a series of U.S. Coast and Geodetic Survey maps made in the 50 years before the quake. The maps, made every decade or so by measuring the angles between landmarks, revealed that the ground miles away from the fault had been moving slowly prior to the 1906 quake, while the ground right next to the fault had been stuck. Geophysicist Harry Reid concluded that strain from some unknown force had been building up. The earthquake occurred when that strain overcame the friction holding the fault in place, causing the ground alongside it to leap forward and catch up with the motion of the ground surrounding it (see diagram above).

This idea is the basis for how we know where

earthquake risk is high in the world today. Reid reasoned that by measuring and monitoring strain over time, areas with a lot of accumulated strain—and thus at high risk of an earthquake—could be spotted. Today we have somewhere around 25,000 continuously recording GPS receivers all over the world doing exactly that.

Meanwhile, the engineers on Lawson's team were busy collecting the most extensive set of damage and shaking reports ever amassed for a single quake. They took note of everything: what type of buildings had suffered the most damage, the direction that headstones had fallen, and which way milk had spilled from pails. They learned that structures without proper bracing and buildings made of unreinforced masonry could least withstand shaking.

They assembled the map opposite of estimated shaking intensity based on the damage they saw. When the map was compared to Lawson's updated geologic map (see page 194), they made a critical discovery: The shaking intensity and damage varied based on the geology beneath the structures. Buildings on solid bedrock fared much better than those on softer sediment. Ground made of soggy landfill, such as the gray area on the shaking map north of Rincon Point on the northeastern

edge of the city, was the most dangerous of all.

While the scientists were learning all of this, San Franciscans were busy erecting replacement structures atop acres of man-made landfill that was virtually guaranteed to cause severe damage in the next big quake. And when that quake happens, the toll will likely be much greater than in 1906, when fewer than a million people lived in the greater Bay Area. Today there are more than seven million. Many structures built in the wake of 1906 still need structural reinforcement. And San Francisco's extremely competitive real estate market encourages people to ignore the uneven dangers of the area's geology.

Estimates of the economic losses from a 1906-size earthquake in the Bay Area today top $200 billion—twice that of Hurricane Katrina—the vast majority of it uninsured. Hundreds of thousands of people will be displaced; hundreds of roads will be closed; the Sacramento Delta levees may fail; thousands could die.

As we've known since the Lawson report was published more than a century ago, the next major quake isn't a matter of if, but when. But the Bay Area is also still home to cutting-edge earth science and structural engineering, and the San Andreas fault continues to inspire geologists and seismologists to break new ground. ✳

Cities Versus Species

AN ATLAS SHOWING WHERE URBANIZATION THREATENS BIODIVERSITY COULD BE A GUIDE TO SAVING WHAT'S LEFT

CREATED *2017*
CREATOR *Atlas for the End of the World project*

In 1570, the Flemish cartographer Abraham Ortelius published the first modern atlas, *Theatrum Orbis Terrarum (Theater of the World)*. The Age of Discovery was just kicking into high gear, and Ortelius's artfully drawn maps showed what many Europeans must have seen as a brand-new world full of recently discovered lands waiting to be colonized and exploited.

That world no longer exists, says Richard Weller, a landscape architect at the University of Pennsylvania and leader of an online project, Atlas for the End of the World. The apocalyptic-sounding title doesn't refer to the end of *the* world, Weller says, but to the end of the world as Ortelius knew it. "It's the end of the world where we thought nature was an infinite resource and we could exploit it without consequence," Weller says.

The main focus of the atlas is the 36 biodiversity hotspots targeted for conservation by the United Nations. The hotspots, like the Indo-Burma hotspot in Southeast Asia to the right, ignore international boundaries; they're defined by scientific consensus as areas rich in plant and animal species that live nowhere else and face significant threats of extinction. As of 2017, only 14 of the hotspots had met the UN goal of protecting 17 percent of the land and inland waterways within them. The atlas identifies exactly where the shortcomings are with detailed maps of each hotspot that show the different ecosystems within them and the threats they face from human activity such as mining, agriculture, and urbanization.

A major theme of the atlas is that conservation and urbanization are intertwined. There are 422 cities of at least 300,000 people within the 36 biodiversity hotspots. Many of these are growing, and few have any systematic urban planning, which sets the stage for future conflicts. Weller and his coauthor used urban growth predictions from researchers at Yale University to map where these conflicts are likely to occur.

This is where Weller thinks his colleagues in landscape architecture and urban planning can play a larger role. "What we do is model different scenarios and look for opportunities to absorb population growth so that it reshapes the city in a certain way," he says. The idea is to steer growth away from the most vulnerable areas. The challenge is that every city is unique and requires its own plan for balancing growth with the impacts on biodiversity.

It won't be easy, Weller says, but any efforts to protect and restore ecosystems are a hopeful sign that our relationship with the natural world has improved since Ortelius's day. ✳

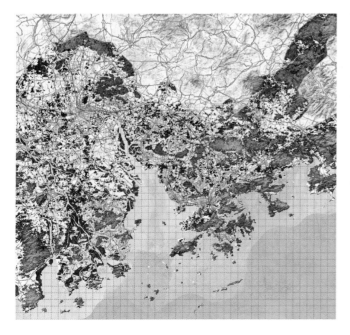

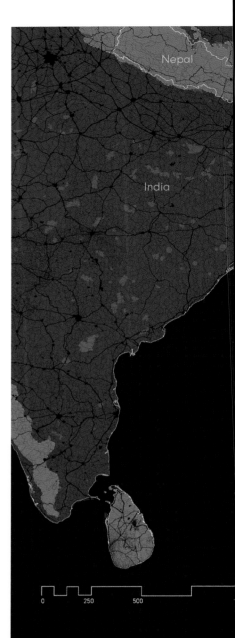

RIGHT In the Indo-Burma biodiversity hotspot in Southeast Asia, just over 13 percent of land is protected (shown in green). The number falls short of the 17 percent goal set by the UN but is closer than in many other areas.

· ·

LEFT Red indicates areas of likely conflict between urban growth and biodiversity in places with remaining native vegetation (shown in dark green) in the region around the Chinese cities of Hong Kong, Shenzhen, and Guangzhou.

INDO-BURMA
2,655,063 km²

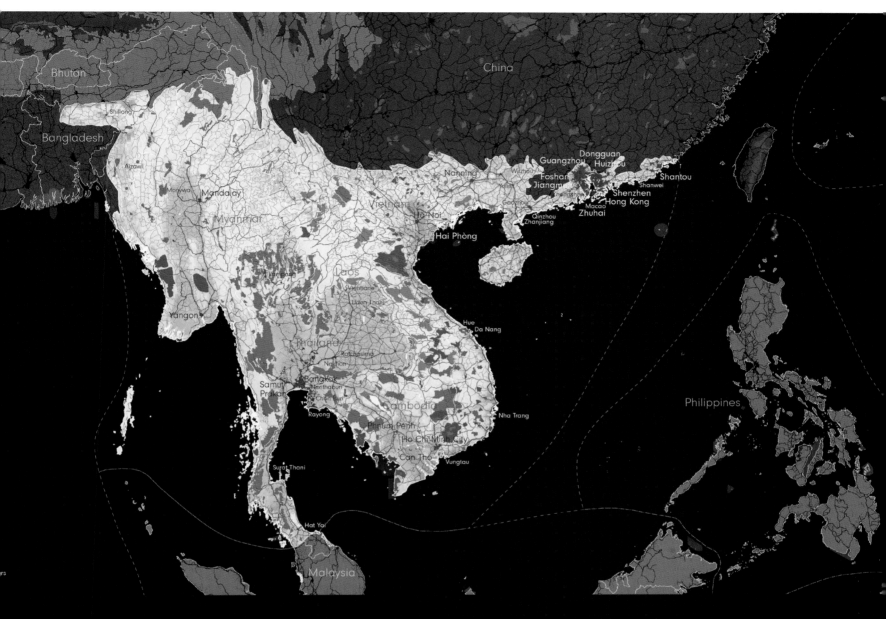

BIODIVERSITY TARGET

2020 TARGET: 17% protected

2015: 13.4% PROTECTED
8.2% I-IV
2.5% V-VI
2.7% NA

- Indo-Burma Hotspot
- Neighboring Hotspot
- Protected Area (IUCN Category I-IV)
- Protected Area (IUCN Category V-VI)
- Protected Area (IUCN Category NA)
- Urban Area
- Agriculture (0-100% landuse)
- —— Roads
- —— Railroads

The Art of Mapping the Brain

THE BEAUTIFUL, ENDURING DRAWINGS OF SANTIAGO RAMÓN Y CAJAL

CREATED *1887–1934*
SOURCE *Instituto Cajal*

Growing up in Spain in the middle of the 19th century, Santiago Ramón y Cajal was obsessed with drawing, a self-diagnosed graphomaniac. He wanted to be an artist, but his father, a physician, was determined that his son would become a doctor. As a young man, Cajal agreed to help his father teach anatomy. He found that he had a talent for drawing anatomical dissections, so he decided to enroll in medical school. Five decades later, Cajal had made nearly 3,000 drawings of the brain, won a Nobel Prize, and changed neuroscience forever.

Early in his career, Cajal gravitated toward the relatively new field of histology, the study of the anatomy of cells and tissues under the microscope. By placing extremely thin slices of stained tissue between two thin glass plates, scientists could see the microscopic structures within. Toward the end of the century, the Italian scientist Camillo Golgi discovered a new method of staining tissue that elucidated individual nerve cells like never before. Suddenly Cajal could see single neurons, wonderfully intricate cells painted black against a light background.

He began drawing what he saw: a stunning variety of sizes, shapes, and patterns of neurons that appeared to have all sorts of different roles in the brain. He drew pyramidal neurons in the cerebral cortex of a rabbit, astrocytes in a human hippocampus, glial cells in the spinal cord of a mouse. He had the advantage of being both a brilliant observer and a skilled artist. By carefully mapping dead brain cells, Cajal began to envision how the living brain works, leading him to several major insights that helped lay the foundation for modern neuroscience.

He surmised that neurons are individual cells that interact with other neurons through close contact rather than a continuous network, as Golgi believed. Cajal made another leap in our understanding of how the brain works by closely studying and drawing neurons in the retina, the thin layer of light-sensitive cells at the back of the eye (opposite).

OPPOSITE Santiago Ramón y Cajal's drawing of the retina maps out the major layers of cells in the light-sensitive structure at the back of the eye, including photoreceptors that are activated by light (layers B, C, and D), relay neurons (F), and ganglion cells (H).

LEFT Inspired by Louis Daguerre's invention of a practical photographic process, Cajal taught himself how to take, develop, and print photographs. He took self-portraits throughout his life, including this one in his early 30s in his laboratory in Valencia, Spain.

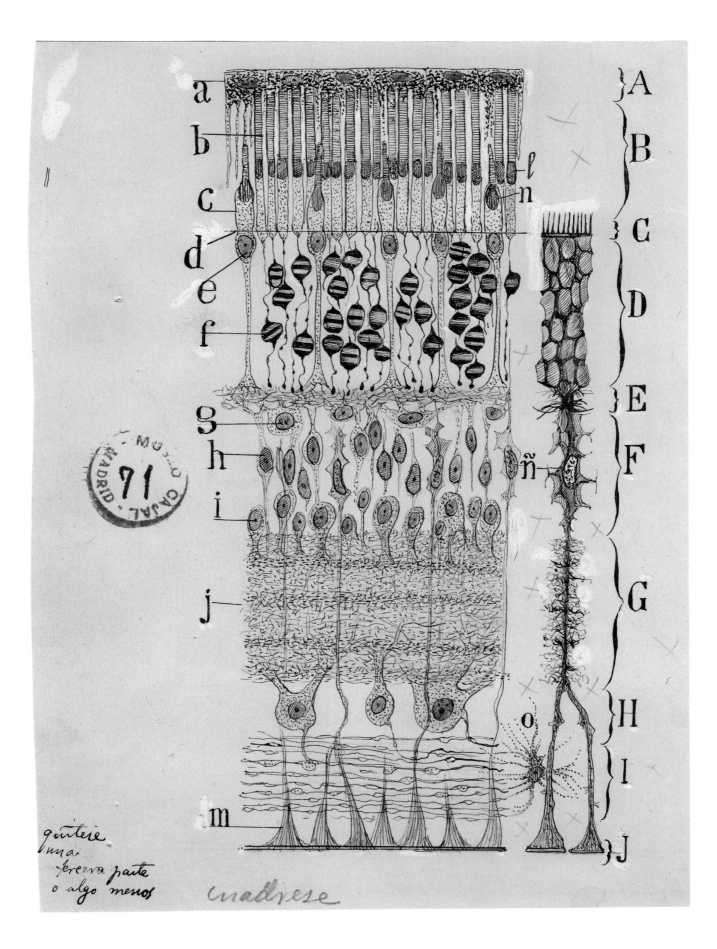

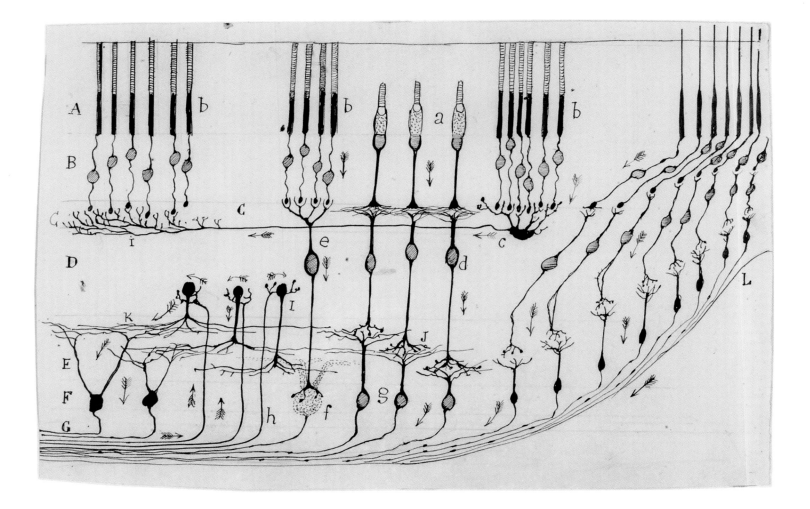

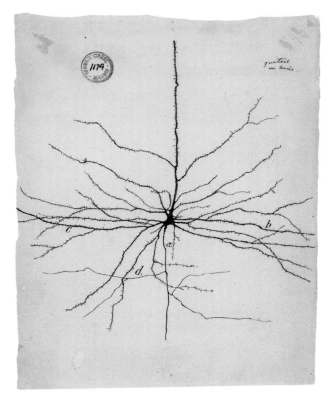

Golgi's stain had shown scientists that neurons have two kinds of appendages: thin, short dendrites that radiate away from the cell body and a single, thicker axon that could be much longer. Cajal observed that the dendrites of neurons in the retina were oriented toward the eye's photoreceptors, which are activated by light entering the eye. The axons extended toward the brain. From this arrangement, Cajal deduced that the purpose of dendrites was to receive information from the world and transmit it to the cell body and that axons would then transmit signals to other neurons. In his diagram of the retina above, Cajal used arrows to map the direction of information flow through the layers of the retina and out to a region of the brain called the thalamus.

"He looked at brains and just inferred things no one else could see," says Harvard University neuroscientist Jeff Lichtman.

A century earlier, Luigi Galvani's experiments using electricity generated during thunderstorms to stimulate muscles in dead frog legs showed that the brain uses electrical signals to transmit information. Cajal's work showed which way those electrical impulses might flow through neurons. He used this revelation to decipher and map out the neural circuits in many other parts of the brain, work that countless scientists have continued to build on.

"He was the explorer," says neuroscientist Larry Swanson of the University of Southern California. "You could almost think of him as Columbus going out and creating those first maps that then people could follow."

In 1906, Cajal and Golgi shared the Nobel Prize for Physiology or Medicine "in recognition of their work on the structure of the nervous system." Though Golgi had been wrong about that structure, his staining method was critical to Cajal's observations. A member of the Nobel committee said of Cajal's contribution to neuroscience, "It is he who has built almost the whole framework of our structure of thinking."

Though countless illustrations, diagrams, and maps of the nervous system have been made since Cajal's time, professors today still use his drawings to help budding neuroscientists navigate their way around the structure and function of the brain. ✳

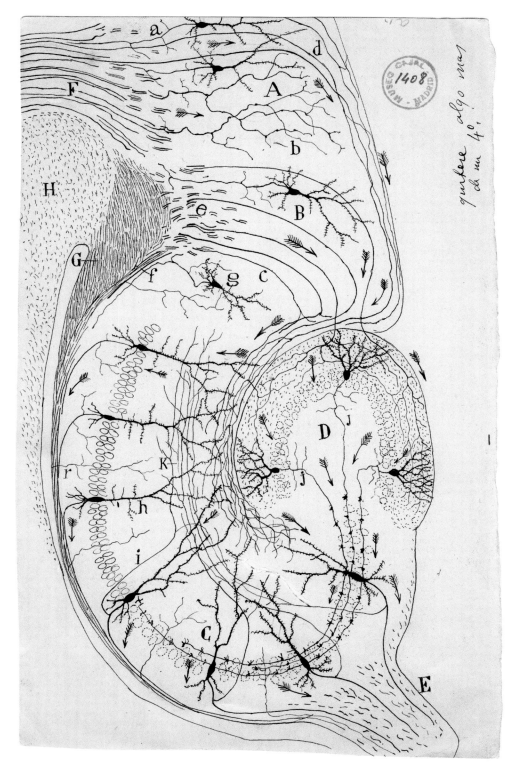

Planetary Cartography

THE GEOLOGY OF THE SOLAR SYSTEM MAKES FOR OTHERWORLDLY MAPS

CREATED *1977–1978*
SOURCE *U.S. Geological Survey*

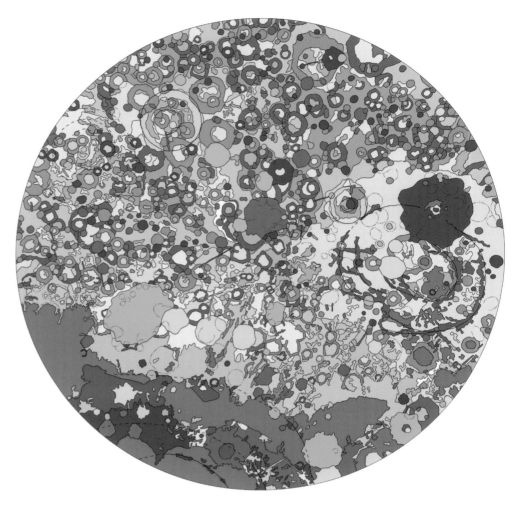

To the untrained eye, geologic maps can resemble abstract art. But closer observation reveals patterns that look natural, even somewhat familiar—unless the map is of another world.

These U.S. Geological Survey maps of the moon are about as alien looking as any map you'll ever see. They're part of a remarkable, psychedelic-looking collection of maps of planets and moons created by geologists in the 1970s and 1980s based on an influx of data from space missions, including the Apollo moon missions and the Mariner 9 Mars orbiter.

The strangeness of these moon maps is accentuated by the absence of symbols, labels, and underlying topography, leaving the colors that represent different rock types and ages. These bare-bones maps were created as the U.S. Geological Survey digitized its catalog of astrogeologic maps for use with modern mapping software. Part of that process separates different types of information into digital layers. These isolated map layers showing just the rock units are striking.

The lunar landscape is dominated by the scars of many thousands of meteors and asteroids that have crashed into it over billions of years, which is why these maps have so many circular shapes. At first glance, they look very different from geologic maps of Earth, but they are based on the same techniques developed to map our planet. They've been adapted, of course, as it's not (yet) possible to walk along a fault on Mars or sample a rock on Mercury. But basic geologic principles hold true on other worlds: The oldest rocks are generally on the bottom, with younger rocks on top.

Scientists use what they know about Earth to extract clues about alien landscapes from images and data collected remotely. Photo-graphs from both land-based telescopes and spacecraft reveal differences in texture, brightness, and topography that help scientists recognize the type and age of the rock formations. For example, the debris that gets thrown out of an asteroid impact crater tends to be rough and bright, and the crater rim is usually tall and sharp. But as time goes by, the rim is worn down and the debris becomes smoother and less reflective. And the relative density of the craters is a clue to the age of the surrounding terrain: Areas with fewer craters are usually younger than areas that have had more time to be pummeled by asteroids.

Geologists are always updating their maps based on new data from lunar missions. When Apollo astronauts brought back more than 800 pounds (360 kg) of rock samples from the moon between 1969 and 1972, geologists used this rare opportunity to adjust and reinterpret their maps. The lessons they've learned have also helped scientists map other rocky planets and moons in the solar system.

Today scientists often have data from x-ray, gamma ray, infrared, and ultraviolet detectors that can help them distinguish the different chemical compositions of extraterrestrial surfaces. Gravitational, magnetic, and digital elevation data reveal even more about the outside and inside of planets. As spacecraft bearing ever more sophisticated instruments explore other worlds, planetary geologic maps will only get better. ✳

ABOVE Impact craters pepper the north side of the moon in this 1978 geologic map. The colors represent different types and ages of rock.

OPPOSITE The big splash of blue on this 1977 map of the west side of the moon is the 580-mile (930 km)-wide Orientale Basin, one of the largest lunar impact craters, formed around 3.8 billion years ago. The bright red at its center (and in the upper right of the map) represents more recent lava flows.

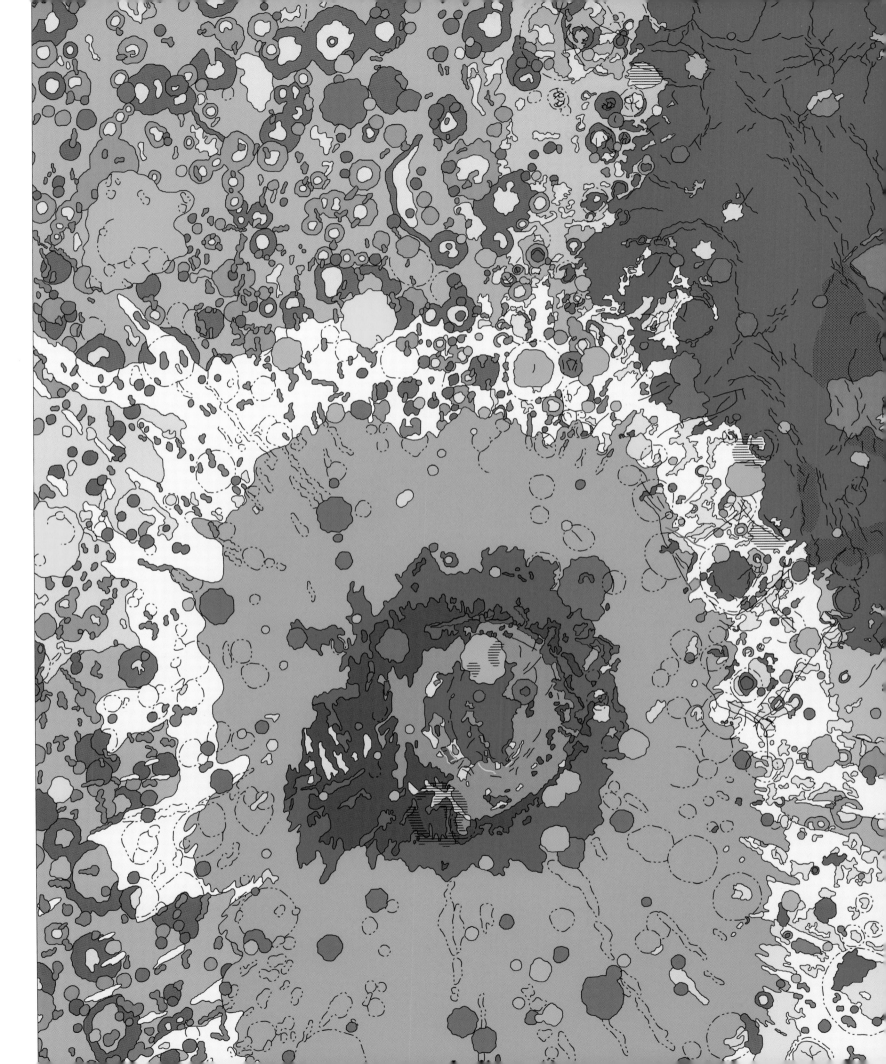

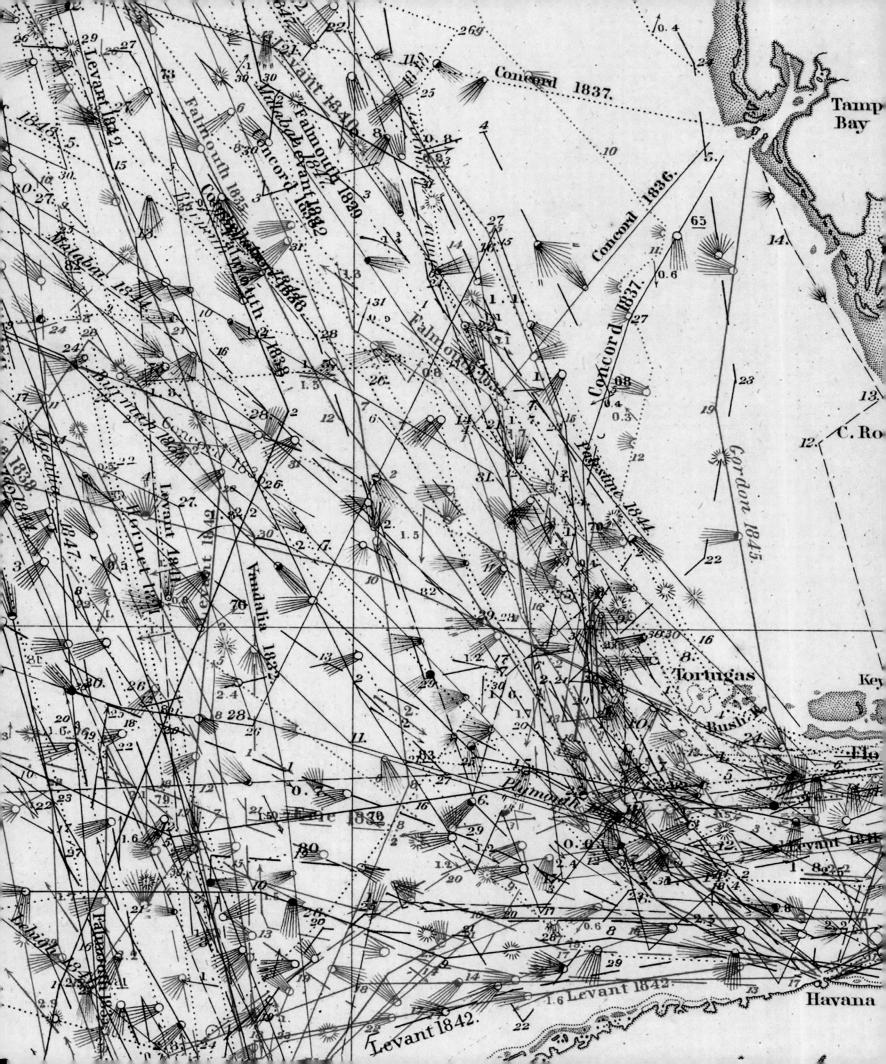

Scientist of the Seas

HOW A U.S. NAVAL OFFICER FOUNDED THE FIELD OF OCEANOGRAPHY AND REVOLUTIONIZED SEA TRAVEL

CREATED *1850s*
SOURCE *American Geographical Society Library and others*

If not for a stagecoach accident that disqualified him for duty at sea, Matthew Fontaine Maury probably wouldn't have become the father of modern oceanography. Maury, the son of a Virginia farmer, had enlisted in the U.S. Navy in 1825 and immediately taken an interest in the principles of navigation. One of his first assignments was on the *Vincennes,* the first American warship to circumnavigate the globe.

Maury seemed destined for a career at sea, but in 1839, he was flung from the top of a stagecoach and suffered a dislocated knee and badly broken leg. It took him years to recover. When he returned to the Navy, he was relegated to a desk job, put in charge of the Depot of Charts and Instruments. A less ambitious man might have sleepwalked through his duties, which involved maintaining the Navy's chronometers—crucial pieces of equipment used to determine longitude at sea—and other navigational tools and records. But Maury saw an opportunity.

A voracious reader, he realized that the depot's disorganized collection of old captains' logs contained an untapped trove of data on navigation at sea. Poring over the logbooks, he began to see patterns. Too often, navigators stuck to the shortest route, only to be delayed by unfavorable winds and currents. Longer routes that took advantage of these forces of nature instead of fighting them were often faster.

The logbooks revealed another navigational complication that was largely unappreciated at the time: Currents and winds shifted with the seasons, so the best route in, say, March might be treacherous in August. What was needed, Maury decided, was a new kind of chart that showed the fastest, safest routes for a given time of year.

Maury's *Wind and Current Chart of the North Atlantic,* first published in 1848, was packed with observations made by hundreds of ship captains (on the zoomed-in detail to the left, the names of individual ships are legible). He used little brush-like symbols to indicate the strength and variability of the wind at specific locations, as reported in the logbooks. The length of the lines indicates wind speed,

Matthew Fontaine Maury's maps of ocean winds and currents, based on entries made by ship captains in their logbooks, helped make sea travel faster and safer. The detail opposite is from an 1850 edition of Maury's *Wind and Current Chart of the North Atlantic* (left). Each colored line indicates a specific voyage. The brushlike symbols reflect notes recorded in the captain's log on wind speed and variability.

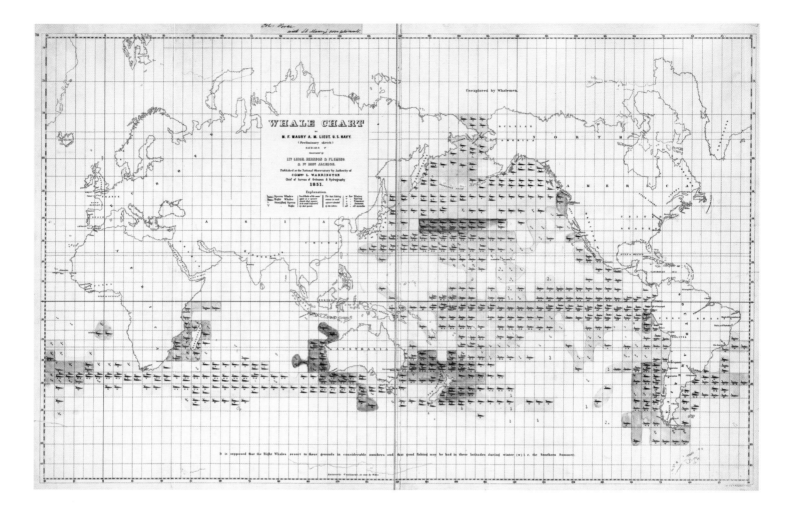

ABOVE During the American Civil War, Confederate raiders used Maury's whale chart to target Northern whaling ships, knowing they'd be likely to find them in parts of the ocean that were home to whales.

OPPOSITE This map from Maury's *Physical Geography of the Sea* shows favorable sailing routes. The tiny ships have their sails trimmed according to how favorable the winds are in that spot—one of Maury's innovations for packing in a lot of information.

LEFT This portrait of Maury was taken around the time he organized the first international conference on marine meteorology in Brussels in 1853. Maury urged other nations to collaborate on gathering data on winds and currents.

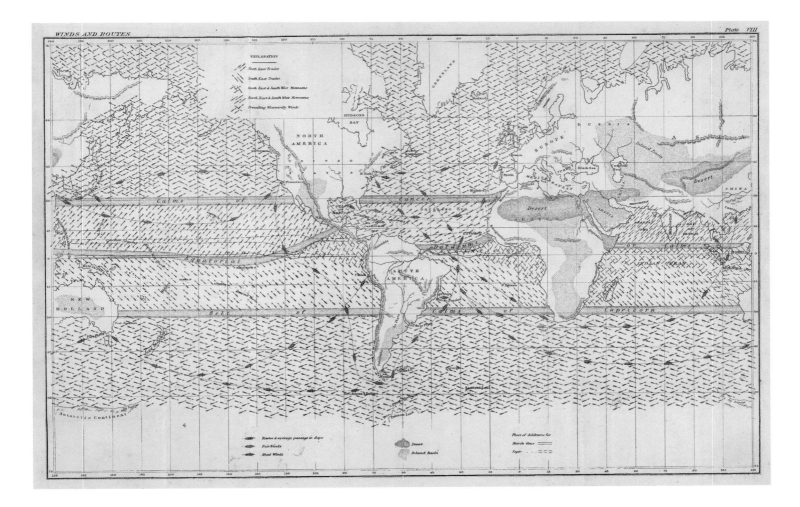

and the width of the brush indicates whether the direction of the wind was consistent or variable.

Sailors had long known about currents and winds, of course, but their knowledge was mostly anecdotal, shared by word of mouth. Nobody looked for patterns across entire oceans or across time. Maury did, then distilled it all down to practical sailing directions. His maps and charts showed sailors the quickest path through the bands of doldrums in the tropics that could bog down sailing ships for days or even weeks. He showed them how to adjust their routes to follow the Gulf Stream as it drifted northward in summer to take advantage of this powerful current on the trip from North America to Europe.

Few sea captains were willing to try Maury's routes at first. Out of habit and superstition, they stuck to the ones they'd been sailing for years. Then, in what became a widely publicized trip, a Baltimore ship captain used one of Maury's routes and saved 17 days on a trip to Rio de Janeiro with a shipment of flour. Emboldened, he trusted Maury again on the return trip and

made it back to Baltimore with a shipment of Brazilian coffee 35 days ahead of schedule. More captains began to sail Maury's routes, and with similar success. When the gold rush broke out in California, the time savings became even more dramatic: Maury's route saved more than 40 days on what had been a six-month trip from the East Coast down around Cape Horn and up to San Francisco.

To refine his charts and extend them to other oceans, Maury distributed logs that sea captains could fill out and return to him. Having seen the benefits of Maury's scientific approach, many were happy to oblige. By 1851 a thousand ships were regularly sending him data. One shipmaster wrote a note of gratitude to Maury, telling him, "I yet feel that until I took up your work I had been traversing the ocean blindfold[ed]."

As the reports flooded in, Maury extended his sea charts to include weather patterns, water temperature, and even whale migrations. In 1855 he published his best-selling *The Physical Geography of the Sea,* the first textbook on oceanog-

raphy. Among other things, it included the first map showing the topography of the seafloor, which was used to determine the placement of the first transatlantic telegraph cable in 1858.

When the American Civil War started, Maury faced an agonizing choice between his native Virginia and the Navy to which he'd devoted his life. With a heavy heart, he handed in his resignation. In the hands of the Confederacy, his maps, made to help U.S. Navy and merchant sailors, quickly became weapons against them. Confederate raiders hunted Union ships throughout the war, sinking hundreds. By defining tracks in the sea for safe travel, Maury's maps showed the Confederates where to find their targets—and where to hide.

Deeply conflicted about the war, Maury spent much of it, and several years after, in exile in England. He finally returned to Virginia in 1868 and lived out his days teaching and writing. Maury died in 1873, but every nautical chart published since reflects his enduring contributions to the science of the seas. ✳

EXPERI

HUMAN

ENCES

Capturing the Human Condition

The idea of mapping things that aren't part of the physical landscape is relatively new in cartography. It took off in earnest only in the mid-19th century as mapmakers began investigating subjects like race, immigration, and criminal activity. Some of these maps were a force for good, and some were quite the opposite. They all reveal something about the human experience that wasn't otherwise apparent.

The map to the right is a perfect example. It's part of a famous late 19th-century inquiry that revealed that poverty was more prevalent in London than most people realized, and more intricately woven into the city's neighborhoods. The maps became instruments for social change, lending weight to antipoverty efforts.

Around the same time, the city supervisors of San Francisco conducted a neighborhood survey with a very different purpose. Launched at a peak of anti-Chinese immigrant sentiment, the survey—and the map that came out of it (see page 214)—supported the foregone conclusion that the city's Chinatown was a den of iniquity and a threat to the rest of the city. If the London poverty maps reflect the better angels of human nature, the Chinatown map reflects its darker impulses.

The maps in this chapter tackle all sorts of social, cultural, and political issues. From beautiful hand-painted scrolls of an ancient Japanese road walked by pilgrims and samurai (see page 218) to modern maps using satellite data to track human activity (see page 230), they reveal something about the human experience at a given time and place. ➺

MAPPING POVERTY
(1898–99, Library of the London School of Economics and Political Science)

In 1886, a wealthy businessman named Charles Booth decided to fund his own survey of living conditions in London because he was skeptical of a recent report that a quarter of the city's residents lived in poverty. In fact, he discovered, it was more than a third. In this detail from a digital reconstruction of Booth's maps, the wealthy Marylebone neighborhood abuts the more diverse Fitzrovia. Yellow indicates well-off areas, reddish areas are middle-class, and blues represent poor areas. Booth reserved black for the "Lowest class. Vicious, semi-criminal."

Opium, Brothels, and Prejudice in Chinatown

A MAP COMMISSIONED BY SAN FRANCISCO CITY SUPERVISORS REVEALS A THINLY VEILED ANTI-IMMIGRANT AGENDA

CREATED *1885*
SOURCE *David Rumsey Map Collection, Stanford Libraries*

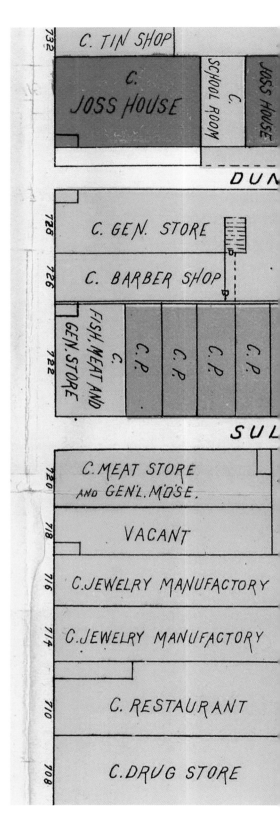

Chinese laborers came to California in droves in the mid-1800s, lured by work building the first transcontinental railroad. Twelve thousand Chinese immigrants worked on the railroad. When the work was done in 1869, many of them settled in San Francisco and set up laundries, shoe repair shops, and other businesses. The City by the Bay may be famously liberal now, but many residents at the time saw this as a serious problem.

Anti-Chinese sentiment was rampant, and the map on pages 216 and 217 was one manifestation of it (a detail is shown to the right). The map covered a six-block area in what was—and still is—San Francisco's Chinatown, accompanying a blatantly racist report issued in 1885 by the city supervisors that purported to show that the area was a hotbed of disease and moral depravity. "The Chinese must go!" was a popular slogan. Many felt that Chinatown was putting the entire city at risk.

Folk temples, or "joss houses," are marked in red and described in the report as an indication of moral decrepitude. "Idols of the most hideous form and feature squat upon their altars," according to the report, which goes on to suggest that these idols granted worshippers license to commit crimes and indulge in all manner of vice.

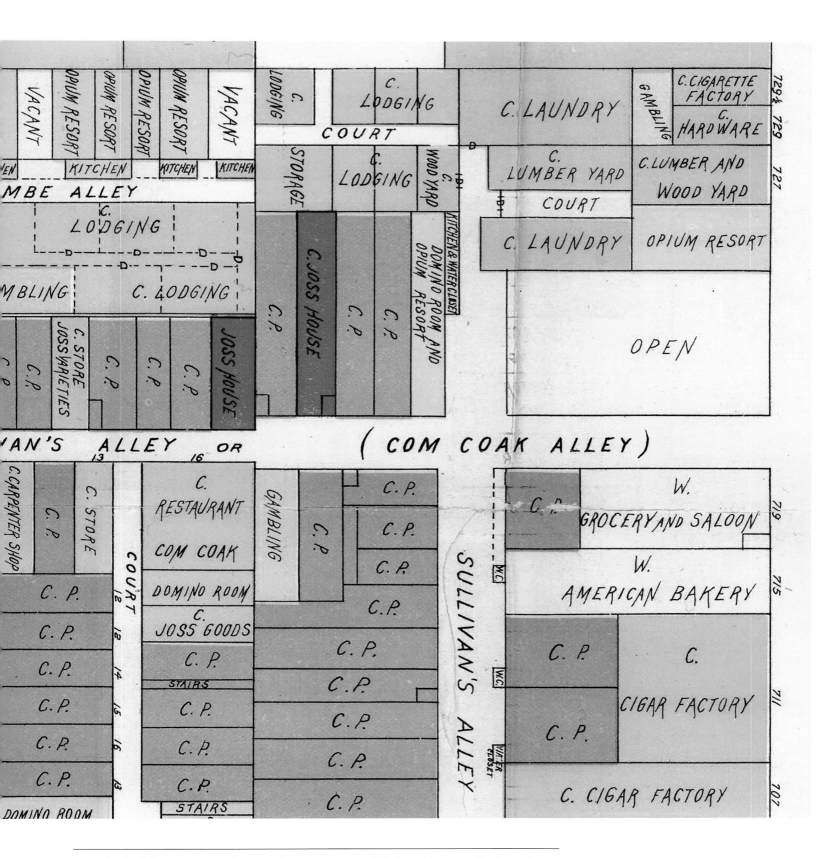

The map contains the following labels:

VACANT · OPIUM RESORT · OPIUM RESORT · OPIUM RESORT · OPIUM RESORT · VACANT · C. LODGING · C. LODGING · C. LODGING · C. LAUNDRY · GAMBLING · C. CIGARETTE FACTORY · C. HARDWARE

KITCHEN · KITCHEN · KITCHEN · COURT · C. STORAGE · C. LODGING · C. WOOD YARD · C. LUMBER YARD · C. LUMBER AND WOOD YARD

..MBE ALLEY · C. LODGING · COURT

C. LODGING · C. JOSS HOUSE · C.P. · C.P. · C.P. · DOMINO ROOM AND OPIUM RESORT · KITCHEN & WATER CLOSET · C. LAUNDRY · OPIUM RESORT

..MBLING · C. LODGING · C. STORE JOSS VARIETIES · C.P. · C.P. · C.P. · JOSS HOUSE · C.P. · OPEN

..AN'S · ALLEY · OR · (COM COAK ALLEY)

13 · 16

C.P. · C.P. · C. STORE · C. RESTAURANT COM COAK · GAMBLING · C.P. · C.P. · C.P. · C.P. · W. GROCERY AND SALOON · 719

C. CARPENTER SHOP · C.P. · COURT · DOMINO ROOM · C. JOSS GOODS · C.P. · C.P. · W. AMERICAN BAKERY · 715

C.P. · 12 · C.P. · STAIRS · C.P. · SULLIVAN'S ALLEY · W.C. · C.P. · C. CIGAR FACTORY · 711

C.P. · 14 · C.P. · C.P. · W.C. · C.P.

C.P. · 15 · 16 · C.P. · C.P. · WATER CLOSET · C.P. · 707

C.P. · 13 · C.P. · C.P. · C. CIGAR FACTORY

DOMINO ROOM · STAIRS

729½ · 729 · 727

ABOVE This detail from an 1885 map shows a section of San Francisco's Chinatown that was packed with opium resorts (yellow), gambling houses (pink), and houses of prostitution (green).

OPPOSITE This photo, taken around the turn of the 20th century, shows the scene outside one of the many joss houses—traditional Chinese temples— marked in red on the map.

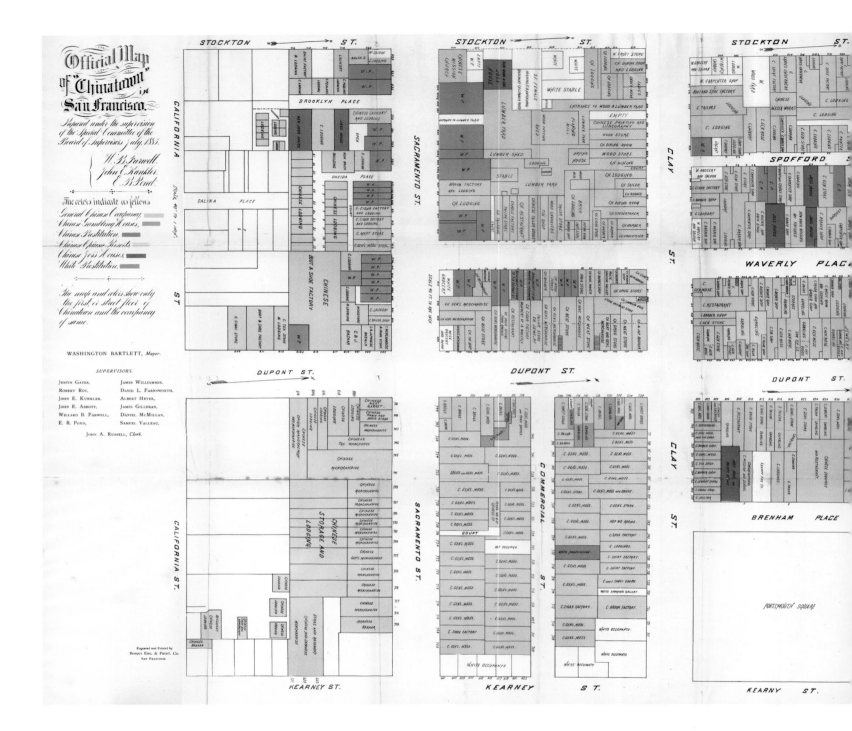

The report claims to be the result of a dispassionate investigation into living conditions in Chinatown. It argues that Chinatown is a reservoir of filth and disease that threatens public health. In hindsight, it's clear that the real issue was something very different: the perception that immigrants were stealing jobs from American citizens.

The panic of 1873 had triggered an economic depression. Many unemployed easterners took the newly completed railroad west to seek work in the promised land of California, only to find that jobs weren't there. Many of the newcomers and other white residents blamed competition from Chinese immigrants, who were willing to work long hours for low wages.

In response to this perceived threat, San Francisco's supervisors passed a string of discriminatory laws in the 1870s. One prohibited merchants from carrying their goods on poles balanced on one shoulder, as was the Chinese custom. Another created an onerous tax on laundries that didn't have a horse (most Chinese laundries did not). Yet another prohibited renting rooms with less than 500 cubic feet (14 cubic m) of space per resident—a common condition in overcrowded Chinatown. In summer 1877, an anti-Chinese riot raged for two days, resulting in four deaths and more than $100,000 in property damage to Chinese-owned businesses. Twenty Chinese laundries were destroyed.

In 1882 Congress passed the Chinese Exclusion Act, which banned immigration of Chinese laborers nationwide. That law, as harsh as it was, did nothing about the immigrants who were already there, so the San Francisco supervisors commissioned a study to bolster the case for driving them out.

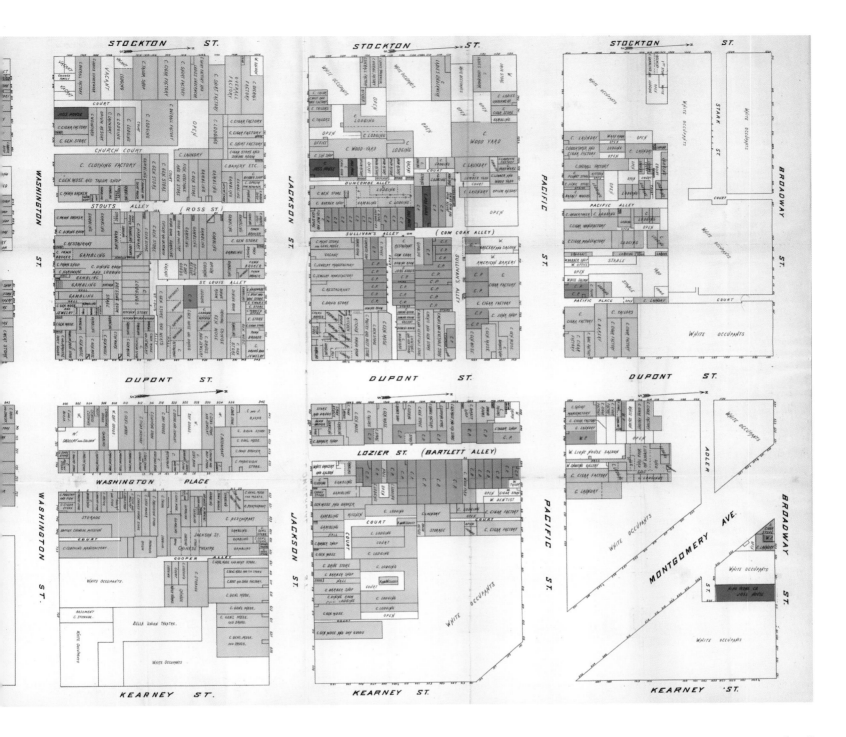

The inspectors documented 27 opium dens, whose conditions ranged from "filthy" to "very filthy." They also found roughly 150 gambling rooms, many equipped with trapdoors so occupants could escape in the event of a police raid. On the topic of prostitution, the report cites a local doctor. "I am satisfied, from my experience, that nearly all the boys in town who have venereal disease, contracted it in Chinatown," he opines. Perhaps more to the point, the report includes a remarkably precise estimate of the number of Chinese workers involved in making clothing and other goods in direct competition with American workers: 2,326.

Ironically, some of these supposed dangers made Chinatown a tourist attraction. Touts offered sensationalized slum tours, and less scrupulous guides led customers into the warren of buildings only to disappear, leaving them to find their own way out.

San Francisco's Chinatown is still a major tourist attraction, but today it's far more family friendly. The opium houses and brothels have been replaced by dim sum restaurants and souvenir shops. In 2010, the city elected the son of Chinese immigrants as its mayor. Yet for all this change, the prejudice and resentment that created the 1885 map are hardly things of the past. They're still very much with us today. ✳

The Chinatown map contains fascinating details about the businesses in the area, which included several stables and a preponderance of cigar factories. Blue squares mark white houses of prostitution. The letters W and C indicate whether a business was white or Chinese (whether this designation refers to the owners, clientele, or both is left unexplained).

The Legendary Tōkaidō Road

ANCIENT JAPANESE MAPS HELPED PEOPLE IMAGINE A FAMOUS TREK WITHOUT LEAVING HOME

CREATED *circa 18th century*
SOURCE *Library of Congress, Geography and Map Division*

Virtual travel was popular in 17th- and 18th-century Japan. People who couldn't afford to take a trip would imagine traveling along one of the country's official roads, called the Gokaidō, with the help of books, pictures, and maps. Everyone from lords and samurai to merchants and peasants could be found on the Gokaidō. Some traveled for practical or official administrative reasons, and others walked the roads as a pilgrimage, to inspire poetry, or just for fun. But a journey on foot along the entire Tōkaidō road—the most important of the Gokaidō—would take an average of 15 days, with several stops for rest and provisions, putting the cost out of reach for many people. Making the journey just once in a lifetime, often as a religious or spiritual pilgrimage, was a common aspiration. But those who couldn't afford it could take a fantasy trip with the help of a pictorial road map full of stories.

"It is something between a guidebook and an illustrated story about travel," says architect and spatial studies scholar Jilly Traganou of Parsons School of Design at The New School.

There was a thriving market for illustrated maps of the Tōkaidō, which stretched 319 miles (513 km) and linked Japan's two capitals, Tokyo (then called Edo) and Kyoto. The original Tōkaidō road maps were beautifully hand-painted for the shoguns, the military dictators of Japanese territories. Eventually many different versions were produced by carving the basic outlines into woodblocks that were then used like stamps to create copies. Depending on their intended audience, more details and sometimes color would be added. They might contain practical information like the prices of inns or the distances between points. Some of them included short stories, poems, or mythology about places on the road. Some had notes on sightseeing opportunities along the way, such as where to find the best views of Mount Fuji or what species of trees grew at the roadside.

Some of these maps were quite long, unwieldy, and clearly not meant for navigational purposes, such as a 117-foot (36 m)-long Tōkaidō road map held by the Library of Congress (a section of which is shown above). This map was probably an early, relatively expensive copy of one of the original maps, Traganou says, and it was likely meant to inspire imaginary journeys. The map depicts the dozens of way stations along the road, as well as river crossings, temples, and trees. The section above has a beautiful illustration of Mount Fuji, with a rainstorm to its right. Traganou suspects the rain was intended to recall a particular story or myth related to that area.

Tōkaidō road maps, which were made throughout most of Japan's Edo period (1603–1863), changed over time based on a public understanding of what people were interested in knowing about the road, Traganou says. Unlike typical maps

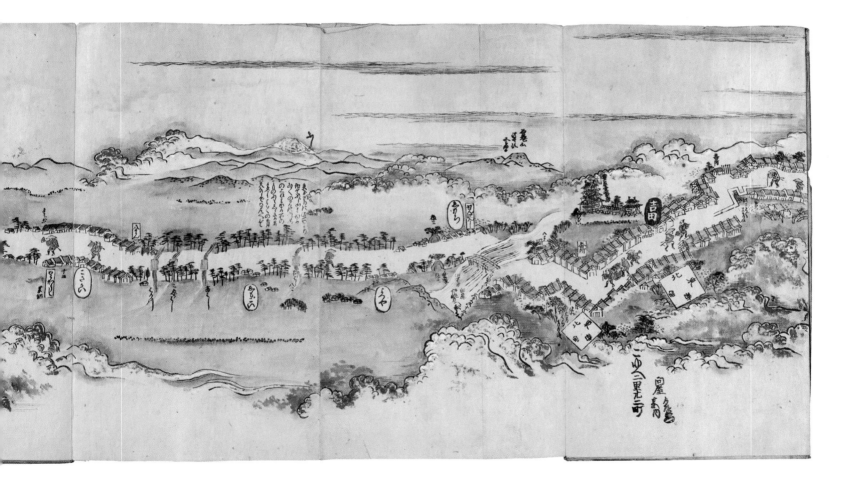

TOP This is a small piece of an 18th-century map of the Tōkaidō road between Tokyo and Kyoto held by the Library of Congress. It is made up of two 10.2-inch (26 cm)-tall scrolls that together are around 117 feet (36 m) long. Unwieldy, hand-painted Tōkaidō road maps like this one weren't designed to be used by travelers but were probably meant to inspire journeys of the imagination and were popular in Japan in the 17th and 18th centuries.

ABOVE This is one section of a Tōkaidō road map held by the University of Manchester. It's a 25.6-foot (7.8 m)-long accordion-folded map that is a later reprint of a 1690 map. Unlike the map at the Library of Congress, this one is filled with depictions of various travelers. The Tōkaidō road was one of the few places in Japan's stratified culture where commoners might come face-to-face with samurai and shoguns.

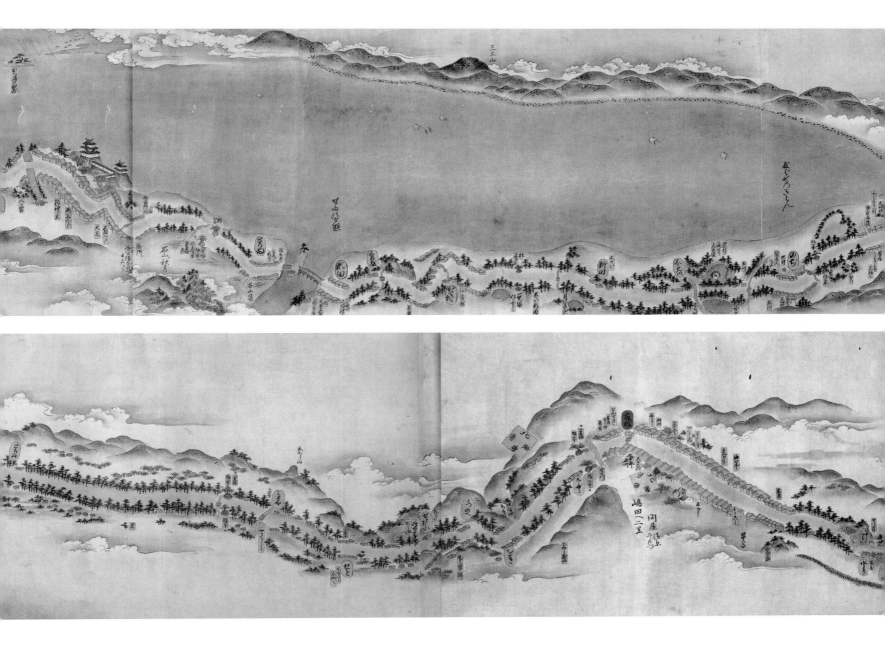

These three sections of the Tōkaidō road map at the Library of Congress cover only around a tenth of its entire length. Maps like this one often included practical information about roadside inns and shops and the distances between them, as well as stories, poems, and mythology related to different places along the road.

of the period that were made and controlled by the authorities, the Tōkaidō maps reflected the cultural interests of their intended audience. The mapmakers often worked with people who weren't typically involved in cartography, such as painters, poets, and travelers of the road.

Other versions of the map depicted the many different kinds of travelers who used the road (see page 219). Part of the appeal of the Tōkaidō was that it was the rare place in Japan where different classes might meet face-to-face. "This is not something that happens in the daily reality," Traganou says, "because the life is quite segregated in this period."

In particular, the Tōkaidō might offer a glimpse of some lords and their samurai. All the lords who controlled different parts of the terri-

tory had to move every few years, along with their families and armies, to Tokyo, where they would live in mansions for a while and be educated by the shogun. This meant that periodically there were massive ceremonial processions as various lords traveled the Tōkaidō to Tokyo.

Merchants, artisans, and other commoners weren't allowed to look at the lords (they had to keep their eyes cast downward), but there were opportunities for them to mingle with the warrior class. Samurai, considered the intellectuals of society, were forbidden by their lords to take part in the vibrant local nightlife, but the road offered a rare opportunity to escape their strict social rules. They would hide their swords to avoid being identified as samurai and sneak out to join the fun. ✳

Trump's America

Alaskan Outpost

Greater Puget Sound
Spokane
Eugene Estuary
Portland Sound
Missoula Lake
Great Falls
Helena
Bezeman
Boise
Billings
Tieton Tarn
Casper
Elko
Salt Lake
San Francisco Bay
Repo Reservoir
Denver Sea
Cheyenne
Colorado Springs
Bakersfield Hook
Las Vegas Harbor
Lake Flagstaff
Los Angeles Bay
San Diego Inlet
Phoenix
Santa Fe Sea
Bay of Tucson
El Paso Bay

Rolette Cove
International Falls
Minot
Bismarck
Standing Rock Pond
Fargo
Boundary Water
Pierre
Sioux Falls
Twin Cities Reservoir
Des Moines Pond
Lakota Lakes
Madison Lake
Omaha
Chicago Sea
Kansas City Isthmus
Champaign Kettle
St. Louis Pond
Indy Puddle
Cincinnati Slough

Detroit Delta
Cleveland Cove
Pittsburgh Puddle
Buffalo Bay
Ithaca Lake
Upstate
Connecticut Strait
Baxter Island
Augusta
Boston Harbor
New York Narrows
Acela Channel
D.C. Delta
Norfolk Sound
Charleston
Louisville Lake
Knoxville
Nashville Pond
Raleigh Bay
Columbia Lake
Wilmington

GREAT AMERICAN PLAINS
Amarillo
Tulsa
Oklahoma City
Fort Worth
Dallas Pond
Memphis Harbor
Miss. Lake
Atlanta Lake
Selma Sea
Jacksonville
San Antonio Lake
Austin Pond
Houston Bay
Laredo Gulf
Corpus Christi
Lake Disney
Tampa Bay
Miami Bay

By Tim Wallace/The New York Times

The Election That Created Two Americas

A PAIR OF UNCONVENTIONAL MAPS SHOWS HOW THE 2016 PRESIDENTIAL ELECTION ALTERED THE POLITICAL LANDSCAPE

CREATED *2016*
CREATOR *Tim Wallace,* New York Times

"For many Americans, it feels as if the 2016 election split the country in two," wrote Tim Wallace in the *New York Times* a week after the nation elected Donald Trump as its 45th president. Wallace, a geographer and cartographer on the *Times*'s graphics team, made these maps to capture the political landscape at a tumultuous moment in U.S. history.

Unlike the red-blue election maps that tend to dominate media reports during elections, Wallace's maps ignore state and county boundaries. Instead, he analyzed election results to estimate where the borders would fall between areas where the majority of people voted for Trump, the Republican candidate, and areas where the majority voted for his Democratic rival, Hillary Clinton. Then he mapped those areas as if they were two different countries.

Wallace's maps capture the growing divide in recent election cycles between urban areas, which lean toward the Democratic Party, and

Clinton's America

Seattle
Portland
Coos Bay
Northwest Sea
Montana Archipelago
Old Glacier Gulf
Reno Island
Salt Lake City
Wyoming Shallows
San Francisco
Bakersfield Bay
Las Vegas
Los Angeles
San Diego
Maricopa Sea
Denver
Albuquerque Island
Santa Fe
Tucson Island
El Paso Island
High Plains Sea
Hawaiian Islands
By Tim Wallace/The New York Times
Lutsen Island
Minneapolis
Milwaukee
Chicago
Des Moines
Detroit
Cleveland
Pittsburgh
Midwest Isles
Cincinnati
St. Louis
Great Bays
Buffalo
Maine Cove
Albany Narrows
New England
Boston
New York
Philadelphia
Washington
Norfolk
Blue Ridge Sea
Raleigh
Carolina Islands
Great American Ocean
Nashville
Memphis
Atlanta
Mississippi Island
Jackson
Alabama Gulf
Georgian Straights
Dallas
Houston
San Antonio
Isla Grande
Tampa
Miami

rural areas, which lean Republican. Clinton's America contains 54 percent of the population, but Trump's America spans 85 percent of the landmass. "Trump's America has holes, but it's a very large part of the country," Wallace says. Clinton's America is more like a far-flung archipelago.

One thing that stands out on the maps is the isolation of cities across the Midwest. On the Trump map, for example, "Louisville Lake" and the "Cincinnati Slough" are completely surrounded by land. When Wallace created similar maps for recent past elections, these political bodies of water were bigger and sometimes interconnected, more like the waterlogged terrain of the Carolinas and the Deep South on the Trump map. Indeed, this landscape of solid Trump support in the Midwest helped turn the election.

On the Clinton map, cities appear as islands, but not every island is a city. The cluster of three midsize islands to the northeast of the "Wyoming Shallows" corresponds to Standing Rock, Cheyenne River, and other Indian reservations in South Dakota. Some of the tiniest islands represent college towns, such as Athens, Georgia, and Lincoln, Nebraska.

Wallace says the maps have been well received by people on both sides of the political divide. For Trump supporters, they show that people who share their views are spread across a vast swath of the country. Clinton supporters can take solace in the fact that while they may be relegated to islands, those islands are numerous and the archipelago is expansive. Perhaps not surprising in such divisive times, what people see on the maps tends to fit what they already believe. ✳

In the wake of the contentious 2016 presidential election, the graphics team at the *New York Times* stuck to neutral geographic terms for the labels on this map (no swamps or badlands, for example). Only one sly reference found its way onto the map: The Acela Channel cuts a path through the Northeast on the Trump map, roughly along the route of its namesake high-speed train line.

Putting People and Cultures on the Map

THE FIRST ATLAS OF ETHNOGRAPHIC MAPS GREW OUT OF ONE MAN'S INTEREST IN THE ROOTS OF HUMAN DIVERSITY

CREATED *1861*
SOURCE *David Rumsey Map Collection, Stanford Libraries*

One of the most innovative thinkers of his time, James Cowles Prichard came close to scooping Charles Darwin on the theory of evolution. Raised a Quaker in England and trained as a doctor in early 19th-century Scotland, Prichard was fascinated by a question that many great minds before his had tackled: How had so many different kinds of people come to be scattered across the globe?

Prichard left a lasting mark on anthropology, helping to develop the relatively new field of ethnology: the study of the origins of, and differences between, peoples and their cultures. In 1843 he published a set of ethnographic maps of the world—the first of its kind.

His map of Africa (the 1861 second edition is shown here) is perhaps the most interesting, given the relatively sparse information available about the continent. By carefully piecing together what was known about its inhabitants at the time, Prichard managed to place 31 different races on the map. Stretching through a huge swath in the center of the map are "Vast Regions Unknown" that include the Mountains of the Moon, an unconfirmed range believed to be the source of the Nile River. These mountains may have referred to any number of actual mountains in Africa, or they may have been just a legend.

Prichard struggled with how to include all the historical information he had gathered on a single map of each continent. "There is one imperfection which cannot be avoided," he wrote in the explanation of the maps. "It is impossible to represent on one map the positions of nations in periods of time very distant from each other. These positions vary through the effect of migrations and conquests."

Often considered the founder of racial studies, Prichard was an early proponent of the idea that all human races had descended from a common ancestor. He was one of the first to argue the "out of Africa" theory that modern humans evolved in East Africa and then migrated to other parts of the world. Following his ideas to their logical conclusion, he believed that the theories about racial superiority espoused by some of his contemporaries were essentially bunk.

Prichard was opposed to slave ownership, which was still practiced by British plantation owners in the Caribbean when he was developing and publishing his theories. And he was an early member of the Aborigines' Protection Society, an international human rights organization founded in 1837.

Measuring and comparing skulls of different races was the typical mode of research for anthropologists at the time, but Prichard pushed beyond this narrow focus, arguing that scientists should also study culture, particularly language. These areas, he said, reveal the shared nature of humanity and the interrelatedness of different races. By showing the similarities between the Celtic languages and Sanskrit, he introduced a new branch to the Indo-European languages.

Amazingly, all of this anthropological work was basically a side gig for Prichard, who was a practicing physician specializing in diseases of the nervous system. Here too he was an innovator, speculating about the existence of a mental disorder called "moral insanity." He was also the first to use the term senile dementia. But even with so much to his credit, Prichard remains a little-known historical figure. Despite his capacity for insight, it seems he fell just short of what would have been his biggest accomplishment: the theory of evolution.

Before Charles Darwin published his breakthrough theory in 1859, many scientists and philosophers had hit on various aspects

FIG. 71.

ABOVE British physician James Cowles Prichard published a massive tome in 1843, *The Natural History of Man*, about the characteristics of different races from around the globe. The book contains many illustrations of people around the world, including this one of a "Souakiny chief" described in Jeddah, Saudi Arabia.

OPPOSITE Prichard made the first ethnographical map of Africa as part of an atlas to accompany his 1843 anthropological text, *The Natural History of Man*. This map is a second edition printed in 1861. It identifies 31 races and reveals how much about the continent remained mysterious to Europeans, with a large section marked "Vast Regions Unknown."

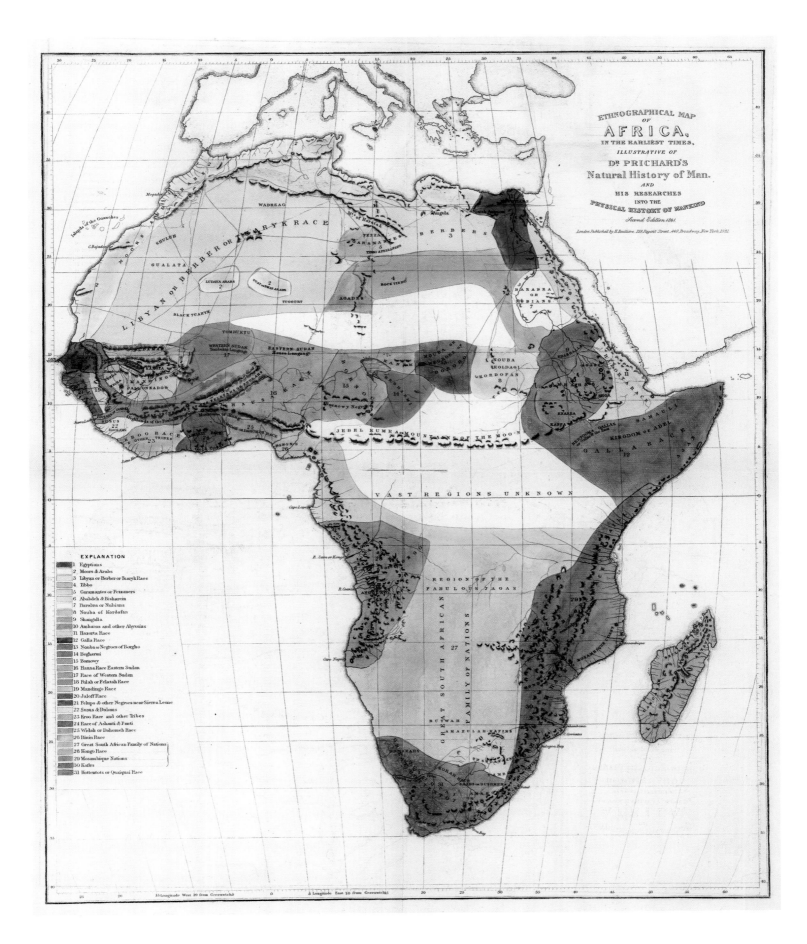

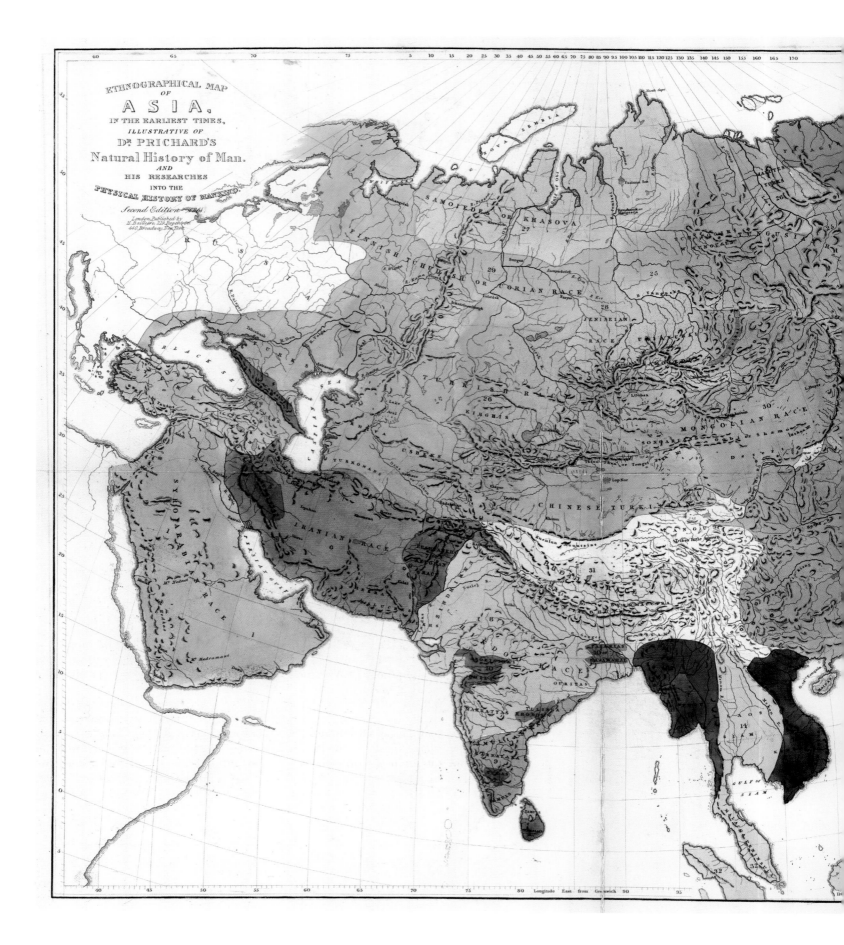

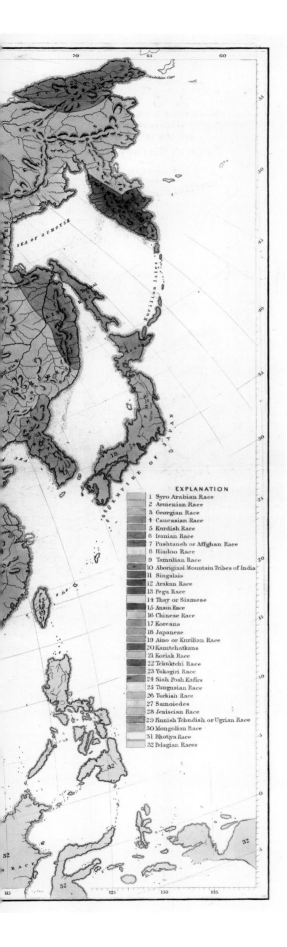

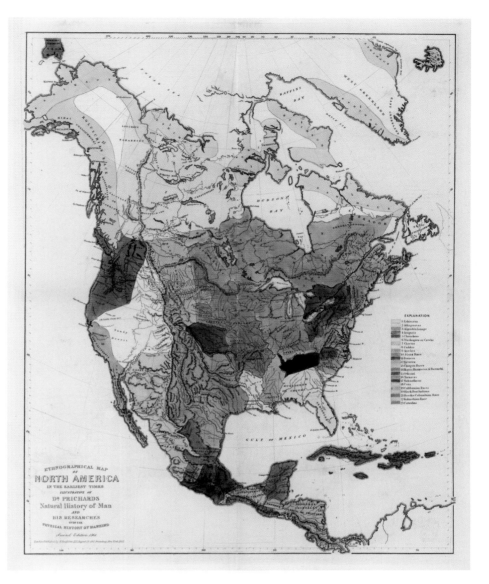

of it. Darwin was the one who put all the pieces together, and consequently his is the only name most people think of when it comes to evolution. But several deep thinkers came rather close to beating Darwin to that "aha" moment, and Prichard was one of those who came closest.

A list of Prichard's ideas and observations about the diversity of species shows that he had all the raw materials needed to understand natural selection. He believed that different races were the result of the different environments people inhabited. He understood that variation among individuals in a species was key. He also recognized that traits people (or plants or animals) were born with could be inherited, but traits that were acquired later in life could not.

But Prichard never put it all together. It seems he was more interested in the anthropological details of his ideas than he was in the mechanism that made it all possible. As historian Conway Zirkle put it in 1941, "Indeed we are justified in marveling how Prichard avoided discovering that natural selection was a major factor in organic evolution." ✳

LEFT Prichard located the origins of 32 races on the second edition of his map of Asia from 1861. It was based on an 1831 map from Julius Klaproth's study of Eastern languages, *Asia polyglotta*.

ABOVE Prichard's 1861 ethnographical map of North America identifies the geographical origins of 23 races. It was based on the best map available of Native Americans by Albert Gallatin in 1836.

Gangs of Chicago

A PIONEERING STUDY IN 1927 MAPPED THE CITY'S GANGS, DOCUMENTING LIFE INSIDE

CREATED *1927*
CREATOR *University of Chicago Map Collection*

In 1927, the streets of Chicago were home to 1,313 gangs. Many of their territories are marked on this map, which accompanied *The Gang,* a book published that year by Frederic Thrasher, a young sociologist who'd just finished his Ph.D. at the University of Chicago. Thrasher's research on how gangs work was pioneering for its time, and it has been influential ever since.

Thrasher divided Chicago's gangland into three sections that he called, somewhat melodramatically, the "North Side jungles," "West Side wilderness," and "South Side badlands." These aren't named on the map, but they form a band around the central business district, the Loop, which is visible along the lakeshore near the center. Gray outlines indicate the predom-inant ethnic groups in those areas, and the red outlines and labels indicate neighborhoods and landmarks as they were known to local residents. Tiny red dots represent the gangs, with triangles representing those that had a designated clubroom and circles those that simply gathered on street corners.

In the book, Thrasher describes well-known gangs in each area. The South Side, for example, was home to the So-Sos, the Onions, the Torpedos, and the XXX's, a beer-running gang (this was during Prohibition). The West Side was home to several Jewish gangs, including the Black Hand Society, which Thrasher describes as a pickpocket outfit. Only a few gangs are named on the map, presumably because there were so many of them, and not all had names.

The North Side was home to several gangs with ties to the Mafia, including the Gloriannas and the Little Italy gang. They were based in Little Sicily, which Thrasher outlined in red just north of the Loop. He also labeled an especially bad part of this neighborhood, known locally as Little Hell, and a nearby site of frequent murders known as Death Corner. Just up the Chicago River to the northwest was "Pojay Town," a Polish enclave that was home to a number of gangs at constant war with West Side gangs on the other side of the river.

One of Thrasher's most enduring arguments was that gangs form not because boys are innately predisposed to them, but due to a mix of geography and social factors. The gangs of Chicago, his research showed, concentrated in a transitional area wedged between the Loop and the more established residential neighborhoods farther out. Here, Thrasher wrote, the schools, churches, and strong communities that elsewhere gave structure and purpose to the lives of boys were failing to capture their imagination and inspire them. Gangs arose to fill the void. Because Thrasher was the first to treat gangs as a subject worthy of serious research, his conclusions had an outsize impact on the field for decades to come.

Thrasher acknowledged the crime and other problems associated with gangs, but he was sympathetic to their members. At times, he even seems to romanticize gang life. "The gangs dwell among the shadows of the slum," he wrote. Yet, he continued, "they live in a world distinctly their own—far removed from the humdrum existence of the average citizen." ✳

The detail from Thrasher's map shows Little Sicily (top center) and Hobohemia, an area just to the southeast that was home to dope gangs.

Seeing in the Dark

SATTELITE MAPS OF NIGHTTIME LIGHTS REVEAL SHIFTING PATTERNS OF HUMAN ACTIVITY

CREATED *2017*
CREATOR *John Nelson*

I n 2011, NASA launched a two-ton (1.8 metric ton) satellite into orbit that can show us Earth at night as we've never seen it before. Among the many powerful instruments carried by the Suomi National Polar-Orbiting Partnership is a low-light sensor that has six times better spatial resolution than previous satellites and can detect differences in the brightness of lights with 250 times better resolution. It can pick up lights as small and faint as those of individual fishing boats at sea from more than 500 miles (800 km) away.

Nighttime light can provide a map of human activity on the planet and track how patterns change over time. NASA scientists have developed techniques to filter out sources of natural light, such as fires and reflected moonlight, leaving only man-made light on the map. These data can be used to monitor all sorts of things like urban growth, illegal fishing, light pollution, and the impacts of war. Even some holidays are visible from space: Light displays brighten some U.S. cities by as much as 50 percent between Thanksgiving and New Year's Day, and some cities in the Middle East are visibly brighter during Ramadan.

Cartographer John Nelson of mapping software company Esri took NASA's night light data from 2012 and 2016 and mapped the change in lights all over the globe. His map of Asia and the Middle East shows where lights have gotten brighter or new lights have appeared (in yellow), as well as where lights have dimmed or disappeared (in blue). Lights that have remained steady are shown in white.

Several areas on the map stand out. War-torn Syria is laced with blue, representing lights that dimmed or went out during the civil war that started there in 2011. India, in contrast, is a web of new light, which may be due in part to efforts to bring electricity to rural areas for the first time. ✳

An algorithm was used to compare pixels on satellite images from 2012 and 2016 to find where lights have gone out (shown in blue) or new lights (yellow) have appeared during that time. Lights that were unchanged during that time period, such as the triangle of the Nile River delta at far left, are colored white.

Lights Out No Change Lights On

he changing nighttime illumination between 2012 and 2016

Rural Romanticism

COUNTY ATLASES FROM THE LATE 1800S PROVIDE A FASCINATING—IF IDEALIZED—LOOK AT LIFE IN RURAL AMERICA

CREATED *1874*
SOURCE *David Rumsey Map Collection, Stanford Libraries*

Jesse J. Phillips fought bravely for the Union in the American Civil War. He had his horse shot out from under him no fewer than five times, and he was shot twice himself, including a debilitating shot through the ankle. Despite it all, he attained the rank of general and returned as a war hero to his native town of Hillsboro in Montgomery County, Illinois.

Phillips's war exploits are described in detail in an atlas of Montgomery County published in 1874. He had since resumed his successful law practice in town, the atlas notes, and apparently he was well liked: "In social life the General is one of the most genial of men, his rare conversational powers and ready wit rendering his society ever pleasant and agreeable."

Atlases like these were wildly popular in rural North America in the late 19th century. Nominally, they were about property—who owned which parcel of land in a particular area. But they turned into something different as publishers realized that people would pay to have a short biography included, or an artist's rendering of their farm, family, or prize pig, for all their neighbors to see.

Michael Conzen, a professor of geography at the University of Chicago, estimates that more than 5,000 pictorial atlases were produced during their heyday, mostly in the Northeast and Midwest. Some atlases described how an area was first settled, which in many parts of Illinois had occurred just a few decades earlier. They gave residents an account—often a somewhat glorified one—of what they and their relatives had accomplished and thus were expressions of civic and personal pride.

The personal virtues of residents is a common theme. Of livestock trader James Milton Kelley, the atlas says: "He never was intoxicated; 'threw a card' in his life, or had a lawsuit—a good example to both children and neighbors." John H. Beatty was the "honorable, high-toned and trustworthy" president of the local bank (see the sketch of his farm to the right).

The images of neat farmhouses and well-tended fields paint a rosy picture of life in late 19th-century rural America. In a way, the atlases were the Facebook of their day: a forum in which people put their best selves forward. You won't get the whole story from their pages, but you'll get a telling glimpse of how people in these communities wanted to be seen and remembered. ✳

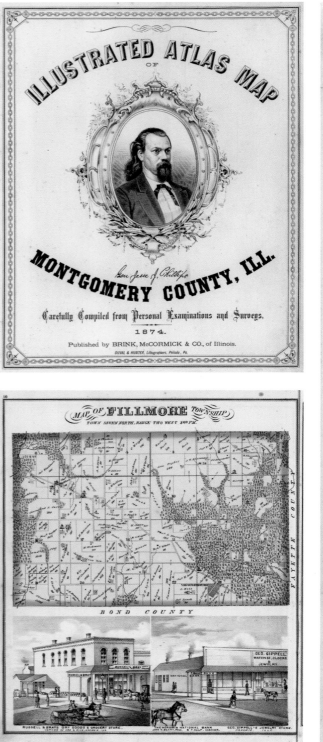

RM OF JOHN H. BEATTY, PRESIDENT OF THE NOKOMIS NATIONAL BANK AND BREEDER OF SHORT HORN CATTLE AND POLAND CHINA HOGS, NOKOMIS TP. MONTGOMERY CO. ILL.

OPPOSITE TOP Prominent citizens received special treatment in this 1874 atlas of Montgomery County, Illinois. Jesse J. Phillips, a Civil War hero and well-liked lawyer, graced the title page.

ABOVE John H. Beatty, president of the local bank (just visible around the corner from the jewelry store on the Fillmore township map at bottom left), also raised Shorthorn cattle and Poland China hogs on 440 acres (180 ha) outside town. Two of Beatty's prized animals, Fancy Boy and Lord Stanley, are portrayed on the map of his farm above.

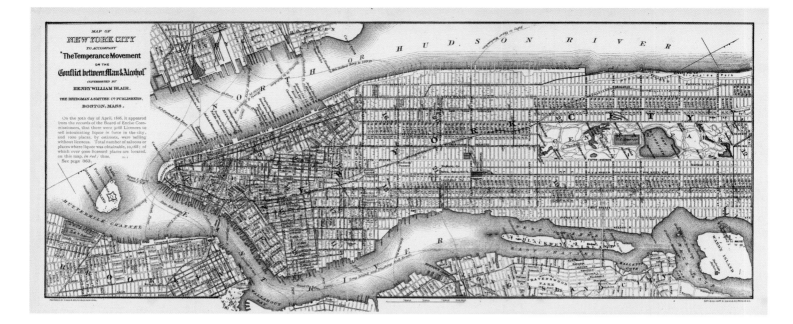

The Rise and Fall of America's Booze Ban

MAPS TELL THE UNLIKELY STORY OF HOW PROHIBITION CAME TO NEW YORK CITY—BUT NEVER REALLY TOOK HOLD

CREATED *1838–1932*
SOURCE *PJ Mode Collection of Persuasive Cartography, Cornell; PBA Galleries; Library of Congress*

New York City was a boozy town at the end of the 19th century, despite attempts to make it dry. The map above accompanied an 1888 book by Henry William Blair, a U.S. senator from New Hampshire and a prominent advocate for the prohibition of alcohol. Blair's book, *The Temperance Movement or the Conflict Between Man and Alcohol,* documents 9,168 saloons licensed to sell "intoxicating liquor" and suggests that another 1,000 saloons were operating in the city without a license. To Blair, this was an unmitigated disaster.

In his book, Blair rails against the evils of alcohol for nearly 600 pages. He uses colorful illustrations to show livers and stomachs diseased by intemperance. He quotes preachers, judges, and other civic leaders on the social depravity that inevitably results when booze flows freely. Disorder! Socialism! Anarchy! New York City was Exhibit A. "The one city of New York is now doing more to destroy the American people than the whole Southern Confederacy accomplished from 1861 to 1865," he writes.

From the beginning of the American temperance movement in the early 19th century to the repeal of Prohibition more than a century later, maps illustrated what advocates saw as the perils of alcohol—and satirized what opponents saw as the folly of a misguided (not to mention buzz-killing) effort to restrict their freedom. New York City was a frequent focus for both sides. "As the nation's cultural capital, financial center, media headquarters, and largest city, it was the foremost battleground in the war against demon rum," writes historian Michael Lerner in his 2008 book *Dry Manhattan*.

The temperance movement had its roots in the Protestant church, and from the beginning, advocates used maps as visual aids to illustrate the moral hazards of alcohol. One colorful example is the allegorical map opposite created in 1838 by John Christian Wiltberger, Jr., a Philadelphia minister. At the far left of the map lies the Ocean of Animal Appetites; at the far right, the Ocean of Eternity. A waterway connects the two, but the route is fraught with danger. Just beyond the Moderation or Temperate Drinking Sound lay the islands of Folly and Evil Company, and beyond them the Sea of Intemperance with its even more ominous islands of Brutality, Larceny, and Murder. (*Don't be duped into thinking an occasional drink is a harmless habit*, Wiltberger seems to be saying.)

Luckily, this is not the only path. The straight-and-narrow Tee Total Rail Road cuts through the province of Prosperity to the Sea of Temperance, where virtuous souls will find the islands of Tranquility and Longevity awaiting them.

The temperance movement scored a coup with the passage of the 18th Amendment, which forbade the manufacture, sale, or transport of alcoholic beverages and became the law of the land in January 1920. But enforcing Prohibition turned out to be something else entirely, and New Yorkers showed special creativity when it came to skirting the law, or at least trying to, Lerner writes in *Dry Manhattan*. A Brooklyn candy shop sold chocolate bunnies filled with whiskey. A Manhattan olive oil dealer filled its tins with rye. On Staten Island, the driver of a hearse carrying 60 cases of liquor got busted.

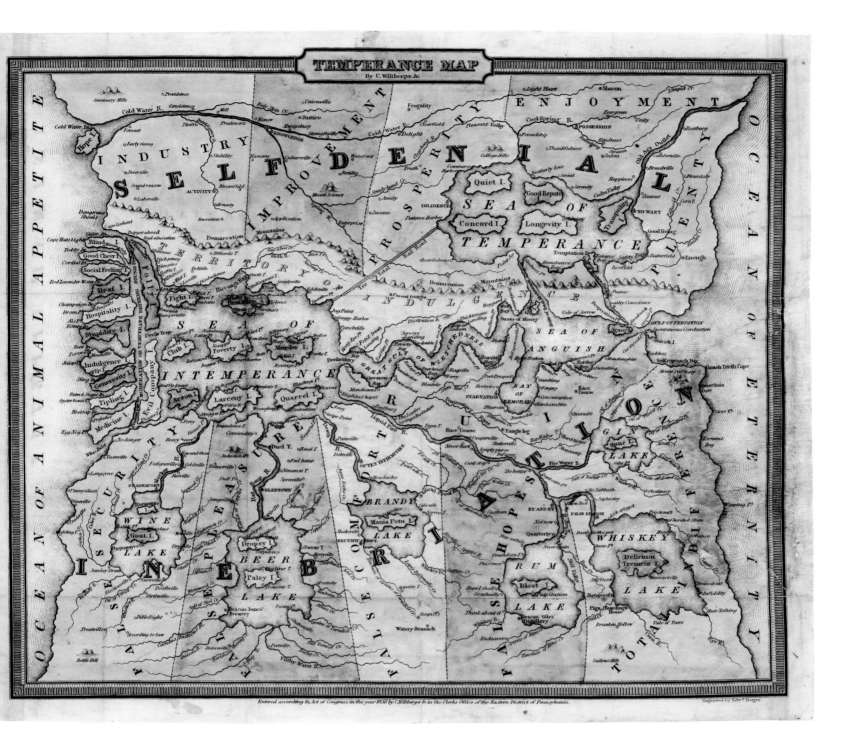

OPPOSITE Saloon maps like this 1888 map of Manhattan were often used by temperance advocates to argue that alcohol flowed too freely in American cities. This one accompanied a report on the evils of alcohol written by a New Hampshire senator, Henry William Blair.

ABOVE This 1838 temperance map by Philadelphia minister John Christian Wiltberger, Jr., illustrates the land of Self Denial (at top) and the land of Inebriation (at bottom). Treacherous waters lie in between, including the Great Gulf of Wretchedness and the Sea of Anguish.

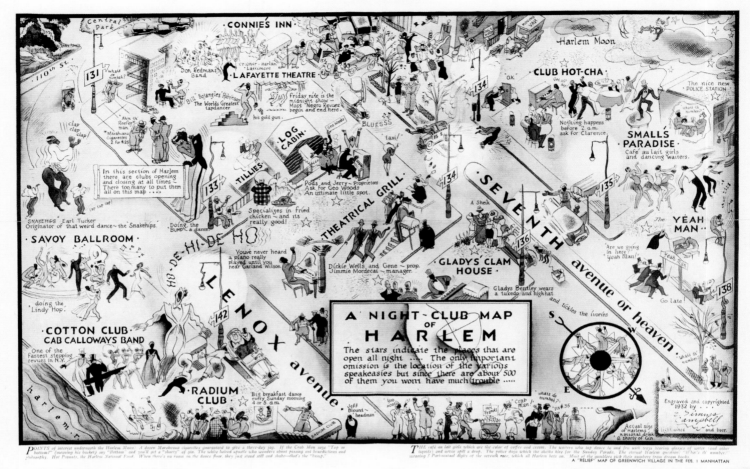

This spirit of rebellion is captured on Prohibition-era maps. The map above was created in 1932 by E. Simms Campbell, an illustrator best known for his later work for *Esquire* magazine. It shows a thriving nightlife centered on now-iconic Harlem jazz venues like the Savoy Ballroom and the Cotton Club, where Cab Calloway leads "one of the fastest stepping revues in N.Y." Nearby, "Snakehips" Earl Tucker practices "that weird dance—the 'Snakehips.'" Campbell's map is filled with caricatures of famous musicians, dubious denizens of the nighttime scene, and helpful tips for partygoers. One thing that's not on the map is speakeasies. "But since there are about 500 of them you won't have much trouble," the map reassures readers.

The map opposite is the allegorical opposite to Wiltberger's map. It depicts the State of Inebriation, in the shape of a human skull, packed with satirical names and puns (the ballpark is called High-Ball Grounds, and a sign near the train station reads: "Absinthe makes the heart grow fonder"). On the left side of the map, the ship *18th Amendment* is "sinking into oblivion"

in the Prohibition Sea. Clinging to the top of the mast is Andrew Volstead, the Minnesota congressman who wrote the law (often called the Volstead Act) that spelled out the rules for enforcing the 18th Amendment.

The difference between these post-Prohibition maps and the earlier ones is striking, says PJ Mode, a map collector who specializes in "persuasive cartography." Maps made before Prohibition—such as Wiltberger's allegorical map and Blair's saloon map, both in Mode's collection—tend to be deadly serious and in favor of enactment. In contrast, nearly all the maps made later tend to be satirical attacks. "Perhaps this reflects the difference between the fervent religious minority that drove enactment and the larger populace that engaged once "prohibition became a reality," he says.

Whatever the case, Prohibition is now a distant memory in New York. If Henry William Blair were alive today, he'd be dismayed to know that at last count, the city had more than 21,000 establishments licensed to sell liquor, wine, and beer. ✳

ABOVE Drunk men strewn across the compass rose are one sign Prohibition didn't stop the party in Harlem. This map advises readers that "nothing happens before 2 a.m." at Club Hot-Cha and suggests they "ask for Clarence." A "Reefer man" works the corner of Lenox and 110th ("Marahuana cigarettes 2 for $.25").

OPPOSITE The sun beams "moon shine" down on the "Gulp Stream," and various types of liquor, cocktails, and wine line the border of this 1931 map that mostly celebrates drinking (though a sea monster called Old Delirium Tremens lurks in the water).

The Urban Smellscape

VOLUNTEERS FOLLOW THEIR NOSES TO MAP THE EVER CHANGING SCENTS OF A CITY

CREATED *2017*
CREATOR *Kate McLean*

Most maps of cities focus on things you can see, like streets, parks, and buildings. This map by British designer and researcher Kate McLean focuses on something far more ephemeral and subjective: smells.

We humans may be primarily visual creatures, but odors are intertwined with some of our most powerful memories, McLean says. Yet they're a tremendously difficult thing to map. Human activities create different smells at different times of day (fresh bread baking early in the morning, followed by exhaust fumes at rush hour), and environmental factors like temperature and wind affect how smells disperse. Then there's the variability in the human olfactory system. "Four people can open the same bin and smell something different," McLean says.

She is experimenting with ways to create olfactory snapshots of cities, and this map represents one attempt. She recruited seven strangers using posts on Facebook and Twitter, and together they walked the freezing streets of Kiev, Ukraine, with her on Christmas Day 2016. Before their smellwalk, as McLean calls it, she briefed the volunteers on their mission, encouraging them to tune out other senses and focus on their sense of smell.

The group started at Independence Square (opposite at bottom center) and ended up at Zhytnyi Market (opposite at top left), taking notes along the way. Each color represents one person, and the dots mark places where they noted a smell. The concentric shapes indicate the strength of the odor, a nod to the contour lines that indicate elevation on topographic maps. Where a modest breeze was blowing by the Dnieper River on the right side of the map, McLean distorted the contour lines accordingly. The text around the outside of the map is color-coded for each smellwalker and describes the odors they recorded over the course of the walk, which ranged from easily identifiable scents like cigarette smoke and grilled meat to more complex combinations like "confectioners' sugar hot dog water."

McLean says she's often asked if every city has a unique smellscape. She sees it as an open question, and one that deserves more attention. She envisions her smell map project evolving into something like the olfactory equivalent of photo-sharing sites like Flickr, where people post snapshots taken from different perspectives at different points in time. With enough snapshots, perhaps a more complete and multifaceted picture will emerge. ✳

The smell descriptions on the map reflect the complexity of the odors that seven volunteers experienced on their smellwalk through Kiev with the mapmaker. They include things like "Tire and hot engine" and "Spicy vegetables, preserves" (see detail below).

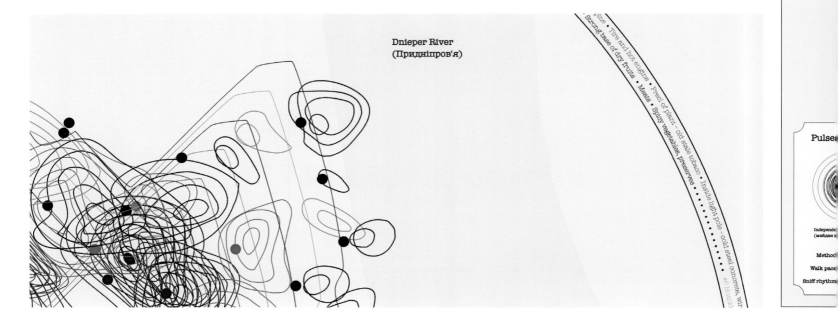

Dnieper River
(Придніпров'я)

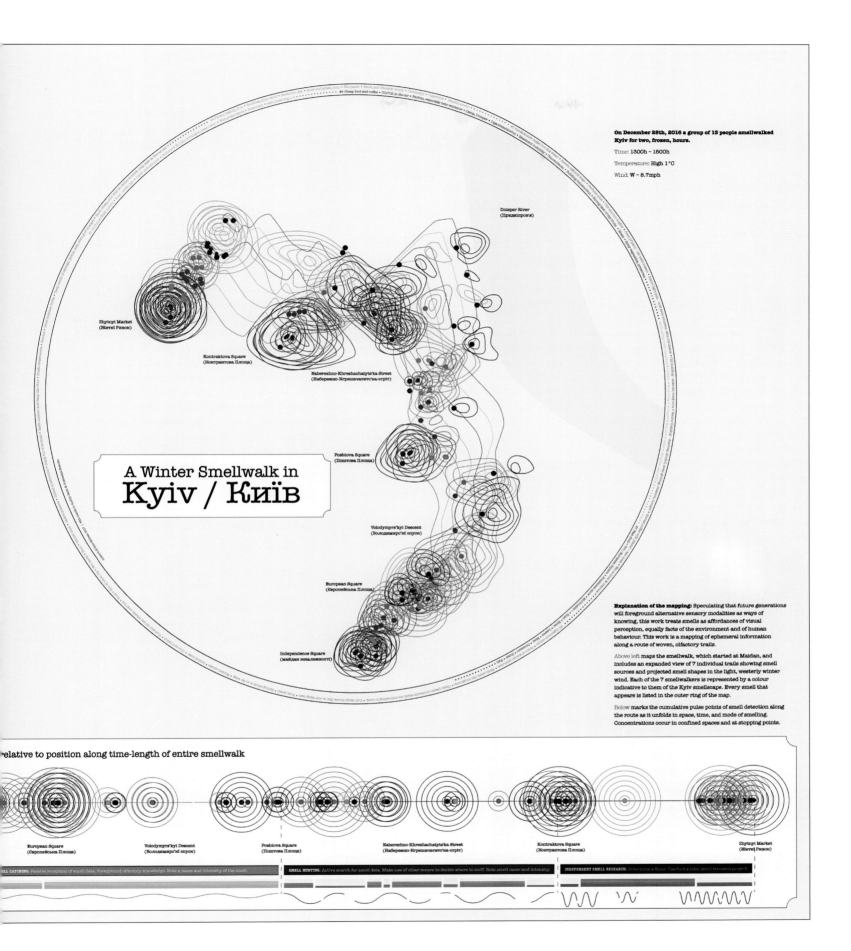

A Winter Smellwalk in
Kyiv / Київ

On December 25th, 2016 a group of 15 people smellwalked Kyiv for two, frozen, hours.

Time: 1300h – 1800h

Temperature: High 1°C

Wind: W – 8.7mph

Dnieper River
(Придніпров'я)

Zhytnyi Market
(Житні Ринок)

Kontraktova Square
(Контрактова Площа)

Naberezhno-Khreshchatyts'ka Street
(Набережно-Крещачатитс'ка-стріт)

Poshtova Square
(Поштова Площа)

Volodymyrs'kyi Descent
(Володимирс'ні спуси)

European Square
(Європейська Площа)

Independence Square
(майдан незалежності)

Explanation of the mapping: Speculating that future generations will foreground alternative sensory modalities as ways of knowing, this work treats smells as affordances of visual perception, equally facts of the environment and of human behaviour. This work is a mapping of ephemeral information along a route of woven, olfactory trails.

Above left maps the smellwalk, which started at Maidan, and includes an expanded view of 7 individual trails showing smell sources and projected smell shapes in the light, westerly winter wind. Each of the 7 smellwalkers is represented by a colour indicative to them of the Kyiv smellscape. Every smell that appears is listed in the outer ring of the map.

Below marks the cumulative pulse points of smell detection along the route as it unfolds in space, time, and mode of smelling. Concentrations occur in confined spaces and at stopping points.

relative to position along time-length of entire smellwalk

European Square
(Європейська Площа)

Volodymyrs'kyi Descent
(Володимирс'ні спуси)

Poshtova Square
(Поштова Площа)

Naberezhno-Khreshchatyts'ka Street
(Набережно-Крещачатитс'ка-стріт)

Kontraktova Square
(Контрактова Площа)

Zhytnyi Market
(Житні Ринок)

SMELL CATCHING: Passive reception of smell data. Foreground olfactory knowledge. Note a name and intensity of the smell.

SMELL HUNTING: Active search for smell data. Make use of other senses to decide where to sniff. Note smell name and intensity.

INDEPENDENT SMELL RESEARCH: Determine a focus. Conduct a mini smell research project.

Parceling Out Paradise

MAPS SHOW THE ANCIENT ROOTS OF MODERN LANDOWNERSHIP ON THE HAWAIIAN ISLANDS

CREATED *1886*
SOURCE *Library of Congress, Geography and Map Division*

The intriguing radial pattern of land division on this 19th-century map of Hawaii is around 600 years old, but it wasn't until the 19th century that anyone attempted to map the island in any detail. Narrow strips of land, known as *ahupua'a*, stretched from the coast up the flanks of the island's volcanic peaks to ensure that each contained a bit of everything Hawaii had to offer, from forests to arable farmland to sea access.

Traditionally all land on the islands was controlled by the king, who assigned stewardship of each ahupua'a to a high-ranking chief. The chiefs designated some lands for their own use and divvied up the rest into small tracts, known as *kuleana,* for individual commoners'

families to live on and cultivate. Each ahupua'a was essentially a self-sustaining unit; tenants traded the fruits of the land among each other and shared with the hierarchy above them through a system of taxation. Lower chiefs made sure the land was used productively and sustainably, even issuing prohibitions against catching specific species of fish during certain seasons.

That all changed in 1848. Under pressure from foreigners who wanted to own land on the islands, King Kamehameha III moved Hawaii away from the traditional system of land tenure and communal subsistence toward Western-style individual landownership. In a process known as the Great Mahele, the king kept some land for himself and divided the rest among the government, the chiefs, and the tenant farmers.

As chiefs began taking legal possession of their ahupua'a and tenants claimed their kuleana lands, determining the boundaries of these properties became a challenge. For most of their history, native Hawaiians had no culture of written language, so knowledge of place names and boundaries was simply passed down through the generations by word of mouth. There were no records or maps of any of it.

There were virtually no qualified surveyors on the islands, so the difficult task of sorting out these boundary issues fell to people with no training. Plots were often mapped separately, with no attempt to relate them to surrounding properties or to mark them on the ground. To make matters worse, the metal content of lava rock can interfere with compass readings, rendering these rudimentary surveys even more suspect.

By 1870, the situation was such a mess that the government, which had been funding itself by selling off its land, no longer knew what property it had left to sell. So the Hawaiian Government Survey was established to systematically map all property on the islands. Using equipment borrowed from the U.S. Coast and Geodetic Survey, the Hawaiian survey team established a network of survey stations and spent nearly three decades comprehensively surveying the islands.

Their maps, like this one of the Island of Hawaii from 1886, are sometimes still referred to today to sort out landownership claims that can be traced all the way back to the Great Mahele. ✳

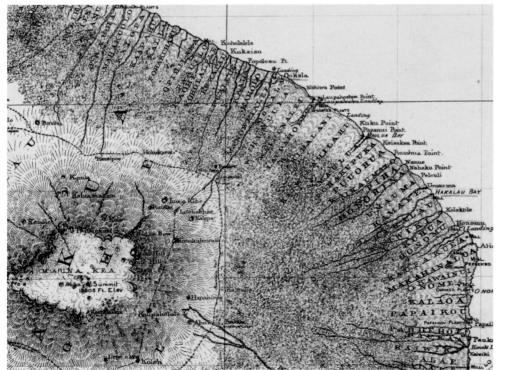

OPPOSITE This 1886 map of Hawaii is one of the first detailed maps of the islands ever made. The surveyors who made it were given the difficult task of mapping boundaries between land units whose locations were based on traditional knowledge that was passed down orally through the generations.

LEFT Hawaii's traditional land-use system was based on *ahupua'a*, units that typically stretched from the coast to the flanks of the volcanoes and were often named for the chiefs that oversaw them, as shown on the northeast coast of the big island of Hawaii.

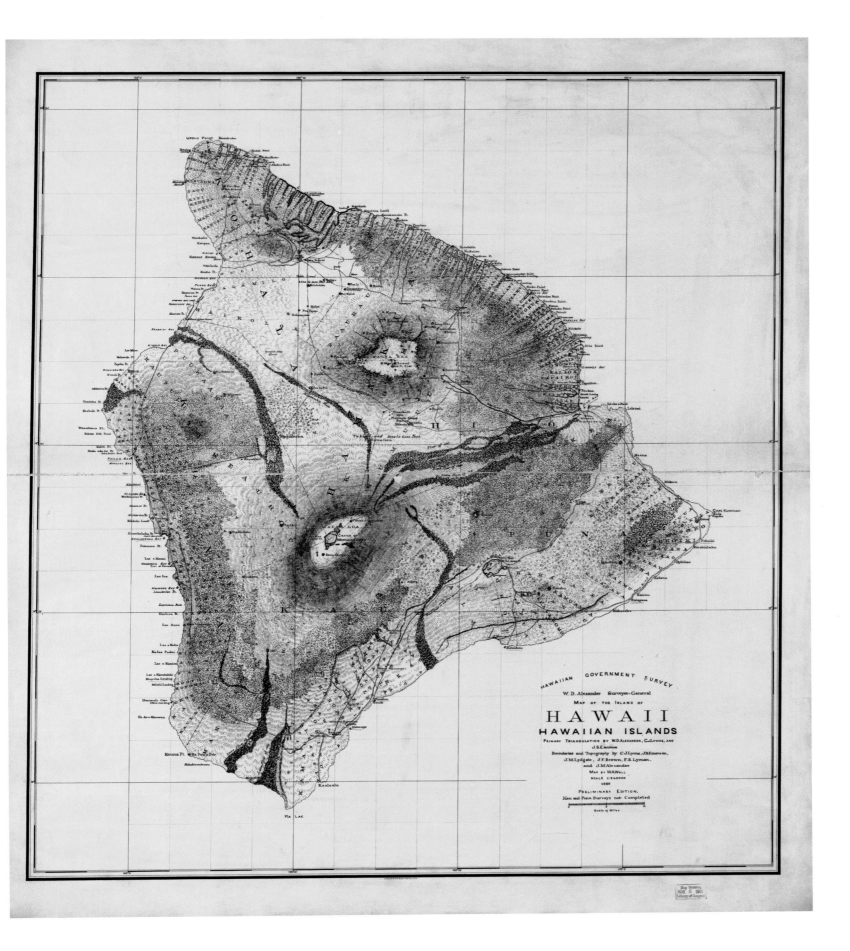

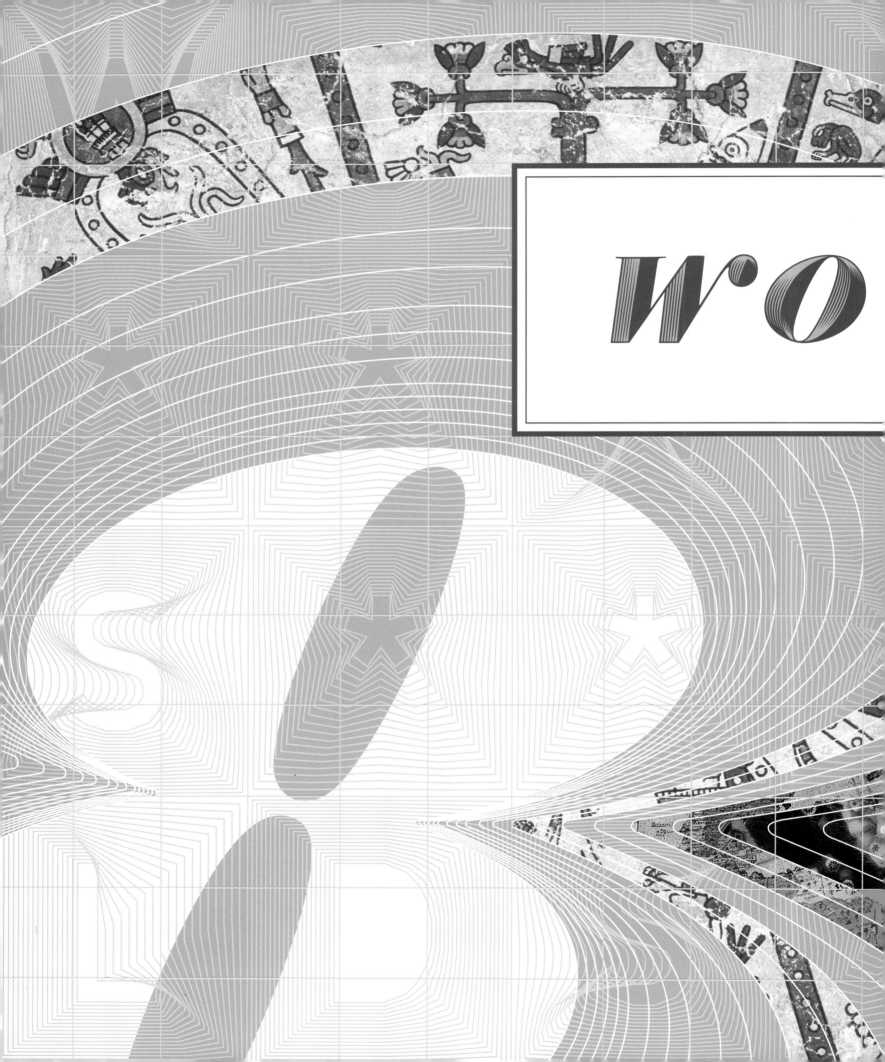

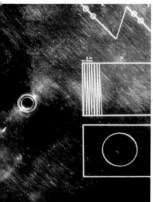

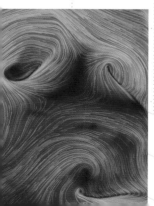

Understanding the World Through Maps

The earliest world maps were speculative affairs, more guesswork than geography. As the Age of Discovery got under way in the 15th century, cartographers refined their maps based on the accounts of explorers. But many gaps remained, and mapmakers often filled them with elaborate decorations and fanciful creatures, perhaps to hide their ignorance. The maps in this chapter reflect this age-old struggle to represent what we know about the world we live in while also imagining other worlds distant in time or space.

These maps tell the stories of turning points in the history of human knowledge, like the invention of the telescope in the early 17th century and how it sparked a race to map the moon and name its features (see page 268), and finally put to rest the long-held notion that the Earth was the center of the universe (see page 256).

They also show mapmakers grappling with the limits of their knowledge, as in the late 19th-century debate over whether long lines seen on the surface of Mars were created by intelligent beings or some natural process (see page 248), and the even thornier problem of how the Apocalypse might unfold (see page 254).

Like all other maps, they reveal much about their makers. Many reflect the biases and beliefs of the people who created them, their hopes and fears about the world they knew—and their desire to know what else is out there. ➤➤

A WORLD ON THE BRINK
(1908, Osher Map Library)

This map shows a view of the world that was about to change forever. It's an early 20th-century replica of the gores—the oblong segments pasted onto a sphere to make a globe—from the oldest surviving terrestrial globe, created in the early 1490s in Germany before word of Christopher Columbus's discovery of the Americas had reached Europe. Where the land masses of North and South America should be, in the top left panel, there is nothing but blue sea (nothing, that is, except the sailing ships, sea monsters, and copious text the cartographer added to fill the void).

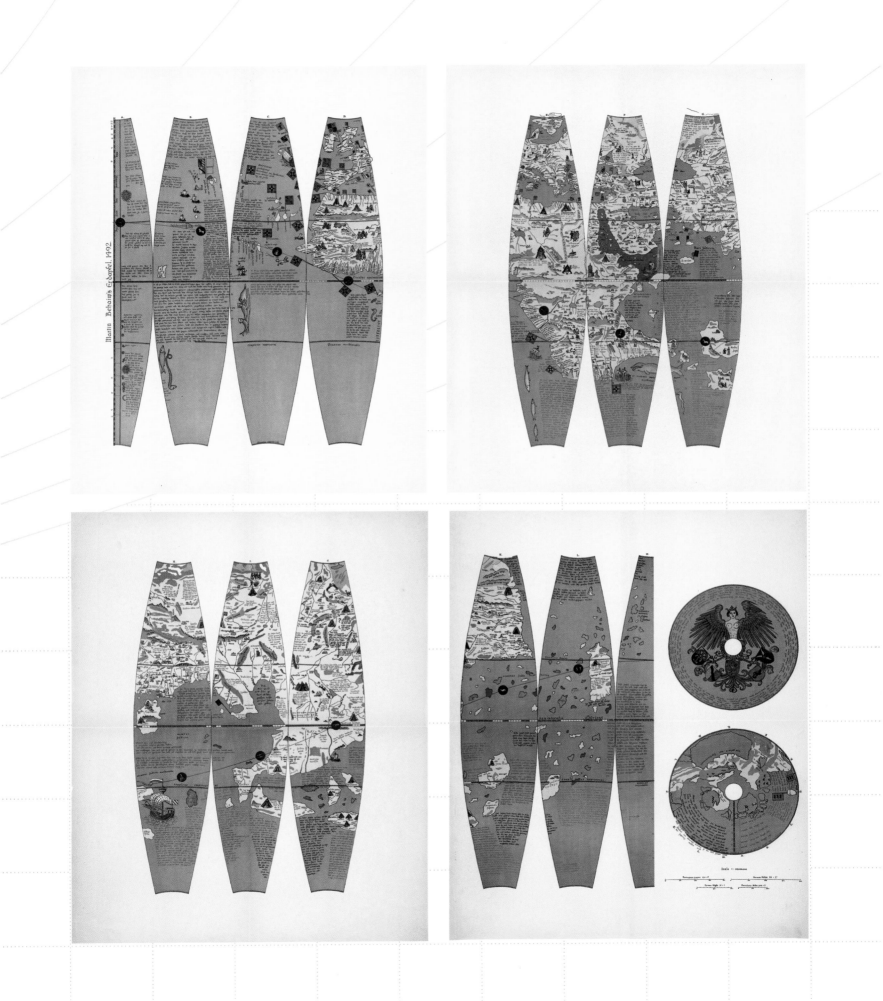

Martin Behaim's Globe. 1492.

Assembling an Ancient View of the World

THE VISION OF A 16TH-CENTURY CARTOGRAPHER HAS BEEN REALIZED, THANKS TO MODERN TECHNOLOGY

CREATED *1587*
SOURCE *David Rumsey Map Collection, Stanford Libraries*

When Urbano Monte made this map in 1587, it may have been the largest map of the world ever made. For 430 years, its 60 individual sheets were bound together as an atlas, never seen as a whole. But in 2017, they were finally assembled—digitally—to reveal the world as Monte saw it.

And what a fascinating world it was. Monte portrays the Earth as seen looking directly down on the North Pole—a highly unusual perspective for the time. His map is packed with fantastical creatures, from unicorns in Siberia to a terrifying bird flying over the Southern Ocean with an elephant in its talons.

"It's unique in many ways," says G. Salim Mohammed, the head and curator of the David Rumsey Map Center at Stanford University, which acquired the map in 2017. It is believed to be the earliest of the three surviving copies of Monte's map.

Monte came from a wealthy and well-connected family in Milan, and like many other gentleman scholars of his day, he had a keen interest in geography. He appears to have been quite geo-savvy: He drew on the works of more famous cartographers, such as Gerard Mercator and Abraham Ortelius, and he included recent discoveries, such as the islands of Tierra del Fuego at the tip of South America, first sighted by the Portuguese explorer Ferdinand Magellan in 1520. Thanks to friends in high places, Monte met with the first official Japanese delegation to visit Europe when they came to Milan in 1585. Perhaps as a result, his depiction of Japan contains many place names that don't appear on other Western maps of the time.

An even more unusual feature of Monte's map is the projection—the method he used to flatten the globe onto a two-dimensional map (see page 264). Monte puts the North Pole at the center with lines of longitude radiating outward. Polar projections became popular in the 20th century, as air travel seemed to bring the world closer together (the emblem of the United Nations uses one), but it was extremely rare in Monte's time.

"I think Monte was really trying to show the circular nature of the Earth," says David Rumsey, the map collector who bought the map and donated it to the Stanford center that bears his name. Monte's projection grossly exaggerates the size of Antarctica, which extends all the way around the outer circle of the map, but that reflects the cartographic thinking of the time. "Most cartographers thought it had to be massive to counterbalance the large landmasses to the north," Rumsey says. This misguided but influential idea dates back to the ancient Greeks.

The digitized composite of Monte's map is now freely available for scholars and anyone else who wants to explore it. The scanned pages fit together almost perfectly, suggesting that's what Monte intended for them all along. ✳

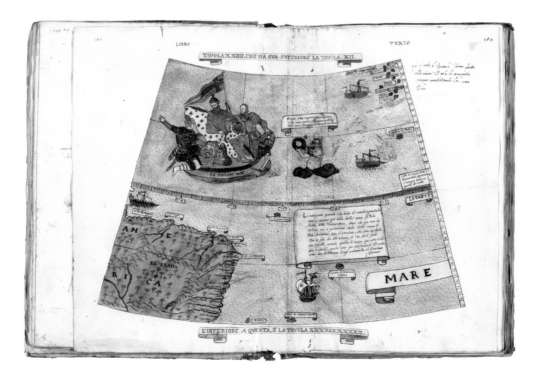

A merman pays tribute to King Philip II of Spain as he floats on a throne in the detail to the left from Urbano Monte's 1587 map, a nod to Spanish dominance of the high seas. Fully assembled, the 60 sheets that make up the map would cover an area that's roughly 9 by 9 feet (3 by 3 m).

When Mars Had Canals

FOR NEARLY A CENTURY, HUMANS BELIEVED THE RED PLANET WAS HOME TO INTELLIGENT BEINGS

CREATED *1867–1965*
SOURCE *Library of Congress; Smithsonian Libraries; Lowell Observatory*

The idea that there might be intelligent life on Mars began to take hold toward the end of the 19th century. Scientists' ability to see the Red Planet's surface had greatly improved in the 300 years since Galileo Galilei first laid eyes on it through a telescope. And how astronomers interpreted what they saw led to a public fascination that peaked in 1938 with the invasion hysteria caused by Orson Welles's radio broadcast of his "War of the Worlds."

Some of the first seeds of that fascination were planted almost 70 years earlier when British astronomer Richard Proctor published the popular book *Other Worlds Than Ours* in 1870. In it, he included the map of Mars below, which he had pieced together in 1867 from drawings of the planet made by an eagle-eyed preacher. Proctor interpreted the light and dark spots on the planet as continents and oceans with ice caps at the poles. He was the first to name

these features, honoring famous astronomers who had contributed observations of Mars with names like Cassini Land and Tycho Sea.

This vision of lands and seas similar to Earth's spurred speculation about the habitability of Mars. In his book, Proctor wrote: "Processes are at work out yonder in space which appear utterly useless, a real waste of Nature's energies, unless, like their correlatives on earth, they subserve the wants of organized beings."

Other Mars geographers, known as areographers, continued in this vein. The maps of French astronomer Camille Flammarion, such as the one on the right from his 1884 book *Les Terres du Ciel,* resemble Proctor's, though they're more detailed. Like Proctor, Flammarion believed the planet could support life. In 1873, he wrote in *La Nature:* "On earth the smallest drop of water is peopled with myriads of animalcules, and earth and sea are filled with countless species of animals and plants; and it is not easy to conceive how, under similar

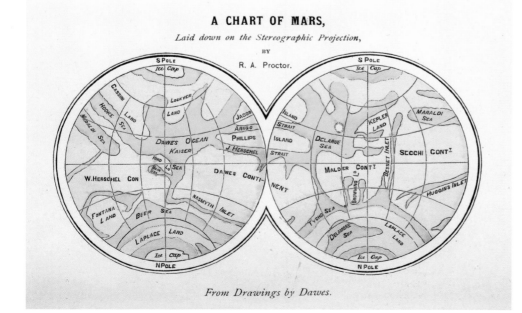

A CHART OF MARS,
Laid down on the Stereographic Projection,
BY
R. A. Proctor.

From Drawings by Dawes.

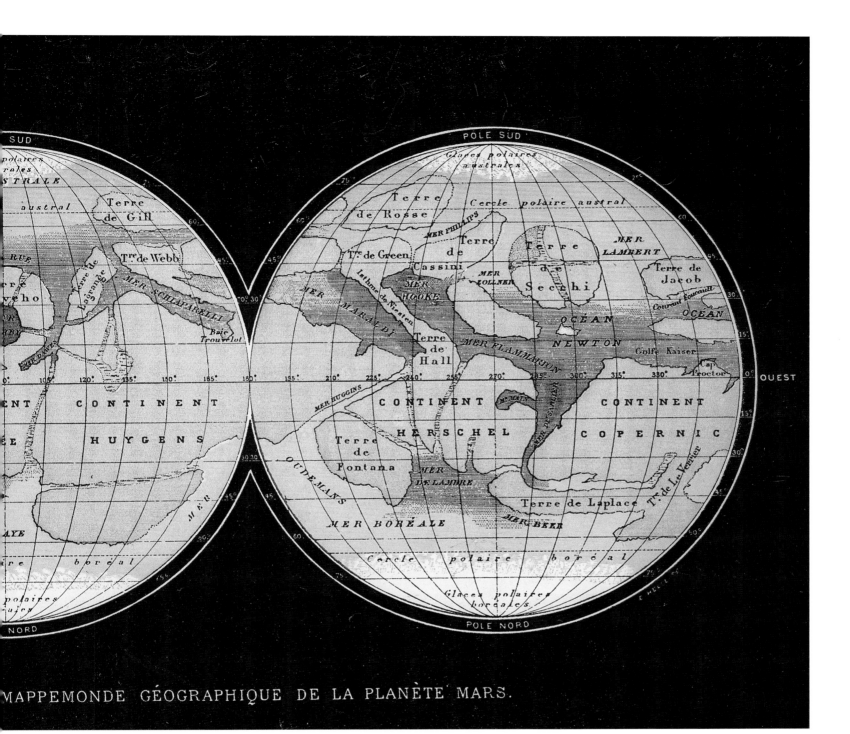

MAPPEMONDE GÉOGRAPHIQUE DE LA PLANÈTE MARS.

OPPOSITE British astronomer Richard Proctor compiled this map of Mars in 1867 from drawings made by a preacher, William Dawes, after whom he named several of the planet's features. Proctor interpreted the light and dark areas on Mars as continents and seas, which made the planet look similar to Earth and led people to wonder if it was also inhabited by intelligent beings.

ABOVE French astronomer Camille Flammarion's 1884 map of Mars bears a resemblance to Proctor's 1867 map (opposite), but it is also a clear predecessor to later maps by Giovanni Schiaparelli and Percival Lowell (see page 250) that led to speculation about the existence of artificial canals on Mars. Flammarion was a proponent of the idea that Mars was habitable.

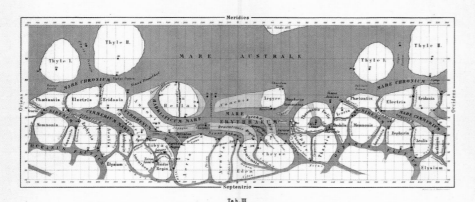

Tab. III

MAPPA AREOGRAPHICA

Exhibens Planetæ Martis Chorographiam inter Polum Australem et Parallelum 40°
Latitudinis Borealis:

Ex propriis Observationibus atque Mensuris ope Tubi Merziani decempedalis
in Speculâ Braydensi Mediolani habitis
composuit, supputavit, atque delineavit J.V. Schiaparelli

1877 - 1878.

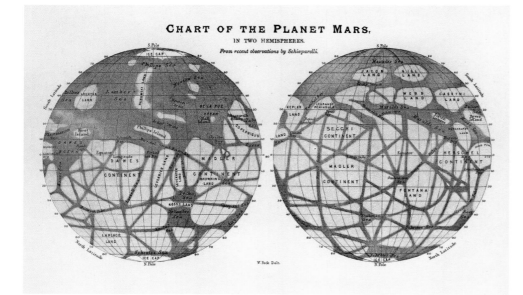

CHART OF THE PLANET MARS,

IN TWO HEMISPHERES.

From recent observations by Schiaparelli.

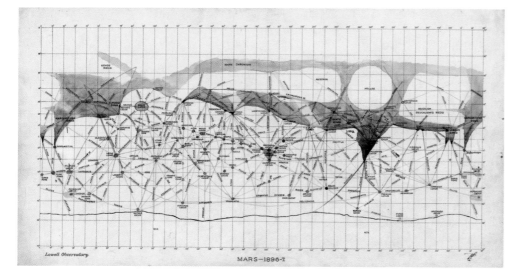

MARS—1896-7

TOP LEFT Giovanni Schiaparelli's 1878 map of Mars has a distribution of features interpreted as land (white) and sea (blue) that are similar to those on Camille Flammarion's 1884 map (see page 249). Many of the names Schiaparelli gave to locations on Mars are still used today.

....

MIDDLE LEFT This map, published in an English astronomy handbook in 1891, shows how the water features separating landmasses on Schiaparelli's maps had become much straighter, leading to questions about their origin. Schiaparelli called them *canali*, an Italian word that can mean either artificial canals or natural channels, fueling speculation that the linear features were Martian-made.

....

BOTTOM LEFT Percival Lowell was a champion of the idea that the linear features on Mars were artificial canals built by intelligent Martians. His 1897 original manuscript resembles Schiaparelli's later maps but contains many more canals. Lowell gave every one of the canals on his maps names including Phlegethon, Gigas, and Thermadon.

....

OPPOSITE This map was made by Earl Slipher in 1962 and published by the U.S. Air Force in 1965 in preparation for the Mariner flyby missions. It is notable because it inexplicably still contains Lowell's linear canals, even though their existence had been debunked by the time the map was made. Text on the map notes, "The linear features are representative of the 'canals' as they have been drawn by many prominent observers of Mars."

conditions, another planet should be simply a vast and useless desert."

All this speculation about life on Mars influenced how subsequent maps of the planet were interpreted. In the late 1870s, Italian astronomer Giovanni Schiaparelli began making maps based on his observations of Mars (at top left) that looked very similar to Flammarion's. But by 1891, the presumed waterways separating landmasses on his maps had become much straighter (at middle left). People couldn't resist interpreting the lines as the work of intelligent beings. They just looked too straight to be natural.

Though he didn't completely rule out the possibility that the lines could be artificial, Schiaparelli was skeptical. But it seems he inadvertently fanned speculation by describing the lines on his maps with the Italian word *canali*. This was translated into English as "canals," which are artificial waterways by definition. In Italian, however, the word is also commonly used to mean natural channels, and this appears to be the meaning that Schiaparelli had in mind.

"It is not necessary to suppose them the

MARS

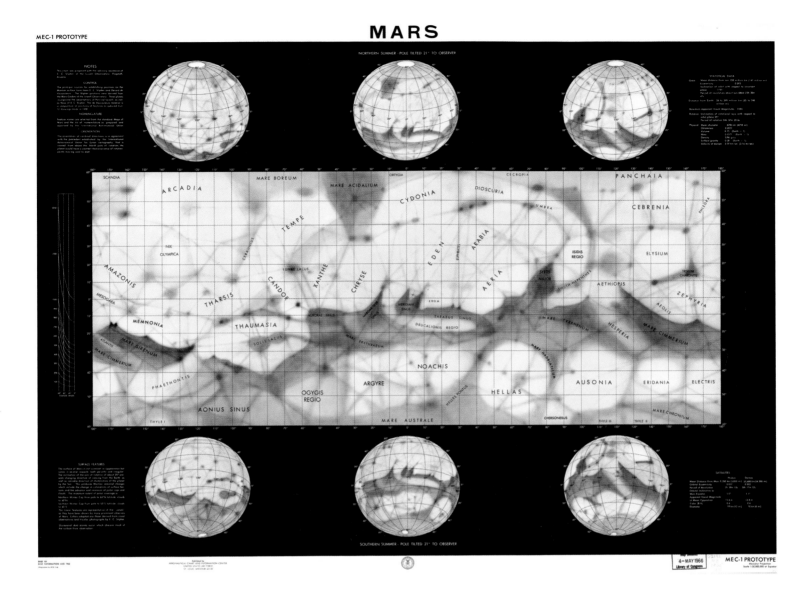

work of intelligent beings," he wrote in 1893. "And, notwithstanding the almost geometric appearance of all of their system, we are now inclined to believe them to be produced by the evolution of the planet, just as on the Earth we have the English Channel and the channel of Mozambique."

The names Schiaparelli gave to locations on Mars largely survive today, but his most prominent legacy is the canali. Their enduring popularity was thanks largely to American astronomer Percival Lowell, who embraced and popularized the idea that the straight lines on Schiaparelli's maps were water conduits built by Martians. In a lecture to the Boston Scientific Society in 1894, Lowell said, "The most self-evident explanation from the markings themselves is probably the true one; namely, that in them we are looking upon the result of

the work of some sort of intelligent beings." Lowell made a map (opposite bottom) in 1897 that is filled with dozens of oases connected by more than 200 canals, each of which he named.

Lowell correctly anticipated that his scientific colleagues would be reluctant "to admit the possibility of peers" inhabiting other planets. But the public loved the idea, and his lectures were often packed. Lowell himself was so taken with the theory that he built an entire observatory in Flagstaff, Arizona, and spent years observing Mars and mapping its surface.

Soon, however, criticism of the canal hypothesis mounted as scientists learned more about Mars. There were the prohibitively cold surface temperatures that would rule out running water, and a scientific demonstration proved the straight lines could be merely the result of an optical illusion. But Lowell continued to write

popular science books, culminating with *Mars as the Abode of Life* in 1908. His ideas persisted in the popular imagination for decades and inspired countless works of science fiction, including the 1938 "War of the Worlds" radio broadcast that dramatized an alien invasion and inadvertently fooled some listeners into believing it was real.

The canals hung around on maps as well, including, surprisingly, the map above made in 1962 for the U.S. Air Force. The map, which looks a lot like some of Lowell's and Schiaparelli's renderings, was made by Earl Slipher, an American astronomer who had joined Lowell Observatory in 1908. The Air Force used Slipher's map in the planning of the first Mariner flyby missions. When the Mariner 4 spacecraft had the first close encounter with the Red Planet in 1985, any lingering doubts about the canals were finally put to rest. ✳

A Pocket-Size Universe

TINY GLOBES OF THE EARTH AND COSMOS WERE A FASHIONABLE ACCESSORY IN 18TH-CENTURY EUROPE

CREATED *circa 1745*
SOURCE *Osher Map Library*

For a well-appointed gentleman in 18th-century England, this pocket globe would have been a fashionable accessory. The black fish-skin case opens to reveal a hollow wooden orb less than 3 inches (7 cm) across. On the case's concave inner surface, the constellations of the northern and southern skies have been artfully drawn and colored.

Pocket globes first appeared in the late 1600s and became especially popular in England and Holland. They may have been used as teaching tools for sailors or geography students, the Dutch map historian Peter van der Krogt writes in the *Bulletin of the Scientific Instrument Society*. But they may have been even more popular as status symbols that reflected the owner's worldliness and a fashionable interest in science. A 1697 advertisement in a Dutch newspaper, quoted by van der Krogt, describes a pocket globe as "most suitable for all amateurs of astronomy and other arts, to be carried always with them just as a watch."

The pocket globe shown here is a later edition of a globe first made in 1731 by Richard Cushee, a British surveyor and mapmaker. It was produced after his death by his wife, Elizabeth, perhaps around 1745, and reflects the geographical knowledge of its time—and

lack thereof. For example, the eastern half of Australia is completely missing. Accurate mapping of Australia was still several decades away, says Ian Fowler, former director of the Osher Map Library at the University of Southern Maine, which holds this globe in its collection. "The currents at the eastern end of the continent and the north are extremely difficult to navigate, which is one of the reasons it took so long," he says.

Elizabeth Cushee did, however, add several updates and enhancements to her husband's globe. California, depicted on the 1731 globe as an island off the coast of North America (a common misconception at the time), has been reconnected to the mainland. She also added arrows illustrating the trade winds, as well as the route of George Anson, a British naval officer who completed a harrowing four-year navigation of the globe in 1744.

What historians find most notable about this globe is Richard Cushee's innovative depiction of the cosmos. Makers of celestial maps had long been bedeviled by a question of perspective. Most chose to show the constellations as they'd be seen from space—or by God—looking down on the Earth. In contrast, Cushee's pocket globe was one of the first to portray them as they'd be seen from Earth by someone looking up, a less lofty but eminently more practical perspective. ✳

Arrows indicate the direction of the trade winds, and a thin dotted line shows the route of British naval admiral George Anson on this later edition of Richard Cushee's pocket globe. The concave inner surface of the fish-skin case (below) portrays the constellations as they would appear from Earth.

Ireland
Moscovy
GREAT TARTAR
E U R O P E
A S I
TURKEY
PERSIA
Taurus M.
MOGUL
Portugal
BARBARY
Biledulgerid
ZAARA or the Des'art
NEGRO LAND
A F R I C A
Nubia
GUINEA
ETHIOPIA
Indian Sea
Socotra I.
Malabar
Bengal
Ceylon
C Comorin
TICK
Almirante Is.
THE EASTERN
OCEAN
Ascension
ETHIOPIAN SEA
I. Trinidada
Is. Helena
Zaire
Monoe mugi
Monomotapa
ZANGUEBAR
Comore Is.
C d'Ambra
INDIAN SEA
I. Mauritius
Tristan da Cunha
CAFFERS
C of Good Hope
C S. Sebastian
St. Paulo
Dina
SOUTHERN OCEAN

Mapping the Apocalypse

AN OBSCURE 15TH-CENTURY MANUSCRIPT DEPICTS THE END OF THE WORLD

CREATED *circa 1486*
SOURCE *Huntington Library*

In 15th-century Europe, the Apocalypse weighed heavily on the minds of the people. Plagues were rampant. The once great capital of the Roman Empire, Constantinople, had fallen to the Turks. Surely the end was nigh.

Dozens of works from that time describe the coming reckoning in detailed text and gory pictures, but one long-forgotten manuscript depicts the Apocalypse in a very different way—through maps. "It has this sequence of maps that illustrate each stage of what will happen," says Chet Van Duzer, a historian of cartography whose 2015 book, *Apocalyptic Cartography,* co-written with Ilya Dines, examines the previously unstudied manuscript.

This cartographic account of the Apocalypse begins with a map that shows the condition of the world between 639 and 1514. The earth is a circle, and Asia, Africa, and Europe are pie wedges surrounded by water. The text describes the rise of Islam, which the author sees as a growing threat to the Christian world—a common view in Europe at the time, after centuries of battles over control of the Holy Land and other territory.

Subsequent maps depict the "Sword of Islam" conquering Europe, followed by the rise of the Antichrist, a massive triangle that extends from pole to pole. Another map shows the gates of Hell opening up on Judgment Day, which the author predicts will occur in 1651. A small, featureless globe depicts the world after that. All the maps in the manuscript are symbolic, but this post-Apocalyptic map takes minimalism to the max. "There's nothing on it, but it's very clearly labeled as a map," Van Duzer says. "It raises the question of what is a map, and it explores that boundary."

The manuscript was made in Lübeck, Germany, between 1486 and 1488, but the author is unknown. Van Duzer suspects it may have been a well-traveled doctor named Baptista who was appointed by Pope Pius II to care for pilgrims at the Franciscan monastery on Mount Zion in Jerusalem. It's written in Latin, so it wasn't meant for the masses.

In addition to the Apocalyptic section, the manuscript includes a section on astrological medicine and a treatise on geography that's remarkably ahead of its time. The author outlines an essentially modern understanding of maps as a means to illustrate something beyond the physical features of the landscape. It's an idea most historians of cartography date to the 17th century, but Van Duzer argues that this collection of Apocalyptic maps pushes that date back two full centuries. "For me this is one of the most amazing passages, to have someone from the 15th century telling you their ideas about what maps can do," he says. ✳

OPPOSITE Triangles represent the predicted rise of the Antichrist between 1570 and 1600 on this map from a 15th-century manuscript.

BELOW Other maps show what follows (from left to right): The four horns of the Antichrist extend to the edges of the Earth; on Judgment Day, the damned stand above an abyss leading to Hell; and a featureless globe is all that remains on a page describing the Last Judgment, Resurrection, and renewal of the Earth.

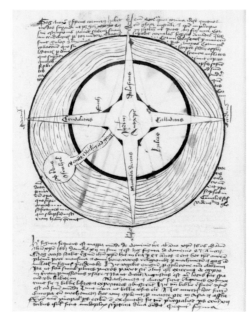
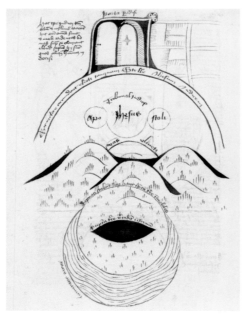

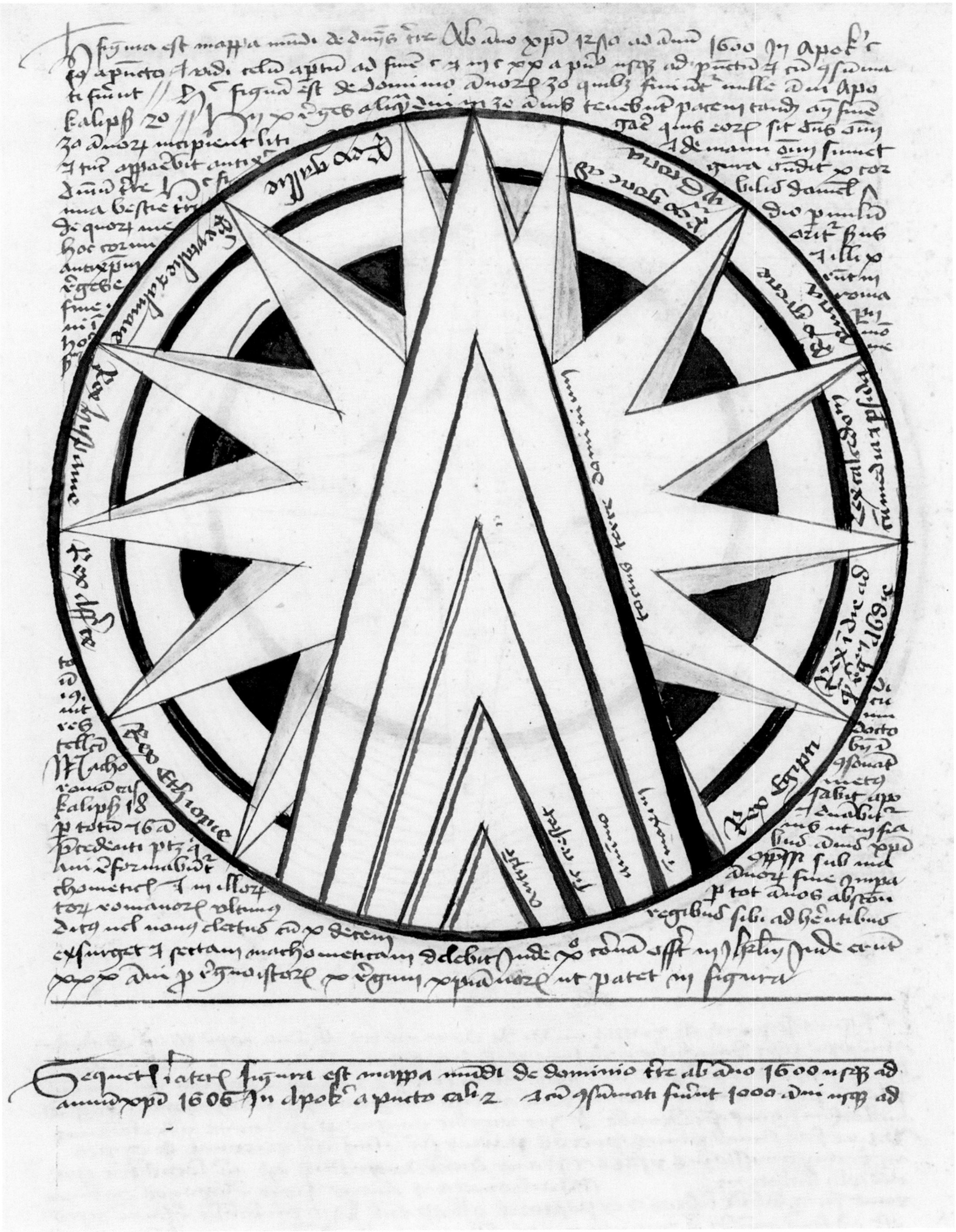

When Worldviews Collide

A SPECTACULAR 17TH-CENTURY ATLAS CAPTURES THE DAWNING REALIZATION THAT THE EARTH IS NOT THE CENTER OF THE UNIVERSE

CREATED *1661*
SOURCE *Octavo/Warnock Library*

For an astronomical atlas made more than 350 years ago, Andreas Cellarius's *Harmonia Macrocosmica* remains surprisingly popular today. You can buy images from its pages printed on everything from calendars and jigsaw puzzles to shower curtains and throw pillows. There's little question that Cellarius's design, and the exquisite work of the engravers and colorists who worked on the best versions of his book, is the reason for its centuries-long appeal. Even map scholars rank it among the most beautiful celestial atlases ever made.

The *Macrocosmica* wasn't quite cutting-edge astronomy, even in its day, writes astronomy historian Robert Van Gent in the introduction to a modern reproduction of the atlas. It does, however, capture the revolutionary shift from the view of the cosmos that had held sway for 1,500 years to a newer, more scientific worldview that put humankind in a decidedly less central place. Most of Cellarius's atlas is devoted to portraying these competing visions of the universe.

The old, on-its-way-out view was that of Claudius Ptolemy, the second-century Greek mathematician and astronomer. The Earth was the center of Ptolemy's universe, and the moon, sun, planets, and stars revolved around it. This view would have made perfect sense to the ancient Greeks as they stood with feet firmly planted on Earth and observed the celestial bodies moving across the night sky. It also happened to fit nicely with Christian theology, which put the Earth at the center of God's creation.

Ptolemy's ideas were still influential by the time Cellarius made the first version of his atlas in 1660. Several maps in the atlas

This map from Andreas Cellarius's 17th-century atlas portrays the new worldview proposed by Nicolaus Copernicus, in which the Earth (just above center, with the moon orbiting it) revolves around the sun, not the other way around. Copernicus himself sits in the bottom right corner, holding a globe. The scholarly figure in the opposite corner may be Aristarchus, a Greek scholar who argued for a sun-centered universe back in the third century B.C. but was widely ignored until Copernicus came along.

ABOVE The Earth is at the center of Claudius Ptolemy's universe, and figures from classical mythology represent the planets.

LEFT Ptolemy had to resort to mathematical contortions, invoking circles within circles, or "epicycles," to make his system fit the observed motions of planetary bodies. Cellarius devoted several plates in his atlas to illustrating these complex motions, including this one showing the epicycles of the moon.

The following labels appear around and within the illustration:

PLANISPHÆRIVM Sive MVNDI TOTIVS, TYCHONIS PLANO

BRAHEVM, Structura EX HYPOTHESI BRAHEI IN DELINEATA.

CAPRI · CORNVS · SAGIT · TARIVS

AQVA · RIVS · SCOR · PIVS

PIS · CES · LI · BRA

ARI · ES · VIR · GO

TAV · RVS · LE · O

GE · MINI · CAN · CER

MARS. MARTIS CIRCVLVS
IVPITER IOVIS CIRCVLVS
SATVRNVS SATVRNI CIRCVLVS

SYSTEMA PLANETA RVM SOLEM HVC DESCENDEN TEM COMI TANTIVM

MERCVRIVS

describe Ptolemy's worldview and its implications for planetary motion.

On the map at the top of the opposite page, the blue Earth is at the center, surrounded by successive spherical shells of water, air, and bright orange-yellow fire. Ptolemy called this inner region below the orbit of the moon (the white circle just beyond the fire) the "sublunary sphere," an ever changing and imperfect realm where all matter was composed of the four classical elements—earth, water, air, and fire—and behaved accordingly (a flame, for example, would reach toward the fiery realm above unless something stopped it).

Beyond the sublunary sphere was a more perfect place where heavenly bodies were composed of an immutable fifth element: ether. The planets inhabited a series of concentric spheres whose revolutions carried the planets in circular orbits around the Earth. Beyond the moon were Mercury and Venus, then the sun. Farther out were the other planets known in Cellarius's time: Mars, Jupiter, and Saturn.

Cellarius used figures from classical mythology to represent the planets to which they lent their names on his map of the Ptolemaic universe. Mars, the god of war, commands a chariot bristling with spears and banners of war, pulled by two wolflike creatures. Venus, the goddess of love and fertility, reclines naked on a chariot drawn by swans. Beyond the orbit of Saturn is the realm of fixed stars, represented by the 12 signs of the zodiac. One problem with this worldview, however, is that perfectly circular

ABOVE The Earth remains at the center of the universe in the system proposed by Tycho Brahe, but the rest of the planets (including Jupiter, with its four moons, near the top) orbit around the sun. The well-dressed, mustachioed figure in the bottom right corner is Brahe, surrounded by his students.

orbits do not account very well for the movement of celestial bodies as seen from Earth. Even in Ptolemy's day, astronomers could see that objects appeared to move faster or slower across the night sky at certain times and, in the case of planets, even change direction. Ptolemy had to tweak the shapes of his orbits and resort to an increasingly complicated geometry of circles within circles, or "epicycles," to make it all work (see bottom map on page 258).

The map on page 256 presents a radically different arrangement. It's based on the work of Nicolaus Copernicus, the Polish astronomer who proposed in 1543 that the Earth orbited the sun, and not the other way around. By the time Cellarius made his atlas more than a century later, this once heretical idea was finally taking hold.

On that map, a large, radiant sun has displaced the Earth from the center, and the Earth and other planets follow circular orbits around it. The moon orbits the Earth (just above center) and four moons orbit Jupiter (at right), having been discovered by the Italian astronomer and polymath Galileo Galilei in 1610, soon after the invention of the telescope.

Astronomers could see the simplicity and mathematical elegance of the Copernican system, but few rushed to embrace it (the fact that an outspoken advocate of a sun-centered universe, the Dominican friar Giordano Bruno, had been tried for heresy and burned at the stake in 1600 may have weighed on their minds). Besides, abandoning Ptolemy would mean abandoning physics as it was understood at the time. If rigid spheres of ether weren't keeping the planets in their places, then what was?

The Danish astronomer Tycho Brahe was among those who admired Copernicus but remained skeptical that the Earth ("that ponderous, lazy body," as he called it) could move around the sun. Brahe proposed a compromise in which the planets revolved around the sun as Copernicus had theorized, but the sun still revolved around the Earth with the other planets in tow. Cellarius shows this arrangement on the map on page 259.

Brahe may have been reluctant to give up on the Ptolemaic view, but he made several observations that contributed to its ultimate undoing. For one, he discovered a comet passing close to Venus in 1577—a major blow to the idea that the planets are embedded in impervious shells of ether.

Other evidence was piling up too—notably Galileo's discovery in 1610 that Venus exhibited phases like those of the moon, an observation that flew in the face of Ptolemy and confirmed that the planet revolved around the sun, not the Earth.

Around the same time, Brahe's protégé Johannes Kepler was working out his laws of planetary motion, which held that planetary orbits are elliptical rather than perfectly circular, making it far easier to reconcile the theory of Copernicus with actual observations. Finally, by the end of the 17th century, Isaac Newton had provided an explanation of the force—gravity—that kept the planets in their orbits and explained why they appeared to move faster when they passed close to the sun. The last nail had been hammered into Ptolemy's coffin.

Cellarius seems to have been only moderately up-to-date on these developments. For instance, he makes no mention of Kepler's work on planetary motion (although he may have meant to do so in a planned second volume that never materialized). The atlas would have been of little use to working astronomers, Van Gent writes, but they weren't the intended audience. In his foreword, Cellarius wrote that he originally created the atlas for his own use and for that of other lovers of astronomy.

Cellarius's atlas also includes eight celestial charts showing the constellations of the northern and southern skies. Four of these use a novel perspective, showing the Earth as seen through a translucent sphere onto which the mythical beasts and figures representing the constellations have been drawn (see map to the left). Cellarius referred to these lavishly illustrated plates as "scenographs," and they're especially coveted by serious collectors.

But it's Cellarius's diagrams of competing worldviews that seem to have had the most enduring appeal with casual consumers. It's a safe bet, though, that most people who hang these colorful images on their walls never stop to wonder what they meant in the context of their time—and whether they're paying tribute to the past with Ptolemy or looking to the future with Copernicus. ✳

In this plate, Cellarius portrays the stars of the Southern Hemisphere as they would be seen looking down on Earth from space, a novel perspective for the time. Antarctica and the tip of South America are visible below the colorfully rendered figures representing the constellations. Cetus, the sea monster just above center, is especially terrifying.

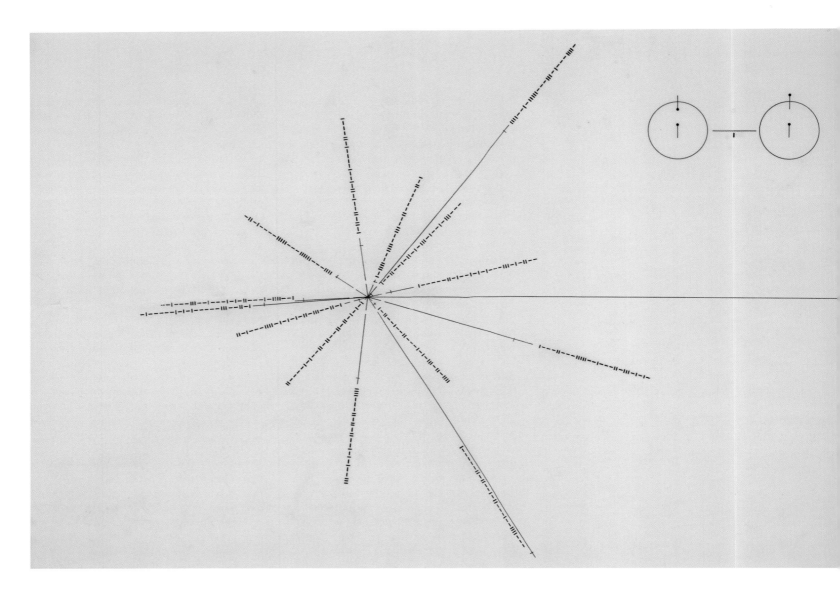

We Are Here

A MAP LAUNCHED INTO INTERSTELLAR SPACE COULD HELP ALIENS LOCATE EARTH

CREATED *1972*
CREATOR *Frank Drake*

The Voyager 1 spacecraft is more than 13 billion miles (21 billion km) from Earth, hurtling through interstellar space at around 38,000 miles an hour (61,000 km/h). It's the farthest any Earthling has ever been, so it's fitting that the spacecraft carries with it the basic unit of human exploration: a map.

But this map is different from any other map ever made. It's meant to reveal where in the cosmos our world is located for any extraterrestrial beings that happen to intercept it.

The map was designed in 1972 by astronomer Frank Drake, who had been tasked along with Carl Sagan to craft a message from humanity to an alien life-form. They decided to include a map that would indicate, "We are here." It was a relatively straightforward idea that required answering a complicated question: How do you create a map that will make sense to an alien species?

Drake, who is best known for his work with the Search for Extraterrestrial Intelligence (SETI) Institute, came up with a clever solution that could precisely locate the sun within the vastness of both space and time. He chose as waypoints the remnants of supernova explosions, known as pulsars because of the way they appear to give off pulses of light. In fact, pulsars send out steady beams of electromagnetic radiation that appear to blink because the pulsars are spinning.

Pulsars, which had been discovered just a few years earlier, appealed to Drake because each one has a unique signature based on the timing of its pulses. And because pulsars slow down at predictable rates over billions of years, E.T. could use them to calculate how long the spacecraft had been traveling by comparing the pulsars' current spin rates to those indicated on the map.

Drake sketched out the sun and 14 different pulsars, calculated the distance between them, and wrote their spin rates in binary code along their connective distance lines (see above). The map was then etched onto a plaque, next to a drawing of a man and a woman, and attached

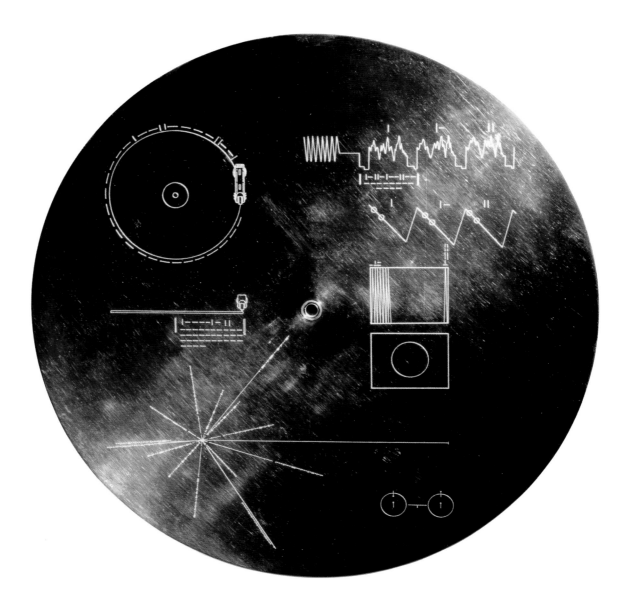

to two spacecraft of the Pioneer mission that would eventually leave the solar system. When the Voyager mission was preparing to send two more craft into interstellar space beyond the solar system—ones that would overtake the Pioneer craft—Sagan envisioned a much grander cosmic dispatch.

He led a committee that spent a year assembling content aimed at giving extraterrestrials a sense of life on Earth. They chose a huge variety of sounds, including thunder, whale song, spoken greetings in 55 languages, footsteps, laughter, Morse code, and music ranging from Bach to Chuck Berry. They selected photos and diagrams of things such as the solar system, the structure of DNA, human anatomy, insects, animals, landscapes, architecture, and people doing everything from eating to running in a track meet. All of it was then recorded on two gold-plated copper records to be fastened to the Voyager ships. Each record was put into an aluminum cover that

was etched with instructional diagrams for how to play the record and decipher the encoded images, a diagram of a hydrogen atom whose spin was used as a clock to convey time in the diagrams, and, of course, Drake's map.

But there's no need to worry that we've handed potentially malicious aliens directions to our doorstep. "Because space is very empty, there is essentially no chance that Voyager will enter the planetary system of another star," Sagan said when the first of the two spacecraft was launched in August 1977. "But . . . the launching of this bottle into the cosmic ocean says something very hopeful about life on this planet."

As Voyager 1—with Voyager 2 just 2.3 billion miles (3.7 billion km) behind it—speeds ever farther away from Earth toward an unknown recipient, the map and record are really for us, to help us understand our world's place in the universe. ✳

ABOVE LEFT This map of dying stars known as pulsars was made in 1972 by astrophysicist Frank Drake to be sent into space with the Pioneer and Voyager missions. The map locates our solar system relative to 14 different pulsars that would presumably be recognizable to intelligent extraterrestrial beings.

ABOVE The covers of the golden records attached to the two Voyager spacecraft have several diagrams etched into them, including Drake's pulsar map (at lower left). Also pictured is a diagram indicating how to play the record (at upper left) and a diagram of the two lowest states of the hydrogen atom (at lower right).

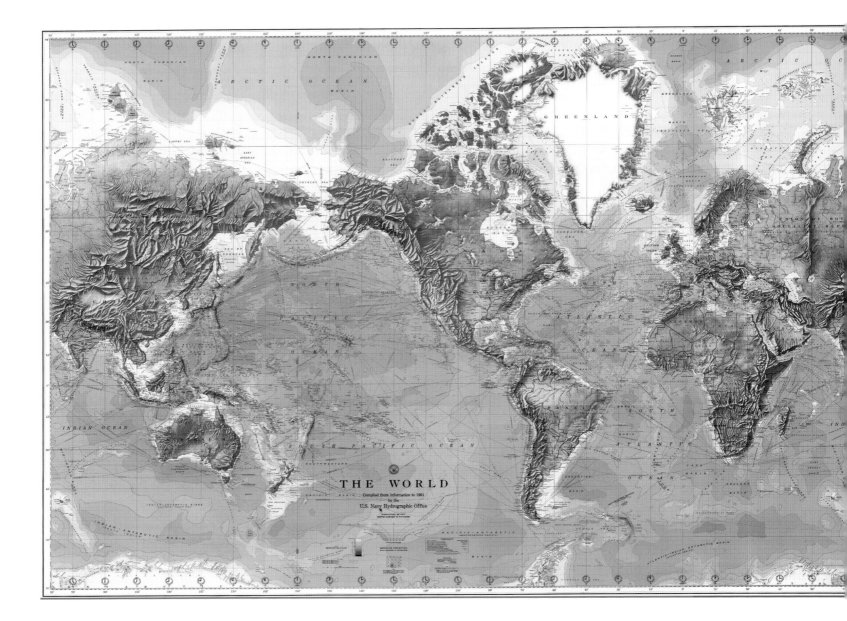

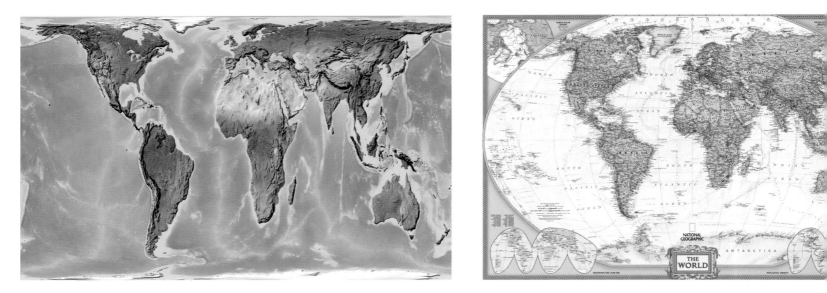

Flattening the World

THE PROBLEM OF REDUCING THE GLOBE TO TWO DIMENSIONS HAS MANY INTERESTING SOLUTIONS

CREATED *1923–2015*
SOURCE *David Rumsey Map Collection, Stanford Libraries; National Geographic; and others*

Every cartographer creating a map of the world faces the same problem: how to flatten the skin of a three-dimensional sphere onto a two-dimensional plane. There's simply no way to do it without stretching, tearing, or otherwise distorting the planet's surface. Unless it's on a globe, every map is an imperfect representation of reality in one way or another.

Different ways of representing Earth's curved surface on a flat map are called projections. To choose one, cartographers have to decide which types of distortion they can live with and which to minimize. Projections can distort five aspects of geography: area, shape, distance, angle, and direction. Reducing one means increasing others.

One of the best known world map projections was designed in the 16th century by German-Flemish cartographer Gerard Mercator as a framework for maritime navigation. Maps that use his projection prioritize angles and direction so that if you were to draw a straight line between two points, you could measure the angle of the line with a protractor and use that bearing to travel between those points in the real world. Mercator's projection remained popular into the 20th century, hanging on walls in many classrooms and, some would argue, distorting students' conception of the world. It was particularly ubiquitous for maps focused on the oceans (see page 188). The U.S. Navy Hydrographic Office adopted it (top left) and eventually pressured the U.S. Coast and Geodetic Survey into using it as well.

The Mercator projection began to fall out of favor in the middle of the 20th century largely due to one of its other notable characteristics: In order to keep direction true, lines of longitude have to be parallel, which means area is increasingly inflated toward the poles. This leads to gross distortions of the relative size of continents and countries, with some absurd results. For example, Sweden appears to be twice its actual size. Europe is also larger than it should be, which was handy for cartographers trying to fit in all of Europe's tiny countries and their names. But some argued that the projection is misleading because it magnifies the perceived importance of northern countries relative to those closer to the Equator.

One remedy for Mercator's polar inflation is a projection that prioritizes area. German historian Arno Peters invented one such "equal-area" projection in 1967 and presented it as a replacement for Mercator's that would more accurately, and fairly, portray the developing world. This aspect made the Peters projection (bottom left) popular with development organizations and educators in the 1980s. The projection made news in 2017 when the Boston Public School System began hanging it in classrooms in place of Mercator maps.

But cartographers, and many others, generally despise the Peters projection because it drastically distorts the shapes of continents, stretching them vertically near the Equator and squashing them horizontally near the poles. The Peters projection may not be pretty, but comparing it to Mercator's is a cogent demonstration of how important the choice of projection can be.

National Geographic's preferred projection, known as the Winkel Tripel (bottom right), is an example of a compromise projection. It minimizes distortion as much as possible by spreading it out among the various geographic factors in an effort to make everything look balanced and achieve an aesthetically appealing portrayal of the world.

Another such compromise projection was created in 1943 by Hungarian American cartographer Erwin Raisz (see page 124), a vocal critic of the Mercator projection. He called his projection the Armadillo for its resemblance to that animal's curved, leathery armor. It adds an element of perspective that makes the

TOP This map of the world published in 1961 by the U.S. Navy Hydrographic Office uses the Mercator projection. This projection distorts the shapes and relative sizes of the continents, enlarging them near the poles, but it preserves directions, making it useful for navigation at sea.

BOTTOM LEFT The Peters projection used for this shaded relief map of the world keeps the total area of the continents and oceans correct relative to each other, but shapes are distorted. The continents are stretched vertically near the equator and compressed horizontally near the poles.

BOTTOM RIGHT National Geographic uses the Winkel Tripel projection for its world maps. The projection is designed to minimize the distortion by spreading it out among all the geographical aspects. In its online store, National Geographic proclaims that on this 2015 map, "Greenland is shown the same size as Argentina and not as the size of all of South America."

projection appear three-dimensional, almost as if Earth had been cracked open and spread apart. "Although the distortions on the peripheries of the [projection] may be extreme, we perceive the correct proportions because we visualize a three-dimensional body instead of a flat map," Raisz wrote in a paper introducing the projection. Though Raisz used the projection for a few thematic maps in his 1944 atlas (opposite bottom), it was mostly intended to inspire experimentation with new projections.

Another way to keep from warping the continents is to break the map into pieces. In 1909 Bernard Cahill, a British architect living in San Francisco, presented a projection made of eight triangles with curved sides arranged in a configuration resembling a butterfly (below). While this interrupted view breaks up the oceans, it minimizes the distortion of the continents. Cahill argued that his Butterfly was a much better map than Mercator's "preposterous chart" for anyone interested in comparisons of things that occur on land: geographers, teachers, political economists, statesmen, students of the Weltpolitik, and especially scientists. "In short, the uses of such a map are endless," he wrote. He formed the Cahill World Map Company to promote the projection, but the Butterfly never caught on.

Other interrupted views fared somewhat better. J. Paul Goode's "orange-peel" projection, which could be arranged to divide the oceans and keep the continents whole or vice versa, was introduced in 1923 and used in Rand McNally's *Goode's World Atlas* through most of the rest of the 20th century. Two examples of Goode's projection can be seen in the bottom corners of the National Geographic world map showing population density and vegetation and land use (page 264).

Perhaps the best known example of an interrupted view was invented by American architect and visionary Buckminster Fuller in 1943 and introduced with a photo essay in *Life* magazine. Fuller's projection is made by first projecting the Earth's surface onto a 20-sided shape made of triangles called an icosahedron. The map can then be unfolded in a number of ways, but he settled on the arrangement shown opposite (top) in 1954, which he named the Dymaxion map. It modifies a few of the triangles to show the proximity and connectedness of the planet's landmass as "one island in one ocean."

There are thousands of different solutions to the problem of flattening Earth's surface. Each offers a different outlook on the world that is sometimes intentional, but often incidental. In a sense, every map starts with a lie, and viewers would do well to keep that in mind. ✳

OPPOSITE TOP Buckminster Fuller's projection breaks the globe into 22 pieces that can be unfolded in various ways. Fuller preferred the arrangement shown here, which he named the Dymaxion map, because it highlights the connectedness of the world's landmasses—a concept he called "Spaceship Earth." The map shown here won the Buckminster Fuller Institute's 2013 Dymaxion map design contest.

OPPOSITE BOTTOM The Armadillo projection used for this map of world agriculture in Erwin Raisz's 1944 *Atlas of Global Geography* is named for its resemblance to that animal's armored skin. It adds a bit of three-dimensional perspective while still showing most of the globe. New Zealand disappears around the corner, so on some Armadillo maps, a "pigtail" with the islands on it is added.

BELOW This 1923 promotional map puts San Francisco at the center of the world using Cahill's Butterfly projection. The projection minimizes distortion by breaking the globe into eight pieces that can be arranged in various ways to keep either continents or oceans intact. The note on the map was written by Cahill to an acquaintance and says, "My plan of the world. I will give $100 to you if you can show me a more accurate one as to form, area, distance, and direction."

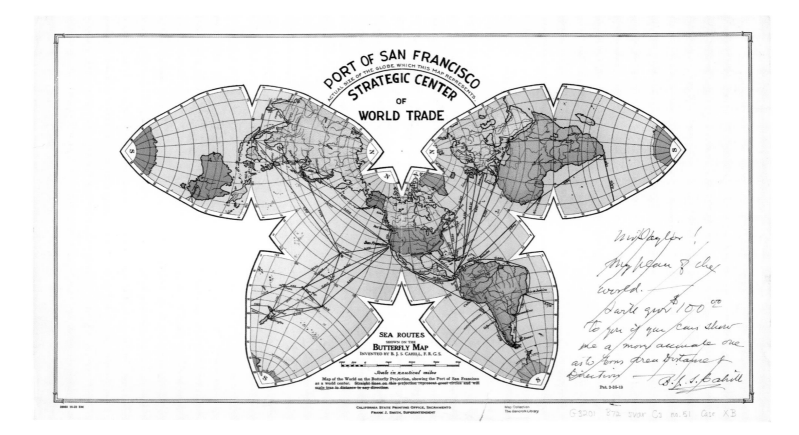

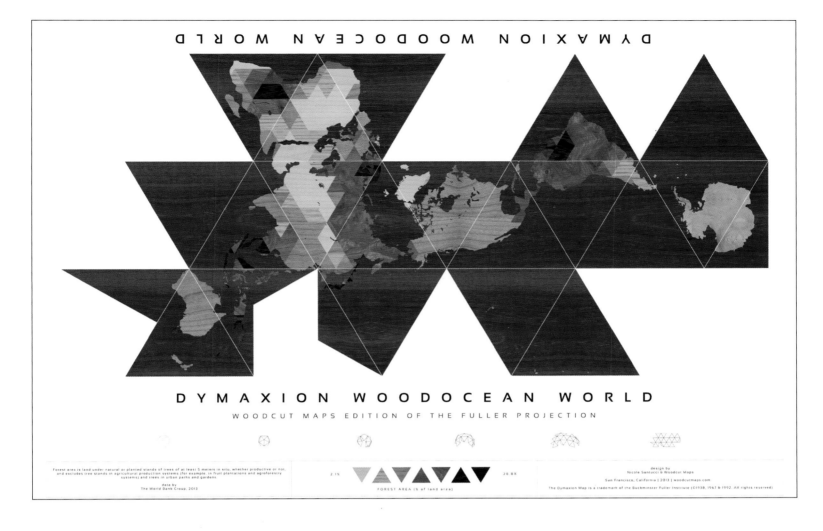

DYMAXION WOODOCEAN WORLD

DYMAXION WOODOCEAN WORLD

WOODCUT MAPS EDITION OF THE FULLER PROJECTION

Forest area is land under natural or planted stands of trees of at least 5 meters in situ, whether productive or not, and excludes tree stands in agricultural production systems (for example, in fruit plantations and agroforestry systems) and trees in urban parks and gardens

data by
The World Bank Group, 2013

2.1%   28.8%

FOREST AREA (% of land area)

design by
Nicole Santucci & Woodcut Maps

San Francisco, California | 2013 | woodcutmaps.com

The Dymaxion Map is a trademark of the Buckminster Fuller Institute (©1938, 1967 & 1992. All rights reserved)

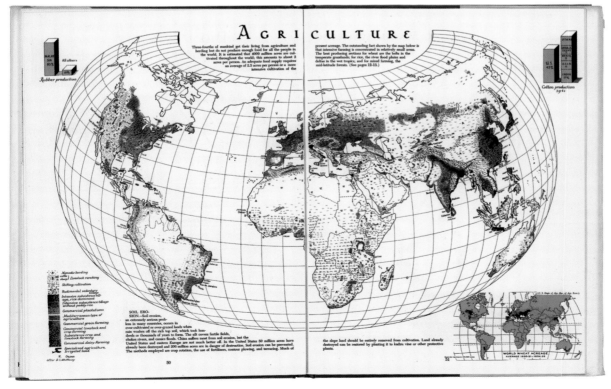

Cl. Mellan Gal. ping. et Sculp.

Phasis Aquis Sextijs An. 1635. Octob. 7. a claro adhuc crepusculo in occasu usq;

Mapping the Moon

FOR AS LONG AS PEOPLE HAVE LOOKED AT THE MOON, THEY'VE SEEN A REFLECTION OF THEMSELVES

CREATED *1610–1742*
SOURCE *Museum of Fine Arts, Boston; Thomas Fisher Rare Book Library; and others*

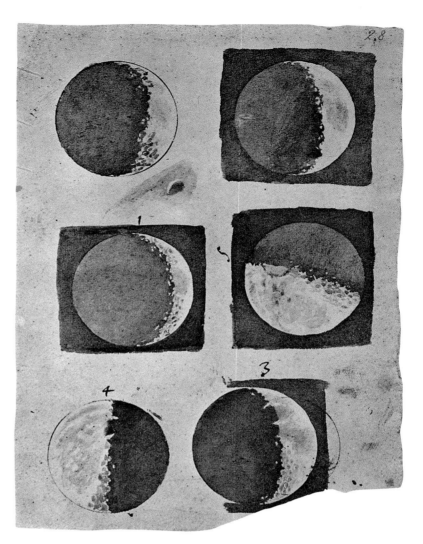

The moon is the only object in space whose surface features are plainly visible from Earth with the naked eye. Stargazers have long gazed up at the night sky and projected their own worldview onto it. In ancient Korean and Japanese legends, the visible splotches on the surface of the moon represent a rabbit making rice cakes. The medieval Catholic saint Albertus Magnus thought he saw a dragon.

This tendency only increased with the invention of the telescope in the early 1600s. After all, far more details of the lunar surface were now visible. Astronomers fought for prestige and immortality as they raced to create ever better portraits of the moon and to stake a claim by naming its features. Not surprisingly, these naming schemes tended to reflect the political, religious, and philosophical leanings of their inventors.

Many of these early depictions blurred the lines between astronomy and art, and many were, in fact, collaborations between astronomers and artists. "They're rendered more beautifully than scientific accuracy would require," says Nydia Pineda De Avila, a historian of selenography, the study of the lunar surface. "They make good gifts for kings."

Italian astronomer Galileo Galilei created a series of drawings of the moon in different phases (right) beginning in 1609 after observing it through a telescope he'd built. Though he wasn't the first to sketch the moon through a telescope—the Englishman Thomas Harriot preceded him by several months—Galileo's artistry brought the topography of the lunar surface into clear view, especially along the terminator (the border between dark and light), inviting comparisons with more familiar terrain.

"The Moon is by no means endowed with a smooth and polished surface, but is rough and uneven and, just as the face of the Earth itself, crowded everywhere with vast prominences, deep chasms, and convolutions," Galileo wrote. He also revived the view of the ancient Greeks that the bright areas on the moon were land and the dark spots were potentially seas.

Galileo's drawings were unrivaled until the French artist and engraver Claude Mellan, working at the behest of astronomers Nicolas-Claude Fabri de Peiresc and Pierre Gassendi, created the beautiful engraving opposite in 1635. Mellan's work was part of a plan to use features of the lunar surface to determine longitude on Earth, a major challenge for mariners at the time, and it far surpasses Galileo's in detail and accuracy.

Hundreds of previously hidden lunar features had become visible thanks to the telescope, and it didn't take long for the learned men of Europe to start squabbling over what to name them. Three naming schemes published within just six years of each other in the mid-1600s set the stage for a debate that would continue for the next century and a half.

The first map of the moon that included labeled features was published in 1645 by Michael Florent Van Langren, an astronomer living in Brussels, then the capital of the Spanish Netherlands.

OPPOSITE Claude Mellan's engravings of the moon are especially impressive given that the telescope he used had a narrow viewing angle that allowed him to see only about a third of the moon at any one time. He made three engravings capturing the moon in different phases. This one shows the moon in its first quarter.

....

ABOVE Galileo's wash drawings, made in 1609, are among the first images of the moon created using a telescope. The rugged lunar topography is most evident along the terminator, the line separating light from dark, prompting Galileo to compare the surface of the moon with that of Earth.

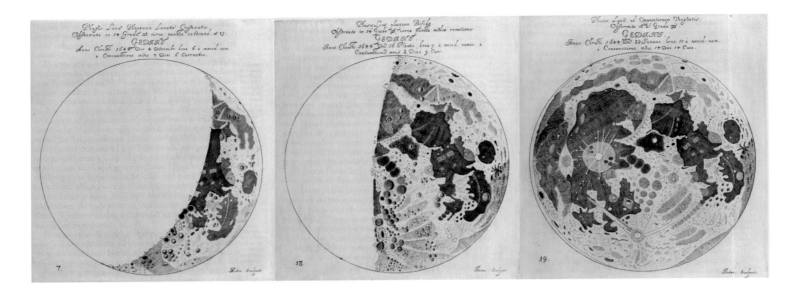

Loyal to the Spanish king, Philip IV, and the Catholic Church, Van Langren named the features of the moon after "illustrious men," including aristocrats, philosophers, and saints. He reserved one of the most prominent features for the king—a large, dark region he called Oceanus Philippicus—and claimed a more modest "sea" and a crater for himself.

Meanwhile, a competing nomenclature was being devised by Polish brewer turned astronomer Johannes Hevelius. Using a telescope of his own invention, Hevelius sketched more than 40 images of the moon in different phases and published them in 1647 in his landmark *Selenographia,* a book that's often credited for being the first lunar atlas. Heve-

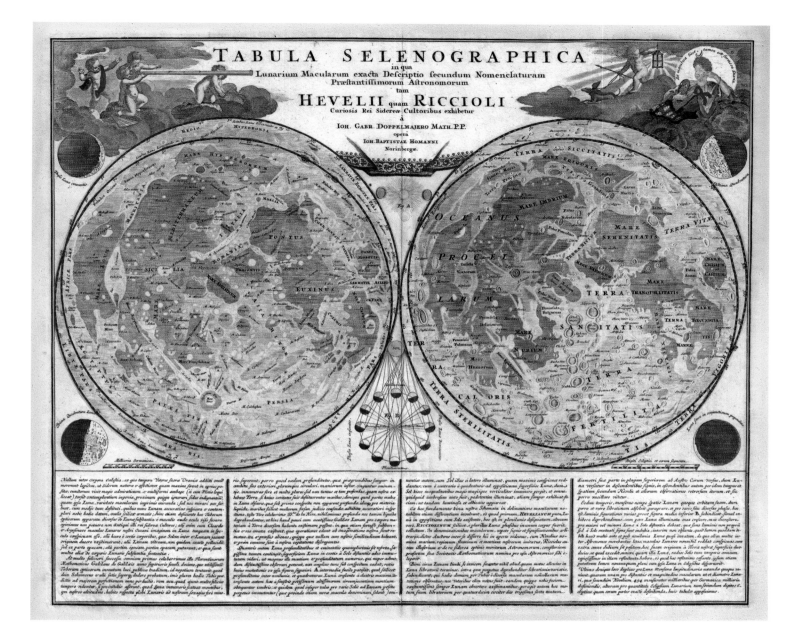

lius proposed his own system for naming lunar features, but he made no mention of Van Langren. Whether he was ignorant of Van Langren's work or intentionally ignoring him isn't clear—but he wrote that he decided against naming lunar features after famous figures of his day for fear of inciting jealousy and anger in those who'd been left off. Instead, he tried to transfer the geography of Earth onto the Moon, using Latin names for geographical features like the Mediterranean Sea (Mare Mediterraneum) and the island of Malta (Malta, Insula).

Hevelius soon had competition from yet another nomenclature devised by a scholarly Jesuit priest, Giambattista Riccioli. In 1651, Riccioli published a lengthy tome on astron-omy that included a labeled map of the moon. Riccioli disregarded Hevelius's scheme, noting the poor correlation between the shapes of lunar features and the places on Earth they'd been named after. Riccioli's nomenclature is more similar to that of Van Langren, but instead of giving preference to Catholic saints and dignitaries, he named the lunar features after people from both ancient and modern times who'd made contributions to astron-omy, regardless of their religious and political affiliations.

For more than a century, astronomers continued to use both the nomenclature of Hevelius and Riccioli on their maps and writ-ings (see above). In the end, however, Riccioli won out. Hevelius's archaic Latin nomen-clature was cumbersome, and his tendency to use a single name for a group of craters became problematic by the end of the 18th century as better telescopes revealed more and more lunar detail. Only four features on the moon still bear the names Hevelius gave them: two mountain ranges (Alpes and Apen-ninus) and two promontories (Agarum and Archerusia).

Most of Riccioli's nearly 250 names, how-ever, can be found on lunar maps today. They form the core of our modern lunar nomencla-ture, alongside nearly 2,000 additional fea-tures that have been spotted and named in the centuries since. ✳

A Mesoamerican Survivor

THIS RARE MAP OF THE AZTEC WORLDVIEW TWICE ESCAPED DISASTER

CREATED *pre-1521*
SOURCE *World Museum, National Museums Liverpool*

In 1940, as German bombs began to hit London, curators at the World Museum in Liverpool worried about the thousands of precious artifacts in their care. Fearing that their city would be targeted, they began moving hundreds of objects into the countryside in North Wales and Cheshire, where bombs were less likely to fall. The museum's three rarest and most valuable artifacts were boxed and carried by hand to Martin's Bank next to the Liverpool Town Hall to be stored in a safe deposit box, where they would stay until the war was over.

Those prized objects were an elaborate Anglo-Saxon brooch, a belt owned by Ramses III, and a more-than-500-year-old document containing an Aztec map of the world (opposite). Known as a codex, it is one of only a dozen or so pre-Columbian books of this type still in existence. If it hadn't been for the move to the bank, there'd be one fewer. On May 1, 1941, the German Luftwaffe began relentlessly bombing Liverpool, demolishing thousands of buildings over seven days. Though the World Museum didn't suffer a direct hit, on May 3, an incendiary bomb landed on the Central Library next door and the ensuing fire engulfed both buildings. Much of what remained in the museum was lost. But the evacuees, including the codex, had been saved.

The Mesoamerican codex is an accordion-style book with 22 double-sided leaves made of deerskin parchment. It begins with the map, which is a conceptual diagram of the worldview of the Aztecs and neighboring Mixtecs. The map divides the surface of the Earth into four quadrants outlined by a Maltese cross, each with a "world tree" that keeps the sky from falling. The Aztec fire lord Xiuhtecuhtli occupies the center of the cross, though scholars believe the map is most likely the handiwork of the Mixtecs.

Two deities flank each tree on the map. In the east (at the top of the map), the sun can be seen rising at the base of the tree. The north is the realm of death and sacrifice, represented by a bowl containing a sharpened bone used to pierce flesh. The west is home to the souls of women who died in childbirth, and the deities are pictured in skirts. The south is known as the "thorny land," and the base of its tree sits in the gaping mouth of the earth monster. Around the edges of the cross is a 260-day ritual calendar marked by animals, objects, and dots. Combining space and time in this way is typical of Aztec and Mixtec culture.

Though codices like the one held by the World Museum were likely very common in the libraries of the Mesoamerican priestly caste, very few survived after Hernán Cortés conquered and destroyed the Aztec capital of Tenochtitlan in 1521. The Spanish burned entire libraries because they disagreed with the religious mythology and views of the universe contained in the books. That this codex miraculously escaped not one fiery disaster, but two, makes it that much more special. ✳

OPPOSITE These two pages from an ancient Aztec codex depict several Aztec gods. The page on the left shows, clockwise from the upper left: Tlazolteotl, a goddess of fertility, sexuality, and filth; Quetzalcoatl, the god of wind and wisdom, also called the Feathered Serpent; Xochipilli, the god of flowers; and the earth goddess Tlaltecuhtli. The page on the right depicts Tezcatlipoca, the god of ancestral memory and time, also called the Smoking Mirror.

ABOVE This 7-inch (17 cm)-tall map of the Aztec view of the universe is part of an accordion-style book known as a codex. Very few examples of these Mesoamerican documents survived after the Spanish arrived in 1521. This codex was donated to the Liverpool World Museum in 1867 by British antiquarian Joseph Mayer, who had bought it from Hungarian collector Gabriel Fejéváry, which is why it is often called the Codex Fejéváry-Mayer.

World of Wind

A GORGEOUS GLIMPSE OF THE INVISIBLE FORCES THAT DRIVE OUR WEATHER

CREATED *2013*
SOURCE *Cameron Beccario*

These beautiful views of Earth are snapshots in time, but they reveal one of the world's ever present stories: the persistent wind patterns that are largely responsible for the world's weather and have shaped the way people travel the globe for centuries.

These images are freeze-frames of an animated web map designed by Tokyo-based software engineer Cameron Beccario using global forecast data from the U.S. National Weather Service and other sources, updated every three hours. Inspired by a similar web animation of the United States and hoping to fill some gaps on his résumé, Beccario decided to build a global map. "Weather is really awesome," Beccario says. "It's terrifying and beautiful at the same time."

Beccario's animation can display all sorts of weather data, including temperature, pressure, humidity, and precipitation, at different heights above the Earth's surface. In the view to the right, the lines depict the shape of the wind field near Earth's surface on September 18, 2017. Faster wind speeds are represented by brighter lines and by color: As wind speed increases, the color goes from blue and green to yellow and red.

In the Atlantic, Hurricane Maria can be seen bearing down on Puerto Rico, just days before it made landfall and devastated the island. The hurricane-force winds at the storm's center are colored red. At the same time, Hurricane Jose threatened the Atlantic coast of the United States before veering north and losing steam.

One of the clearest trends the map shows is the dominance of winds blowing from east to west throughout the tropics. These easterlies are known as trade winds, a moniker based on the 14th-century use of the word *trade* to mean something like "course" or "path." By the time Matthew Fontaine Maury charted these winds and the corresponding ocean currents in the mid-19th century (see page 206), they had become important for European merchants shipping their goods across the Atlantic, which neatly matches the modern meaning of the word *trade*.

Directly south of the trade winds, the prevailing direction flips and westerlies (winds blowing from west to east) dominate. This pattern is often referred to as the Roaring 40s because the winds generally flow between the latitudes of 40 and 50 degrees. These winds were extremely important for the spice trade in the 17th century when European ships, such as those of the Dutch East India Company, sailed around the southern tip of Africa and then caught the westerlies to quickly head east to the East Indies. The view centered on the South Pole on October 9, 2017, at left, shows these winds beautifully, and hints at another reversal of direction at the poles where the prevailing winds are easterly once again. ✳

RIGHT The winds blowing across Earth's surface on September 18, 2017, are depicted on this map of the Western Hemisphere. Wind speed is indicated by the brightness of the flow lines and by color, increasing from blue and green to yellow and red. Hurricane Maria can be seen heading toward Puerto Rico, and Hurricane Jose sits off the U.S. East Coast.

....

LEFT The westerly winds swirling around Antarctica on October 9, 2017, in this image are known as the Roaring 40s because of their latitude. The winds are particularly strong due to the lack of landmasses to slow them down, making them a boon to sailing ships heading east.

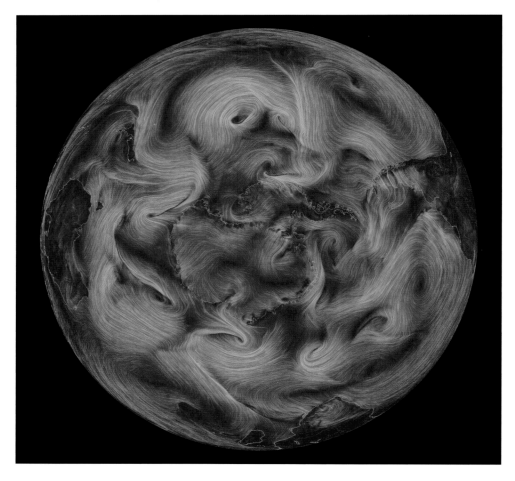

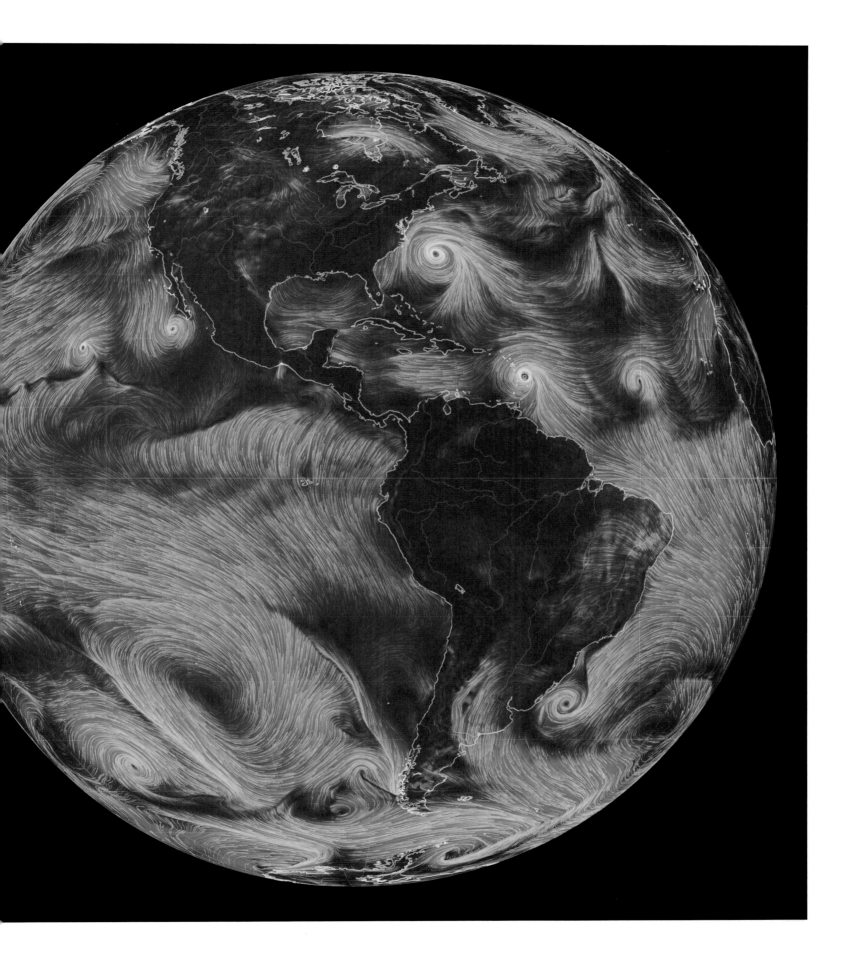

ART

AND

IMAGI

Cartography Gets Creative

By their nature, maps invite us to picture the worlds they represent and wonder what they're like. They can lay the foundation for entire imaginary worlds, provide a way to explore the real world from different perspectives, or inspire new ideas about the future. Artists are drawn to the creative side of mapmaking, discovering endless ways to portray a place.

The maps in this chapter range from imaginative depictions of actual places to fantastical maps of imaginary terrain. A treacherous fictional world is charted on an enormous map of Westeros from the TV series *Game of Thrones* (see page 290). Though the terrain is pure fantasy, the map is inspired by the historical works of medieval cartographers. A map of the city of Jerusalem during the time of Christ (see page 286) was created by a 16th-century priest who had never been to the city himself and based his work on others' descriptions with a dose of his own imagination. In the 19th century, an inventor imagined a self-sustaining utopian community and hoped it might someday become a reality (see page 296). A contemporary artist uses textiles to map a hopeful future for San Francisco Bay (see page 294).

Maps offer a familiar way to make imaginary places tangible and relatable. They also afford us ways to explore the wonders and possibilities of the real world, allowing us to see it in countless different lights. ➻

A WRINKLE IN TIME
(2015, Andrew DeGraff/Zest Books)

Artist Andrew DeGraff maps the paths of characters as they make their way through the plots of our favorite books and movies. This map of Madeleine L'Engle's beloved science-fiction novel *A Wrinkle in Time* charts the travels of schoolgirl Meg Murry as she and her brother attempt to rescue their father, who is being held captive on the planet Camazotz. The 11 characters' paths are each represented by a different color, and the time-wrinkling "tesseracts" that the siblings (Meg in red, Charles Wallace Murry in blue) use to hop between planets are illustrated as wrinkles in their routes.

MEG MURRY
CHARLES WALLACE MURRY
CALVIN O'KEEFE
MRS. WHATSIT
MRS. WHICH
MRS. WHO
MR. MURRY
MRS. MURRY
SANDY MURRY
DENNYS MURRY
AUNT BEAST

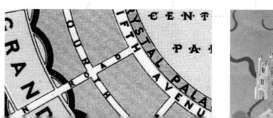

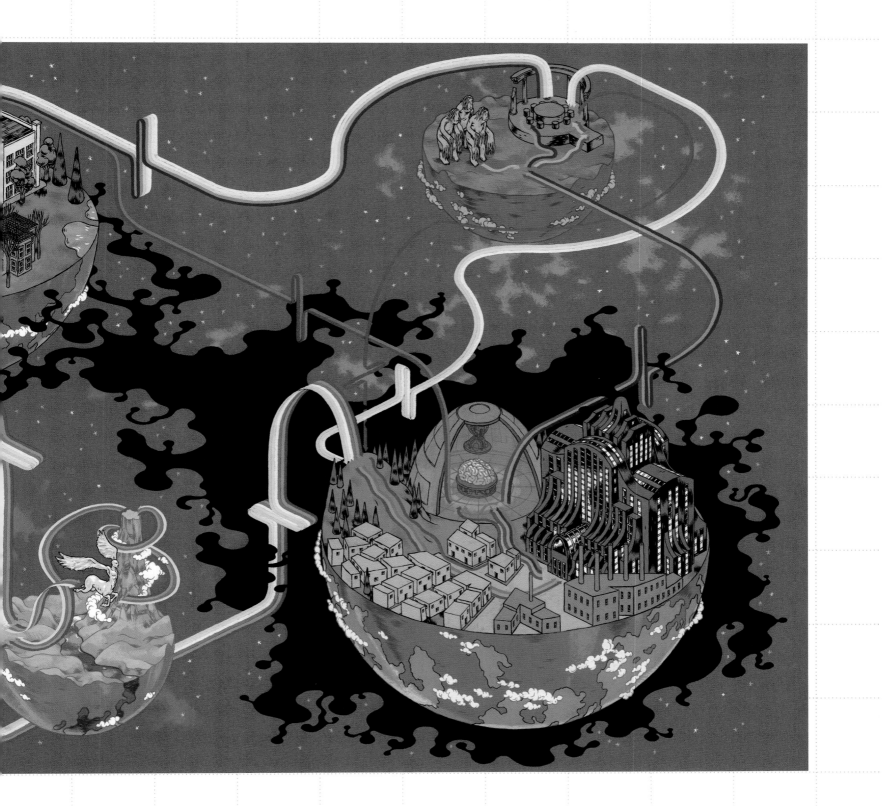
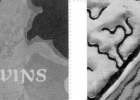
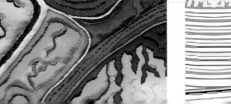

A Map of Many Secrets

A HAND-DRAWN MAP CAPTURES THE RAW ENERGY AND EMOTION OF LIFE IN LONDON

CREATED *2015*
CREATOR *FULLER*

There's a lot to see in this map of London, and there's a lot you would never see without the artist's help. It was created over 10 years by Gareth Fuller, a British artist who explored every corner of the city on foot and bicycle. It captures his personal experience of the city, from nights out at music clubs to the anguish of the 2005 terrorist attack on the Underground. "It's really about how I was feeling about London, and what the culture of London meant to me at the time," says Fuller, who was 25 when he started the map in 2005.

The River Thames, snaking from left to right, anchors the map to reality, along with the Central Underground line running just above it and the Northern line running from the top of the map to the bottom. The map is packed with cultural and historical references. Many familiar landmarks appear, but rarely without a slightly subversive twist. The Houses of Parliament have been reimagined as a circus tent, and Big Ben's clock face is occupied by a large question mark. Look closely and you'll find sly references to the rat race, the surveillance state, and the influence of money.

There are darker references too. Near the center, a Tube car looks as if it's coming out of a tunnel and up off the map. The two figures in the window have bombs for heads, a reference to the terrorist attacks on the Underground. Two crosses on the map represent the tragic deaths of two young women Fuller knew. "There's some very, very personal stuff on here," he says, including some things he'd rather not point out for the world to see.

Fuller thinks of his map as a cartographic love letter, despite the painful parts. "A love letter might contain a lot of wonderful thoughts," he says, "but it can have a lot of angst and sadness as well." ✳

One of the cultural references on Fuller's artistic map of London is a pig floating between the towers of Battersea Power Station on the south bank of the Thames, an homage to the Pink Floyd album *Animals*, which featured the same building on its cover.

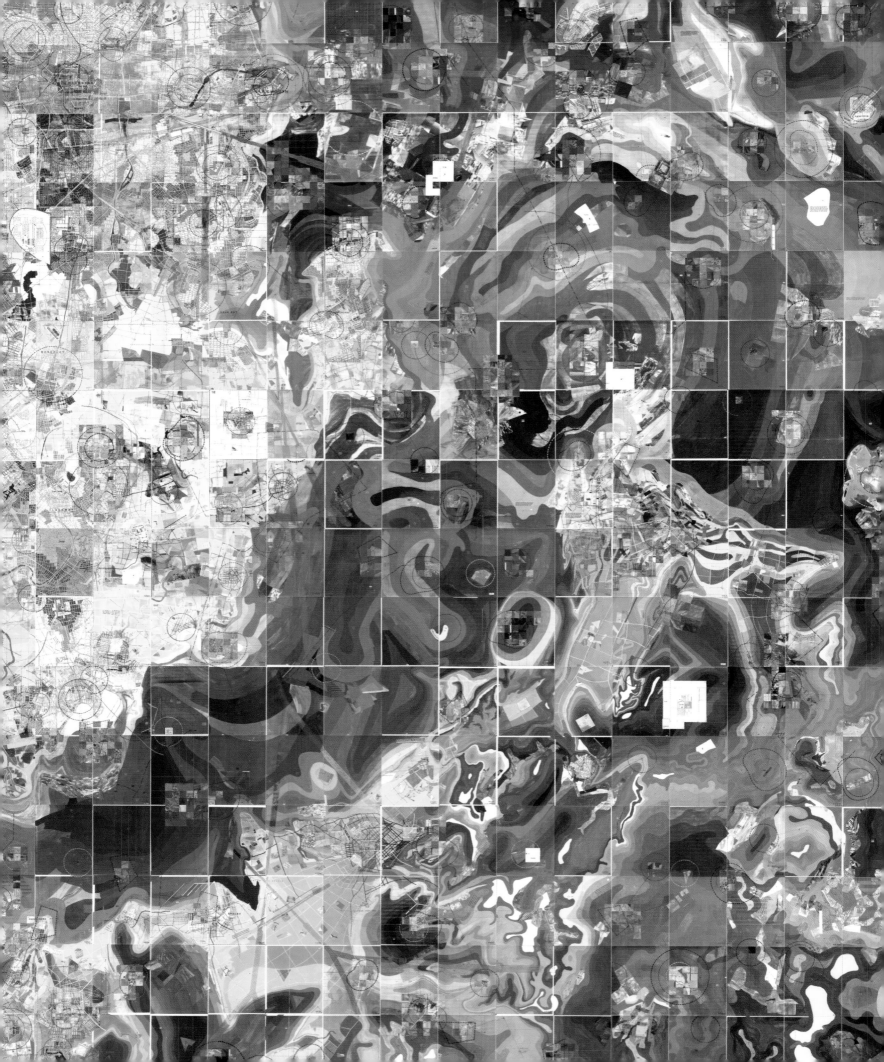

Jerry's Map

ONE MAN HAS SPENT 35 YEARS (AND COUNTING) MAPPING AN IMAGINARY WORLD

CREATED *1963–present*
CREATOR *Jerry Gretzinger*

The way Jerry Gretzinger tells it, the map just sort of happened to him. It started as a doodle drawn one day in a Michigan ball bearing factory in 1963, where he was bored at his summer job monitoring the machines. He drew buildings and roads, rivers and railroads. When the page was filled, he continued onto the next one, then the next. Today, 55 years after he started it, "Jerry's Map" covers around 3,500 panels, stretching 55 feet (17 m) across. And it's still growing.

Jerry's imaginary world is a sprawling, ever changing mix of literal and abstract elements, made with paint, pen, and collage. There are hundreds of cities—such as Ukrania, Sabratha, and Wybourne—with a combined population that has topped 17 million. Beyond the urban areas are bright green agricultural lands, swirling blue bodies of water, and mountainous terrain in rust-colored hues. The periphery of the map grows increasingly abstract, with swaths of purples and browns painted over pieces of cereal boxes and beer cases.

As Jerry's life evolved, so did the map. After his stint at the ball bearing factory, he went to the University of California, Berkeley to study architecture and brought the map with him. Then he joined the Peace Corps, and the map followed him to Tunisia. "It was like a security blanket," he says. "It was a familiar, if imaginary, place."

By the 1980s, the map had grown to around 800 paper panels. Jerry was living in New York City, selling his handmade shoulder bags, which became a hit on Madison Avenue. All the while he worked on his map nearly every day, adding train stations, airports, schools, and fields. One day he got the urge to try something different. He cut some images from a magazine—mostly pictures of arms and legs that reminded him of sand dunes—and collaged them onto a panel. It was the first abstract part of the map. "It unleashed a whole new world of images for me," he says.

Soon Jerry's life also took a new turn. He met his second wife, and they started a one-of-a-kind clothing business, and then a family. The first of their two sons was born in 1983, and time to work on the map grew scarce. It was pushed to the back of his desk, then into a box. Soon it was entirely out of the picture.

The map lay dormant for 20 years until one day in 2003 when one of his sons found it in the attic of their home on the Hudson River, Jerry says. "He brought this dusty box down, and said, 'Dad, what is this?'" And just like that, the map was back. By then Jerry was semiretired with plenty of spare time, and no longer had clothes to design as a creative outlet. He dusted off the map and got back to work.

Before the hiatus, he had been looking for a way for existing cities on the map to grow and change, gaining highways, airports, and suburbs. Now he realized he could do it without losing the work he'd already done, by printing copies of panels he wanted to alter and archiving the originals.

Excited by the possibilities, Jerry quickly grew impatient with how long it was taking to work through the entire stack of 8-by-10-inch (20 by 25 cm) panels. He wanted a way to speed things up without having to choose which part of the map to work on, so he devised a way to jump around through the stack of panels at random using a deck of cards. "If I drew a Jack, I would go down 11 panels. Or if it was a three, then I would only go down three panels and move the others to the bottom of the stack," Jerry says.

OPPOSITE Jerry Gretzinger has been creating a map of an imaginary world for decades. After his map was exhibited in public, he started gaining fans and inspiring others to try their hand at crafting imaginary worlds. There's even an online community on the Reddit news and discussion website (called r/Jerry Mapping) that is "dedicated to creating maps in the style of Jerry Gretzinger."

LEFT Jerry arranges his map in 2012 for an exhibition at the Massachusetts Museum of Contemporary Art when it had around 2,600 panels. The map has since grown to more than 3,500 panels and measures more than 55 feet (17 m) across—too big to be displayed in one piece anymore.

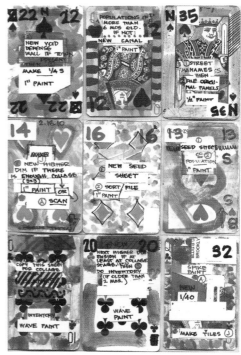

After a while, he began adding instructions to the cards in the deck that told him what to do with each panel he worked on. It could be anything from adding municipal facilities to a town or painting part of a panel, to collaging material onto the map or adding a new panel to the edge. He developed a system of rules that guides how the map evolves. "I'm not having to think about where I want it to go," Jerry says. "I stand back and I watch it be transformed."

One of the more unusual instructions in the deck is to add a void to the map by covering part of a panel with a blank white space. If he draws that card for a panel that already has a void, that void grows bigger, sometimes wiping out an entire city. The only way to stop a void is with a defense wall. If the cards don't deliver defenses to a city in time, it disappears. If a void gets big enough, a new city can begin to grow within it. "I'm always intrigued to see how it turns out," Jerry says. "What direction, what form it takes over time."

About a decade ago, friends convinced him that the public would also be intrigued by his map. He began showing it at museums, galleries, and art shows. Jerry's Map has been exhibited everywhere from New Mexico and New York to Paris and Nagoya, Japan. The map has been shown in its entirety only once, at the Massachusetts Museum of Contemporary Art in North Adams. But that was back in 2012 when it was a mere 2,600 panels. Now, most of the time it's just pieces of the map on display; it's simply too big for most public spaces. Jerry himself has no way to see the whole thing at once.

Meanwhile the map, and the mapmaking rules, continue to evolve. Jerry has started cutting up his journal and slowly adding pieces to the map. He's also added bits of old letters, some dating back 50 years. The map has long been a part of his life story. Now his story is a part of it, too. ✳

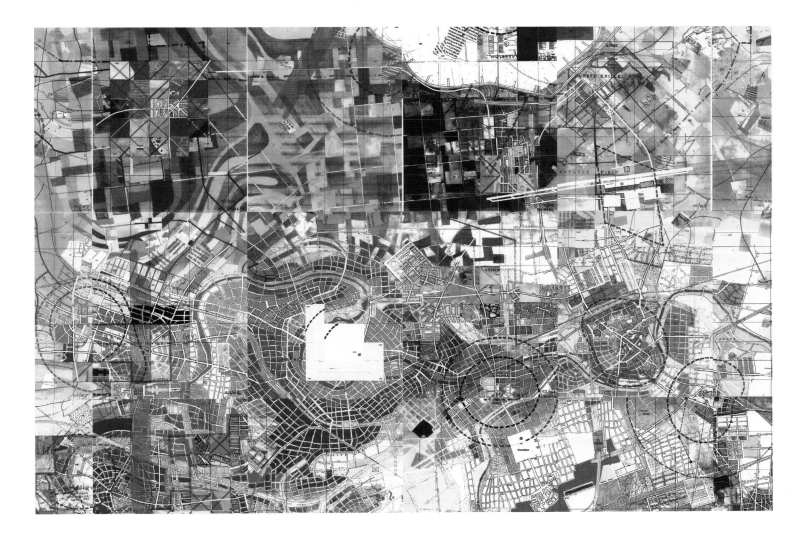

ABOVE The results of Jerry's method of reworking existing parts of his map at random can be seen in this section of the map. Neighboring panels have some continuous features, but some have new color schemes or extensive collage work that set them apart from the panels that surround them. The white stair-shaped area is a void that is beginning to blot out part of a city. At the top of the map, defense walls have stopped the spread of a void that threatened the towns of Reyesville and Ironcorn.

LEFT On this single panel of Jerry's Map, which measures 8 by 10 inches (20 by 25 cm), scraps of Jerry's emails and other documents have been incorporated into the rural areas on the outskirts of New Penfold and Casa Manny. The notation "S5/W11" in the lower right of the panel indicates that this panel is in the southwest quadrant of the map.

Jerusalem in the Time of Christ

A EUROPEAN PRIEST LOOKS 1,500 YEARS INTO THE PAST AND IMAGINES THE HOLY CITY AT THE BIRTH OF CHRISTIANITY

CREATED *1584*
SOURCE *National Library of Israel*

Christiaan van Adrichom almost certainly never visited Jerusalem before making this map in 1584. He was a Catholic priest working in Cologne, in what is now Germany, at a time when the Holy Land had been in Muslim hands for centuries, making it a difficult and potentially dangerous place for Christian pilgrims to visit. Nevertheless, Adrichom managed to create an enormously popular map that not only allowed European Christians to imagine a trip most of them would never be able to take, but also took them back in time to picture the city as it existed during the time of Christ.

The map is packed with at least 270 landmarks and references to Christian tradition, all numbered and keyed to captions in a booklet that accompanied it. Adrichom drew from the work of previous mapmakers, as well as from the Bible and accounts by earlier scholars and pilgrims.

The map looks down on Jerusalem from the west, with east at the top of the map. The orderly grid of streets appears to be based on an overly simplified description of the city by first-century historian Flavius Josephus (see the more realistic map on page 289). In contrast to the thick limestone buildings that would have dominated Jerusalem in the time of Christ, the buildings on Adrichom's map are suspiciously similar in style to the more ornate architecture of 16th-century Europe.

Key episodes from the life of Jesus are strewn across the map. He arrives at Jerusalem on a donkey, as described in the New Testament, surrounded by disciples and preceded by a figure spreading branches in the road ahead of them (number 214, near the top of the map, just right of center, and shown in detail on page 288). The Last Supper, where Jesus predicted his betrayal by Judas, appears just inside the city walls near the map's bottom right-hand corner (number 6), and Jesus' trial before Pontius Pilate, the Roman governor who ordered his execution, plays out just left of center

Christiaan van Adrichom's 1584 map includes many references to historical events—the tents of armies that have invaded the city at different times can be seen around the perimeter of the walled city—but the focus is on the story of Christ, from his arrival (near the top of the map, just right of center) to his crucifixion on Mount Calvary (at the bottom left corner).

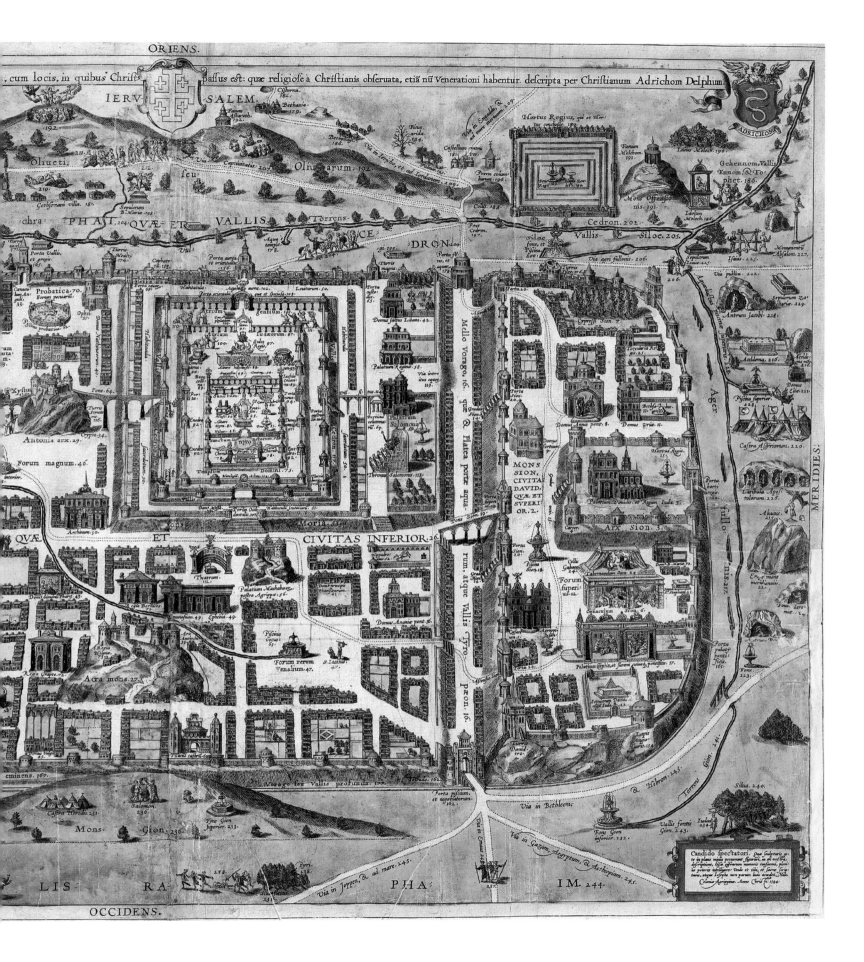

ABOVE Details from Adrichom's map depict episodes from the life of Christ, including (clockwise from top left) his arrival at Jerusalem on a donkey on Palm Sunday, accompanied by his disciples; the Last Supper; Christ's trial before Pontius Pilate; and the crucifixion on Mount Calvary, which plays out in several scenes that end with his mother, Mary, holding his body (number 255).

(number 115). From there, Adrichom portrays Jesus carrying a wooden cross to Mount Calvary (number 235, outside the city walls in the bottom left corner), where he was crucified, as depicted by images of 14 distinct events. That number is one that seems to have stuck. Even today, some Christians observe Good Friday by reenacting Jesus' path, pausing to pray at 14 Stations of the Cross.

Adrichom illustrates events from the final days of Jesus' life as if they are happening simultaneously, but he performs even greater feats of time warping. The invaders who conquered Jerusalem through its history encircle the city together, all at once. The Assyrians who invaded in the eighth century B.C. have set up their tents on the right side of the map (number 220), while the Chaldeans who laid siege to the city in the sixth century B.C. are camped out on the left (number 258), not far from the Roman conquerors who arrived in A.D. 70 (number 259).

Jerusalem was a minor city in the Ottoman Empire in Adrichom's time, but its religious significance meant it still loomed large in the European imagination. Since the invention of the printing press a century earlier, histories, travel guides, and other books about the Holy Land had become increasingly popular and available for people to buy. But what Europeans were looking for in these works wasn't something they could actually use to plan a trip, writes historical geographer Rehav Rubin of the Hebrew University of Jerusalem in a 1993 article in the biblical archaeology magazine *Bible Review*. "Few Europeans actually traveled to Jerusalem. They bought maps and books reflecting their interest in the ideas and events associated with the Holy City—not its physical details."

Adrichom's map did exactly that. It was printed in several editions over the following centuries and translated into several languages, a testament to its popularity. For nearly 300 years, the vision of Jerusalem held by European Christians was shaped to a large degree by this colorful and highly imaginative map. ✳

ABOVE The Franciscan monk Francisco Quaresmius published this more realistic map of Jerusalem in 1639, based in part on his travels to the Holy City. Like Adrichom's map, it includes numbered references to events in the life of Christ and includes historical references from different time periods. The orientation of this map is the opposite of Adrichom's, however, with west at the top and east at the bottom.

Charting the Lands of Ice and Fire

MEDIEVAL MAPS INSPIRE THE CARTOGRAPHY OF THE BLOCKBUSTER TV SHOW

CREATED *2016*
CREATOR *Jim Stanes for HBO*

Geography is so important to the plot of HBO's *Game of Thrones* TV series that the title sequence features a flyover of an animated map of the show's sprawling imaginary world, highlighting the territory relevant to each episode. The show is also littered with maps used by dynastic noble families as they ponder strategy.

The main storyline of the series is a bloody struggle for control of the Seven Kingdoms of Westeros, fought among a shifting cast of characters who scheme and maneuver to sit upon the Iron Throne. The premiere of the show's seventh and penultimate season, aired in 2017,

showcases a huge, striking map of the territory, painted on the stone courtyard floor of one of the most tenacious contenders, Cersei Lannister. She and her twin brother, Jaime, stand over it, gazing at the land beneath their feet, all of which Cersei views as rightfully theirs.

A set piece as big as this one is usually a good candidate for computer-generated imagery that's digitally added to the scene after it's shot. But this map is real: a hand-painted, 29-by-34-foot (9 by 10 m) physical map installed in the *Game of Thrones* studio in Belfast, Ireland. It's one of dozens of maps designed and created for the series by U.K.-based graphic artist Jim Stanes. The geography

used in the show's cartography is derived from a map included in George R. R. Martin's A Song of Ice and Fire books that the wildly popular TV series is based on. The style and feel of the show's maps are inspired by actual historical cartography. "We look at old maps as a daily sort of preoccupation," Stanes says.

Game of Thrones takes place in an unspecified but presumably medieval era, and several historical maps from that period have influenced Stanes's work for the series. The combination of early science and cartography with religion, myth, and legend is appealing, he says. "I love them because they're mysterious, still. They are maps that do not really know the whole picture, so they're guesses, and we get a lot of interesting things happening because of that."

One of the maps Stanes has drawn inspiration from is the Gough Map of Great Britain (see page 292), named after the collector who donated it to the Bodleian Library at the University of Oxford in 1809. Its author and precise age are unknown, but scholars believe it was made in the late medieval era of the 14th and 15th centuries. The map may have been owned by ambitious British royalty, making it a fitting model for Cersei's map. According to the British Library's Peter Barber, an expert on medieval maps, "The Gough map speaks to the imperial

OPPOSITE This map of Westeros, the disputed territory in the TV series *Game of Thrones,* was created to look medieval, the period when the story presumably takes place. The map's designer took cues from actual historical maps, with one exception: Contour lines showing elevation weren't commonly used on maps until hundreds of years later.

RIGHT Once it was designed, the Westeros map took more than three weeks' work by two painters to complete before it was installed in the *Game of Thrones* studio in Belfast, Ireland. This photo shows the map as it appeared on the show in 2017. In the scene, the final corner is being painted.

ambitions of English kings and their clerks."

The shape of the land on the Gough Map may look unfamiliar, mostly because it's oriented with east at the top. Rotate it 90 degrees clockwise, and the English coastline becomes recognizable. It even looks a little like Westeros: Hadrian's Wall separates England from less defined northern territories including Scotland, just as the towering barricade of ice known as the Wall separates Westeros from the frigid northern wilds. Another similarity between the two maps is in the depiction of cities and towns. It was common for medieval mapmakers to use profiles of important buildings to represent locations, and Stanes captures this beautifully with his hand-drawn cities. His Winterfell looks as grand as Gough's London (opposite top).

"I'm fascinated by the world imagined by those mapmakers and feel that a lot of maps from that period are the most beautiful objects ever made," Stanes says.

Another map that has influenced Stanes is the Hereford Mappa Mundi, a late 13th-century map of the world that is the largest known medieval map still in existence. The 5.2-by-4.4-foot (1.6 by 1.3 m) map was made by clergymen at the Hereford Cathedral in England, where it still resides today. Like the Gough Map, locations are marked with the profiles of buildings, but they are far more lavishly decorated. The most elaborate is the city of Babylon topped by the Tower of Babel, which compares nicely to Stanes's illustration of Kings Landing, the capital of the Seven Kingdoms (opposite bottom).

Rather than drawing straight profiles of buildings, Stanes depicted the cities on the courtyard map at more of an angle. This bird's-eye view helps connect them to the flyover of the animated map in the show's title sequence. For the details of each city, Stanes took cues from the animated map as well as scenes from the show. Once he finished drawing the individual cities and designing the base map, everything was digitally combined and printed at full size for the producers' approval. Then two painters got to work on 2-foot (0.6 m)-square tiles, painting a half-dozen at a time, which were then laid down in the studio. From initial conception to final brush strokes, the whole project took around two months to complete.

All that work came with a bonus for Stanes: a brief cameo in the season seven premiere. Fittingly, he plays the mapmaker, painting the last corner of the courtyard map as Cersei Lannister looks on. When her brother Jaime enters the courtyard and sees the map, he dismisses Stanes's character with a nod as he asks his sister, "What is this?"

"It's what we've been waiting for our whole lives. It's what Father trained us for, whether he knew it or not," she replies. "It's ours now. We just have to take it."

But as they pace around the map, assessing the geography and pondering their relationships with neighboring noble families, their precarious position becomes clear. "Enemies everywhere," Cersei says bitterly. "We're surrounded by traitors. East, south, west, north." ✳

ABOVE East is at the top of this medieval map of Great Britain. Called the Gough Map after a previous owner, it has been dated to the 14th or 15th century. The coastline of England is relatively accurate, but Scotland is an unrecognizable blob, suggesting the map was made for an Englishman, possibly British royalty.

....

OPPOSITE TOP The illustration of Winterfell on the Westeros map (at right) bears a resemblance to the depiction of London on the medieval Gough Map (at left). The use of profiles of recognizable or important buildings to represent major cities was common on medieval maps.

....

OPPOSITE BOTTOM The city of Babylon topped by the Tower of Babel is represented by the most elaborately illustrated structure on the map known as the Hereford Mappa Mundi (at left), which was made around 1300. Kings Landing, the capital city of the Seven Kingdoms, is likewise given special attention on the map of Westeros (at right).

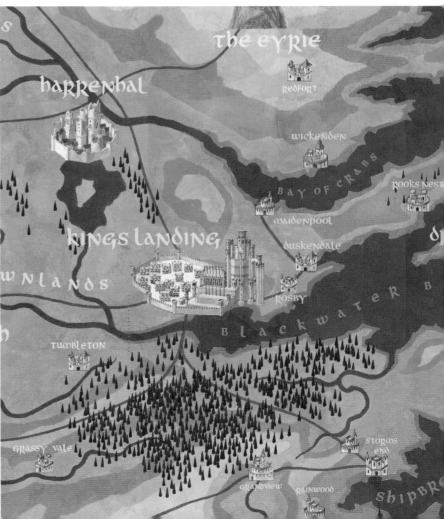

San Francisco Bay, Sewn in Silk

TEXTILE MAPS IMAGINE THE BAY'S INDUSTRIALIZED SHORELINE BEING RECLAIMED BY NATURE

CREATED *2005–2013*
CREATOR *Linda Gass*

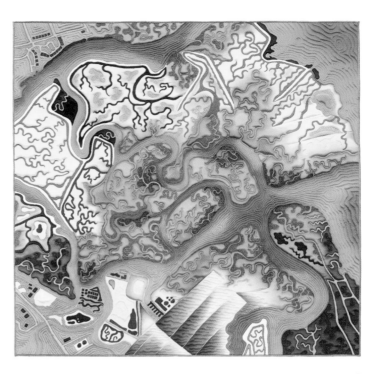

Before humans arrived, the San Francisco Bay was a thriving estuary ringed with wetlands. Since then, more than 90 percent of those natural marshy areas have disappeared. The edges of the bay are now a patchwork of salt ponds, office parks, airports, and hiking trails, with a few small wetland preserves sprinkled in. The story of how that landscape has changed, and might continue to evolve in the future, is woven into the quilts of California artist Linda Gass.

"I first became interested in the bay after being mesmerized by the mysterious view of the industrial salt ponds I saw from the airplane window," Gass says. "What were those unreal colors and shapes?" She later learned that the ponds, which produce sea salt through evaporation, take on the bright reds, oranges, and greens of the microorganisms that live in them.

A set of maps made by the San Francisco Estuary Institute showed her that over the past two centuries, much of the natural wetlands around the bay have been either diked and drained, filled in, or transformed into salt ponds. Intrigued, Gass began researching old aerial photographs and maps, incorporating what she learned into her art. Her goal is to help people understand the importance of the bay—to animal species, water quality, and flood protection—and the impact that humans have had on it. "My approach is to use beauty to encourage people to look at the hard issues that we face," she says.

To create what she calls "stitched paintings," Gass paints white silk, then sews in details and textures. For the project shown here, she focused on an area of the bay near Redwood City known as Bair Island, which was drained by a rancher named Fred Bair nearly a century ago. Her first piece (opposite) shows the area as it looked in the 1970s: salt ponds brightly colored by different microorganisms, former ranchland, and a few remaining fragments of wetlands. The aptly named Corkscrew Slough runs through the center of Bair Island.

In 1982, citizens of Redwood City voted to stop a modern development planned for Bair Island. In 2007, the land was incorporated into a refuge, and efforts to restore it got under way. In the second piece in her series (top right), Gass imagines a future landscape where the wetlands have begun to reclaim the

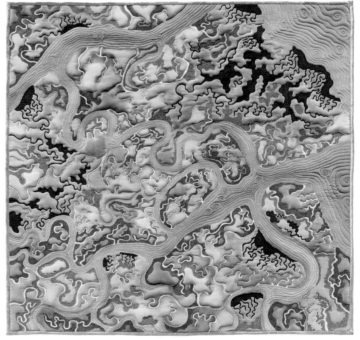

salt ponds and the surrounding sloughs are returning to health.

"Although it's my imagined landscape, I didn't totally make it up," Gass says. "I researched historical photographs of that area to understand what the wetlands looked like before the salt ponds were built." These old aerial photos were black and white, so to understand what the natural colors of a San Francisco Bay wetland would be, she visited one of its few remaining untouched marshes.

The third piece (above) is a completely imagined return to wilderness. "It's a landscape of how nature, impatient with how long it's taking us to restore the wetlands, is just starting to do it herself." ✳

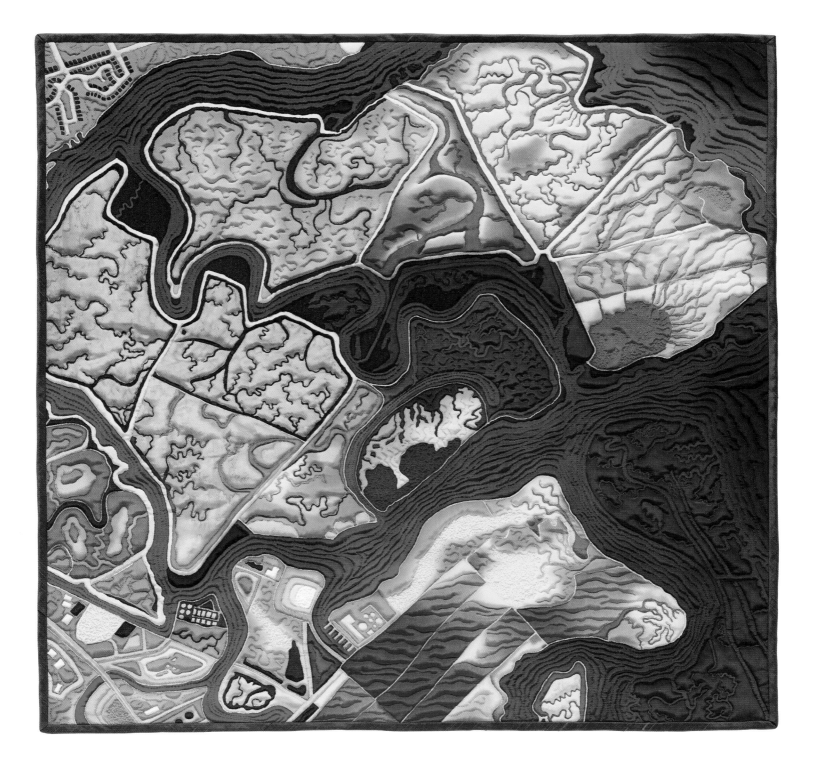

This series of "stitched paintings" by artist Linda Gass shows an imagined evolution of the edge of San Francisco Bay. The first piece (above), based on photographs from the 1970s, shows salt ponds brightly colored by the microorganisms living in them. The second piece (opposite top) shows how the area might look as nature begins to reclaim it in the future. The final piece (opposite bottom) shows a landscape even farther in the future that has been almost completely restored to natural wetlands.

Garden City Utopias

A LONDON STENOGRAPHER'S MAPS ENVISION COMMUNITIES THAT COMBINE THE BEST OF TOWN AND COUNTRY LIVING

CREATED *1898*
CREATOR *Ebenezer Howard*

Ebenezer Howard was a stenographer and part-time inventor living in London when he published these community planning maps in 1898. They appeared in Howard's book *To-morrow: a Peaceful Path to Real Reform,* which describes his vision for utopian communities that combined the best elements of urban and rural life. Howard called them Garden Cities, and they've been an inspiration to urban planners ever since.

The country, as Howard saw it, offered benefits like bright sunshine, fresh air, and natural beauty, but it lacked high-paying jobs, social opportunities, and amusements. Towns and cities offered much of what the country lacked in regard to employment and society, but also came with high rents and foul air (Howard lived in London at the height of the Industrial Revolution). He also counted "slums & gin palaces" as downsides.

Howard imagined a third kind of community that would combine the best of these two worlds and be largely self-sufficient. He suggested starting a hypothetical city on 6,000 acres (2,400 ha) of land to be purchased by the inhabitants. At the center, covering about 1,000 acres (400 ha), would be the Garden City itself, home to about 30,000 people. Howard drew his cities as circles, but each diagram acknowledged that the actual shape would vary according to local conditions.

The map to the right shows a wedge-shaped ward of a Garden City. At the center is a large garden surrounded by public and cultural institutions like the town hall, library, and museum. A large central park surrounds these buildings and is itself encircled by a crystal palace, a glass

---

Ebenezer Howard envisioned his Garden Cities as concentric circles of residential neighborhoods (pink rings) surrounding a large, central public space. The city would be surrounded by 5,000 acres (2,000 ha) of agricultural land—home to another 2,000 people— and connected to other cities by roads and a railway.

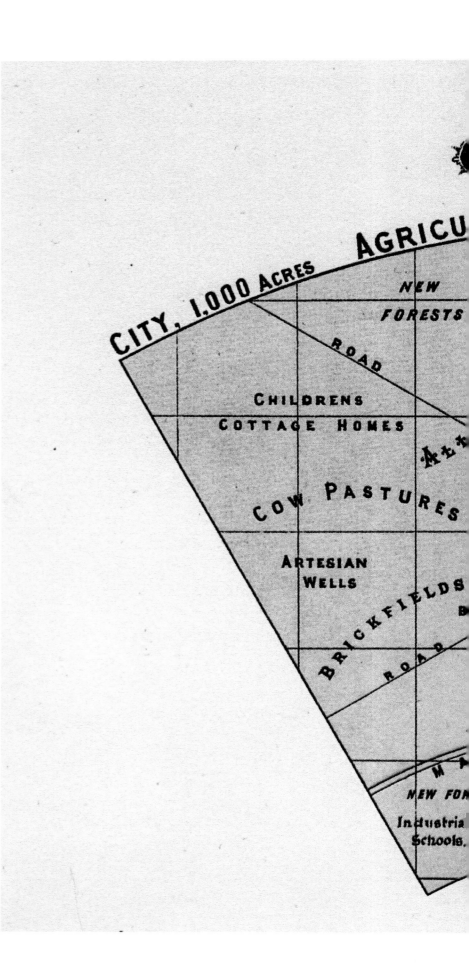

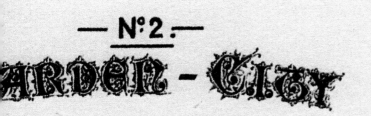

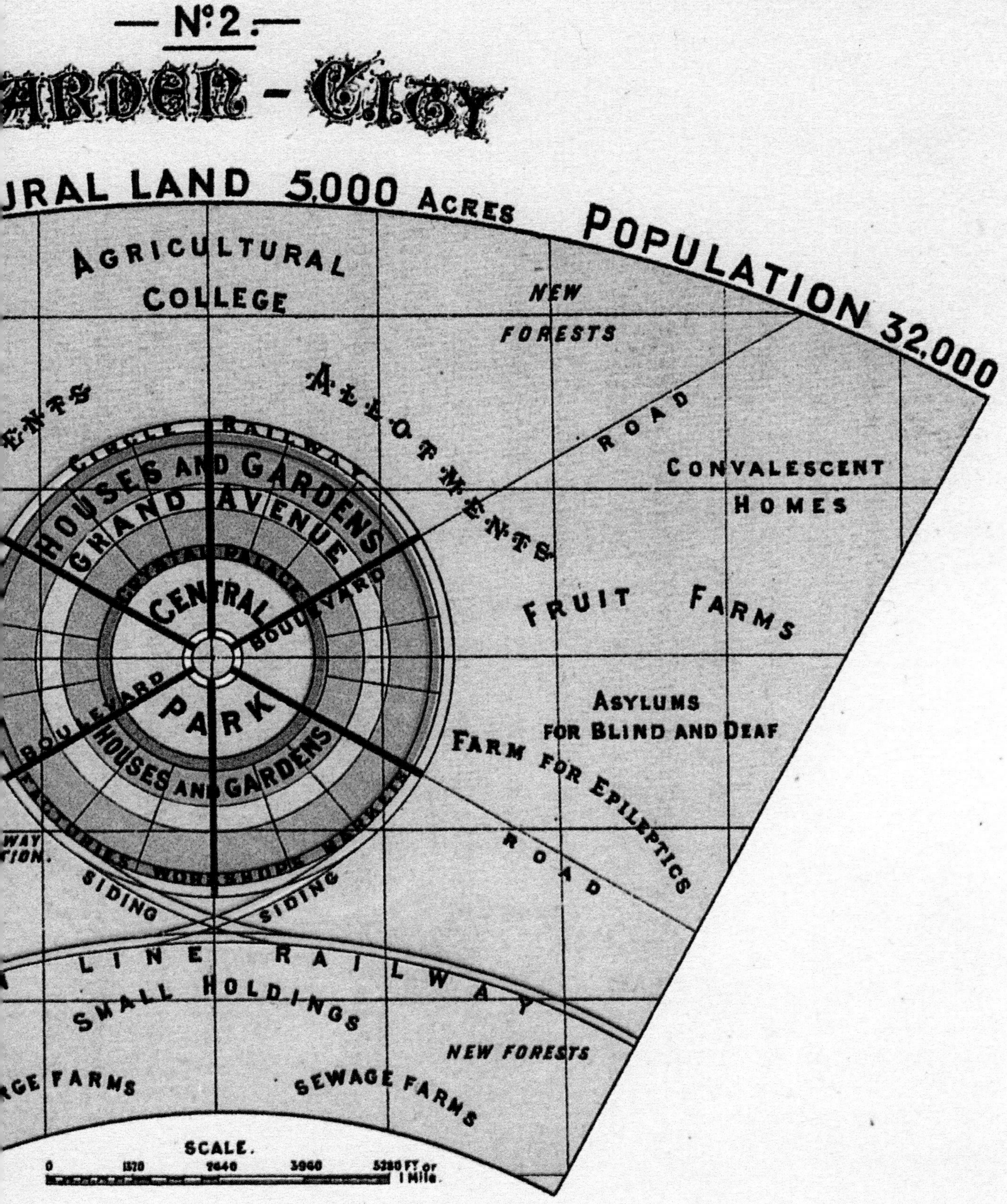

GARDEN - CITY

RURAL LAND 5,000 ACRES

POPULATION 32,000

AGRICULTURAL COLLEGE

NEW FORESTS

ENTS

ALLOTMENTS

CIRCLE RAILWAY

HOUSES AND GARDENS

GRAND AVENUE

ROAD

CONVALESCENT HOMES

CENTRAL

BOULEVARD

FRUIT FARMS

PARK

BOULEVARD

HOUSES AND GARDENS

ASYLUMS FOR BLIND AND DEAF

FARM FOR EPILEPTICS

WAY TION.

SIDING

SIDING

ROAD

LINE RAILWAY

SMALL HOLDINGS

NEW FORESTS

RGE FARMS

SEWAGE FARMS

SCALE.

0   1320   2640   3960   5280 FT. or 1 Mile.

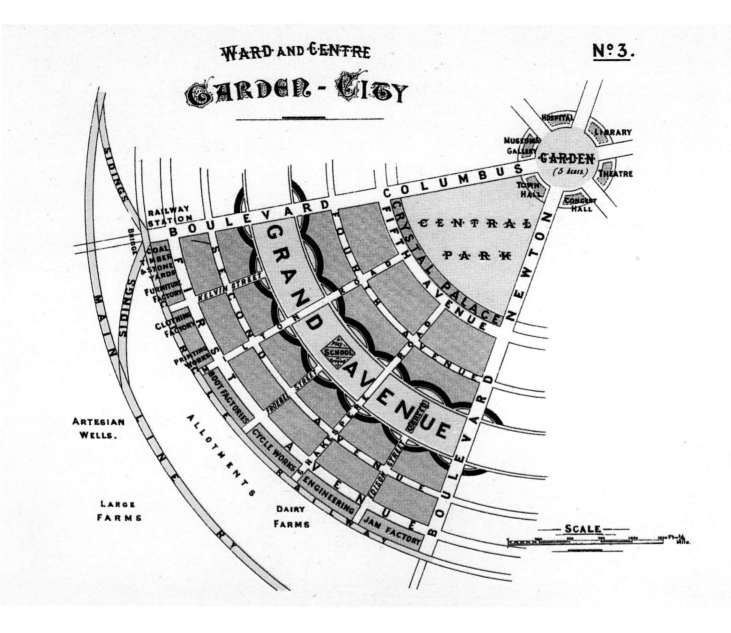

arcade that would allow people to enjoy the area "even in the most doubtful of weathers." Concentric rings of residential streets surround this public space. An enormous Grand Avenue cuts a 420-foot (130 m)-wide green belt through this area, providing space for churches, schools, and still more gardens. Because of the avenue's circular design, no resident would live more than 720 feet (220 m) away from it.

The outermost circle of the Garden City is reserved for factories and other workplaces. Some, like the cycle works and jam factory, seem quaintly Victorian, although they'd fit in just fine in some modern neighborhoods where

artisan goods are back in style. Rail stops along this outer ring would connect the Garden City to others like it (opposite left). The spaces in between the cities would be kept rural, providing a place for orchards and farms, as well as a smattering of institutions and homes for the unfortunate (including "waifs," "inebriates," and the "insane").

When it came out, the book got mixed reviews. Some saw Howard's ideas as naively idealistic and totally unworkable for established cities like London. "His plans would have been in time if they had been submitted to the Romans when they conquered Britain," one critic wrote

in the newsletter of the Fabian Society, a socialist group advocating for social reform.

Howard was undaunted by such critiques. He traveled across England giving lectures and promoting his idea. While reportedly unremarkable in appearance, he had a powerful speaking voice and a natural gift for eloquence. Howard helped raise money and support to establish the first Garden City at Letchworth, about 40 miles (64 km) north of London, in 1903 and a second at Welwyn in 1920. Both successfully implemented Howard's key ideas, if not the idealized geometry of his maps, and they still exist today.

Dozens of other Garden Cities have been

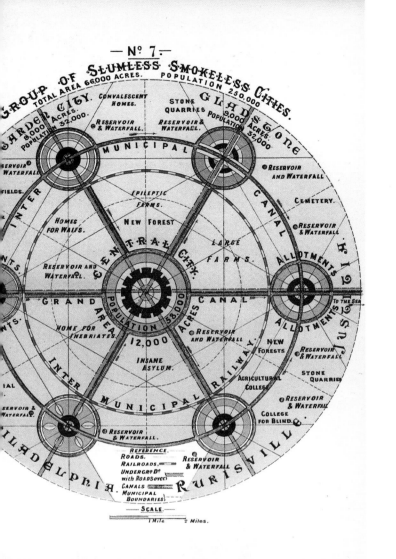

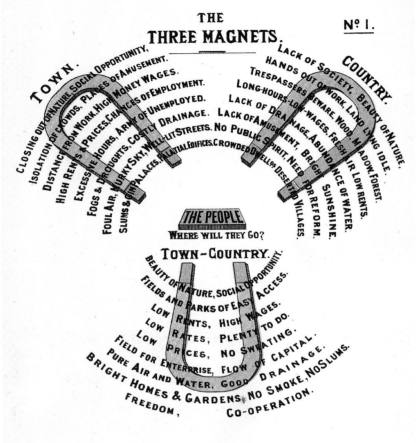

founded in the United Kingdom and elsewhere since Howard's death in 1928, but his ideas also influenced urban planning and revitalization efforts in existing cities throughout the 20th century. They can be seen, for example, in the urban growth boundaries established by the Oregon legislature in the 1970s to preserve a rural greenbelt surrounding cities of a certain size, and in the push to revive city parks and other green spaces across the United States. Howard's vision of a perfect balance of rural and urban life may remain an elusive ideal, but it's no less attractive today than it was when he proposed it more than a century ago. ✳

OPPOSITE This close-up shows the concentric rings of a Garden City in greater detail. The town hall, hospital, library, and other public buildings in the central garden are visible, as are the businesses and railway station around the outer ring.

ABOVE LEFT This map shows what a network of Garden Cities might look like, connected by railways, roads, and an "inter municipal canal." This "group of slumless, smokeless cities" would be home to 250,000 people, but still include a great deal of open space.

ABOVE RIGHT Howard likened "Town" and "Country" to two magnets, each with its own attracting and repelling forces. His Garden Cities were meant to create a third magnet, "Town-Country," that would offer the best of both worlds, including "low rates, plenty to do. Low prices, no sweating."

The Elusive Death Star Plans

THE SUPERWEAPON SCHEMATICS PLAY A HUGE ROLE IN THE STAR WARS SAGA, BUT WE RARELY SEE THEM

CREATED *2015*
SOURCE *Lucasfilm*

The original *Star Wars* movie opens with a crawl of yellow text that sets the stage for the action to come. A civil war is under way, we learn, and the rebels have just scored their first victory against the evil Galactic Empire. "During the battle, Rebel spies managed to steal secret plans to the Empire's ultimate weapon, the DEATH STAR," the text reads as it scrolls into infinity.

Forty-odd years later, it's hardly a spoiler to say that those plans are essential to the plot. The Death Star is indeed a deadly weapon, equipped with a powerful laser that can vaporize an entire planet. But it has a fatal flaw: The stolen plans reveal a narrow cooling shaft where a well-placed proton torpedo could set off a chain reaction that would blow the whole thing up. In the movie's thrilling finale, attacking rebel pilots fly through a narrow trench that leads to the opening of the cooling shaft with Imperial TIE fighters in hot pursuit.

In this cutaway schematic, the cooling shaft appears as a thin line running almost vertically from the top of the Death Star down into the main reactor, which powers its planet-destroying laser.

Such a detailed schematic never appears in the movie. This imagining of the Death Star's inner workings was used by Lucasfilm to create posters promoting *Rogue One,* the 2016 movie that tells the story of how the rebels stole the Death Star plans from the Imperial Archive and smuggled them to safety (earlier versions of the schematic were used for other promotions and merchandise, including a 2013 Death Star owner's manual).

The *Rogue One* storyline was inspired by the text crawl in the 1977 movie, now known as *Star Wars: A New Hope* to distinguish it from all the sequels and prequels. John Knoll, who co-wrote, executive-produced, and served as visual effects supervisor for *Rogue One,* saw *New Hope* when he was a boy, and the line about the rebels stealing the plans fired his imagination. "I thought that could be a pretty good movie by itself," he says.

But despite the importance of the Death Star plans, only a few partial glimpses of them ever appear onscreen. The longest sequence in *New Hope* comes near the end, when a rebel commander briefs the pilots before their attack. A wire frame graphic on a screen behind him shows the narrow trench the pilots will have to navigate to reach their target.

The few brief shots of the plans in *Rogue One* pay homage to the early computer graphics of the 1977 movie. That was intentional, Knoll says, because the events of *Rogue One* directly precede those of *New Hope.* "We were trying to be true to the graphic design style of *New Hope,*" Knoll says. "There was a desire to not have graphics that would look out of place in the original film."

That makes sense, of course, but for any fans left wondering what those highly sought-after plans actually look like, this may be as close as you're going to get. ✳

The Death Star's planet-vaporizing laser looks like a concave eye on the surface, and the huge cylindrical apparatus that makes it work is visible in this cutaway view. The circular chamber at the center of the planet-size superweapon is the "hypermatter" reactor that powers the laser.

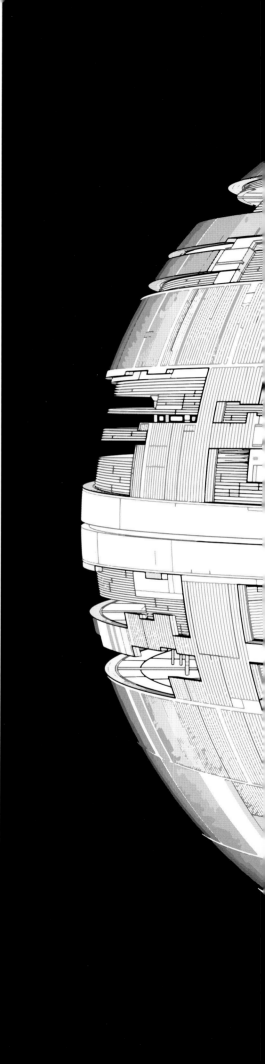

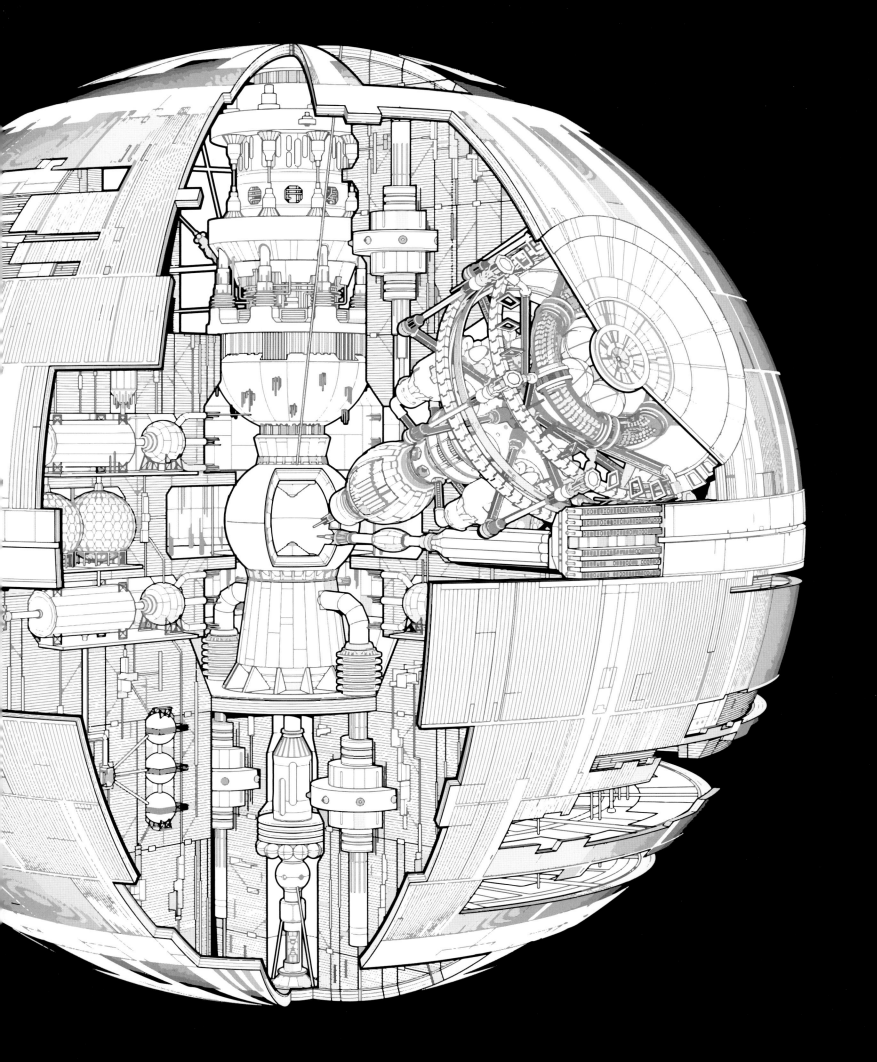

An Epic Mapmaking Journey

AN ARTIST IMMERSED HIMSELF IN NORTH AMERICA'S LAND-SCAPES AND CULTURES TO CREATE A REMARKABLE MAP

CREATED *2018*
CREATOR *Anton Thomas*

It took Anton Thomas four years to finish his hand-drawn map of North America. In that time, he filled every inch of the 5-foot (1.5 m)-tall map with forests, mountains, lakes, animals, and cities, all carefully rendered with colored pencil and ink.

As he drew the landscape from the West Coast eastward, his drawing skills improved—so much so that when he reached the East Coast, he decided to redo the western half of the continent. "That set me back almost a year," Thomas says of all the erasing and scratching out of ink with a sharp knife. But it was worth it in the end, he says. The map, which he plans to sell prints of, has launched a new career for him as a mapmaker.

Thomas has been obsessed with maps since he was around seven years old, and he couldn't be happier to have found himself combining art and cartography. "I love every part of the research and the drawing," he says.

The project was inspired by a six-month trip Thomas took to the United States in 2011. He was 21 years old, and it was his first time leaving his native New Zealand. He fell in love with the United States and afterward couldn't stop thinking about it. So when a roommate asked him to spruce up their old refrigerator with some art, Thomas started drawing a freehand map of North America. "I ended up spending a month just drawing this map on the fridge," he says. "People who saw the fridge kept saying, 'That's amazing! Can you do my fridge?'"

This close-up of the northeast portion of the United States on Anton Thomas's map of North America shows the incredible level of detail he included. He drew the skylines of hundreds of cities and animals as well as countless trees, mountains, deserts, plains, and prairies. He has called the years-long project "a love letter to the continent."

The seed was planted, and in 2014 Thomas started making the real map, on paper. The first step was to project an outline of the continent onto a large sheet of paper hung on the wall, then trace the coastlines, rivers, and political borders. Everything else was drawn freehand.

Thomas drew the skylines of 600 cities and towns, making sure that all the iconic, important, and meaningful structures were included, like San Francisco's Golden Gate Bridge and Seattle's Space Needle. For the rest, he did extensive online research and did his best to immerse himself in places from afar. He listened to local music, watched movies set in those locations, and sought out local food specialties. "I try to cast a wide net, learn what I can and draw content representative of a place," he says. "Content that would be familiar to a local."

For example, Thomas drew the big letter "M" that hovers 600 feet (183 m) above Missoula, Montana, on the slope of Mount Sentinel, and the switchbacks leading up to it. In the Pacific Northwest's Cascade Range, each of its main peaks—including Mount Rainier, Mount Hood, and Mount St. Helens—is recognizable on the map (see page 305). "I feel they all have a certain character, and I worked hard to try to capture that," he says.

While researching Cuba, he rewatched the movie *Buena Vista Social Club* and spent hours listening to Cuban music. He sought out Cuban food and even bought and smoked an expensive Cuban cigar. He thought of it as a "method actor" approach to cartography. When it came time to illustrate Havana, instead of simply putting a few musical notes on the map Thomas drew the symbols for the rhythmic pattern of rumba, a style of music that originated there.

The map also features more than 400 animals, including 25 bears, 12 caribou, eight moose, four jaguars, and many other species. Every state and national bird is represented,

even Costa Rica's clay-colored thrush, which seemed like a waste of that country's limited space on the map. "I found it very strange that a boring old thrush would be the national bird of a country that's home to around 5 percent of Earth's species," Thomas says. Neighboring countries had more colorful and charismatic birds, like the scarlet macaw in Honduras, Panama's harpy eagle, and Belize's toucan. The thrush turned out to be a perfect choice for other reasons: It's a friendly bird with an alluring song and is commonly seen in cities and towns. "It resonates with people's actual lives," he says.

But not every symbol on the map is a happy one. Texas and Illinois are dotted with smokestacks belching pollution into the air. The *Exxon Valdez,* which spilled hundreds of thousands of barrels of crude oil in 1989, is sinking into Alaska's Prince William Sound. The cloud from a

OPPOSITE TOP The landscape of Mexico on Thomas's map includes pre-Columbian ruins, such as Monte Alban outside Oaxaca. Pico de Orizaba, a volcano that is the third-tallest peak in North America, rises south of the city of Xalapa. Mexico City's historic center is recognizable, with a modern skyline lurking behind it. In the countryside, there are native animals including a kinkajou, a jaguarundi, a northern tamandua, and a mountain trogon.

OPPOSITE BOTTOM One of the most challenging parts of the map for Thomas to draw was the intricate Arctic coastline. This part of the Arctic in northernmost Canada is sparsely populated by people, but has plenty of interesting animals, including polar bears, musk oxen, short-tailed weasels, and spotted seals. Though there are mainly just very small towns and outposts, Thomas still took care to represent them accurately.

RIGHT Thomas started drawing North America from the West Coast of the United States. By the time he filled in the territory all the way to the East Coast, his drawing had improved and his style had evolved so much that he ended up redoing the western half of the map. Now the skylines in California, Washington, Oregon, and Nevada are cleaner and the animals are smaller and more accurately placed.

nuclear bomb test rises from the Nevada desert.

Thomas struggled with how to represent the scars left by conflict and natural disasters. In Haiti's Port-au-Prince, he acknowledged the damage from the 2010 earthquake by including the ghostly outline of buildings that had collapsed. Throughout the map, he tried to strike a balance between pretty pictures and geographic reality. "The whole thing is just full of interesting puzzles and conundrums," he says. "It can get pretty philosophical sometimes."

After years of painstakingly drawing thousands of details on the North American continent, he's ready for some new territory. Some smaller projects would be a nice break from the scale of this project, he says. Perhaps New Zealand will be next.

For his next really big map, Thomas has his eye on South America. He thinks he could knock that one out in just 12 or 18 months. ✳

Nellie Bly's Race Around the World

A BOARD GAME MAPS A PIONEERING JOURNALIST'S WHIRLWIND JOURNEY

CREATED *1890*
SOURCE *David Rumsey Map Collection*

In 1889, trailblazing journalist Nellie Bly set out to circle the globe in record time, a stunt inspired by the popular Jules Verne novel *Around the World in Eighty Days*. Circling the globe in such a short time had only recently begun to seem possible with the completion of the Suez Canal and railways like the transcontinental railroad across North America. But if a woman were the first to do it—traveling alone, no less—it would be a sensation.

Bly's editor at the *New York World* initially balked at the idea, suggesting that any woman would surely bring too much baggage and fail to make all her connections. He eventually relented, and Bly famously packed a small case of essentials she could carry in one hand and wore a single dress she made the day before her departure. "I always have a comfortable feeling that nothing is impossible if one applies a certain amount of energy in the right direction," she later wrote.

Bly left New York City on November 14 on a steamer bound for London. Over the coming months, the public was captivated by her journey, their imaginations fired by her dispatches from abroad. The *World* did what it could to stoke the frenzy, printing coupons readers could use to place bets on the exact time of Bly's return to New York (more than 900,000 people entered, hoping to win a free trip to Europe), as well as a board game based on her trip that could be cut out of the paper. The more colorful version shown here, mounted on cardboard, was produced after her return.

The game maps Bly's planned itinerary as a spiral. The journey starts with an ocean voyage to London; proceeds by train to Brindisi on the heel of Italy's boot; then goes by ship through the Suez Canal; across the bottom of Asia and up to Yokohama, Japan; across the Pacific to San Francisco; and then finally by train back to New York. Each space on the board represents a day of the journey, many of which instruct players to jump ahead a few spaces or go back, mostly due to changes in weather. Although the game was first printed during Bly's trip, she did in fact return to New York in just over 72 days—exactly as the board suggests.

In Bly's day, the few women working as journalists were mostly relegated to writing gossip columns, recipes, and tips on homemaking. Bly blazed a new path not only with her trip, but also with an undercover exposé of the horrid conditions at a mental hospital and frontline reporting during World War I. Circling the globe made Bly famous in her day, but her most enduring contribution may have been the inspiring example she set for future generations of women who would dare to do things society told them they couldn't. ✳

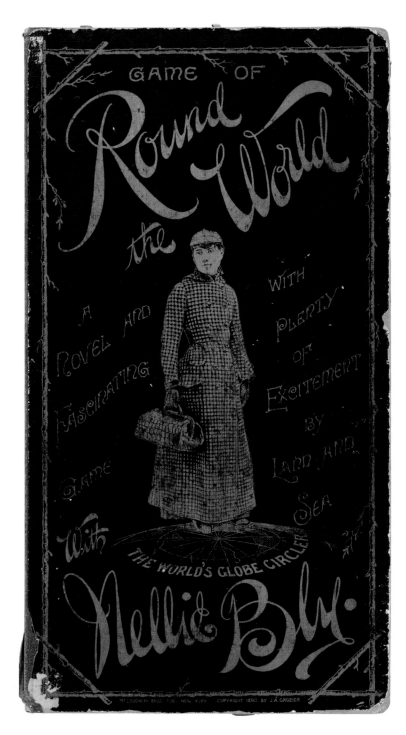

Nellie Bly, clutching her handbag, appears on the cover of the board game (above) and at the starting point in the top left corner of the board (at right). She was 35 when she embarked on her trip. The man in the top right corner is Jules Verne, author of *Around the World in Eighty Days* and inspiration for Bly's journey. Bly visited him in Amiens, France, near the beginning of her trip.

The map shows various Venus surface features labeled with goddess names, including:

UILATA FLUCTUS — Cherokee Stone-Clad Female Monster
...VARD Armenian
NEDA Macedonian
MEHSETI PATERA — Ganjevi
TULI MONS — Samoan Goddess of Creation
KOTI FLUCTUS — Creek Water-Frog Helpful Spirit
MADDERAKKA CORONA — Sami Goddess of Birth
...TTER Beatrix
...AUFEY REGIO — ...RSE GIANTESS
TINGOI VALLIS — Mande River Spirit
NANG-BYON CHASMA — White Tai (Vietnam) Moon Goddess
KALA Koryak
VAR MONS — Scandinavian Love Goddess
SHIH MAI-YU — Chinese Physician
SEYMOUR Jane
GUDRUN Norse
MORTIM-EKVA FLUCTUS — Mansi Mistress of Bird's Country
SATI VALLIS — Egyptian River Goddess
CLIO Greek
NGONE Wolof
KODU Wolof
AURELIA — Mother of Julius Caesar
NINZI Burma
VASILUTSA Moldavian
GUINEVERE PLANITIA — BRITISH WIFE OF KING ARTHUR
VAKARINE VALLIS — Lithuanian word for Venus
CHIUN CORONA — Hebrew Fertility Goddess
BENTEN CORONA — Japanese Love & Fertility Goddess
LYDIA Greek
SOMAGALAGS MONTES — Bella Coola Earth Mother (formerly Somagalags Corona)
EINGANA CORONA — Australian Aboriginal Snake Goddess
BENNU VALLIS — Egyptian word for Venus
COMNENA Anna
VERIKO Georgian
DE LALANDE — Marie-Jeanne
OLOSA COLLES — Yoruba Lagoon Goddess
ENID Celtic
CUNITZ Maria
RHODA Greek
BARAUKA Hausa
SIF MONS — Teutonic Goddess
Finno-Ugric Harvest Spirit
GULA MON... — Babylonia Earth Mother Creative Forc...
SILVIA CORONA — Roman Earth Goddess
OKSANA Ukrainian
MARIANNE Greek
NADINE French
HENG-O CHASM... — Chinese Moon Godd...
HELLMAN Lillian
HENG-O CORON... — Chinese Moon Godd... (named for Heng-O Cha...)

45W 40W 35W 30W 25W 20W 15W 10W 5W

The Goddesses of Venus

POWERFUL WOMEN FROM MANY CULTURES ARE REPRESENTED IN THE PLANET'S FEATURES

CREATED *2017*
SOURCE *Eleanor Lutz*

Venus is home to scores of powerful women. Dzalarhons, the volcano goddess of the indigenous Haida people of the Pacific Northwest, resides just below the home of Ojuz, deity of frost and cold wind to the people of Tajikistan. Nearby are Gbadu, the goddess of guessing to the Fon people of the West African country of Benin, and Mafdet, the Egyptian goddess of judicial authority and executions. All have given their names to actual features on the surface of Venus, and you can find them opposite top right on this imaginative map by scientific designer Eleanor Lutz.

Lutz was a biology Ph.D. student at the University of Washington in 2017 when she made it. She'd made her first planetary map the year before, a map of Mars inspired by Victorian-era maps that introduced people to far-off lands they'd likely never visit. The Venus map has a very different look. "I wanted to use an aesthetic that referenced elements of Cold War propaganda posters, as a nod to the political history of Venus exploration," she says. Most exploratory spacecraft sent to Venus were sent by the Soviets during the space race in the 1960s and 1970s. Their landing sites are marked with circular shields on the map. Several of the landers crashed, but even those that didn't were soon destroyed by the scorching heat (which can exceed 800°F/430°C) and crushing atmospheric pressure (about 90 times that on Earth).

These landers are vastly outnumbered by the goddesses, mythical heroines, and other female namesakes of the planet's physical features. By decree of the International Astronomical Union, the scientific body that sets the naming conventions for celestial bodies, nearly all features on Venus are named after real or imaginary women.

Lutz says she was intrigued by how the goddesses hinted at what might have been important to their culture, like the beekeeping goddess of the Adyghe, an ethnic group native to what's now the southwest corner of Russia. "It was also fun to see that some things seemed to be almost universally important—there are a lot of fertility goddesses and water goddesses on the map."

Mortal women are represented, too. Craters over 12 miles (20 km) wide are named after famous women and appear on the map in yellow. These include Mona Lisa, Virginia Woolf, and Billie Holiday. Smaller craters, shown in red, are given common women's names from different cultures. And so it is that Fatima, Magdalena, and even Linda all have a home on Venus. ✳

The naming rules for Venus are very specific. Tesserae, areas with tile-like terrain, are named after goddesses of fortune and fate and marked on the map with a white circle inside a dark square. Coronae are oval features named after fertility or earth goddesses and marked by a symbol with four dark circles.

roman Empress

Tibetan Goddess
of Compassion
(the sea Dayaks of Borneo)

MERISA FLUCTUS
Adyghe Beekeeping Goddess

FAUFAU Polynesian

BEREGHINYA PLANITIA
SLAVIC WATER SPIRIT

ESTHER Persian

AYASHE Hausa

CORINNA
Greek Poet

MAMITU TESSE
Akkadian Destiny
Goddess

SHEILA C

GUOR LINEA
Northern European Valkyrie

IRNINI MONS
Assyro-Babylonian
Goddess of
Cedar-Tree
Mountains

HIRIATA Polynesian

METELITSA
DORSA
East Slavic
Snowstorm Deity

HUAREI
Polynesian

VENERA 4 · Венера-4
SUCCESSFUL
Survived for
93 MIN
USSR · 1967

BRADST
Anne

**NEHALENNIA
CORONA**
Teutonic Fertility
Goddess

DEVORGUILLA
Irish Heroine

SAPPHO PATERA
Lyric Poet

**NINMAH
CORONA**
Sumer-Akkadian
Mother Goddess

MARGARITA
Greek

AGOE Eve

CARMENTA FARRA
man Goddess of Springs

ANALA MONS
Hindu Fertility Goddess
(formerly Anala Corona)

**LIBERA
CORONA**
Roman Fertility
Goddess

DE AYALA
Josefa

**PAVLOVA
CORONA**
Anna Pavlova
(formerly Pavlova Crater)

ISO
CO
Ibibi
Fert
God

EISTLA
REGIO
NORSE GIANTESS

FESTA
Italian Painter

VIRTUS LINEA
Roman War Goddess

**CHANGKO
CORONA**
Kachin Mother of
all Humans

BADB LINEA
Irish War Goddess

AKUBA Eve

MANTON Sidnie

GWYNN Nell

MAFDET TESSERA
Egyptian Goddess of
Judicial Authority &
Executions

**CALAKOMANA
CORONA**
Pueblo Corn Goddess

**SUNRTA
CORONA**
Hindu Fertility
Goddess

**BELET-ILI
CORONA**
Mesopotamian Nature
& Fertility Goddess

KELEA
Maui
Chieftess

KALI MONS
Hindu Goddess,
Mother of Death

**RABZHIMA
CORONA**
Tibetan Great
Mother Goddess

AMINATA Mandinka

AFIRUWA Hausa

OSHUN FARRA
Yoruba Water Goddess

GAIA CORONA
Greek Earth &
Fertility Goddess

OJUZ DORSA
Tajik Deity of Frost
& Cold Wind

FARIDA Azeri

**NAMJYALMA
FOSSAE**
Tibetan Victorious Mother

CALLAS Maria

**DZALARHONS
MONS**
Haida Volcano
Goddess

GBADU TESSERA
Fon (Benin) Goddess
of Guessing

**PTESANWI
MONS**
Lakota White
Buffalo Wom

PIAF Edith

NEPRA VALLIS
East Slavic Goddess of Dnieper River

5E 10E 25E 30E 35E 40E 45E 50

VENERA 5 · Венера-5
SUCCESSFUL
Survived for
53 MIN
USSR · 1969

**NEKHEBET
FLUCTUS**
Egyptian Vulture
Goddess

SALUS TESSERA
Roman Health &
Prosperity Goddess

**KUAN-YIN
CORONA**
Chinese Fertility
Goddess

LARA Latin

VENERA 6 · Венера-6
SUCCESSFUL
Survived for
51 MIN
USSR · 1969

EVIKA Tatar

VALERIE French

VANESSA
Greek

GRAHAM PATERA
Martha

BANUMBIRR VALLIS
Arnhemland word for Venus

THOURIS CORONA
Egyptian Fertility Goddess

VASHTI Persian

**THERMUTHIS
CORONA**
Egyptian Fertility &
Harvest Goddess

**NABUZANA
CORONA**
Ugandan Crop
Goddess

**ATARGATIS
CORONA**
Hittite Fertility
Goddess

XANTIPPE
Wife of Socrates

REBECCA Hebrew

LESLIE English

**MUKYLCHIN
CORONA**
Udmurt Fertility
Goddess

MAGDALEN
Spanish

LINDA Latin

KAREN Greek

**DUDUMITSA
DORSA**
Bulgarian
Rain Deity

FRANK Anne

GILLIAN L

TINATIN
PLANITIA

FATUA CORONA
Roman Fertility Goddess

ADAMSON Joy

MUNTER Gabriele

LAURENCIN Marie

GEORGIAN EPIC HEROINE

ANDAMI
Iranian Doctor

BATHSHEBA
Hebrew Queer

FATIMA Arabic

MEDHAVI
Ramabai

**JUKSAKKA
CORONA**
Sami Goddess o
Birth

**MINU-ANNI
TESSERA**
Assyrian Fate Goddess

MICHELLE French

ALPHA
REGIO

BRYNHILD FOSSAE
Norse Warrior Maiden

SCARPELLINI
Caterina

IRST LETTER OF THE
GREEK ALPHABET

KIMITONGA
Polynesian

VIRGA Lithuanian

**MAMA-ALLPA
CORONA**
Peruvian Harvest
Goddess

ANICIA
Greek Physician

**UMAY-ENE
CORONA**
Kazakh Childcare
Goddess

NADIA Russian

SOPHIA Greek

ZENOBIA
Queen of Palmyra

SEORITSU FARRA
Japanese Stream Goddess

KALOMBO Bantu

PUREV Mongolian

STUART
Mary, Queen of Scots

EVE CORONA
Hebrew First Name
(formerly Eve Crater)

**PASOM-MANA
TESSERA**
Hopi Goddess of
Dreams & the Insane

ZEMLIKA
CORONA
Latvian Earth

Further Reading

GENERAL RESOURCES

ONLINE

Mason, Betsy, and Greg Miller. "All Over the Map." nationalgeographic.com /all-over-the-map.

David Rumsey Map Collection: www .davidrumsey.com.

Library of Congress: "Worlds Revealed." blogs.loc.gov/maps.

Osher Map Library: www.oshermaps.org.

Norman B. Leventhal Map Center, Boston Public Library: www.leventhalmap.org.

New York Public Library Map Division: www.nypl.org/about/divisions/map -division.

PRINT

Antonis, Antoniou, and R. Klanten, eds. *Mind the Map.* Gestalten, 2015.

Benson, Michael. *Cosmigraphics: Picturing Space Through Time.* Abrams, 2014.

Black, Jeremy, and others. *Great City Maps.* DK Publishing, 2016.

Blake, John. *The Sea Chart.* Conway, 2016.

Hall, Debbie, ed. *Treasures from the Map Room.* Bodleian Library, 2016.

The History of Cartography series. University of Chicago Press.

Hornsby, Stephen. *Picturing America: The Golden Age of Pictorial Maps.* University of Chicago Press, 2017.

Sumira, Sylvia. *Globes: 400 Years of Exploration, Navigation, and Power.* University of Chicago Press, 2014.

Van Duzer, Chet. *Sea Monsters on Medieval and Renaissance Maps.* British Library, 2014.

SELECTED BIBLIOGRAPHY

1 | WATERWAYS

14-17   Fisk, Harold N. "Geological Investigation of the Alluvial Valley of the Lower Mississippi River." U.S. Army Corps of Engineers, 1944.

Morris, Christopher. "Reckoning with 'the Crookedest River in the World': The Maps of Harold Norman Fisk." *The Southern Quarterly* (Spring 2015), 30-44.

Barry, John M. *Rising Tide: The Great Mississippi Flood of 1927 and How It Changed America.* Simon & Schuster, 1998.

18-21   Howse, Derek, and Norman Thrower, eds. *A Buccaneer's Atlas: Basil Ringrose's South Sea Waggoner.* University of California Press, 1992.

Lynam, Edward. "William Hack and the South Sea Buccaneers." In *The Mapmaker's Art: Essays on the History of Maps.* Batchworth Press, 1953.

Lloyd, Christopher. "Bartholomew Sharp, Buccaneer." *Mariner's Mirror* (1956), 291-301.

22-23   Wolter, John. "The Heights of Mountains and the Lengths of Rivers." *Quarterly Journal of the Library of Congress* (July 1972), 186-205.

Rumsey, David. "Heights of Mountains, Lengths of Rivers." 2009. www.davidrumsey.com/ blog/2009/9/5/heights-of -mountains-lengths-of-rivers.

24-29   Osher Map Library. "The Northwest Passage: Navigating Old Beliefs and New Realities." Exhibit, 2016-2017. www.oshermaps.org/exhibitions/ arctic-exploration.

30-31   Russell, Ron. "Neglected Treasures." *SF Weekly,* January 16, 2008.

Covarrubias, Miguel. *Pageant of the Pacific.* Pacific House, 1940.

32-35   Hofmann, Catherine, Helene Richard, and Emmanuelle Vagon. *The Golden Age of Maritime Maps: When Europe Discovered the World.* Firefly Books, 2013.

38-41   McCullough, David. *The Path Between the Seas: The Creation of the Panama Canal, 1870-1914.* Simon & Schuster, 2001.

Allen, Cyril. "Félix Belly: Nicaraguan Canal Promoter." *Hispanic American Historical Review* (February 1957), 46-59.

Meyer, Axel, and Jorge A. Huete-Pérez. "Conservation: Nicaragua Canal Could Wreak Environmental Ruin." *Nature* (February 20, 2014), 287-289.

42-43   Theberge, Albert E. "The Coast Survey 1807-1867." NOAA. http:// library.noaa.gov/About/Mission/ Coast-Geo-Survey/Coast-Survey -1807-1867-TOC

2 | CITIES

50-55   Berg, Scott. *Grand Avenues: The Story of the French Visionary Who Designed Washington, D.C.* Random House, 2007.

60-63   Ebel, Kathryn. "Representations of the Frontier in Ottoman Town Views of the Sixteenth Century." *Imago Mundi* (2008), 1-22.

Ayduz, Salim. "Nasuh Al-Matrakî, A Noteworthy Ottoman Artist-Mathematician of the Sixteenth Century." Muslim Heritage. www.muslimheritage.com.

Rogers, J. M. "Itineraries and Town Views in Ottoman Histories." In *The History of Cartography,* vol. 2, book 1, edited by J. B. Harley and David Woodward. University of Chicago Press, 1992.

66-69   "Kowloon Walled City" (multimedia documentary). *Wall Street Journal.* http://projects.wsj.com/kwc.

Kowloon Walled City Expedition: https://kowloonexpedition.word press.com.

70-73   Seasholes, Nancy. *Gaining Ground: A History of Landmaking in Boston.* MIT Press, 2003.

Boston Groundwater Trust: www .bostongroundwater.org.

74-75   Barber, Peter. *London: A History in Maps.* British Library Publishing, 2012.

Rosen, Jody. "The Knowledge, London's Legendary Taxi-Driver Test, Puts Up a Fight in the Age of GPS." *New York Times,* November 10, 2014.

3 | CRISIS AND CONFLICT

80-83   Desjardin, Thomas. *These Honored Dead.* Da Capo Press, 2003.

Hartwig, Scott. "High Water Mark: Heroes, Myth and Memory." National Park Service, 2008. www .npshistory.com/series/symposia/ gettysburg_seminars/12.

84-89   Davies, John, and Alexander Kent. *The Red Atlas: How the Soviet Union Secretly Mapped the World.* University of Chicago Press, 2017.

Miller, Greg. "Inside the Secret World of Russia's Cold War Mapmakers." *Wired,* July 18, 2015.

90-93   Osborn, Carlyn. "Anna Beek and the War of the Spanish Succession." Library of Congress, March 25, 2016. https://blogs.loc.gov/ maps/2016/03/anna-beek.

Falkner, James. *The War of the Spanish Succession, 1701-1714.* Pen and Sword Military, 2015.

94-97   Ward, Laurence. *The London County Council Bomb Damage Maps, 1939-1945.* Thames & Hudson, 2016.

98-99   Moore, Ryan. "World War I: Understanding the War at Sea Through Maps." Library of Congress, January 18, 2017. https://blogs.loc.gov/ maps/2017/01/world-war-i -understanding -the-war-at-sea -through-maps.

Breemer, Jan. *Defeating the U-Boat: Inventing Antisubmarine Warfare.* Naval War College Press, 2012.

100-103   Abrams, Leonard. *Our Secret Little War.* International Geographic Information Foundation, 1991.

Pearson, Alastair. "Allied Military Model Making During World War II." *Cartography and Geographic Information Science* (2002), 227-241.

Reed, Harrison. "The Development of the Terrain Model in the War."

Geographical Review (October 1946), 632-652.

104-107   Wigan, Kären, ed. "Japanese Imperial Maps as Sources for East Asian History: The Past and Future of the Gaihōzu." *Cross-Currents: East Asian History and Culture Review* (March 2012).

108-109   The Refugee Project: www.the refugeeproject.org.

4 | LANDSCAPES

114-115   Patterson, Tom. "A View From On High: Heinrich Berann's Panoramas and Landscape Visualization Techniques for the U.S. National Park Service." *Cartographic Perspectives* (Spring 2000), 38-65.

Troyer, Matthias. "The World of H. C. Berann." www.berann.com/life.html.

116-117   Thorington, J. Monroe. "John Auldjo, Fortunate Traveller." *Alpine Journal* (November 1952), 459-464.

118-123   Washburn, Bradford. "Resurvey of the Heart of the Grand Canyon, 1971-1978." National Geographic Society and Boston Museum of Science, 1979.

Wilford, John Noble. "Copters and Lasers Map Grand Canyon." *New York Times,* July 19, 1972.

Washburn, Bradford. *An Extraordinary Life.* WestWinds Press, 2005.

124-127   Garver, Joseph. "Plainly Visible Patterns: The Cartography of Erwin Josephus Raisz." *Mercator's World* (September/October 1999).

Raisz, Erwin. "The Physiographic Method of Representing Scenery on Maps." *Geographical Review* (April 1931), 297-304.

Robinson, Arthur. "Erwin Josephus Raisz, 1893-1968." *Annals of the Association of American Geographers* (March 1970), 189-193.

132-135   "Eduard Imhof—Swiss Cartographer." *Treffpunkt.* Swiss television documentary with English subtitles, 1983. https://vimeo .com/164529891.

Imhof, Eduard. *Cartographic Relief Presentation.* Esri Press, 2007.

136-137   Beveridge, Charles, Lauren Meier, and Irene Mills. *Frederick Law Olmsted: Plans and Views of Public Parks.* Johns Hopkins University Press, 2015.

Olmsted and America's Urban Parks. Directed by Rebecca Messner and others. PBS, 2011. www.olmsted film.org.

138-141   James Niehues: www.jamesniehues .com.

142-143   Mode, P. J. "Birds-Eye View From Summit of Mt. Washington." Cornell University Library, April 4, 2014.

https://digital.library.cornell.edu/catalog/ss:19343463.

5 | ECONOMIES

148-151 Baker, Oliver. *Atlas of American Agriculture.* U.S. Government Printing Office, 1936.

Baker, Oliver, Ralph Borsodi, and M. L. Wilson. *Agriculture in Modern Life.* Harper and Brothers, 1939.

152-157 Friendly, Michael. "Visions and Re-Visions of Charles Joseph Minard." *Journal of Educational and Behavioral Statistics* (Spring 2002), 31-51.

Andrews, R. J. "Seeking Minard" and "Finding Minard." Infowetrust.com, March 15, 2017.

Robinson, Arthur. "The thematic maps of Charles Joseph Minard." *Imago Mundi* (1967), 95-108.

158-161 Kahrl, William, ed. *The California Water Atlas.* California Governor's Office of Planning and Research, 1979.

162-163 Deák, Antal. "The Mineral Maps of L. F. Marsigli and the Mystery of a Mine Map." In *Lecture Notes in Geoinformation and Cartography,* edited by E. Liebenberg, P. Collier, and Z. Török. Springer, 2014.

Stoye, John. *Marsigli's Europe, 1680-1730: The Life and Times of Luigi Ferdinando Marsigli, Soldier and Virtuoso.* Yale University Press, 1994.

164-167 Miller, Greg. "Historical Atlases Rescued from the Trash Could Be a Boon to Historians." *National Geographic,* March 3, 2017.

Brinkley, Douglas. *Wheels for the World.* Penguin Books, 2004.

Fitzpatrick, Gary. "Sanborn Samplers." Library of Congress. www.loc.gov/collections/sanborn-maps/articles-and-essays/sanborn-samplers.

168-171 Jarvis, Paul. *Mapping the Airways.* Amberley Publishing, 2016.

172-173 Dobb, Edwin. "The New Oil Landscape." *National Geographic* (March 2013), 28-59.

174-175 Rappaport, Erika. *A Thirst for Empire: How Tea Shaped the Modern World.* Princeton University Press, 2017.

6 | SCIENCE

180-183 Koch, Tom. *Cartographies of Disease: Maps, Mapping, and Medicine.* Esri Press, 2017.

Cairo, Alberto. "Heroes of Visualization: John Snow, H. W. Acland, and the Mythmaking Problem." Peachpit.com, May 29, 2013.

184-189 Tharp, Marie. "Connect the Dots: Mapping the Seafloor and Discovering the Mid-Ocean Ridge." In *Lamont-Doherty Earth Observatory of Columbia: Twelve Perspectives on the First Fifty Years, 1949-1999,* edited by Laurence Lippsett. LDEO of Columbia University, 1999.

Felt, Hali. *Soundings.* Holt, 2012.

190-193 MappingRome: http://mappingrome.com.

Stanford Digital Forma Urbis Romae Project: https://formaurbis.stanford.edu.

194-197 Lawson, Andrew. *The California Earthquake of April 18, 1906: Report of the State Earthquake Investigation Commission.* Carnegie Institution of Washington, 1908.

Zoback, Mary Lou. "The 1906 earthquake and a century of progress in understanding earthquakes and their hazards." *GSA Today* (April/May 2006), 4-11.

Mason, Betsy, and others. "A Century Ago, a Moment Away." *Contra Costa Times* (special section), April 18, 2006.

198-199 Atlas for the End of the World: http://atlas-for-the-end-of-the-world.com/index_0.html.

200-203 Swanson, Larry, and others. *Beautiful Brain: The Drawings of Santiago Ramón y Cajal.* Abrams, 2017.

Instituto Cajal "Legacy of Cajal." www.cajal.csic.es/ingles/legado.html.

204-205 Greeley, Ronald, and Raymond Batson, eds. *Planetary Mapping.* Cambridge University Press, 1990.

206-209 Hearn, Chester. *Tracks in the Sea: Matthew Fontaine Maury and the Mapping of the Oceans.* International Marine, 2003.

Maury, Matthew F. *Physical Geography of the Sea.* Harper, 1855.

7 | HUMAN EXPERIENCES

214-217 Farwell, Willard. *The Chinese at Home and Abroad: Together with the Report of the Special Committee of the Board of Supervisors of San Francisco on the Condition of the Chinese Quarter of that City.* A. L. Bancroft & Co., 1885.

Shah, Nayan. *Contagious Divides: Epidemics and Race in San Francisco's Chinatown.* University of California Press, 2001.

218-221 Traganou, Jilly. *The Tōkaidō Road: Traveling and Representation in Edo and Meiji Japan.* Routledge, 2004.

222-223 Wallace, Tim. "The Two Americas of 2016." *New York Times,* November 16, 2016.

224-227 Zirkle, Conway. "Natural Selection Before the 'Origin of the Species.'" *Proceedings of the American Philosophical Society* (April 25, 1941), 77-123.

228-229 Thrasher, Frederic. *The Gang: A Study of 1,313 Gangs in Chicago.* University of Chicago Press, 1927.

230-231 Nelson, John. "Lights On & Lights Out." Adventuresinmapping.com, April 18, 2017.

Carlowicz, Michael. "New Night Lights Maps Open Up Possible Real-Time Applications." NASA.gov, April 12, 2017.

232-233 Conzen, Michael. "The County Landownership Map in America: Its Commercial Development and Social Transformation." *Imago Mundi* (1984), 9-31.

Conzen, Michael. "The All-American County Atlas: Styles of Commercial Landownership Mapping and American Culture." In *Images of the World: The Atlas Through History,* edited by John Wolter and Ronald Grim. Library of Congress, 1997.

234-237 Lerner, Michael. *Dry Manhattan: Prohibition in New York City.* Harvard University Press, 2008.

Blair, Henry. *The Temperance Movement; or, The Conflict Between Man and Alcohol,* W. E. Smythe, 1888.

Graham, Robert. *Liquordom in New York City.* Church Temperance Society, 1883.

238-239 McLean, K. "Sensory Maps." http://sensorymaps.com.

240-241 Cummins, Patrick, and Mary Cummins. "Surveying in the Former Kingdom of Hawaii." *American Surveyor* (January/February 2006), 12-20.

Alexander, W. D. "A Brief History of Land Titles in the Hawaiian Kingdom." In *Surveyor General's Report, Interior Department.* P. C. Advertiser Co., 1882.

8 | WORLDS

246-247 Ruderman, Barry, David Rumsey, and Katherine Parker. *A Mind at Work: Urbano Monte's 60-Sheet Manuscript World Map.* 2017.

Digital composite of Urbano Monte world map: www.davidrumsey.com/luna/servlet/s/j552ds.

248-251 Digital Museum of Planetary Mapping: planetarymapping.wordpress.com.

252-253 Van der Krogt, P. "Globes, Made Portable for the Pocket." *Bulletin of the Scientific Instrument Society* (1985).

254-255 Van Duzer, Chet, and Ilya Dines. *Apocalyptic Cartography: Thematic Maps and the End of the World in a Fifteenth-Century Manuscript.* Brill, 2015.

256-261 Van Gent, Robert. *Andreas Cellarius, Harmonia Macrocosmica.* Taschen, 2016.

Kanas, Nick. *Star Maps: History, Artistry, and Cartography.* Springer, 2012.

Kuhn, Thomas. *The Copernican Revolution: Planetary Astronomy in the Development of Western Thought.* Harvard University Press, 1957.

262-263 Drake, Nadia. "How a NASA Spacecraft May Help Aliens Find Earth." *National Geographic,* August 14, 2017.

NASA. "The Golden Record." https://voyager.jpl.nasa.gov/golden-record.

264-267 Kretschmer, Ingrid, Daniel Strebe, and others. "Projections." In *The History of Cartography,* vol. 6, part 2, edited by Mark Monmonier. University of Chicago Press, 2015.

Monmonier, Mark. "Mercator Projection." In *The History of Cartography,* Vol. 6, edited by Mark Monmonier. University of Chicago Press, 2015.

Monmonier, Mark. *How to Lie with Maps,* 2nd ed. University of Chicago Press, 1996.

268-271 Whitaker, Evan. *Mapping and Naming the Moon: A History of Lunar Cartography and Nomenclature.* Cambridge University Press, 1999.

Montgomery, Scott. *The Moon and the Western Imagination.* University of Arizona Press, 1999.

272-273 World Museum. "Bombed Out! World Museum and the Blitz." National Museums Liverpool. www.liverpoolmuseums.org.uk/wml/collections/blitz/index.aspx.

Mundy, Barbara. "Mesoamerican Cartography." In *The History of Cartography,* vol. 2, book 3, edited by David Woodward and G. Malcolm Lewis. University of Chicago Press, 1998.

274-275 Beccario, Cameron. "EarthWind Map." earth.nullschool.net.

9 | ART AND IMAGINATION

280-281 Map, art, and works by FULLER: www.fullermaps.com.

282-285 Gretzinger, Jerry. "Jerry's Map." *Cartographic Perspectives* (2014), 68-70.

Jerry's Map: www.jerrysmap.com.

286-289 Rubin, Rehav. "Fantasy & Reality—Ancient Maps of Jerusalem." *Bible Review* (April 1993).

De Peuter, Stanislas. "The Holy Land as Seen by Christiaan van Adrichem." *BIMCC Newsletter,* no. 28 (May 28, 2007).

290-293 Gough Map: www.goughmap.org.

Hereford Mappa Mundi: www.themappamundi.co.uk.

294-295 Gass, Linda. "Art About San Francisco Bay." www.lindagass.com/NewWork.html.

296-299 Howard, Ebenezer. *To-morrow: A Peaceful Path to Real Reform.* Swan Sonnenschein, 1898.

Fishman, Robert. *Urban Utopias in the 20th Century: Ebenezer Howard, Frank Lloyd Wright, Le Corbusier.* MIT Press, 1982.

300-301 Windham, Ryder, Chris Reif, and Chris Trevas. *Imperial Death Star Owner's Workshop Manual.* Haynes Publishing, 2013.

302-305 Anton Thomas Cartography Art: www.antonthomasart.com.

306-307 Bly, Nellie. *Around the World in Seventy-Two Days and Other Writings.* Penguin Classics, 2014.

308-309 Lutz, Eleanor. "The Goddesses of Venus: A Topographic Map." March 6, 2017. http://tabletopwhale.com/2017/03/06/goddesses-of-venus.html.

Acknowledgments

SINCE WE LAUNCHED our blog about maps in 2013, we've been the lucky beneficiaries of the warmth and enthusiasm of the cartography community. Professional cartographers, map scholars, collectors, librarians, and archivists have all encouraged us and helped us learn. Their willingness to share their expertise with a pair of newcomers has been invaluable and is reflected throughout this book. Though we still have a lot to learn (and any errors in this book are ours alone), we are very grateful for their generosity.

Many individuals were important to the creation of this book, but none more so than David Rumsey. From the time he invited us to see his collection five years ago through the process of writing this book, David has encouraged our interest in maps and graciously shared his knowledge and maps with us. Many of the maps featured in this book are from his incredible collection.

We would also like to thank Ian Fowler of the Osher Map Library (who has since moved to the New York Public Library), who took an interest in this project from the start and suggested a number of maps in this book. PJ Mode supplied several maps from his Persuasive Cartography collection at Cornell University and helped provide information about them. In addition to the people mentioned and quoted throughout the book, we owe thanks to many others for sharing their knowledge and assisting in a variety of other ways, including Chet Van Duzer, Michael Fry, Ryan Moore, Julie Sweetkind-Singer, G. Salim Mohammed, Matthew Edney, Stephen Hornsby, Kate Cordes, Alex Tait, R. J. Andrews, Ken Field, Simon Kettle, Vanessa Wilkie, Joe Marquez, Bonnie Burns, Ron Grim, Mark Monmonier, Joe Dunbar, Karen Pinto, Shizuka Nakazaki, Kevin Morrow, David Neikirk, Whitney Autin, Susan Powell, Michael Warner, Lorenz Hurni, Walt Roman, and Ross Stein.

This book contains well over 200 maps and would not have been possible without the help and generous permission of numerous people including Marcy Bidney, Sam Brown, Michael Buehler, Luzia Carlen, Fernando de Castro, Bret Crimmins, Amahl Drake, Frank Drake, Nadia Drake, David Hodnefield, Rika Ito, Hazel Kayes, Kent Lee, Ricardo Martínez, Amy Muldoon, Tom Patterson, Rob Simmon, AmyLee Walton, and John Warnock, as well as the families of Miguel Covarrubias, Macdonald Gill, Eduard Imhof, and Erwin Raisz. We are also very grateful to all the contemporary cartographers whose work is featured in the book.

We are indebted to several public resources, in particular public and university libraries. This book was greatly aided by the digitization of maps by many of these institutions, and our research on historical maps and cartographers would have been much more difficult without access to books, journal articles, and research tools hosted by these libraries, as well as free online sources such as Archive.org, Hathi Trust, and Google Books.

We also owe many thanks to the team at National Geographic Books including Robin Terry-Brown, whose vision helped shape and nurture this project in the early stages, and Michelle Cassidy, who deftly and enthusiastically shepherded it from start to finish. A book with so many highly specific and unusual images could not have been done without the excellent photo editing and rights acquisition team led by Susan Blair and Meredith Wilcox. Our text editor Kate Armstrong helped bring out the best in these stories. Creative director Melissa Farris and our designers Joe Newton and Gail Anderson rose to the challenge of crafting a beautiful and coherent design in spite of many oddly and inflexibly shaped maps.

In many ways, this book is the culmination of the work we've been doing over the past five years, first at *Wired* for our blog Map Lab and then at *National Geographic* for our blog All Over the Map. We've had a lot of help and encouragement along the way from countless people, for which we are extremely thankful. We'd especially like to acknowledge Nick Stockton, Susan Schulten, Matt Knutzen, Adam Mann, Andy Woodruff, Anthony Robinson, and members of the North American Cartographic Information Society. We're grateful for the support we've received from National Geographic's online team, past and present, including Erika Engelhaupt, Gabe Bullard, Jeremy Berlin, Natasha Daly, and Dan Gilgoff. We've also benefited from the wisdom of Damien Saunder, Ted Sickley, and other past and present members of the brilliant cartography team at National Geographic.

Both authors are thankful for the support of their loved ones throughout this project. Greg is grateful for the encouragement and support of his friends and family, especially his wife, Rebecca, who put up with him working many weekends, canceling many plans, and being unable to talk about anything besides maps for the better part of a year. He could not have done it without her. He also thanks his dog Rio for reminding him to get outside once in a while and not take it all so seriously.

Betsy would like to thank her family for their love and support, her friends for their encouragement, and her dog Hogan for making sure she took time for a walk outside every day, despite the deadlines. She is especially grateful for the love, support and encouragement of her partner, Bryan Gardiner. From suggesting maps for the book, to reading and editing stories, to patiently listening to Betsy talk endlessly about maps, she can't thank him enough for all of his help.

About the Authors

BETSY MASON and GREG MILLER co-author the blog All Over the Map at *National Geographic* (nationalgeographic.com/alloverthemap). They co-founded the blog at *Wired* in 2013. Follow them on Twitter and Instagram @mapdragons.

BETSY MASON is a science journalist based in the San Francisco Bay Area. She covers a broad range of topics including earth sciences, animal behavior, cartography, and beer. Her work has appeared in numerous publications such as *Science, Nature, New Scientist, Discover, Wired,* and *Science News.*

Betsy was a senior editor at *Wired* in charge of online science coverage from 2008 to 2015 and led the science section to several Webby Awards. Previously she was the science and national laboratories reporter at the *Contra Costa Times* in the San Francisco Bay Area, where she won the American Geophysical Union's David Perlman Award for coverage of earthquake risk in California.

She has a master's degree in geology from Stanford University and completed the graduate science writing program at the University of California, Santa Cruz. She was a Knight Science Journalism fellow at MIT for the 2015–2016 academic year. She has been a board member of the Council for the Advancement of Science Writing since 2013.

Betsy's interest in cartography stretches back to drawing maps of her childhood bedroom, home, and backyard. Learning to make geologic maps in college sparked her interest in the earth sciences and deepened her love of maps. She's learning to make digital maps now, but she still always likes to have the relevant paper map on hand whenever she travels.

Read more of her work at www.betsymason.com.

GREG MILLER is a science and technology journalist based in Portland, Oregon. Previously he was a senior writer at *Wired* and a staff writer at *Science.* In addition to writing about maps, Greg writes about neuroscience and other areas of biological, behavioral, and social science.

He has won several honors for his work, including a share of the Magazine Journalism Award from the National Academies of Science, Engineering, and Medicine in 2013 in recognition of a special issue of *Science* devoted to research on human conflict. Greg's article examined how unmanned drones are changing the psychology of warfare. Greg is also a former Rosalynn Carter Fellow for Mental Health Journalism, and he has traveled to Sri Lanka, India, China, and Indonesia to report on cultural differences in psychiatry and the challenges of treating mental illness in developing countries.

Before becoming a journalist, Greg earned a Ph.D. in neuroscience at Stanford University and completed the graduate science writing program at the University of California, Santa Cruz.

Greg's interest in maps goes back to childhood, when he used to pore over maps in the backseat of the car on family vacations. He credits maps with inspiring his wanderlust and curiosity about the world. In the course of researching this book, maps have rekindled his interest in history, art, astronomy, and other subjects he was never very good at in school.

Read more about his work at www.gregmiller.co. Follow him on Twitter @dosmonos.

Illustrations Credits

DRMC = David Rumsey Map Collection, www.davidrumsey.com
DRMCSL = David Rumsey Map Collection, David Rumsey Map Center, Stanford Libraries
LCGM = Library of Congress Geography and Map Division

Cover
Front
(UP) Stanford University Libraries; (CT) LCGM, cw0322000; (LO) Swiss Alpine Museum, Bern, photo by Vincenz Schwab; (Inner Circle) London Metropolitan Archives; (Outer Circle) Made by Bert Spaan for Waag Society, Amsterdam, 2013

Back
Main: Courtesy, DRMCSL; Strips (L to R): Courtesy, DRMCSL; Library of Congress, Geography and Map Division, 2016432165; National Geographic Maps; Courtesy, DRMCSL.

2-3 (Inner circle to outer), from pages 16, 125, 204, 25; 4-5, Image Copyright, 2013, Weldon Cooper Center for Public Service, Rector and Visitors of the University of Virginia (Dustin A. Cable, creator); 6-7, Courtesy DRMCSL; 9, NG Maps; 10-11 (L to R), from pages 30-31, 42-3, 16; 12-13 (UP), Courtesy, Barry Lawrence Ruderman Map Collection, David Rumsey Map Center, Stanford Libraries; 12-13 (LO-L to R), from pages 25, 30-31, 38-9, 42-3, 35, 17 LO LE; 14-16, U.S. Army Corps of Engineers, ERDC; 17 (UP LE), Planet Labs, Inc., 9/29/17 (https://creativecommons.org/licenses/by-sa/4.0/legalcode); 17 (LO LE), 17 (RT), U.S. Army Corps of Engineers, ERDC; 18, National Maritime Museum, Greenwich, London; 19, British Library, London, UK/© British Library Board. All Rights Reserved/Bridgeman Images; 20, National Maritime Museum, Greenwich, London; 21, HM918 The Huntington Library, San Marino, California; 22-3, Courtesy DRMCSL; 24-9, Osher Map Library and Smith Center for Cartographic Education; 30-31, © Maria Elena Rico Covarrubias, photo courtesy DRMC; 32-5, Osher Map Library and Smith Center for Cartographic Education; 36-7, Created by Muir-Way.com, Design by Jared Prince, Data by Roman Perkhaliuk; 38-9, Courtesy DRMCSL; 40, Produced by ProQuest as part of ProQuest Serial Set Digital Maps Collection. www.proquest.com. Published with permission. Further reproduction is prohibited without permission. (UP-https://congressional.proquest.com/congressional/docview/t45.d46.2826_s.rp.1944_map_8), (LO-https://congressional.proquest.com/congressional/docview/t45.d46.2826_s.rp.1944_map_7); 41, Cornell University - PJ Mode Collection of Persuasive Cartography; 42-3, Courtesy DRMCSL; 44-5 (L to R), from pages 65, 74-5, 56-7; 46 (L to R), from pages 68-9, 48-9, 60-61, 74-5; 46-7, LCGM ct000338; 48-9, Made by Bert Spaan for Waag Society, Amsterdam, 2013; 50-51, LCGM, ct001865; 52, LCGM ct002488; 53 (UP), LCGM ct005090; 53 (LO), National Geographic Map retrieved from LCGM, ct005040; 54-5, National Geographic Map retrieved from LCGM, ct004682; 56-7, San Francisco Maritime National Historical Park; 58, Courtesy DRMCSL; 58-9, Smithsonian Institution, National Museum of American History, Photographic History Collection; 59 (UP), Courtesy DRMCSL; 59 (LO), James Allan; 60-61, Istanbul University Library of Rare Books; 62, Map of Aleppo, ca 1600 (color litho), Ottoman School/Private Collection/Bridgeman Images; 62-3, Images & Stories/Alamy Stock Photo; 63, TSM H.1608 View of Nice, from the Suleymanname (Life of Suleyman) 1545 (gouache on paper), Al-Silahi, Nasuh (Matraki) (16th century)/Topkapi Palace Museum, Istanbul, Turkey/Dost Yayinlari/Bridgeman Images; 64-5, Eric Fischer, Base map © OpenStreetMap (https://creativecommons.org/licenses/by-sa/2.0/legalcode); 66-9 (UP), Hitomi Terasawa, courtesy Iwanami Shoten, Publishers; 69 (LO), Jodi Cobb/National Geographic Creative; 70-71, LCGM gm71002188; 71, Map reproduction courtesy of the Norman B. Leventhal Map & Education Center at the Boston Public Library; 72 (LE), Map reproduction from the Mapping Boston Collection of the Norman B. Leventhal Map & Education Center at the Boston Public Library; 72 (RT), Map reproduction courtesy of the Norman B. Leventhal Map & Education Center at the Boston Public Library; 73 (UP LE), NOAA's Office of Coast Survey Historical Map & Chart Collection, http://historicalcharts.noaa.gov; 73 (UP RT), Greater Boston area map © Mapbox © OpenStreetMap, see https://www.mapbox.com/about/maps/ and https://www.openstreetmap.org/copyright; 73 (LO), © The Muriel G. and Norman B. Leventhal Family Foundation. Cartography by MapWorks, Herb Heidt and Eliza McClennen, Norwell, Massachusetts; 74-5, Reproduced by permission of Geographers' A-Z Map Co. Ltd. Licence No. B8245. © Crown copyright and database rights 2018 OS 100017302.; 76-7 (L to R), from pages 106 up, 87 lo, 92 lo; 78 (UP to LO), from pages 107, 101, 84-5, 94-5, 98-9; 79, Cornell University—PJ Mode Collection of Persuasive Cartography; 80-81, LCGM cw0322000; 82 (UP), LCGM cw0322000; 82 (LO), LCGM cw0322000; 83 (LE), Courtesy Gettysburg National Military Park; 83 (RT), LCGM cw0322000; 84-7 (UP), East View Geospatial, www.geospatial.com; 87 (LO), U.S. Geological Survey; 88, East View Geospatial, www.geospatial.com; 89, John Davies, http://redatlasbook.com; 90-91, LCGM 2008621715; 92 (UP), LCGM 2008621715; 92 (LO), LCGM 2008621715; 93, LCGM 2008621715; 94-6 (UP), London Metropolitan Archives; 96 (CTR), © Historic England; 96 (LO), Andrew Holt/Getty Images; 97, London Metropolitan Archives; 98, LCGM 2016432163; 98-9, LCGM 2016432165; 100-101, LCGM, control number 2008628434; 101, Bryan Gardiner; 102 (UP), Figure 20 from *Geographical Review* article "The Development of the Terrain Model in the War" by Harrison P. Reed, Wiley, 1946; 102 (LO), AP Photo; 103, Courtesy Imperial War Museum, Neg. #CH_015885; 104-7, Courtesy Stanford University Libraries; 108-109, Hyperakt and Ekene Ijeoma; 110-11 (L to R), from pages 120, 114-15, 132-3; 112 (UP to LO), from pages 136-7, 114-15, 143, 132-3, 118-19; 113, Courtesy Boston Rare Maps Incorporated, Southampton, Massachusetts; 114-15, National Park Service; 116-17, Typ 825 32.1757, Houghton Library, Harvard University; 118, Museum of Science, Boston, photo by David Ochsner; 118-19, 120, NG Maps; 121, Charles O'Rear; 122, Jim Mendenhall/National Geographic Creative; 123 (UP), Brad Washburn sketches photographed by Mark Thiessen, NG Staff; 123 (LO), Jim Mendenhall/National Geographic Creative; 124-127 (LE), Courtesy Raisz Landform Maps and DRMC; 127 (RT), Courtesy Raisz Landform Maps; 128-131, Stephen Gladieux; 132-3, Swiss Alpine Museum, Bern, photo by Vinzenz Schwab; 133, ETH Library, Image Archive; 134-5, ETH Library, Maps; 136-7, Design for Prospect Park in the City of Brooklyn, Olmsted, Vaux & Co., 1871; B PP-1871.Fl; Brooklyn Historical Society; 138-41, James Niehues; 142-3, Cornell University—PJ Mode Collection of Persuasive Cartography; 144-5 (L to R), from pages 164, 154-5, 160; 146 (UP to LO), from pages 168-9, 166, 161, 148-9, 155; 147, Cornell University—PJ Mode Collection of Persuasive Cartography; 148-51, Courtesy DRMC; 152-3, LCGM ct002136; 154-6, Ecole nationale des ponts et chaussées, Fol.10975; 157, LCGM ct000242; 158-161, Courtesy DRMC; 162-3, Getty Research Institute; 164-167 (UP), Historical Information Gatherers; 167 (LO), LCGM sb000010; 168-71, Courtesy of British Airways, Amberley Publishing, and Paul Jarvis; 172-3, Virginia W. Mason/National Geographic Creative; 174-5, Courtesy DRMC; 176-7 (L to R), from pages 198, 194-5, 180-81; 178 (L to R), from pages 201, 196, 205, 185; 178-9, Courtesy Stanford University Libraries; 180-81, "Map of Oxford, to illustrate Dr. Acland's Memoir on cholera in Oxford in 1854," 1856, Historic Maps Collection, 2010-0388Q, Department of Rare Books and Special Collections, Princeton University Library; 182 (UP), British Library/Granger. All Rights Reserved; 182 (LO), "Map of Oxford, to illustrate Dr. Acland's Memoir on cholera in Oxford in 1854," 1856, Historic Maps Collection, 2010-0388Q, Department of Rare Books and Special Collections, Princeton University Library; 183, Memoir on the cholera at Oxford, in the year 1854, with considerations suggested by the epidemic, 1856, Historic Maps Collection, 2010-0388Q, Department of Rare Books and Special Collections, Princeton University Library; 184, Joe Covello/Black Star; 185, NG Maps; 186, Heezen, B. C., Tharp, M., and Ewing, M., Lamont Geological Observatory, Columbia University (now the Lamont-Doherty Earth Observatory), 1965, The Floors of the Oceans, I. The North Atlantic: Geological Society of America Special Paper 65, pl. 22, https://doi.org/10.1130/SPE65-p1; 187, Physiographic Diagram of the South Atlantic Ocean, by Bruce C. Heezen, Marie Tharp, Lamont Geological Observatory, Columbia University (now the Lamont-Doherty Earth Observatory), published by the Geological Society of America, 1961. Reproduced by permission of Marie Tharp Maps, LLC, 8 Edward Street, Sparkill, New York 10976; 188-9 LCGM 2010586277; 190-91, Forma Urbis Romae, Detail, by Rodolfo Lanciani, 1901. Digital representation developed by University of Oregon, Stanford University, and Dartmouth College. Reprinted by permission of the University of Oregon http://mappingrome.com/; 192, Courtesy DRMC; 193 (UP), Istituto Nazionale di Archeologia e Storia dell'Arte, Roma, Fondo Lanciani, inv. Roma XI.100.7; 193 (LO), © Roma, Sovrintendenza Capitolina ai Beni Culturali; 194-6, Courtesy DRMCSL; 197 (LE), Based on U.S. Geological Survey graphic; 197 (RT), U.S. Geological Survey; 198-9, Richard J. Weller, Claire Hoch, and Chieh Huang, ATLAS FOR THE END OF THE WORLD; 200-203, Self-portrait and original drawings of Santiago Ramón y Cajal belong to the Legado Cajal, conserved at the Instituto Cajal (Consejo Superior de Investigaciones Científicas-CSIC/Spanish Research Council), Madrid, Spain; 204, Geologic Map of the North Side of the Moon, by Baerbel K. Lucchitta (1978), USGS Map I-1062; 205, Geologic Map of the West Side of the Moon, by David H. Scott, John F. McCauley, and Mareta N. West (1977), USGS Map I-1034; 206-7, American Geographical Society Library, University of Wisconsin-Milwaukee Libraries; 208 (UP), LCGM; 208 (LO), Naval History and Heritage Command; 209, Osher Map Library and Smith Center for Cartographic Education; 210-11 (L to R), from pages 216-17, 236, 226-7; 212 (L to R), from pages 214-15, 226-7, 238-9, 237; 212-13, Charles Booth's Poverty Maps courtesy of the Library of the London School of Economics and Political Science (LSE); 214, Arnold Genthe/Library of Congress Prints and Photographs Division, 7a08939; 214-17, Courtesy DRMCSL; 218-9 (UP), LCGM 2002531180; 218-19 (LO), Digital capture by Heritage Imaging, The University of Manchester Library; 220-21, LCGM 2002531180; 222-3, From the *New York Times*, November 16, 2016 © 2016 *The New York Times*. All rights reserved. Used by permission and protected by the Copyright Laws of the United States. The printing, copying, redistribution, or retransmission of this Content without express written permission is prohibited.; 224, Illustration from *The Natural History of Man* by James Cowles Prichard, 1843; 225-7, Courtesy DRMCSL; 228-9, University of Chicago Map Collection; 230-31, Courtesy Esri, cartography by John Nelson; 232-3, Courtesy DRMCSL; 234-5, Cornell University—PJ Mode Collection of Persuasive Cartography; 236, PBA Galleries; 237, LCGM; 238-9, A Winter Smellwalk in Kyiv © Kate McLean 2017; 240-41, LCGM 2005625310; 242-3 (L to R), from pages 273, 246-7, 260-61; 244 (UP to LO), from pages 270, 263, 260, 246-7, 274; 245, Osher Map Library and Smith Center for Cartographic Education; 246-7, Courtesy DRMCSL; 248, R. A. Proctor, from drawings by W. R. Dawes, 1864/65; 248-9, From *Les terres du ciel* by Camille Flammarion, 1884; 250 (UP), 1877-1878 Mars map by Giovanni Schiaparelli; 250 (CTR), Chart of Mars-Plate 12 from *A Popular Handbook and Atlas of Astronomy* by William Peck, 1891; 250 (LO), Lowell Observatory Archives; 251, LCGM 2013593160; 252-3, Osher Map Library and Smith Center for Cartographic Education; 254 The Huntington Library, San Marino, California, HM 83 f.10v (LE), HM 83 f.11v (CTR); HM 83 f.12r (RT); 255, The Huntington Library, San Marino, California, HM 83 f.10r; 256-61, Octavo/Warnock Library; 262-3, Frank Drake; 263, NASA/JPL; 264, © Michael Schmeling, www.aridocean.com; 264-5 (UP), Courtesy DRMCSL; 264-5 (LO), NG Maps; 266, Collection of maps, diagrams, and globes relating to the Butterfly Map, and its development and promotion/B.J.S. Cahill, G3201.B'12 svar.C3 no.5. Courtesy of The Bancroft Library, University of California, Berkeley; 267 (UP), The Fuller Projection Map design is a trademark of the Buckminster Fuller Institute. ©1938, 1967 & 1992. All rights reserved, www.bfi.org.; 267 (LO), Courtesy Raisz Landform Maps and DRMC; 268, Claude Mellan, French, 1598-1688, The Moon in its First Quarter, 1636, Engraving, 23.5 x 17x5 cm (9 1/4 x 6 7/8 in.), Museum of Fine Arts, Boston, Harvey D. Parker Collection - Harvey Drury Parker Fund, P4596/Photo (c) 2018 Museum of Fine Arts, Boston; 269, Wellcome Collection (https://creativecommons.org/licenses/by/4.0/legalcode); 270 (UP), Thomas Fisher Rare Book Library, University of Toronto; 270 (LO), SSPL/Getty Images; 271, VCG Wilson/Corbis via Getty Images; 272-3, National Museums Liverpool, World Museum; 274-5, Cameron Beccario, earth.nullschool.net; 276-7 (L to R), from pages 289, 306-307, 299 le; 278-9 (UP), Map ©2015 by Andrew DeGraff. Used with permission from Zest Books LLC from *Plotted: A Literary Atlas* by Andrew DeGraff. All rights reserved.; 278-9 (LO-L to R), from pages 298, 291, 295, 300-301, 286-7, 285 lo; 280-81, FULLER; 282-5, Courtesy Jerry Gretzinger, www.jerrysmap.com; 286-9, Courtesy National Library of Israel; 290-91, Courtesy of HBO. Map image © 2018 Home Box Office, Inc.; 292-3 (UP LE), Bodleian Images; 293 (UP RT), Courtesy of HBO. Map image © 2018 Home Box Office, Inc.; 293 (LO LE), © The Dean and Chapter of Hereford Cathedral and the Hereford Mappa Mundi Trust; 293 (LO RT), Courtesy of HBO. Map image © 2018 Home Box Office, Inc.; 294 (UP), Copyright © 2013 Linda Gass, Photo by Don Tuttle; 294 (LO), Copyright © 2008 Linda Gass, Photo by Don Tuttle; 295, Copyright © 2005 Linda Gass, Photo by Don Tuttle; 296-9, From *To-Morrow: A Peaceful Path to Real Reform* by Ebenezer Howard, 1898; 300-301, Courtesy of Lucasfilm Ltd. LLC, STAR WARS© & ™ Lucasfilm Ltd. LLC; 302-305, Anton Thomas www.antonthomasart.com; 306-307, Courtesy DRMC; 308-9, Copyright 2017 Eleanor Lutz. References: Venus 1:5 million-scale Magellan Imagery: USGS and IAU Gazetteer of Planetary Nomenclature. Venus Nomenclature search function: USGS and IAU Gazetteer of Planetary Nomenclature. Altimetric Radar Image Map of Venus (1997, USGS Series #I-2444) and Topographic Map of Venus (1997, USGS Series #I-2444).

Index

Boldface indicates illustrations.

Since 1888, the National Geographic Society has funded more than 13,000 research, exploration, and preservation projects around the world. National Geographic Partners distributes a portion of the funds it receives from your purchase to National Geographic Society to support programs including the conservation of animals and their habitats.

National Geographic Partners

1145 17th Street NW

Washington, DC 20036-4688 USA

Get closer to National Geographic explorers and photographers, and connect with our global community. Join us today at nationalgeographic.com/join

For information about special discounts for bulk purchases, please contact National Geographic Books Special Sales: specialsales@natgeo.com

For rights or permissions inquiries, please contact National Geographic Books Subsidiary Rights: bookrights@natgeo.com

Library of Congress Cataloging-in-Publication Data

Names: Mason, Betsy, author. | Miller, Greg (Greg L.), author.

Title: All over the map : a cartographic odyssey / Betsy Mason, Greg Miller.

Description: Washington, D.C. : National Geographic, 2018.

Identifiers: LCCN 2018007300 | ISBN 9781426219726 (hardback)

Subjects: LCSH: Cartography--History. | BISAC: REFERENCE / Atlases. | HISTORY / Historical Geography. | SOCIAL SCIENCE / Anthropology / Cultural.

Classification: LCC GA201 .M373 2018 | DDC 526.09--dc23

LC record available at https://lccn.loc.gov_2018007300

Printed in Malaysia

18/IVM/1

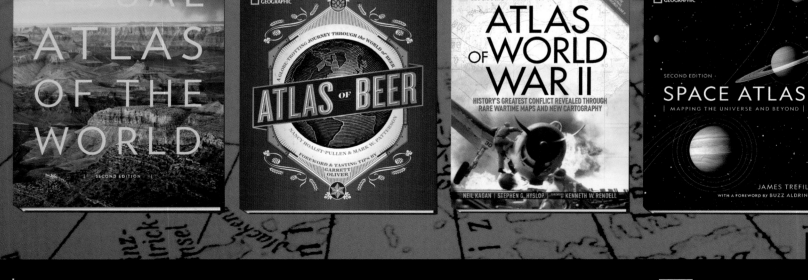